THE
EMOTION
THESAURUS:

A Writer's Guide to Character Expression

SECOND EDITION

ANGELA ACKERMAN
& BECCA PUGLISI

THE EMOTION THESAURUS: A WRITER'S GUIDE TO CHARACTER EXPRESSION.
Copyright 2012, 2019 © by Angela Ackerman & Becca Puglisi

First edition published in 2012
Second edition published in 2019

ISBN: 978-0-9992963-4-9 (Second Edition)

Edited in part by Michael Dunne

Book cover design by: JD Smith Design
Book formatting by: JD Smith Design

ACKNOWLEDGEMENTS

First and foremost, we want to thank readers of *The Bookshelf Muse* and *Writers Helping Writers* for their support, encouragement, and kind words. You made us see the need for a book version of *The Emotion Thesaurus*, and your belief in us made it happen.

We also want to acknowledge the very important members of our first critique group: Helen (Bookish), Roy (Grampy), Madeline (Maddog), Joan (Unohoo), and Laura (Goofus). These Critique Circle writers helped us kick start this list and our respective writing careers. Our deepest appreciation also goes to our friend Sharon, who encouraged us when we needed it most.

We also owe a huge debt to the writing community at large. The writers we have met online, at conferences, at face-to-face groups, and in our own communities have been so generous with their knowledge and optimism, enabling us each to grow as writers. We love being part of this group.

And finally, the biggest shout out goes to our families, who supported us though they couldn't see the vision, encouraged us when we struggled, and provided the business savvy we were lacking. We owe it all to you.

~To AAD and SDJ, with all our love~

THE WRITERS HELPING WRITERS®
DESCRIPTIVE THESAURUS SERIES

Available in nine languages, sourced by universities, and recommended by editors and agents all over the world, this bestselling series is a writer's favorite for brainstorming fresh description and powering up storytelling.

The Positive Trait Thesaurus: A Writer's Guide to Character Attributes

The Negative Trait Thesaurus: A Writer's Guide to Character Flaws

The Urban Setting Thesaurus: A Writer's Guide to City Spaces

The Rural Setting Thesaurus: A Writer's Guide to Personal and Natural Places

The Emotional Wound Thesaurus: A Writer's Guide to Psychological Trauma

The Occupation Thesaurus: A Writer's Guide to Jobs, Vocations, and Careers

The Conflict Thesaurus:
A Writer's Guide to Obstacles, Adversaries, and Inner Struggles (Vol. 1)

The Conflict Thesaurus:
A Writer's Guide to Obstacles, Adversaries, and Inner Struggles (Vol. 2)

Emotion Amplifiers: A Companion to The Emotion Thesaurus

TABLE OF CONTENTS

INTRODUCTION TO THE SECOND EDITION

When we first released *The Emotion Thesaurus* almost seven years ago, it was with enormous trepidation. This was our first nonfiction project, and what we didn't know about self-publishing would have filled its own book. What we did recognize was our own difficulty conveying character emotion in a way that would engage readers. This problem is a big one, because only when the character's emotions are clearly shared can readers become more involved. We wanted to ensure that our character's feelings would trigger the reader's own emotional memories, encouraging empathy that would draw them deeper into the story. Based on a hunch that other writers also had this problem, we set out to provide a solution with *The Emotion Thesaurus*. It wasn't clear just how common the problem was until we saw the response to our book—a response that continues to amaze and humble us.

Our hypothesis confirmed, we dug deeper into this topic, and as we expanded our own knowledge, it became clear that we had more to share. Hence, our decision to release an updated edition of *The Emotion Thesaurus*.

The instructional material in the first part of the book continues to offer its unique how-to cocktail of writing emotion and show-don't-tell tips but with some powerful new additions. It's been expanded to include a section on how dialogue can and should be used to convey a character's feelings. We've also explored the critical part subtext plays in natural conversation and how it can be written to show hidden emotion. And because backstory figures so heavily into characterization, we've added information on what research should be done to establish your character's wounding events and emotional range, which will allow you to write their responses realistically and consistently.

As for the emotions themselves, we now have a total of 130 entries, each of which contains a list of the physical cues, thoughts, and internal sensations that, chosen thoughtfully, will enable you to create the perfect responses for your character. We've added power verbs so you can choose stronger words to describe associated actions, and sets of escalating and de-escalating emotions to help you visualize where a character might naturally go next.

In short, we hope you'll find the second edition of *The Emotion Thesaurus* to be even more useful than its predecessor. Our goal, as always, is to give you the methods and brainstorming tools that make it easier to write emotional moments that are fresh and evocative.

THE POWER OF EMOTION

All successful novels, no matter what genre, have one thing in common: emotion. It lies at the core of every character's decision, action, and word, all of which drive the story. Without emotion, a character's personal journey is pointless. Stakes cease to exist. The plot line becomes a dry riverbed of meaningless events that no reader will take time to read. Why? Because above all else, readers pick up a book to have an emotional experience. They read to connect with characters who provide entertainment and whose trials may add meaning to their own life journeys.

As emotional beings, feelings propel us. They steer our choices, determine who we spend time with, and dictate our values. Emotion also fuels our communication, allowing us to share meaningful information and beliefs with others. And while it may seem that most exchanges happen through conversation, studies show that up to 93% of communication is nonverbal. Even in instances where we try not to show our feelings, we are still sending messages through body language and vocal cues. Because of this, each of us becomes adept at reading others without a word being said.

As writers, we must take our innate skills of observation and transfer them to the page. Readers have high expectations. They don't want to be told how a character feels; they want to experience the emotion for themselves. To make this happen, we must ensure that our characters express their feelings in ways that are both recognizable and compelling to read. Thankfully, the media for conveying emotion are customizable, so with a bit of elbow grease, writers can craft original, authentic responses personalized to every individual in the story.

VEHICLES FOR SHOWING EMOTION

Dialogue is what we use to articulate our ideas, thoughts, beliefs, and needs, all of which are driven by our emotional state. What we feel always propels us, but it is rare to refer to those feelings directly in conversation. So while dialogue is a proven vehicle for sharing a character's emotions, it rarely should do so alone. To convey feelings well, a writer should also utilize nonverbal communication, which can be broken down into four additional vehicles: vocal cues, body language, thoughts, and visceral reactions.

Vocal Cues are shifts in the voice that supply readers with valuable hints about the speaker's emotional state. In conversation, there isn't always time to think about how to react, so while a person might disguise their true feelings by choosing their words carefully, their tone of voice or the flow of words won't be as easy to control. Hesitations, a voice that changes tone or pitch, words that suddenly slide out faster—all of these are terrific indicators that a character's emotions have changed and there's more to the exchange than meets the eye.

Vocal cues can be especially useful for showing the feelings of a non-point-of-view character, since, in most written viewpoints, their direct thoughts cannot be shared with the reader.

Body Language is how our bodies outwardly respond when we experience emotion. The stronger the feeling, the more we react and the less conscious control we have over movement. Because characters are unique, they will express themselves in a specific way. Combine the vast number of physical signals and behaviors found in this book with the individuality of each character, and a writer's options for showing emotion through body language and action are virtually limitless.

Thoughts act as a window into the mental process that corresponds with an emotional experience. A character's internal monologue is not always rational and can skip from topic to topic with incredible speed, but utilizing that mental response to express emotion is a powerful way to convey how they see their world. Thoughts also add a layer of meaning by illustrating how people, places, and events affect the POV (point-of-view) character and can help showcase their voice.

Visceral Reactions are the most powerful form of nonverbal communication and should be used with the most caution. These internal sensations (heart rate, light-headedness, adrenaline spikes, etc.) are raw and uncontrolled, triggering the fight-flight-freeze response. Because these are instinctive reactions, all people experience them. As such, readers will recognize and connect with them on a primal level.

The very nature of these heightened responses requires writers to take special care when using them. Relying too much on internal sensations can create melodrama. Also, because visceral reactions are limited, a writer can inadvertently use clichéd phrasings when describing them. A light touch is needed with this type of nonverbal communication, as a little goes a long way.

CHARACTER RESEARCH: WHAT TO KNOW TO WRITE AUTHENTIC EMOTION

In the real world, no two people are alike, which means each of us expresses emotion in our own way. Some people find it perfectly natural to share what they feel with those around them, experiencing little to no discomfort with their emotions being on display. Others find the idea of revealing what they feel horrifying and will avoid situations that could lead to such vulnerability. Most fall somewhere between these extremes. This spectrum of expressiveness is called an **emotional range**, and it will influence not only which feelings a person overtly shows but when and how they will manifest. While each person tends to stick to a specific area of the spectrum overall, situations where emotions are heightened can cause a shift one way or the other.

Interestingly, while we are each unique in our expressiveness, this individuality originates from the same place for everyone: our collective pasts. Upbringing, education, experiences, beliefs, and personality will all determine who we are and how we go about showing our emotional selves to the world.

As writers, one of our biggest goals is to create characters who are true-to-life, so we want to strive for this individuality when we consider how they will express themselves. The best way to do this is to spend time digging into each character's backstory and uncover details that will show us how to design their reactions.

Backstory planning often gets a bad rap, because some writers dump that information into a scene as exposition, believing that readers must know every detail to fully understand the forces at work in the character's life. The reality is that most backstory is for the writer, not the reader. Like a GPS is helpful for navigating a new city, understanding key details about a character's life prior to the story's start makes it easier to write actions, choices, and decisions that will align with who they are. Not only will this draw readers in through active characterization, it also creates intimacy and puts the character's emotions directly on display through specific behaviors and mental processes.

The amount of backstory planning each character requires will vary depending on their role in the story, but since everyone is a product of the past, there are two universal areas worth exploring: the **important people** in your character's life and the **impactful experiences** that have stayed with them.

Because we're social creatures, when it comes to navigating life, we tend to look to others, especially those who are closest to us. They help us form beliefs and values and teach us how to behave and what to feel. Unfortunately, the people who have the most access and influence are not always the most supportive or functional, meaning not all our life lessons are positive ones. This is important to remember when thinking about who from your character's past served as an example or influenced them. Specifically ask yourself: *Who shaped my character's views on emotion, and did they pass on functional or dysfunctional attitudes and behaviors?*

For example, a character whose parent belittled her every time she cried as a child learns an unspoken lesson: it is better to hide emotion than share it openly. After being repeatedly invalidated in this way, the character will most likely become evasive or even lie about what they feel because they believe anything else will lead to ridicule and judgment.

Likewise, people who serve as positive influences for your character will convey healthy ideas about emotion. A character with an older brother who vocalized his feelings and used them to positively sway others will see that emotions are powerful and can become a vehicle for change. Provided our character looked up to his older sibling, he will likely adopt this same attitude and behave the same way, understanding that other people will connect to him better if he shows what he feels.

Just as important people in your character's life helped shape how they express emotion, certain experiences can also be formative. Imagine a natural disaster, perhaps a flood that destroys much of your character's neighborhood. In the aftermath, he's utterly devastated by the destruction of his home and feels powerless at seeing the grief of his neighbors who have suffered a similar loss. When TV crews show up, he can't hold back what he feels, and he breaks down on camera, which causes an outpouring of support from the rest of the city. People come forward to bring food, offer everyone a place to stay, help with clean up, and donate needed items. Not only will this wave of compassion and empathy help alleviate the character's despair, it will instill the belief that sharing your feelings results in getting what you need most. After this experience, it's very likely he will feel more comfortable displaying his emotions openly.

In addition to these two important backstory considerations, here are other areas worth brainstorming so you can zero in on how to show each character's feelings.

BASELINE REACTIONS

To understand how a character might react to the big moments of conflict and upheaval in the story, we need to establish a baseline of how they behave in everyday situations. Take the typical "long line at a grocery store checkout" scenario. In front of your character are six people, including the current customer who not only has more than the allotted fifteen items, he's constantly requesting price checks on them. How will your character react? Will he wait quietly, hating the slowness but knowing it would be futile to speak up? Or after a minute of fidgeting and fuming, will he drop his basket on the floor and shout at the cashier to open more registers?

In the first case, the character's baseline becomes obvious: it will take a lot more than a few wasted minutes to rile him up. But if the second reaction is his default, we know that when life starts chucking lemons at him, his rage cannon will fire.

Establishing this baseline will help you maintain consistency throughout the story. And if you want to push a character closer to one end of their personal emotional range, you'll know how hard the screw should be turned. So imagine a few benign scenarios that could be part of your character's normal day—a car that won't start, being late for an appointment, waking up sick, or plans changing at the last minute. It's worth the effort to imagine your character in situations like these to get a feel for how they will react.

DEMONSTRATIVE OR RESERVED

Another aspect to consider when determining emotional range is the natural level of expressiveness for your character. Some people are more reserved while others are demonstrative, and this preference shapes the types of expression they'll use.

Imagine a character learning that her adult children who have been living abroad will be returning home for Christmas. A reserved character may sit down to handle the surprise, a full smile brightening her expression. Her voice could warble as she speaks or she might reach out to her husband and give his hand a quick squeeze. A demonstrative character would react with more vigor, jumping up to crush her husband in a hug or making animated hand gestures as she rattles off every thought in her mind surrounding the happy news. Understanding your character's tendencies will help you plan body language and verbal cues accordingly.

COMFORT ZONES

Not everyone feels comfortable sharing emotion in all situations. Your character's expressiveness will likely shift depending on where they are and who they're with. In private, people generally don't hold back, but being around others can trigger a high degree of self-consciousness. If they feel exposed or are worried about being judged, they might rein in their emotions. However, if your character is surrounded by people they trust or others experiencing the same emotions, he or she will be more comfortable expressing their feelings. As a rule, if the character believes it's safe to show what they feel, they typically will; if they don't, they won't. Plan your scenes with this in mind.

Remember that the character's comfort zone will also extend to dialogue. Some people prefer to communicate more of what they feel while others remain tight-lipped. Likewise, your character will be more comfortable opening up to certain people, so let the nature of their relationships dictate how much is shared in each conversation. For ideas on how to convey hidden emotion through dialogue, see the section on subtext.

STIMULUS VS. RESPONSE

Not all characters have the same interests, fears, or beliefs, so how they feel in a given scenario will vary, eliciting different reactions. Imagine a spider crawling across the table where three of your characters are eating lunch. Carla is the first to notice it meandering through the wasteland of takeout wrappers and salt packets. She sucks in a strangled gasp and jerks back, causing her chair legs to shriek. The second to see it is Diane, who leans away and crosses her arms. Finally, Therese spots the leggy creature. She smiles, plucks a discarded straw wrapper off the table and nudges the spider in a direction away from the group.

The same moment, the same stimulus…and three different responses. This is the nature of emotion. Carla's response is fear-driven. Diane displays wariness, assessing the spider as a non-threat while still protecting her personal space, clearly not wanting the creature to come closer. Therese is not bothered at all and only wants to send the spider on its way before one of her companions (likely Carla) demands its execution.

When it comes to various circumstances, we can't assume that every character will have the same reaction or even feel the same emotion. Life experiences and personality will ultimately decide how your character responds to any given stimulus. It may complicate things when members of the story's cast view the same situation through their own lens, but this incongruency can benefit writers, providing another great way to highlight the originality of emotion-driven behavior.

EMOTIONAL SENSITIVITIES AND INSECURITIES

A final way to ensure a unique emotional range for your character is to understand what insecurities and sensitivities lurk within. Every character will have soft spots: emotions that are avoided because they are uncomfortable or generate insecurity. Whenever one of these emotions crops up in a scene, your character will feel cornered, causing an instinct response to kick in: Fight, flee, or freeze.

These powerful, volatile reactions are an excellent way to show your character's deeper layers and can often offer readers clues about an **emotional wound**—a painful event that your character experienced but has never moved past. Like an anchor dragged through life's choppy waters, this old trauma creates relationship friction and holds her back from happiness and achievement. If you're writing a change arc, the emotional wound can derail your character's life. It must be examined and overcome if she is to grow and change into someone stronger who can handle the challenges standing between her and the story goal.

To illustrate the power of emotional sensitivities and how they can be used, consider this example:

> After the ceremony, everyone mingled, their voices filling the garden. Linda drew in the scent of magnolias from her bouquet and then exhaled, casting out the last of her jitters. The wedding had gone perfectly; the wind behaved, no guest was short a chair, and no one in the bridal party had tripped or suffered a wardrobe malfunction during their walk down the grassy aisle. She could finally relax.
>
> Sarah, the bride, stood in the middle of the lawn talking to a few guests. Sunlight glowed against her cheekbones and glinted off the scatter of crystals sewn into her dress and veil, a truly beautiful bride. After all her friend had been through these last years—losing her mother, the multiple miscarriages—Sarah deserved this perfect day with Tom.
>
> Linda checked on the photographers setting up near the old oak and judged them close to ready. As maid of honor, she needed to keep everyone on a timeline, so she went to gather up the bride.
>
> Before she could get there, Sarah bolted toward an older woman wearing a matronly purple dress and enveloped her in a hug. "Nana, you made it!"
>
> *Nana.* The word knifed through Linda, jolting her to a stop.
>
> "Silly girl. A delayed flight couldn't keep me from making it to your special day." She pulled back and cupped Sarah's cheeks. "Such a beauty."
>
> Sarah took her grandmother's weathered hands in her own. "I hope you know what it means to me, that you're here. You've always taken care of me, and—"
>
> "I love you, girl. Always will. Enough for both your mother and me."
>
> Linda's eyes grew hot, a contrast to the cold weight crushing her lungs. This moment, this beautiful moment, was killing her.
>
> "Oh gosh, Nana. Let me find my maid of honor so I can introduce you. She's like a sister to me, and the only reason I'm still sane."
>
> Linda darted behind a group of wedding guests. The buzz of conversation

drowned out Sarah calling her name, and Linda quickened her pace, heading for the French doors that would take her inside. The light was too bright, the rose garden too filled with sweetness. She couldn't breathe. She also couldn't tell her best friend that meeting her grandmother would be the most painful thing she could ask Linda to do.

It's clear in this example that something traumatic happened in Linda's past that involved her grandmother. Whatever it was, the stain of it is so great that watching her best friend share a loving, supportive moment with her Nana is too painful to bear, and so she flees.

Not only does this situation shine a spotlight on Linda's emotional sensitivities, it also provides a window into her past in a very active, non-dumpy way. Readers will now want to know more and keep reading in hopes of discovering exactly what happened. They will also root for Linda, hurting when she hurts, and wishing for her to find happiness so she can be freed from her difficult past.

Once you've established your character's sensitivities, you can use them to write scenes that evoke powerful feelings. This is easily done via the setting. Embedding **triggers** (like Sarah's grandmother) to awaken these insecurities or touch on a past wound allows you to reveal the point-of-view character's feelings. It also helps readers see exactly what is causing the elevated reaction.

USING DIALOGUE TO WRITE EMOTION

Once you've figured out who your character is and how their emotional responses are likely to manifest, you're ready to start writing. As was mentioned previously, communication happens both verbally and nonverbally, so writers need to be adept at using both to show a character's emotional state. Let's start with the former.

Dialogue is the primary way we communicate with others, using it to share ideas and information. It's also a big part of how we connect with people. This desire for closer relationships is why we go for coffee with friends, date our spouses, and nag at our kids to tell us about their day: we want to strengthen our connections, and the surest way of doing that is by sharing our feelings with each other. This happens because displaying our emotions requires vulnerability—peeling back the outer layers of shielding to reveal one's fragile heart—which almost always results in a deepening relationship.

One of the most natural ways to reveal your character's emotions is through their conversations with others. And it's important to get this element right, because readers are keenly aware of how these verbal exchanges work in real life. If you want to write dialogue that showcases your characters' feelings and rings true for readers, keep the following tips in mind.

UTILIZE PERSONALITY AND BACKSTORY

There's a reason you did all that research discussed in the previous section—because who your character is will determine how they respond emotionally to their circumstances. As an example, consider someone who must initiate a tricky conversation with their boss. How the exchange goes will be largely determined by the character's personality. Here's how it might look for someone who is timid or uncertain:

> Jason tapped on the doorframe. The battle-axe didn't look up, just kept slashing through numbers on her sales report.
> "Um, Mrs. Swanson?"
> No response.
> He shifted his weight, wondering how to proceed. He couldn't mess this up. He couldn't miss another of Kristina's games.
> Jason shuffled half a step into her office. "Um…about this weekend? I know your email said I needed to work, but…Well, I kind of already have plans—"
> "Cancel them," she said in a tone that was as forgiving as her Sharpie.
> When he didn't answer, she looked up. His gaze dropped to the rug.

This conversation makes sense for a character with Jason's personality. But if the character were confident and not afraid of confrontation, it would go differently:

> Dominic gave the door a rat-a-tat before opening it. "Hey, Mrs. Swanson."
> Silence.
> He cleared his throat, clenching his hand around the doorknob. "I can't work this weekend. I have plans."
> "Cancel them," she said, not bothering to look up.

Heat shot through his insides, bringing him to his full height. "You can't make me work last minute." His voice was louder now, and he didn't care. "I can stay late on Monday but not this weekend. Best I can do."

That got her attention. She gave him her patented glare, and he glared right back. If she thought she could intimidate him with a staring contest, she'd never met his twelve-year-old.

Both characters begin this scenario with nervousness, but that emotion manifests differently based on the character's personality. This is why it's so important to do your background research beforehand, so you'll know your character's tendencies and how they're likely to respond when a curveball comes.

COMBINE THE VERBAL AND NONVERBAL ELEMENTS

When we think of dialogue, we almost always equate it with speech. But the truth is that dialogue consists of more than just the words being spoken. Body language is another component that's a part of every exchange. Omitting it will result in unnatural dialogue that will yank readers right out of the story. As an example, take a look at Jason's conversation with only the speech included:

"Um, Mrs. Swanson?"

"Um…about this weekend? I know your email said I needed to work, but… Well, I kind of already have plans—"

"Cancel them."

While this still conveys Jason's nervousness, it says very little about his personality, and it reads awkwardly because this isn't how dialogue works. People shift positions when they speak, move around, and may even interact with objects as a way to focus. These movements, important for underscoring emotion, can also characterize, killing two birds with one stone and adding dimension to the scene.

The small actions that occur within a conversation are referred to as "beats" by Browne and King, authors of the excellent resource *Self-Editing for Fiction Writers*. Beats serve many purposes, one of which is to reveal how a character feels about the words they're saying. Jason's beats (the tentative tap on the door, the shifting weight and shuffling footsteps, his inability to hold her gaze) express his nervousness loud and clear. Cumulatively, they accomplish a secondary purpose by also revealing personality.

Vocal cues—changes in the voice and speech patterns—are also in evidence when the character is feeling emotional. We see this in Jason's hesitations and Dominic's volume getting louder.

So as you're crafting a conversation, consider your character's words carefully, but also think about what the emotion might be doing to their voice. And be sure to include beats that confirm for the reader what the character is feeling while also telling a little something about who they are.

TAKE IT EASY ON THE TAGS

Since we're talking about the words between the words, let's touch briefly on dialogue tags. These are the attributions that let you know who's talking—*he said*, *she muttered*, *they shouted*, etc. There are a lot of choices, and some of them do express emotion. Hissed words express a clear feeling, as do those that are mumbled, yelled, or sung. But after a while, these unusual tags begin to stand out and can give your writing an overworked or melodramatic feel.

This doesn't happen as much with the simple *said*, which is so common as to be virtually invisible on the page. Unless you overdo it, it can be used by all characters and won't feel repetitive. As far as expressive tags go, a good rule of thumb is to save them for important scenes or moments of high emotion. Use them sparingly and they'll work for your story instead of against it.

Another thing to remember is that tags aren't always necessary. If you're worried about readers being confused about who's talking, you can take care of this with well-written beats. Looking back at the previous examples, though quite a few words are exchanged, there is only one direct tag in each. But because of the associated beats, the conversations are easy to follow.

USE VOCAL CUES TO SHOW CHANGES IN EMOTION

As was mentioned earlier, the voice itself is another tool that can be used to show a character's emotional state. It's one of the first things to change when a strong feeling comes on, and initially, it's very hard to mask. If you can capture that brief moment when control of the voice is lost, you can indicate clearly to the reader that an emotion is in play. Consider doing so by experimenting with the following vocal elements.

Pitch: Does the voice get high and shrill or go low and rumbly?

Volume: Does the character move from a moderated volume to almost yelling? Does the voice drop to a near whisper? Is it clear that they're struggling to maintain a reasonable volume?

Tone: Does a clear tone turn breathy or husky when someone is aroused? When the character is close to tears, does the voice become brittle or cracked? Does it lose all expression and become flat when anger hits?

Speech Patterns: Does your verbose character suddenly clam up? Does her timid, verbally stumbling counterpart start running at the mouth? Does poor grammar appear in a well-educated character's dialogue? Does a stutter or lisp announce itself?

Word Choice: What words might slip into a character's vernacular when they're feeling emotional that they wouldn't normally use? Profanity and slurs? Words and phrases from their first language? Pat clichés?

If you've established a baseline for your character's normal speech and vocal patterns, a change can clue readers in that there's been an emotional shift. A word of warning, though: many of these cues can be used for multiple feelings. A trembling voice could indicate sadness, fear, uncertainty, anger, or nervousness, and without more information, the reader won't know which one the character is experiencing. For this reason, it's important to pair vocal cues with thoughts (if the point of view being used allows you to do so) or body language. Providing the situational context will also clarify things for readers.

MAKE YOUR DIALOGUE WORK HARDER

Conversations in real life are complex; while they're mostly about sharing or gaining knowledge, that's seldom the sole purpose of an exchange. Yet we often use dialogue in stories to do just that: reveal information to either the reader or another character. This can result in an info dump, with the author dropping a heavy load of backstory or narrative in the middle of the action. Info dumps are discouraged because they're boring and they slow the pace, causing reader interest to flag.

This doesn't mean that dialogue isn't a good vehicle through which to share information, because it is. That just shouldn't be the only purpose. To keep your verbal exchanges sharp and multi-dimensional, ask yourself the following question: What do my characters want from this conversation?

People have different reasons for communicating with each other. Some do it to connect while others just want to be affirmed (*Wow, Anne, that's so insightful!*). An overbearing person might seek control by dominating verbal interactions with his peers. Someone else might want to appear self-important by sharing juicy tidbits with their neighbors. On and on it goes.

When you know your character's goal in a conversation, you'll have a better idea of what they might do to achieve it: steering the exchange in a certain direction, manipulating the other party, avoiding topics, disengaging at a certain point, etc. This knowledge will give you a better idea of how the conversation will go.

It's also important to note that the participants may be looking for different things. This can lead to inherent conflict, since opposing goals will result in someone—possibly both characters—not getting what they want. Imagine Character A initiating a conversation because she's romantically interested in Character B, while Character B is responding because being friendly with Character A will get him something he wants (esteem, business connections, an alibi, etc.). Someone is going to be thwarted in this scenario—either immediately or down the road—and frustrated desires typically result in an influx of emotion, which is always good for piquing reader interest.

So, absolutely, use those verbal exchanges to reveal the information you want to get across, but don't do it in a vacuum. Keep the conversation interesting by considering each character's goal and using that knowledge to infuse emotion into the exchange.

SUBTEXT: WHAT LIES BENEATH

Writing realistic and evocative dialogue isn't easy. The mechanics can be tricky, but ample resources exist to help, and with enough practice, it can be mastered. But there's another truth we need to keep in mind if we're going to write dialogue effectively, and that is simply this: our communications with others are rarely straightforward. On the surface, it may seem like we're engaging in some simple back-and-forth, but if you look deeper, our conversations are, to some degree, carefully constructed. We withhold information, hide our emotions, dance around what we really mean, avoid certain topics, downplay shortcomings or emphasize strengths—all of which lead to exchanges that aren't totally honest.

Given this knowledge, if we write conversations between our characters that are completely candid, they're going to fall flat because that's not the way people generally deal with each other. Subtext is a huge part of dialogue, and it's often tied in some way to emotion, so we need to be able to include it in our characters' interactions.

Simply defined, **subtext** is the underlying meaning. In a conversation, you have all the obvious things happening on the surface—the words, the "acceptable" emotions on display. But then there are all the hidden elements that the character isn't comfortable sharing: their true opinions, what they really want, what they're afraid of, and emotions that make them feel vulnerable. These underlying elements are the subtext, and they're important because the character wants and is actively seeking (often on a subconscious level) to keep them hidden. This results in seemingly contradictory words and actions as the character tries to overtly convey something that isn't 100% true.

As an example, take a look at this exchange between a teenaged daughter and her dad.

"So how'd the party go?"

Dionne plastered on a smile and buried herself in her Instagram feed. "Great."

"See, I knew you'd have a good time. Who was there?"

Her mouth went dry, but she didn't dare swallow, not with Dad watching her over his coffee mug. Despite the hour, his eyes were bright and searching, twin spotlights carving through the mocha-infused fog.

"The usual. Sarah, Allegra, Jordan." She shrugged. *Nothing to see here. Move along.*

"What about Trey? I ran into his mom at the office yesterday and she said he was going."

"Um, yeah. I think he was there." She scrolled quicker, the images blurring by.

"He sounds like a good kid. Maybe we could have him and his mom over for dinner."

Her stomach lurched. "Oh, I don't know." Her phone trembled and she abandoned it, sitting on her hands to keep them still. "We don't really hang with the same crowd."

"Oh." Dad grabbed an apple from the bowl before heading out. "Well, think about it. Couldn't hurt to branch out and get to know some new people."

Once his feet hit the stairs, Dionne blew out a shaky breath. How could her dad be so smart at work and so stupid about people?

Clearly, Dionne isn't being honest with her dad. She's conveying that everything's fine, but under the surface, we see a different story: something happened at the party, it involved a boy she's now avoiding, and she doesn't want her father to know about it. While Dad is kept in the dark, the reader becomes privy to Dionne's true emotions: nervousness, fear, and possibly guilt.

This is the beauty of subtext in dialogue. It allows the character to carry on whatever subterfuge she deems necessary with others while revealing her true emotions and motivations to the reader. It's also a great way to naturally add tension and conflict. Without the subtext, this scene is fairly boring, just two people having a morning chat. With it, we can almost see the story playing out, with Dionne desperately trying to keep her secrets while it becomes increasingly difficult—maybe even unhealthy—to do so.

So how do we include subtext in our characters' conversations without confusing the reader? Ironically, it's fairly straightforward. It just requires combining the vehicles for showing emotion that were shared earlier—dialogue, vocal cues, body language, thoughts, and visceral reactions. To see them in action, let's take a closer look at how they were used with Dionne.

First, we have her dialogue, which is unreliable; to some degree, we all go a little Pinocchio when we start talking, and Dionne is no exception. Her words subtly scream *status quo*: nothing happened at the party and she doesn't feel anything in particular. But her body language (the plastered-on smile, frantic social media scrolling, trembling hands) and visceral reactions (dry mouth, lurching stomach) tell a different story. Her thoughts are also purely honest; being private, this is how thoughts work.

The nonverbal vehicles are like annoying little brothers and sisters, tattling on the dialogue and revealing true emotion. When you put them all together, they fill out the character's narrative and paint a complete picture for readers to see.

OTHER TECHNIQUES TO SHOW HIDDEN EMOTION

Over- and Underreactions

When you've done the background work on a character, you know how they'll react to ordinary stimuli and will be able to write reliable responses. Readers become familiar with the character's emotional range and have an idea what to expect. So when the character responds to a situation in an unexpected way, it sends up an alert for readers that says, "Pay attention! This is important."

Sometimes this occurs with an overreaction; a seemingly normal situation comes along and the character freaks out. Not only does this tell the reader that something unusual is going on, it also creates an opportunity for the character to fly off the handle and cause more problems, worsening their situation.

Underreactions are more subdued and so contribute less ancillary conflict, but they are just as effective at revealing hidden emotion. Imagine a situation the reader knows should stun or disturb the character, but when it happens, they get…nothing, or an obviously controlled reaction. A downplayed response shows just as clearly that the character is afraid to show their true feelings and so can be a good way to hint at undisclosed emotion.

Every story should include these scenarios that set the character off and cause them to react in unusual ways. Most of the time, the triggers will be tied to their backstory. The research you conducted on their wounds and sensitivities can provide you with specific situations or people that can be used to provoke the character in the story.

Tics and Tells

No matter how adept a character is at hiding their feelings, they all have their own tells—subtle and unintentional mannerisms that hint at deception. As the author, you should know your characters intimately. Take a close look at them and figure out what might happen with their body when they're being dishonest.

It could be a physical signal or behavior, such as covering the mouth, spinning a wedding ring, or biting the lip. Maybe it's one of the vocal cues discussed earlier. It might be a true tic, like a muscle twitch or excessive blinking. Figure out what makes sense for your character, then employ that tell when they're hiding something. Readers will pick up on it and realize that, when it's in play, everything is not as it seems.

Fight, Flight, or Freeze Responses

In the most general sense, the fight-flight-freeze response is the body's physiological reaction to a real or perceived threat. We see this in everyday interactions: when a person invades someone's space, stops what they're doing mid-action, or literally flees the scene. It also happens on a smaller scale in our conversations.

Remember that every character has an underlying purpose for engaging with others. When that purpose is threatened or the character feels unsafe, the fight-flight-freeze reflex kicks in. You can utilize this to great effect if you know which response your character tends toward.

Fight responses are confrontational in nature and may include the character turning toward an opponent to face them directly, squaring up her body to make herself look bigger, or insulting the person to put them on the offensive. Characters who lean toward flight will have reactions centering around escape: changing the subject, disengaging from a conversation, stepping back to take oneself out of the group, or fabricating a reason to leave. If the character's fear or anxiety is triggered, they may simply freeze up, losing their ability to process the situation or find the words they need and being unable to act until something external happens to free them.

When characters exhibit a fight-flight-freeze response in conversation, even if their emotions aren't obvious, the reader will recognize that they're feeling threatened. This not only builds empathy on the character's behalf, it may also create intrigue as the reader pays closer attention to figure out why they're responding this way.

Passive-Aggressive Reactions

Passive aggression is a covert way of expressing anger. If a character is angry but doesn't feel comfortable showing it, they'll often default to certain techniques that will allow them to get back at the person without revealing how they really feel. By employing sarcasm, framing insults as jokes, giving backhanded compliments, and not saying what they really mean (*We're good,* or *I'll get right on that*), characters are able to express their feelings in an underhanded way that others may not recognize or know how to deal with.

This can be a tricky technique to use, because, by definition, passive aggression masks the truth. But you can reveal it through a character's thoughts, the physical signals they exhibit in private (particularly just after an interaction), and the cues they express when the other person isn't looking.

ADDITIONAL IDEAS FOR BRAINSTORMING FRESH EMOTION

With so many aspects to juggle, describing emotion in an evocative way can be a challenge. It's hard work to write something fresh-yet-familiar that puts readers into the character's emotional shoes so they can share the moment. Our thesaurus entries will help you brainstorm emotional expressions that can be transformed into unique descriptions befitting your character, but if you need ideas to supplement that information, try one of the following techniques.

MINE YOUR MEMORIES

Sit back from the keyboard for a minute and think about what emotion your character is feeling. There may be several, but one will be the root cause of the others. When you identify it, think about a time when you experienced this same emotion. Then, if you're comfortable doing so, recreate that moment in your mind and allow your body to respond to the memory. For example, let's pretend that we're dealing with guilt. What do you notice about your body— is there a faint, sour taste in your mouth? Is your stomach bunching up? Does your throat feel painful or constricted?

If it helps, get up and wander around. Pay attention to how your body moves in this instance of remembered guilt: are your arms curled around your torso or is your posture slumped? Are your eyes closed or open? Do you feel itchy, tingly, or uncomfortable?

Don't forget to pay attention to your thoughts; they can create a window for readers to look through and see exactly what your character is feeling and what's causing their reactions. Are you fixating on the people involved, perhaps someone you let down? Are you thinking about how awful it would be if others knew your secret? In fact, what would you do if someone came into the room right now and asked you about this situation?

Keep mining, paying attention to all aspects of yourself, inside and out, until you find an expression or response that would work well for your character. Then write it in an original way that fits their personality and emotional range.

PEOPLE WATCH

While you don't want to be labeled as creepy, watching people can yield great ideas for body language (and dialogue, if you happen to overhear their conversation). Look for everyday opportunities: waiting for your bill to arrive at a restaurant, shopping at a store, standing at a counter while a barista makes your coffee. Be respectful, but don't shy away from locations that could provide high emotion, because people who are visibly upset, excited, or frustrated are treasure troves of unique body movements.

If you do manage to overhear a conversation, pay special attention to vocal cues and speech patterns. Challenge yourself to spot pitch shifts, hesitations, throat-clearings, and other clues that are masking hidden emotions or are alluding to the speaker's true intentions.

TAKE NOTES DURING SCREEN TIME

Another terrific way to observe how people express a range of emotions is to pay attention to TV shows and movies. Unless they're purposely breaking the fourth wall, actors won't have the benefit of sharing an internal monologue with the audience. This means they must show what they feel through action and dialogue. Keep a pen and pad handy and jot down any well-expressed cues you might want to fold into your own storytelling.

If you aren't much of a moviegoer, you can also take notes as you read, paying attention to how other authors describe body language, expressions, vocal cues, internal sensations, and thoughts. While you should never reuse them verbatim in your own work, tracking strong, evocative description is a good way to recognize skillful showing and will give you a better idea of how to do the same but in your own way.

COMMON PROBLEMS WITH
WRITING NONVERBAL EMOTION

It should be clear by now that both verbal and nonverbal communication are necessary and can be used in tandem to convey character emotion. We've discussed the verbal component at length. Now let's look at some of the common traps associated with nonverbal emotion and how to bypass them.

TELLING

By definition, nonverbal emotion can't be told. It has to be shown. This makes it difficult to write because telling is easier than showing. Here's an example:

> Mr. Paxton's eyes were sad as he gave her the news. "I'm sorry, JoAnne, but your position with the company is no longer necessary."
> Instantly, JoAnne was angrier than she'd ever been in her life.

This exchange is fairly easy to write—but not so easy to read. Readers are smart and can figure things out for themselves. They don't want to have the scene explained to them, which is what happens when a writer tells how a character feels. Another problem with telling is that it creates distance between the reader and your characters, which is rarely a good idea. In the preceding example, the reader sees that Mr. Paxton is reluctant to give JoAnne the bad news and that JoAnne is angry about it. But you don't want the reader to only see what's happening; you want them to feel the emotion and experience it along with the character. To accomplish this, writers need to show the character's physical and internal responses rather than stating the emotion outright.

> JoAnne sat on the chair's edge, spine straight as a new pencil, and stared into Mr. Paxton's face. Sixteen years she'd given him—days she was sick, days the kids were sick—making the trip back and forth across town on that sweaty bus. Now he wouldn't even look at her, just kept fiddling with her folder and rearranging the fancy knickknacks on his desk. Maybe he didn't want to give her the news, but she wasn't gonna make it easy for him.
> The vinyl of her purse crackled and she lightened her grip on it. Her picture of the kids was in there and she didn't want it creased.
> Mr. Paxton cleared his throat for the hundredth time. "JoAnne…Mrs. Benson…it appears that your position with the company is no longer—"
> JoAnne jerked to her feet, sending her chair flying over the tile. It hit the wall with a satisfying bang as she stormed out of the office.

This scene gives the reader a much better opportunity to share in JoAnne's anger. Through the use of thoughts, sensory details, a well chosen simile, specific verbs, and body cues that correspond with the featured emotion, readers can see that JoAnne is angry, but they also feel it—in the straightness of her spine and the cheap vinyl in her grip, in the force it takes to send

An example like this also reveals a lot about the character. JoAnne is not well-to-do. She has children to support. She may be angry, but she's also strong minded, family-oriented, and proud. This information rounds out JoAnne's character and makes her more relatable to the reader.

Showing takes more work than telling, as word count alone will indicate, but it pays off by drawing the reader closer to the character and helping to create empathy. Once in a great while, it's acceptable to tell the reader what the character is feeling: when you have to pass on information quickly, or when you need a crisp sentence to convey a shift in mood or attention. But the other ninety-nine times out of a hundred, put in the extra work and you will reap the benefits of showing.

CLICHÉD EMOTIONS

The grin that stretches from ear to ear
A single tear pooling in the eye before coursing down the cheek
Quivering knees that knock together

Clichés in literature are vilified for good reason. They're a sign of lazy writing, a result of settling on the easy phrase because coming up with something new is too hard. Writers often fall back on clichés because, technically, these tired examples work. That grin implies happiness as certainly as knee knocking indicates fear. Unfortunately, phrases like these lack depth because they don't allow for a range of emotions. The single tear tells you that the person is sad, but how upset is she? Sad enough to sob? Shriek? Collapse? Will she even be crying five minutes from now? To relate to your character, the reader needs to know the depth of emotion being experienced.

When writing a certain emotion, remember to think about your body and what happens to it when you're feeling that way. For any given emotion, there are literally dozens of internal and external changes that, when referenced, will show the reader what your character is feeling. The lists in this thesaurus are great for providing ideas, but your own observations are just as helpful.

Secondly, know your character. Individuals do things differently—even mundane activities like brushing their teeth, driving, or making dinner. Emotions are no exception. Not every character will shout and throw things when angry. Some speak in quiet voices. Others go completely silent. Many, for various reasons, will cover their anger and act like they're not upset at all. Whatever your character is feeling, describe the emotion in a way that is specific to him or her, and you're almost guaranteed to write something new and evocative.

MELODRAMA

If all emotions were of average intensity, they'd be easier to describe. But emotions vary in strength. Take fear, for instance. Depending upon the severity of the situation, a person might feel anything from unease to anxiety to paranoia or terror. Extreme emotions will require extreme descriptors, while others are relatively subtle and must be described as such. Unfortunately, many writers make the mistake of assuming that to be gripping, emotion must be dramatic. Sad people should burst into tears. Joyful characters must express their glee by jumping up and down. This kind of writing results in melodrama, which leads to a sense of disbelief in the reader because, in real life, emotion isn't always so demonstrative.

To avoid melodrama, recognize that emotions run along a continuum, from mild to extreme. For each situation, know where your character is on that continuum and choose appropriate descriptors. Just as extreme emotions call for extreme indicators, temperate emotions should be expressed subtly. The indicators for intermediate emotions will lie somewhere in the middle.

It's also very important that your character follows a smooth emotional arc. Consider the following example:

> Mack tapped his thumb against the steering wheel, one arm dangling out the window. He smiled at Dana but she just sat there, twisting that one loop of hair around her finger.
>
> "Worried about your interview?" he asked.
>
> "A little. It's a great opportunity but the timing's awful. There's too much going on." She sighed. "I've been thinking about cutting back. Simplifying."
>
> "Good idea." He nodded along with the radio and waved at the biker thundering past on his Harley.
>
> "I'm glad you agree." She faced him. "I think we should break up."
>
> His foot slipped off the gas pedal. The air grew heavy, making it hard to breathe. The car veered toward the middle line and he let it drift, not caring whether he lived or died.

Unless Mack has a psychological reason for doing so, he shouldn't jump from placidity to depression in a matter of seconds. A realistic progression would be to move from contentment to shock, then disbelief, and finally to grief. Done thoughtfully, this emotional arc can be shown with relatively few words:

> "I'm glad you agree." She faced him. "I think we should break up."
>
> His foot slipped off the gas pedal. "What are you talking about?"
>
> "Mack. We've been headed this way for awhile, you know that."
>
> He gripped the steering wheel and took deep breaths. Sure, things had been rough lately, and she kept talking about needing some time to herself, but she always came around. And she'd definitely never uttered the words *break up*.
>
> "Look, Dana—"
>
> "Please, don't. You can't talk me out of it this time." She stared at the dashboard. "I'm sorry."
>
> His insides twisted. He darted a look at her, but she was curled against the door now, both hands resting easy in her lap.
>
> They were totally breaking up.

Make sure that your character's feelings progress realistically. Map out the emotional journey within the scene to avoid elevated emotional responses that don't make sense.

All of this is not to say that real life doesn't produce extreme emotion. Birth, death, loss, change—some situations call for intense responses that may go on for awhile. Many writers, in an admirable attempt to maintain believability, try to recreate these events in real time. This results in long paragraphs or even pages of high emotion and, inevitably, melodrama. Though real life can sustain this kind of intensity for long periods of time, it's nearly impossible for the written word to do so in a way that readers will accept.

In these situations, avoid melodrama by abbreviating. This method is often used for other real-life scenarios—conversations, for instance. Small talk is left out to keep the pace moving forward. Mundane tasks are also cut short, because the reader doesn't need (or want) to see the entire car washed, a piece at a time, while Bob ponders a problem at work. In the same way, extensive emotional scenes should be long enough to convey the appropriate information, but not so long that you lose the audience. Write the emotion well, develop empathy in your reader, maximize the words that you do use, but don't overstay your welcome.

OVER-RELIANCE ON BODY LANGUAGE

It can't be overstated: body language is incredibly important for showing the character's emotion to readers. Without it, conversations will read as stilted and unnatural, and for readers to figure out a character's emotional state, they'll have to rely solely on the words being spoken—which we know aren't always reliable.

As in so many areas of writing, context is king, and the conveying of emotion is no exception. Without the proper context, readers can't be sure which emotion the character is feeling. Are the fidgety fingers a sign of excitement, nervousness, unease, or impatience? Even if it's combined with an elevated heartbeat, that doesn't narrow the field. The missing piece that the reader needs is the *why*: Why is the character exhibiting these behaviors? Proper context answers this question, and it's often provided through the character's thoughts and dialogue.

When a person is gripped by a strong emotion, they don't tend to think in terms of that feeling. An excited person doesn't think to himself, *I'm so excited!* because he already knows it. Instead, he thinks about the cause of the excitement—perhaps by mentally counting down the days to a loved one's visit or summarizing a recent phone call from a college admissions office.

Physical reactions show what emotion is present, and the thoughts show why it's there. Both must be included for it all to make sense.

OVER-RELIANCE ON DIALOGUE OR THOUGHTS

Because nonverbal writing is harder to master, it makes sense that some writers shy away from it, choosing to rely more on thoughts or dialogue to express what a character is feeling. But an over-reliance on either leads to problems.

> "Are—Are you sure?" I asked.
> "Without a doubt," Mr. Baker replied. "It was neck-and-neck right up to the end, but you came out ahead. Congratulations, William!"
> "I can't believe it," I said. "Valedictorian! I'm so happy!"

Word choice is important in expressing emotion, but it will only go so far. After that, the writer is reduced to weak techniques like telling the reader what's being felt (*I'm so happy*) and over-using exclamation points to show intensity. Without any action to break up the dialogue, the conversation also sounds stilted.

On the other hand, conveying emotion solely through thoughts has its problems, too.

> My pulse was pounding somewhere in the 160 range. I did it! Valedictorian! I was sure Nathan would come out ahead—he was a phenom in the physics lab, and he'd been a ghost at school all month, practically living in the library.
>
> I threw my arms around Mr. Baker. I'd think about this later and cringe with embarrassment, but right now, I didn't care. I'd done it! Take THAT, Nathan Shusterman!

Technically, there's nothing wrong with this sample. Bodily cues, both internal and external, are included. It's clear to the reader that William is excited. Yet it doesn't ring true. Why? Because this monologue screams for verbal interaction with others. Mr. Baker is there and has clearly been talking to William. For William to be so incredibly excited and not say anything comes across as...odd.

Internal dialogue is an important part of any story. There are many scenes and scenarios where a paragraph or more of contemplation is appropriate. This isn't one of them. For this scene, and for the majority of scenes, emotion is much more effectively conveyed through a mixture of dialogue, thoughts, vocal cues, and body language.

> My pulse jittered somewhere around the 160 mark. No, I'd heard him wrong, been tricked by an over-active, sleep-deprived, twisted imagination.
>
> "Are—" I cleared my throat. "Are you sure?"
>
> "It was neck-and-neck right up to the end, but you came out ahead. Congrat- ulations, William."
>
> The leather chair squeaked as I collapsed into it. Valedictorian. How'd I beat out Nathan, who'd been a ghost all month, practically living in the library? Not to mention that A- I scraped in physics.
>
> "But I did it," I whispered.
>
> Mr. Baker stood to shake my hand. I jumped up and threw my arms around him, lifting him off the floor. Later, I'd remember this and die of embarrassment, but right now I didn't care.
>
> "I did it. Take THAT, Nathan Shusterman!"
>
> "Knew you had it in you," he said in a strangled voice.

When expressing emotion, vary your vehicles, using both verbal and nonverbal techniques for maximum impact.

MISUSING BACKSTORY TO ENHANCE READER EMPATHY

Every character is unique, influenced largely by events from the past. One surefire way to gain reader empathy is to reveal why a character is the way he is. Take the movie *Jaws*, for example. The first glimpse we have of shark hunter Quint, he's raking his none-too-clean fingernails down a chalkboard. Hardly endearing. As the movie progresses, the viewer's dislike is justified through his crass manners and bullying of young Mr. Hooper. But once he tells his story of the sinking of the *Indianapolis* and his many days and nights treading water with the sharks, the viewer understands how he became so hardened. His behavior hasn't changed and we still don't like him very much, but we empathize with him now. We wish him better than what life has served up to him.

This is just one example of the importance of backstory in building reader empathy. People are products of their past. As the author, it's important for you to know why your characters are the way they are and to pass that information along to readers. For more help on developing your character's backstory and discovering his resulting personality, we recommend checking out the other books in our thesaurus series.

The difficulty comes in knowing how much of the past to share. Many writers, in an attempt to gain reader empathy, reveal too much. Excessive backstory slows the pace and can bore readers, tempting them to skip ahead to the good stuff. Undoubtedly, Quint's path to crusty and crazy contained more than that one unfortunate event, but the rest didn't need to be shared. That one story, artfully told, was enough.

In order to avoid using too much backstory, determine which details from your character's past are necessary to share. Dole them out through the context of the present-time story to keep the pace moving. For inspiration, consider your favorite literary characters, even those who may have been unlikable. Revisit their stories to see what clues from the past the author chose to reveal, and how it was done.

Backstory is tricky to write well. As is true of so many areas of writing, balance is the key.

USING THE EMOTION THESAURUS

We've established that emotion powers a scene and, when written well, propels readers out of apathy and into the character's emotional experience. Writing authentic emotion is not always easy, but to create breakout fiction, writers must come up with fresh ideas to express their characters' feelings.

Emotion is strongest when both verbal and nonverbal communication are used in tandem. The Emotion Thesaurus can supply that critical nonverbal element writers need to fire up an emotional hit that will leave a lasting impression on readers. Here are some final ideas on how to use this book to its fullest:

IDENTIFY THE ROOT EMOTION

Certain situations can arouse a single, easily identifiable emotion. But more often than not, human beings feel more than one thing at a time. If you are struggling with how to convey this conflict to the reader, take a step back and identify the root emotion. This is the catalyst that dictates any other feelings your character might also experience. Once you've found the root emotion, look to the corresponding thesaurus entry for a range of suggestions. The **May Escalate To** field can also provide a logical progression for where your character's feelings might be headed. Once you've clearly shown the root emotion, you can layer in other emotions to a lesser degree and map out the full experience. Similarly, if the situation shifts or is heading toward a resolution of sorts, you can source the **May De-Escalate To** field to see what emotions might come next.

UTILIZE THE SETTING

If you're looking to add natural emotion in a scene, the setting may provide the answer. Many writers don't put much thought into where their scenes take place, believing that any number of locations could be used to equal effect. But this is shortsighted. Why not include a setting that already contains inherent emotion for the character—maybe one that is painfully rooted in the past? Doing so can set them up for disappointment, trigger old wounds, or put their feelings on edge and increase their chances of doing something foolish—all of which can serve your story well.

Settings can also be used on a micro-level. Instead of the location itself holding significance, perhaps the items and people within it do. Or maybe it contains the props you need to highlight a character's emotional state. Someone in the kitchen might sweep a wine glass off the counter in a fit of rage. An office setting could also work, though the same anger may require some control, ranging from a slammed office door to tense posture and fingers pounding the keyboard. When referring to the entries in this thesaurus, a writer should keep in mind the character's setting in order to create organic and unique emotional responses.

LESS IS MORE

Using too many cues to describe a character's feelings can slow the pace and dilute the reader's emotional experience. Sometimes this happens when a writer fails to identify and focus first on the root emotion. Other times, it's the result of choosing too many weak descriptors.

language and vocal cues for the reader to interpret. Watch for overlong emotional passages that slow the action. Always think like a reader, and keep those pages turning.

TWIST THE CLICHÉ

Whenever possible, writers should use fresh ideas to convey emotion. But let's face it…some descriptors work well. That's why they crop up in novels again and again. Each thesaurus entry includes a myriad of possible cues; if you find yourself leaning toward a traditional response like eye rolling or fist clenching that can be seen as cliché, twist it first.

Take shivering, for example—a common visceral indicator to imply fear or discomfort. Shivers run up the spine, down the spine…these are tired phrases that can turn off readers. Sure, the sensation fits, but why not come up with something new? Why couldn't a shiver swarm over the back of the legs? How about using a simile that likens a shiver to leaf-cutter ants marching along a vine? Better yet, don't call it a shiver at all. Instead, describe the sensations of tightening skin or hair being raised. Never be afraid to experiment. There are many ways to take an old expression and twist it into something unique.

VIEW ENTRIES AS A LAUNCHING POINT

Body movement, actions, visceral sensations, and thoughts are as individual as the characters experiencing them. The list accompanying each thesaurus entry is not designed as a one-size-fits-all set of options. It is meant, rather, to prompt writers to think about the many possible behavioral beats at their disposal so they can choose the most suitable options and transform them into an evocative and unique emotional description.

Each character comes from a different background and has a unique personality, meaning some options in the entries will be a good fit while others will not. Their comfort level around others will also influence how they express emotion. With this in mind, entries should serve as a brainstorming tool and encourage writers to take the next step and create fresh, individual ways to show a character's emotional state.

TRY RELATED EMOTIONS

If you're struggling to find the perfect physical response, visceral reaction, or thought, try reading through the entries of similar emotions. Each entry contains different cues. Studying the lists for related feelings may spark an idea for something new.

ADD AN AMPLIFIER

Getting your character into the right emotional state isn't necessarily easy because they don't always go willingly. When they need an extra push, consider adding an amplifier. Emotion amplifiers are states that stimulate emotion and make a character more volatile. Hunger, boredom, pain, illness, etc. will deplete a character's emotional reserves and ramp up the stress, putting them on edge and impacting their decision-making abilities. Keep possibilities like these in mind when you need to drive your character's emotions.

VISCERAL REACTIONS AS PHYSICAL INDICATORS

Sometimes, the strongest emotional responses are instinctive (visceral) ones that occur mostly internally and are therefore difficult for others to notice. This becomes a problem for writers who want to show a character's emotion while remaining true to their third- or first-person point of view. In these cases, writers should focus on visceral reactions that have a physical "tell" attached to them. For example, sweating, blushing and shakiness have an external component that can be seen by others. Utilizing these cues allows a writer to describe a visceral reaction without damaging the integrity of the point of view. Because of the external signs that accompany these unique internal sensations, we have included them in the **Physical Signals and Behaviors** field.

A FINAL WORD

We created this book to help writers brainstorm stronger expressions of their characters' emotions, and we urge you to remember that these entries are meant to be a starting point, not a cut-and-paste tool. Using the book as such would only lead to boring, one-note writing, and your story deserves to shine! While writing compelling descriptions always takes more work (since it requires us to dig deeper), it's worth the effort, and your readers will thank you for it.

We hope *The Emotion Thesaurus* will become a useful companion on your writing journey, traveling with you from one book to the next. Happy writing!

THE
EMOTION
THESAURUS

ACCEPTANCE

DEFINITION: Letting go willfully; making peace with change to obtain balance and understanding

PHYSICAL SIGNALS AND BEHAVIORS:
One's shoulders and torso loosening slightly as tension ebbs
Taking in a cleansing breath
Nodding
A smile that grows
Stretching, shaking out one's arms, rolling the shoulders, or curling the toes to release tension and embrace a new mindset
Lifting one's head to make eye contact
One's gaze going from unfocused to focused
Eyes that brighten after making the decision to move forward
Verbalizing one's decision to let go: *You know, I'm okay with it,* or *This will work out.*
Moving closer to other people; no longer feeling as though one needs distance
Welcoming others into one's space (offering a hand, gesturing someone to come near, etc.)
Mirroring another's body language to build rapport (facing them, adopting their gestures)
Shaking someone's hand
Making a joke to lighten the mood
Grinning genuinely
Offering a suggestion as a peace offering: *Why don't we go for lunch? I'm buying.*
Touching to offer personal contact (e.g., a light touch on their arm or shoulder)
Politeness with others; listening intently
Sitting with one's palms facing up
Lifting one's hand to the chest
Engaging in conversation
A light tone of voice
Open body posture (arms away from the body, legs slightly apart, chest out, etc.)
Giving someone an embrace or accepting one
Being honest with others
Lighthearted laughter
Strong eye contact during conversation
Asking for advice out of true interest or to make someone feel valued
Discussing and making plans with others

INTERNAL SENSATIONS:
A chest that loosens or feels lighter
Breath that comes a little easier

MENTAL RESPONSES:
A lessening need to review past struggles and obstacles
Being cautiously optimistic

Experiencing a mood boost when realizing that certain worries or stressors can be let go
A willingness to forgive (oneself or others) to move forward
A desire to share the moment with others
Thoughts turning to the new situation and how one can best move forward
Being ready to let go of past upsets

ACUTE OR LONG-TERM RESPONSES FOR THIS EMOTION:
Confidence
Feeling happy and full of purpose (having a clear direction, knowing what goals to pursue, etc.)
Forging strong, genuine relationships
Clear-headedness and optimism
The ability to let go of anger and worry more quickly
Feeling more connected to others or the world
A willingness to trust (other people, a process, one's decisions, etc.)

SIGNS THAT THIS EMOTION IS BEING SUPPRESSED:
A heavy, thoughtful sigh
Tapping one's lip with a finger in thought
Asking further questions for clarification on something or to delay giving a response
Pursing the lips and tipping the head from side to side, as if weighing one's choices
Lighthearted teasing: *I guess you can live here. We needed someone to change the litter box anyway.*
Setting mock conditions: *Okay, you can move out, but you must promise to call every Sunday!*
Dragging out one's words to pretend that coming to a decision is a struggle
Pretending to pout or otherwise hide one's enthusiasm
Keeping one's choices and feelings a secret until the time is right
Asking for more time to think it over

MAY ESCALATE TO: Satisfaction (230), Peacefulness (202), Connectedness (70), Excitement (126)

MAY DE-ESCALATE TO: Doubt (108), Reluctance (218), Regret (214), Uncertainty (264), Vulnerability (276)

ASSOCIATED POWER VERBS: Brighten, care, embrace, grin, hold, hope, hug, join, laugh, lift, listen, meet, nod, plan, profess, rise, share, smile, squeeze, tease, touch, welcome

WRITER'S TIP: *When you raise the stakes in the story, don't forget to also show the POV character's emotions grow more intense. Whenever there's more on the line, there's more weight tied to the feelings being experienced.*

ADMIRATION

DEFINITION: A feeling of warm approval and appreciation

PHYSICAL SIGNALS AND BEHAVIORS:
A smile that reaches the eyes (which are glossy and bright)
Prolonged eye contact
Eyebrows that flash up and hold
Head tilting slightly to the side
Leaning forward
Nodding slightly while grinning
A flush visible in the cheeks
Reaching out to the one who is admired
Offering a compliment
Lowering the head briefly
An enthusiastic, warm greeting
Inviting another into one's personal space
Lightly shaking one's head and smiling upon thinking of the other person
Active listening (nodding while the other speaks)
Mirroring the body language of the one admired
Laying a hand on the back or shoulder of the other
Clasping hands behind the back
Shifting weight to lean toward the one admired
Open body posture (facing toward another, a welcoming stance)
Relaxed arms
A warm squeeze at the end of a handshake
Asking questions and requesting opinions
Asking for more detail, allowing the other more air time
Being agreeable
Adjusting clothing (straightening, smoothing) to make a good impression
Laughing more often
Caretaking: *Can I get you something, a drink?*
Offering praise: *You did great up there, a natural speaker!*
A warm tone of voice
Friendliness
Being more talkative than normal
Not interrupting
Going out of one's way (staying late, making time for another during busy periods, etc.)
Respecting the time of the one admired: *You have lots of people to see so I'll let you go.*
Being more understanding and forgiving if a conversation or meeting is rushed

INTERNAL SENSATIONS:
The heart rate picking up slightly
Stomach flutters
Body heat rising

MENTAL RESPONSES:
Lending more weight to the opinions and actions of the one admired
Being open-minded and trusting
A desire to learn from or be privy to personal details or opinions
A feeling of well-being while in the presence of the admired
Feeling gratitude for the opportunity to spend time together

ACUTE OR LONG-TERM RESPONSES FOR THIS EMOTION:
Clapping, cheering, fist pumping
A handshake using both hands
Making favorable comparisons: *I hope one day I'm in your position* or *Wow, you're just so good at that. Maybe if I stick close enough I'll pick up your skill!*
Inviting closeness: *I'd love to have you over for dinner sometime.*
Prioritizing the other person and making time for them
Bringing the one admired up in conversation with others and singing their praises

SIGNS THAT THIS EMOTION IS BEING SUPPRESSED:
Breaking eye contact to look away briefly
Busying oneself so one isn't caught staring
Waiting at the fringe of a group but not moving toward the subject to engage
Taking deeper breaths to try and slow one's heartbeat
Listening in to a conversation with the one admired but not directly conversing with them
Hesitating before jumping into the conversation or introducing oneself

MAY ESCALATE TO: Eagerness (112), Adoration (32), Inspired (168), Envy (122)

MAY DE-ESCALATE TO: Valued (270), Pleased (206), Curiosity (74), Satisfaction (230)

ASSOCIATED POWER VERBS: Adore, applaud, aspire, bestow, brag, build up, clap, commend, congratulate, envy, flatter, gaze, greet, honor, imitate, invite, linger, marvel, praise, profess, recognize, recommend, respect, salute, thank, vouch, watch, welcome

> **WRITER'S TIP:** *If your character wants to give up, give them a reason to go on. What core beliefs do they hold that they will go to the mat to defend? What injustices or atrocities are just too morally painful to bear?*

ADORATION

DEFINITION: The act of worship; to view as divine

NOTES: The subject of adoration can be a person or thing

PHYSICAL SIGNALS AND BEHAVIORS:
Lips parting
A slack or soft expression
Walking quickly to erase the distance
Mirroring the subject's body language
Touching one's mouth or face
Reaching out to brush, touch, or grasp
Steady eye contact, with the pupils appearing larger
Leaning forward
Stroking one's own neck or arm as a surrogate
Pointing one's torso and feet toward the subject; having an open body posture
A flushed appearance or radiant glow
Inhaling deeply—anchoring oneself in the moment and taking in the scent of the subject
Nodding and smiling while the subject speaks
Releasing an appreciative sigh
Laying a hand over the heart
Frequently moistening the lips
Pressing the palms lightly against the cheeks
Skimming one's fingertips along the jaw line
Eyes that are bright and glossy
Showing agreement (murmuring affirmations, offering words of support, etc.)
Speaking praise and compliments
Keeping trinkets, pictures, or articles that one associates with the subject
Constantly talking about the subject to others
Displaying rapt attention (a lifted chin, body stillness, good posture, etc.)
Losing awareness of the external environment or other people
Visible shakiness
Reduced blinking
Closing the eyes to savor the experience
Speaking with a soft tone
A voice that cracks with emotion

INTERNAL SENSATIONS:
A quickening heartbeat
Breathlessness
Feeling one's pulse in the throat
Having a dry mouth
One's throat growing thick
Growing warmer as one's body temperature rises

MENTAL RESPONSES:
A desire to move closer or touch
Fixating one's thoughts on the subject
Acute listening and observation
Ignoring distractions
An inability to see the subject's flaws or faults

ACUTE OR LONG-TERM RESPONSES FOR THIS EMOTION:
Obsession or possessiveness
Fantasizing
Believing that the feelings are mutual
A sense of destiny (of belonging together)
Stalking
Writing and sending letters, email, and gifts
Taking risks or breaking laws to be near or with the subject
Weight loss
Poor sleep patterns
Jealousy towards those who frequently interact with the subject
Taking on traits or mannerisms of the subject
Carrying something that represents the subject (a picture, jewelry, etc.)

SIGNS THAT THIS EMOTION IS BEING SUPPRESSED:
Clenching or hiding one's hands to hide sweating or shaking
Avoiding conversations about the subject
Watching or observing from afar
Staying out of the subject's proximity
Blushing
An unsteady voice
Sneaking looks at the subject
Creating chance run-ins
Writing secret letters, keeping a personal journal, etc.
Lying about one's feelings regarding the subject

MAY ESCALATE TO: Love (180), Obsession (194), Desire (86), Frustration (134), Hurt (156)

MAY DE-ESCALATE TO: Conflicted (66), Disappointment (96), Embarrassment (118)

ASSOCIATED POWER VERBS: Adore, awe, covet, crave, enchant, enthrall, grasp, idolize, infatuate, need, obsess, pine, reach, spellbind, stroke, tease, touch, worship, yearn

WRITER'S TIP: Body cues should create a strong mental picture. If the movement is too drawn-out or complicated, the emotional meaning behind the gesture may be lost.

AGITATION

DEFINITION: Feeling upset or disturbed; a state of unrest

PHYSICAL SIGNALS AND BEHAVIORS:
A reddening of the face
A sheen of sweat on the cheeks, chin, and forehead
Flexing one's fingers repeatedly
Rubbing the back of the neck
Patting pockets or digging in a purse, looking for something lost
Clumsiness due to rushing (knocking things over, bumping tables, etc.)
A gaze that bounces from place to place
An inability to stay still
Jamming or cramming things away without care
Abrupt movement (e.g., causing a chair to tip or scuff the floor loudly)
Flapping one's hands or displaying jerky movements
Becoming accident prone (e.g., bashing one's hip on a desk corner)
Dragging the hands through the hair repeatedly
Forgetting words; being unable to articulate one's thoughts
Backtracking to try and undo something said in haste
Adjusting one's clothing
Avoiding eye contact
Speaking in a wavering voice or talking roughly
Not knowing where to look or go
Guarding one's personal space—e.g., crossing the arms to block contact
Taking too long to answer a question or respond
Throat-clearing
Overusing *ums*, *ahs*, and other verbal hesitations
Turning away from others
A bobbing Adam's apple
Pacing
Making odd noises in the throat
Rapid lip movement as one tries to find the right thing to say
Flinching if touched
Feet that shift and move when one is standing or sitting
Minimizing another's compliments and refusing to be placated
Fanning oneself or unbuttoning a top shirt button
Tugging at a tie, collar, or scarf as clothing begins to feel restrictive
Rolling one's eyes when the person isn't looking

INTERNAL SENSATIONS:
Excessive saliva
Feeling overheated
Stiffening hair on the nape
Light-headedness

Short, fast breaths due to a tightness in the chest
Sweating
Tingling skin as sweat forms
A jittery feeling in one's belly

MENTAL RESPONSES:
Mounting frustration that causes thoughts to blank
Compounding mistakes due to rushing
A tendency to lie to cover up or excuse one's behavior and overreactions
Anger at oneself for freezing up (negative self-talk)
Trying to pinpoint the source of discomfort
Mentally ordering oneself to calm down and relax

ACUTE OR LONG-TERM RESPONSES FOR THIS EMOTION:
Flight responses (looking for an escape route or fleeing the room)
Snapping at others
Adopting a defensive tone
Not caring about damage (e.g., scattering papers and files during a frantic search)
Being on edge due to the constant agitation

SIGNS THAT THIS EMOTION IS BEING SUPPRESSED:
Changing the subject
Making excuses
Joking to lighten the mood
Staying busy with tasks to avoid dealing with the source of the emotion
Shifting attention to others and putting them in the spotlight
Responding minimally when the subject comes up or the person makes an appearance

MAY ESCALATE TO: Flustered (132), Frustration (134), Anxiety (48), Anger (40)

MAY DE-ESCALATE TO: Admiration (30), Defensiveness (78), Resignation (224), Regret (214), Unease (266)

ASSOCIATED POWER VERBS: Annoy, berate, bother, bristle, chafe, cram, curse, disturb, erode, faze, fester, flush, flutter, frustrate, fume, grate, incite, irritate, jam, jerk, offend, rankle, rattle, rile, ruffle, shake, stew, tap, toss, twitch, undercut, vex, wince

WRITER'S TIP: *A ticking clock can ramp up the emotions in any scene. As the character hurries to complete a task or meet a need, mistakes caused by rushing might open the door for a richer emotional ride.*

AMAZEMENT

DEFINITION: Overwhelming astonishment or wonder

PHYSICAL SIGNALS AND BEHAVIORS:
A widening of the eyes
A slack mouth
Becoming suddenly still
Sucking in a quick breath
A hand covering one's mouth
Stiffening posture, with visible tension in muscles
Giving a small yelp
Gulping, stuttering, or sputtering
Rapid blinking followed by open staring
Flinching or starting, the body jumping slightly
Taking a step back
A slow, disbelieving shake of the head
Voicing wonder: *I can't believe it!* or *Look at that!*
Pulling out a cell phone to record the event
Glancing to see if others are experiencing the same thing
Pressing a hand against one's chest, fingers splayed out
Leaning in
Moving closer, reaching out, or touching
Eyebrows rising
Lips parting
A wide smile
Spontaneous laughter
Pressing one's palms to one's cheeks or the sides of the head
Jerky hand movements near the face
Speechlessness
Repeating the same things over and over
Walking a step or two only to turn around and come back
Squealing dramatically

INTERNAL SENSATIONS:
A heart that seems to freeze, then pound
The sound of blood rushing in one's ears
Rising body temperature
Tingling skin
Stalled breaths
Adrenaline spikes
A dry mouth

MENTAL RESPONSES:
Momentarily forgetting all else
Wanting to share the experience with others
Giddiness
Disorientation
Euphoria
An inability to find words

ACUTE OR LONG-TERM RESPONSES FOR THIS EMOTION:
A racing heartbeat
Shortness of breath
The knees going weak or even collapsing
Feeling overwhelmed, as if the room is closing in
Light-headedness due to a loss of spatial awareness

SIGNS THAT THIS EMOTION IS BEING SUPPRESSED:
Holding oneself tight (self-hugging)
Walking in jerky, self-contained strides
Clasping one's hands and pressing them tightly to one's chest
Looking down or away to hide one's expression
The eyes widening a bit before control is asserted
The mouth snapping shut
A stony expression
Taking a seat to hide the emotion
Making excuses if one's reaction is noticed
Forcing a cough to give oneself a moment to regain control

MAY ESCALATE TO: Curiosity (74), Disbelief (98), Excitement (126), Awe (54)

MAY DE-ESCALATE TO: Happiness (142), Gratitude (136), Satisfaction (230), Curiosity (74), Inspired (168)

ASSOCIATED POWER VERBS: Admire, astound, awe, blink, daze, dazzle, delight, disbelieve, enamor, entertain, gape, gasp, gaze, haunt, hypnotize, intrigue, jerk, marvel, murmur, peer, share, spellbind, spring, stagger, study, stun, touch, twist, witness, wonder

WRITER'S TIP: To add another layer to an emotional experience, look for symbolism within the character's current setting. What unique object within the location can the character make note of that perfectly embodies the emotion they are feeling inside?

AMUSEMENT

DEFINITION: Appealing to the sense of humor; experiencing entertainment or delight

PHYSICAL SIGNALS AND BEHAVIORS:
A shiny or rosy face
Raised or wiggling eyebrows
Snorting or laughing
Chuckling or cackling
Displaying a wide grin
Exchanging knowing looks with others
Witty commentary and observations
Turning away and bursting out in laughter
A playful pinch, nudge, or shove
Squinting, eyes lit with an inner glow or twinkle of mischief
Smirking or offering a bemused smile
Clutching at another person for support
Gasping for air
Slapping one's knees or thighs
Drumming one's feet against the floor
Falling against someone, shoulder to shoulder
"Drunken" behavior (weaving, staggering, etc.)
Repeating the punch line or a select word to spur more laughter
A high voice
Holding one's sides
Whimpers of mirth
Spewing food or drink if laughter hits while eating or drinking
Falling to the ground and rolling on the floor
Sniffing as one's nose runs
Crashing into things; being clumsy but not caring
A wide-eyed look that gets others dissolving into laughter again
Bending double and gripping one's knees
Making gestures or funny expressions to escalate the laughter
Holding onto a chair or wall for support
Giggling, making faces, and winking
Plucking at clothes to cool oneself down

INTERNAL SENSATIONS:
A pain in the ribs or stomach
Wheezy breaths
The body temperature jumping up
Weakness in the limbs, especially the knees

MENTAL RESPONSES:
A need to sit down

Replaying the humorous event
Embellishing the event in one's mind, increasing the mirth
Wanting to keep the amusement going by adding to it with others
Feeling lighter; one's worries or concerns evaporating for the moment

ACUTE OR LONG-TERM RESPONSES FOR THIS EMOTION:
Uncontrollable laughter
Laughing so hard it becomes soundless
The body quaking
Shaking the head emphatically
A loss of body control (weak muscles, having a hard time staying upright, etc.)
Begging people to stop
An inability to form words
Breathlessness
Eyes tearing
A sweaty, disheveled appearance
Loss of bladder control
Needing to leave the room

SIGNS THAT THIS EMOTION IS BEING SUPPRESSED:
Clamping the lips together
Holding a hand up as if to say *No more!*
Shaking the head
Swallowing laughter
Wiping at the mouth
Avoiding eye contact with others
Covering the mouth and biting one's lips to hide a smile
A reddening of the face
Turning away to collect oneself
Confining a laugh to a snort
Pressing a fist against the lips

MAY ESCALATE TO: Happiness (142), Satisfaction (230), Elation (114), Moved (186)

MAY DE-ESCALATE TO: Admiration (30), Connectedness (70)

ASSOCIATED POWER VERBS: Banter, beam, cackle, catcall, chuckle, clap, dance, entertain, giggle, grin, heckle, holler, hoot, howl, impress, joke, kid, laugh, mime, mimic, nudge, poke, prank, shout, smile, smirk, snigger, snort, tease, tickle, titillate, titter, wheeze

WRITER'S TIP: *To add tension to a scene, include someone who carries emotional weight with your character. Who frightens them, creates anxiety, or makes them more volatile?*

ANGER

DEFINITION: Strong displeasure or wrath, usually aroused by a perceived wrong

PHYSICAL SIGNALS AND BEHAVIORS:
Flaring nostrils
Noisy breathing
Sweating
Sweeping arm gestures
Handling objects or people roughly
A high chin
Legs that are planted wide
Baring one's teeth, glaring
Repetitive, sharp gestures (shaking a fist, etc.)
Cutting people off when they speak
Jerky head movements
Eyes that seem to bulge
Flexing the fingers or arm muscles
Cracking one's knuckles
Rolling up one's sleeves or loosening a collar
Eyes that are cold, hard, or flinty
Entering another's personal space to intimidate them
A tightness in the eyes or expression
A reddening of the face
Lips that flatten or curl
Closed body posture (crossing the arms, etc.)
Pounding one's fists against thighs, table, a wall, etc.
Slamming doors, cupboards, or drawers
Punching, kicking, and throwing things
Stomping or stamping
A vein that pulses, twitches, or becomes engorged
Laughter with an edge
A shaking or raised voice; yelling
Deepening one's tone
Picking fights (verbal or physical)
Snapping at people
Visible sweat on one's skin

INTERNAL SENSATIONS:
Grinding one's teeth
Muscles quivering
Pulse speeding
A pounding heartbeat
The body tensing
Heat flushing through the body

MENTAL RESPONSES:
Irritability
Poor listening skills
Jumping to conclusions
Irrational reactions to inconsequential things
Demanding immediate action
Impetuosity
Taking inappropriate action or risks
Fantasizing violence

ACUTE OR LONG-TERM RESPONSES FOR THIS EMOTION:
Exploding over little things
Ulcers and hypertension
Skin problems, such as eczema and acne
Damaging one's own property to vent
Longer recovery time from surgeries, accidents, and other trauma
Road rage
Taking anger out on innocent bystanders

SIGNS THAT THIS EMOTION IS BEING SUPPRESSED:
Using a carefully controlled tone
Drawing in slow, steady breaths
Passive-aggressive comments
Avoiding eye contact
Withdrawing from the conversation
Excusing oneself for a brief time
Headaches
Experiencing sore muscles and pain in the jaw

MAY ESCALATE TO: Rage (212), Hatred (144), Obsession (194), Vengefulness (272)

MAY DE-ESCALATE TO: Bitterness (58), Emasculation (116), Frustration (134), Irritation (172), Annoyance (44)

ASSOCIATED POWER VERBS: Blaze, consume, explode, flare, inflame, provoke, quake, rage, redden, restrain, rile, seethe, shout, simmer, surge, tremble, trigger, vent

WRITER'S TIP: *Pay special attention to the events leading up to an emotional response. If the plotting feels contrived, the character's reaction will seem contrived as well.*

ANGUISH

DEFINITION: Emotional or mental distress; acute suffering

PHYSICAL SIGNALS AND BEHAVIORS:
Manic pacing
Rubbing the back of one's neck
Tugging one's hair
Not eating or drinking
Visible sweating
Skin bunching around the eyes
A pained stare
Hands clenching into fists
Rubbing the wrists or wringing the hands
Restless fingers
Jumping at sounds
Grinding one's teeth or clenching the jaw
A corded neck
Moving about; being unable to settle in one place
Muscles jumping under the skin
Curling one's toes
Repeatedly touching an object that symbolizes safety
Audible stress in one's voice and tone
Picking at one's lips, skin, or nails
Clutching at oneself (self-soothing reactions)
Shivering, moaning, sobbing, or weeping
Yelling or shouting; becoming emotionally unstable
Checking and rechecking the time
Asking those in authority for updates
Shoulders that curl over the chest
Bringing one's legs up close to the body's core
Turning away from others while muttering
Seeking corners in confined spaces
Beating at walls or surrounding objects for a release

INTERNAL SENSATIONS:
Sore muscles, stiffness, and cramping
Pain in the back of the throat (difficulty swallowing)
Elevated body temperature
Nausea

MENTAL RESPONSES:
Thinking irrationally
Praying, bargaining, and making mental promises

Fixating on the source of suffering
A willingness to put oneself in harm's way for emotional relief

ACUTE OR LONG-TERM RESPONSES FOR THIS EMOTION:
Screaming for release
A gaunt appearance, wasting away, and premature aging
Posture that bends or crumples
Vomiting or dry heaving
Hyperventilation
Poor coloring; dark circles under the eyes
Wrinkles and sagging around the eyes and mouth
Alcohol, drug, or medication dependency
Bald patches
Facial tics or repetitive mannerisms (hair tugging, body rocking, etc.)
Cutting, scratching, or other self-destructive behaviors
Depression and suicidal thoughts or attempts

SIGNS THAT THIS EMOTION IS BEING SUPPRESSED:
Wincing
Gritting one's teeth
Facial tension
Uncontrolled shivering and hand tremors
Furtive movements
Hiding expressive gestures like hand wringing
Bitten nails with bleeding quicks
A downturned mouth or pinched lips
Pressed lips that tremble
Engaging in hard manual labor (to expend energy and exhaust oneself)
Minimal speaking (one-word answers, shaking or nodding the head, etc.)
Chain smoking or heavy drinking

MAY ESCALATE TO: Desperation (90), Tormented (260), Depressed (84), Hysteria (158)

MAY DE-ESCALATE TO: Hurt (156), Guilt (140), Unease (266), Uncertainty (264), Vulnerability (276), Self-Pity (238)

ASSOCIATED POWER VERBS: Blister, burn, consume, distress, endure, groan, howl, inflict, moan, overcome, pain, pierce, seize, sob, strangle, suffer, suffocate, torment, writhe

WRITER'S TIP: *Don't be afraid to challenge your character's morals. Putting them in situations that are outside their comfort zone will make them squirm, and the reader will too.*

ANNOYANCE

DEFINITION: Aggravation or mild irritation

PHYSICAL SIGNALS AND BEHAVIORS:
A pinched expression
Sighing heavily or with exaggeration
Statements suggesting impatience: *Here, I'll do it.*
Narrowing eyes
Tapping a foot
Swatting at the air as if to remove obstacles
Tics and tells (a throbbing forehead vein, fingering a collar, etc.)
One's lips pressing into a white slash
Clenching the jaw
Grimacing, sneering, and frowning
Complaining
Folding the arms across the chest
Hands that briefly clench
Making pointed suggestions to alleviate the annoyance
Tugging at clothing (jerking down a cuff, forcing a zipper up, etc.)
Cocking one's head and then shaking it
Raising one's eyebrows and giving a glassy stare
A gaze that flicks upward
Minutely shaking the head
Changing one's stance (shifting weight or position)
Propping the head up with a fist
Opening the mouth to criticize, then stopping short
Taking a deep breath and holding it in
Finger-tapping a tabletop
A smile that slips or appears forced
Snapping a pencil tip, using unnecessary force
Pacing
Light sarcasm
Asking a question that has a painfully obvious answer
A sharp tone
Speaking in short phrases
Visible tension in the neck, shoulders, and arms
Rigid posture
Rubbing the brow as if to ward off a headache
Avoiding the person or object of annoyance
Pressing a fist to the mouth

INTERNAL SENSATIONS:
A headache

Raised body temperature
Sensitivity to noise

MENTAL RESPONSES:

Berating thoughts
Straying attention
Thinking of an excuse to leave
Making unkind mental comparisons
Wishing to be somewhere else

ACUTE OR LONG-TERM RESPONSES FOR THIS EMOTION:

A reddening face
Rough handling of objects
Taking over someone else's job or duties
Grinding one's teeth
Throwing the hands up in a gesture of surrender
Stalking off to get some air
Shutting down; not speaking or responding

SIGNS THAT THIS EMOTION IS BEING SUPPRESSED:

Nodding tightly, as if holding back from speaking an insult
Switching to another job to keep one's hands and thoughts busy
Attacking a task to divert one's energy
Forcing oneself to remain in the presence of the annoyance
Faking interest; barely holding impatience at bay
Carefully controlling one's voice and tone
Focusing one's gaze elsewhere in an attempt to ignore the source of annoyance

MAY ESCALATE TO: Frustration (134), Anger (40)

MAY DE-ESCALATE TO: Conflicted (66), Indifference (164), Acceptance (28)

ASSOCIATED POWER VERBS: Avoid, bother, bristle, clench, complain, discomfort, displease, exhale, fidget, fluster, grate, grind, grit, grumble, intrude, irritate, mutter, nettle, pester, prickle, push, rasp, reach, rub, scrape, sigh, taunt, tire, unnerve, unsettle

WRITER'S TIP: *Don't get caught up on the eyes to convey emotion. While eyes are often the first thing we notice in real life, they provide very limited options for description possibilities. Instead, dig deeper, showing how the character behaves through their body movement, actions and dialogue.*

ANTICIPATION

DEFINITION: Hopeful expectation; to await eagerly

PHYSICAL SIGNALS AND BEHAVIORS:
Sweaty palms
Trembling hands
Crossing and uncrossing one's legs
Frantic planning for the event
List-making
Clasping one's hands to the chest
Being unable to think or talk about anything else
Fidgeting as if movement will make things go faster
Bouncing on one's toes
A bright-eyed look as one engages with others or the environment
Fussing with clothes and rearranging things
Waiting at a window, hovering at the door or by the phone
Checking and rechecking one's hair or makeup in a mirror
Gossiping with others, sharing excitement, and giggling
Closing the eyes and squealing or releasing a mock growl
Jittering a foot against the floor
Covering one's face and then peeking
Biting one's lip
Fake swooning
Asking questions: *How long? When? What is it?*
Wetting the lips
Closing the eyes and sighing
Pacing
Rhythmic movements (swinging one's legs back and forth, etc.)
Obsessive clockwatching, or checking and rechecking email
Phoning or texting friends to talk about what's coming
Grabbing another person and saying *Tell me!*
Leaning in
Picking at food because one is too excited to eat
Begging someone for details, an answer, or to get a look at something

INTERNAL SENSATIONS:
A fluttery, empty feeling in the stomach
Breathlessness
A pounding heart
Tingling all over

MENTAL RESPONSES:
Daydreaming

Fearing that something will happen to screw things up
A lack of concentration
Imagining what will happen
Becoming self-critical (questioning clothing choices, one's abilities, etc.)

ACUTE OR LONG-TERM RESPONSES FOR THIS EMOTION:
Sleep loss
Frustration or impatience
Short-temperedness and irritability
Neglecting everything else (responsibilities, friends, family, etc.)
Fantasizing or building up the event far beyond its reality
Overthinking (e.g., organizing every minute detail)
Going overboard in preparation (e.g., dressing over-the-top)

SIGNS THAT THIS EMOTION IS BEING SUPPRESSED:
Sitting unnaturally still
Pressing one's lips together
Rubbing sweaty hands on one's clothes
Pretending to read a book or watch TV
A corded neck
Clamping one's hands tightly together
Avoiding conversation
Sneaking glances at a clock or doorway
Feigning boredom
Telling oneself that it doesn't matter
Acting interested in something else
Rolling one's shoulders and neck as if they're stiff

MAY ESCALATE TO: Excitement (126), Desire (86), Jealousy (174), Pleased (206)

MAY DE-ESCALATE TO: Disillusionment (104), Disappointment (96), Indifference (164)

ASSOCIATED POWER VERBS: Arouse, await, beam, beg, bounce, buzz, clench, excite, expect, flutter, gleam, glow, grin, heighten, hope, lean, quiver, race, shiver, sparkle, speculate, stir, strum, tense, thrill, tingle, tremble, whet, wonder

WRITER'S TIP: *If a critique partner voices confusion over the emotional reaction of one of your characters, check to make sure the stimulus trigger is prominent. Showing the cause-effect relationship is vital when conveying authentic emotion.*

ANXIETY

DEFINITION: An intense feeling of unease and worry, sometimes without cause

PHYSICAL SIGNALS AND BEHAVIORS:
Rubbing the back of the neck
Crossing the arms, forming a barrier to others
Standing with one arm clasping the other at the elbow
Clutching a purse, coat, or other object
Wringing one's hands or rubbing at the skin in a self-soothing way
Twisting a watch or ring
Hands repeatedly rising to touch one's face
Fingering a necklace (especially if it is a symbol of comfort)
Rolling one's shoulders
Glancing at the clock, phone, or doorway
Holding the stomach and bending forward slightly
Clutching one's hands
Rocking in place
Twisting one's neck, as if it's sore
Biting at the lips or nails
Head shaking
Shifting, unable to get comfortable
Blowing out a series of short breaths to gain control
Digging in a purse or pocket to keep the hands busy
Becoming easily distracted
Adjusting clothes, as if they chafe
Rubbing one's arms and looking around
Bouncing a curled knuckle against the mouth
A darting gaze
Increased awareness of one's environment
Starting at noises or sudden movements
Excessive swallowing
Repeatedly checking a phone for messages
Impatience
Praying

INTERNAL SENSATIONS:
Feeling too hot or too cold
Restless legs
Dizziness
A churning stomach
Increased thirst
Tingling in one's limbs
A tightening chest and accelerated breathing

MENTAL RESPONSES:
Thinking about worst-case scenarios
Engaging in self-blame
Seeking reassurance from others
Time feeling like it's slowing down
Irrational worries
Mentally beating oneself up for being unable to control this feeling
Replaying the events that caused this feeling

ACUTE OR LONG-TERM RESPONSES FOR THIS EMOTION:
Excessive sweating
A ragged appearance
Talking to oneself under the breath
Rocking in one's seat
Heart palpitations, hyperventilating, or even panic attacks
Emergence of fears, phobias, or OCD-like symptoms

SIGNS THAT THIS EMOTION IS BEING SUPPRESSED:
Tightness in the eyes
Avoiding conversation
Finding somewhere to be alone
Doing things to appear normal (e.g., ordering food but not eating it)
Feigning interest in something nearby
Closing one's eyes in an attempt to stay calm
Smoothing or stroking one's hair as a soothing gesture

MAY ESCALATE TO: Fear (128), Desperation (90), Paranoia (200), Panic (198), Hysteria (158)

MAY DE-ESCALATE TO: Wariness (280), Vulnerability (276), Relief (216), Gratitude (136)

ASSOCIATED POWER VERBS: Bother, brood, carve, chase, choke, dig, distract, drill, fluster, gnaw, grate, insist, jar, jerk, jump, natter, pace, pester, pound, press, question, rattle, rub, shake, speculate, squeeze, startle, strain, struggle, sweat, twist, unsettle, upset, wring

WRITER'S TIP: *For each scene, identify the emotion you need to show and think in terms of three…what three ways have you reinforced the character's feelings through verbal and nonverbal communication?*

APPALLED

DEFINITION: An emotionally disturbing shock due to something offensive

PHYSICAL SIGNALS AND BEHAVIORS
Flinching or jerking back from the source
The lips curling or pulling back in disgust
An audible intake of breath
A gaping mouth
Eyes bulging, followed by rapid blinking
Looking away or down while stepping back
The eyebrows drawing close together
The jaw going slack
Slowly yet forcibly expelling all breath as one tries to process what's happening
One's lips moving as words refuse to immediately form
One's posture straightening, the muscles visibly tightening
Clasping a hand over one's own mouth
Grabbing the fabric of one's shirt in a fist (at chest level)
Briefly covering one's mouth and then moving the hand to one's breastbone
Putting a hand out as if to ward off what one has witnessed or was told
Swallowing before speaking
Asking *What?* sharply (if the shock resulted from something another said)
Saying *Oh my God*, or *Did you see what he did?* as one tries to process
One's shoulders rolling forward as the chest caves, making the neck seem to shrink
Rubbing at the chest
Appearing to go white in the face
Legs drawing together as one's stance tightens
Rubbing hands against one's clothing as if trying to rid them of something
Backing away; increasing personal distance from the source
Turning away and raising the hands to the face
Responding with broken sentences as one tries to find the right words
Raising a hand to the temple and shaking one's head
One's voice rising in volume
Gesturing wildly as one discusses the situation with others

INTERNAL SENSATIONS:
The gut tightening as one forces out all breath
A dry mouth
Light-headedness as one's breath briefly gets trapped in the lungs
One's palm (or fist) growing hot from a forced exhale
A feeling of disorientation
A flush of heat in the face and neck as shock transforms into anger

MENTAL RESPONSES:
Mentally replaying what one has just witnessed or experienced
Sharpened focus on and scrutiny of the source
One's thoughts leaping forward to possible repercussions of what one has just learned
Not wanting to be touched
Feeling a rush of disappointment in those responsible
Looking for someone or something to blame
A need for answers, to know why, to understand how this outcome came about

ACUTE OR LONG-TERM RESPONSES FOR THIS EMOTION:
The eyes growing hot and tearing up
Becoming extremely inarticulate or incapable of speaking altogether
Going over the moment again and again in one's mind
Berating oneself for not seeing this coming or for misplacing one's trust
Disbelief leading to disillusionment (in others, a specific person, society, etc.)
Growing angry and confrontational (fight)
Needing to escape because one can't deal with the situation (flight)

SIGNS THAT THIS EMOTION IS BEING SUPPRESSED:
Eyes that widen slightly
Tightness in the face
A gaping mouth that is quickly closed
The lips pressing into a tight, flat line
Rapid swallowing
Not speaking to avoid giving away one's feelings
Turning away from the source or avoiding eye contact to try and collect oneself
Hesitating or clearing the throat to compose oneself before changing the subject or redirecting attention elsewhere

MAY ESCALATE TO: Anger (40), Disgust (102), Resentment (222), Defiance (80)

MAY DE-ESCALATE TO: Disbelief (98), Disappointment (96), Disillusionment (104)

ASSOCIATED POWER VERBS: Back away, balk, blanch, bristle, flinch, gape, gasp, horrify, offend, rankle, rattle, recoil, repel, shake, shock, shrink, sicken, snap, squawk, stagger, startle, stumble, stutter, swallow, taint, unseat, unsettle, wince

WRITER'S TIP: *Emotions aren't always pure or beautiful; sometimes characters feel things that will reveal their dark side. Don't be afraid to show these moments when it's important to the story. Readers will recognize they come from a place of truth and appreciate the author's honesty to write them.*

APPREHENSION

DEFINITION: A stress state caused by the anticipation of misfortune or adversity

PHYSICAL SIGNALS AND BEHAVIORS:
Watching the clock or door (or checking one's phone for a text, etc.)
Chewing the inside of a cheek
Wetting or biting the lips
Rocking slightly with a faraway look (an inward gaze)
An uneven stride or hesitating before moving
A fixed look of concentration
Growing unusually quiet
Offering a flash of a smile that doesn't reach the eyes
Needing to get up, move, or do something
Gripping the hands together
Repeatedly pinching the skin between the thumb and forefinger
Picking at one's cuticles
Touching the face frequently (scratching a cheek, rubbing an eyebrow, etc.)
A strained voice
Impatience with others
Rapping one's fingers against the thigh, or tapping a loose fist against the lips
Taking periodic deep breaths with long exhales
Smoothing down one's clothing
Changing one's clothing frequently (if one will be judged for one's appearance)
Grimacing; displaying a pained look
Fidgeting and touching things; needing to keep one's hands busy
Going into planning mode (talking out options, making notes to oneself, etc.)
Starting tasks only to abandon them due to a lack of focus
Being unable to engage fully with others (relaxing, conversing, sharing activities, etc.)
Picking at food due to a lackluster appetite or displaying the opposite in the form of restless snacking
Drinking too much coffee, smoking too much, vaping far more than usual, etc.
Difficulty following conversations unless they center on one's worries
Rubbing one's arms as if they're cold
Needing to talk things out with others (even strangers) to process feelings
Asking others for their take on the situation
Soliciting information from people in the know to better understand what one is up against
Turning to those who have navigated this situation or challenge before
Listing possible problems and obstacles on paper
Talking to oneself

INTERNAL SENSATIONS:
A tightness or tingling in the chest
Dryness in the mouth caused by frequent swallowing

Light-headedness
An upset stomach
Feeling itchier than normal

MENTAL RESPONSES:
A fixation on whatever is causing the apprehension
Creating a mental tally of what could go wrong
Thinking back to other experiences where apprehension was warranted
Proactively building strategies to deal with possible complications
Engaging in self-talk to encourage positive thinking and optimism (which only half-works)
Sensitivity to loud or unusual sounds
Thoughts that won't turn off
Wishing time would hurry up
Difficulty sleeping, or falling asleep but quickly waking up again
Over-preparing (studying, over-packing, checking and re-checking documents, etc.)

ACUTE OR LONG-TERM RESPONSES FOR THIS EMOTION:
Second-guessing one's decisions and actions
Being risk-averse and taking extra precautions
Reversing a choice due to irrational superstitions or the idea that "safe is better than sorry"
Being impatient with others; displaying rudeness
Lashing out over small things

SIGNS THAT THIS EMOTION IS BEING SUPPRESSED:
Asking questions in a roundabout way that circle one's concerns or fears
Trying to stay active to distract oneself from worry
Nodding to oneself and speaking with optimism
Apologizing and making an excuse for any unusual behavior that draws attention
Feigning fatigue or boredom to appear at ease to others
A smile that appears frozen or that disappears quickly

MAY ESCALATE TO: Dread (110), Fear (128), Tormented (260)

MAY DE-ESCALATE TO: Vulnerability (276), Relief (216), Unease (266)

ASSOCIATED POWER VERBS: Agitate, clasp, conceal, confess, disguise, dread, fidget, fuss, grow, lean, obsess, overthink, pace, pinch, question, redo, reevaluate, rethink, reverse, seize, shift, startle, strain, tighten, tremble, undo, unsettle, voice, wait, watch, waver, worry

> **WRITER'S TIP:** *The emotional spectrum is vast, yet often we only see more prominent "core" feelings being described. Go off the map! Incorporate a variety of feelings to provide a richer experience for your readers.*

AWE

DEFINITION: Euphoric-like wonder at being in the presence of something vast enough to change one's perceptions or understanding of the world

NOTES: Awe can enlighten or terrify (based on whether the character can handle what they have experienced), since it often leaves a person feeling small and insignificant. For the negative emotional reaction, please see the HORROR entry (149).

PHYSICAL SIGNALS AND BEHAVIORS:
Ceasing all movement
Tension leaving one's body
The shoulders dropping
One's mouth falling open slightly (a slack jaw)
The neck tipping back
A deeper intake of breath
Unabashed staring
Slowly releasing a deep breath
Being rendered speechless (or becoming less articulate)
Forgetting to blink; having a fixed gaze
Laying a hand against the breastbone
Grabbing the sides of one's head and then sliding one's fingers down the cheeks
Remaining still for an extended time, not wishing to interrupt the surreal moment
Being overcome with a desire to get closer (taking a step, reaching out, etc.)
Moving carefully (having a lighter touch, taking slower steps, etc.)
Speaking softly as to not break the spell
Repeating *Wow,* or *This is unbelievable.*
Fumbling a hand toward someone else to draw their attention to the source or event
Sitting down to observe and absorb, casting aside other priorities
Wrapping one's arms around oneself
Uncontrolled trembling
Slowly sliding from a standing to a sitting position
Squatting down, as if to rest one's legs while taking in the spectacle

INTERNAL SENSATIONS:
Goosebumps sliding along the back of the neck
The heart rate picking up
Light-headedness
An expanding feeling in the chest
Feeling fully awake and energized in the aftermath (adrenaline rush)
Swallowing to relieve dryness from one's mouth hanging open

MENTAL RESPONSES:
Concerns and worries falling away

Feeling utterly present in the moment
Heightened senses; acute awareness of sensory stimuli (colors, smells, sensations, etc.)
Noticing and cataloging "the little things" as part of the experience
A desire to share the moment with others; feeling a sense of connection
Curiosity being awakened, resulting in mental questions and observations
Ignoring discomforts and distractions easily; staying fully focused on the experience

ACUTE OR LONG-TERM RESPONSES FOR THIS EMOTION:
A willingness to take risks if it increases one's connection to the event or experience
Legs that wobble (going weak due to overstimulation)
Tears sliding down one's face
Being so present in the moment one forgets to record the experience on a cell phone
A desire to travel, have new experiences, or connect with the world in a meaningful way
Increased generosity and compassion
Being more willing to help others
One's mind returning to the experience afterward to revisit the feeling
Feeling different than before, like one is more awake or aware
In the aftermath, experiencing a "reset" of what's important in life

SIGNS THAT THIS EMOTION IS BEING SUPPRESSED:
Turning away, breaking eye contact (with effort), and shrugging
Sneaking glances at the event or situation rather than keeping one's focus there
Speaking when there's no need, just to "break the spell"
Minimizing the importance of the current moment by relaying a past story or experience that was more awe-inducing
Fidgeting on purpose to appear restless or bored (flicking open a lighter lid and closing it over and over, jangling keys, exploring one's pockets, etc.)

MAY ESCALATE TO: Euphoria (124), Adoration (32), Desire (86), Obsession (194)

MAY DE-ESCALATE TO: Moved (186), Connectedness (70), Admiration (30), Happiness (142), Peacefulness (202), Satisfaction (230), Humbled (152)

ASSOCIATED POWER VERBS: Astound, bask, calm, comfort, dazzle, fascinate, floor, gape, gawk, hearten, inspire, listen, mesmerize, mystify, praise, revel, savor, shiver, silence, spellbind, strike, stun, stupefy, thrill, tingle, touch, transfix, tremble, whisper, wonder

WRITER'S TIP: *When you're describing a character's emotional reaction through the eyes of another character, think about the depth of their relationship. If it's close, a simple hair tuck or half-wave could be steeped in meaning which the point of view character can then share with the reader.*

BETRAYED

DEFINITION: A state of wounded outrage at being dehumanized and disrespected by someone of value

NOTES: When a character feels betrayed, reactions will vary depending on how personal the relationship was. This state often embraces a progression of complicated emotions: shock, disbelief, and denial that eventually turn to acceptance, hurt, or outrage.

PHYSICAL SIGNALS AND BEHAVIORS:
One's posture stiffening suddenly
Flinching (especially if the betrayal is revealed through something said)
A shocked, deeply pained look (the eyebrows drawing together, an inward stare, etc.)
Closing the eyes while lowering one's head
Poking a tongue against a cheek while exhaling
A deliberate, angry shaking of the head, with the mouth forming a round "O"
Letting out a forceful breath
Difficulty forming words immediately
Forearm muscles that twitch and grow taut
The head cocking to the side
Making fists (possibly quaking and whitening from the tension)
Lips that are pinched tight
An intense, cold stare
Rubbing at the hair on one's crown and then grabbing a fistful
Kneading at one's chest
Holding one's head while seated and asking *Why?* or saying *I can't believe this.*
Quick, jerky movements
Increasing personal distance (backing up, creating space between oneself and others, etc.)
Shielding the body (crossing one's arms, moving to stand behind a chair, etc.)
Clumsiness that escalates one's rage
Throwing or shoving something for release
A voice that grows rough or thick
Speaking in short bursts or letting out a long tirade
Needing to sit down but being unable to stay seated for long
Swearing, name-calling, and making verbal judgments
Clenching or grinding one's teeth
Rising in height, the spine going stiff as anger takes hold
Pinching the bridge of one's nose and pushing out slow, deep breaths to try and calm down
Revealing secrets or sensitive information about the person to others

INTERNAL SENSATIONS:
Pressure or pain as one sucks in the cheeks to bite down on them in anger
A sharp pain or sudden tightness in the chest
Blurring vision and a sensation of heat as one tries to fend off tears

Growing hot as the body temperature rises
Pain in the palms from fingernails digging into skin (clenched fists)

MENTAL RESPONSES:
A primal urge to hit or destroy something (fight)
Vacillating between disbelief, hurt, and rage
A desire for revenge
Feeling deeply vulnerable and exposed
Recalling past interactions with the betrayer and analyzing them for missed signs
Wanting to be alone to process what's happened (flight)

ACUTE OR LONG-TERM RESPONSES FOR THIS EMOTION:
Negative self-talk for not seeing this coming or for offering trust in the first place
Self-loathing for a perceived inner weakness (naivety, gullibility, etc.)
Fantasizing about the betrayer getting what they deserve
Making plans to bring the betrayer's actions to light so they are held accountable
Seeking revenge and engaging in violence

SIGNS THAT THIS EMOTION IS BEING SUPPRESSED:
Going from animated and engaged to withdrawn and nonverbal
Taking longer than normal to respond in a conversation
Making an excuse to leave
Laughing it off
Showing false empathy: *I'm sure he had a good reason,* or *She must have been in a bad place.*
Acting as if this outcome was expected
Being the bigger person even though it hurts deeply (responding with grace)

MAY ESCALATE TO: Appalled (50), Rage (212), Vengefulness (272)

MAY DE-ESCALATE TO: Disillusionment (104), Insecurity (166), Wariness (280), Powerlessness (208), Bitterness (58)

ASSOCIATED POWER VERBS: Ache, alienate, blindside, bruise, carve, clench, cripple, crush, cut, daze, demoralize, destroy, devastate, erode, eviscerate, falter, grieve, hinder, impede, insult, jeopardize, offend, rattle, ravage, resent, retaliate, scathe, shake, shock, strike, suffer, tarnish, undermine, upset, violate, weaken, wound

WRITER'S TIP: *All people, and therefore all characters, make associations when exploring their world. For each setting, think about any emotional attachments a character may have to it based on their past experiences. Then, use these associations to evoke mood.*

BITTERNESS

DEFINITION: Deep hostility and unhappiness caused by unfair treatment

PHYSICAL SIGNALS AND BEHAVIORS:
Snarky commentary designed to take away from someone else's good mood
A pinched mouth and sour expression
A direct stare that lacks warmth
Speaking matter-of-factly
A tightness in one's eyes
Looking upward and disparagingly shaking one's head
Taking offense easily
A closed body posture (arms crossed in front of the chest, increased personal distance, etc.)
Minimizing the accomplishments of others: *That's because her daddy's well connected.*
Complaining constantly
Sneering
A set jaw
Saying things like *There's nothing to forgive* but not meaning it
Having strong opinions about everything
Interrupting, especially when someone is sharing something positive
Sharp or stiff movements that allude to controlled anger
Being unable to relax, especially when one is close to the source of the emotional pain
Fixating on the perceived injustice (stalking someone on social media who was involved in a betrayal, for example)
Pointing out the faults and flaws of others
Telling people what they should do or how they can do it better
False smiles or enthusiasm at someone's good news
A hard edge to one's voice and words
Starting arguments or being argumentative
Lashing out at others over little things to mask one's pain regarding the real issue
Nursing grudges and bringing up the past
Rarely saying *Thank you* or showing gratitude
Choosing not to help when one could (especially if one feels slighted by the individual making the request)
Being quick to lay blame
Angry outbursts that are out of proportion to the circumstance
Being two-faced
Stiffness when touching others, such as when one is accepting or giving a hug
Being prone to illness

INTERNAL SENSATIONS:
Tightness in the chest
A jaw that aches
Headaches or body pain

MENTAL RESPONSES:

Believing that someone else is to blame for one's circumstances
Having trust issues
Believing others could have intervened and prevented one's pain
Refusing to take responsibility for negative outcomes
A desire to get even or force someone else to experience one's pain
An inability to forgive
Being quick to judge
Jealousy and envy over even the smallest things
Moods that often run either hot or cold

ACUTE OR LONG-TERM RESPONSES FOR THIS EMOTION:

Isolation
Playing the martyr; being unable to move on from an event
Being unable to engage in small talk with others
Negativity that seeps into all aspects of one's life
Health issues
Losing friendships (due to one's negativity, a toxic outlook, etc.)

SIGNS THAT THIS EMOTION IS BEING SUPPRESSED:

Making passive-aggressive comments
Giving small, tight smiles
Speaking positively but showing negativity through one's actions (e.g., offering congratulations while furiously drying dishes or dashing off a memo)
Giving backhanded compliments: *Good job. I didn't think you had it in you.*
Making oneself scarce once good news is shared

MAY ESCALATE TO: Anger (40), Rage (212), Vengefulness (272)

MAY DE-ESCALATE TO: Resentment (222), Irritation (172), Disappointment (96), Self-Pity (238)

ASSOCIATED POWER VERBS: Berate, betray, blame, boil, bristle, complain, disbelieve, dredge, fester, flame, flare, gall, glower, heat, insult, irritate, jab, judge, mutter, point, poke, provoke, quarrel, resent, seethe, shock, smolder, spar, spit, sputter, struggle, sulk

WRITER'S TIP: With emotion, get personal. A tragic situation like a news story about a lost child on TV will affect everyone, but if the child is someone special to the character who is watching, the effect is tenfold.

CERTAINTY

DEFINITION: A state of absolute belief; to be without doubt

PHYSICAL SIGNALS AND BEHAVIORS:
A strong decisive nod or rapid nodding
Unwavering eye contact
A lack of hesitation to commit or volunteer
Speaking in absolutes: *The vote will go through*, or *There's no way to recover from this.*
Thrusting the chest out
Touching others to get their attention (grabbing an arm, etc.)
Having good posture (shoulders back, drawing up to full height, etc.)
Head lifted high, exposing the neck
Being decisive (making decisions quickly, not needing to ask for advice or input)
Even breathing, exuding calm
A wide, open stance
Quietly observing; not needing to prove oneself
Inviting questions and being willing to answer them
Moving closer to others or showing a willingness to let others in one's personal space
Responding to questions quickly and firmly
Citing facts and past experiences to back up one's belief in conversation
Speaking confidently and positively, without any need for subterfuge or insults
Waving a hand dismissively when others show doubt
Smiling at concerns or worries to display their groundlessness
Having an answer for every question
Becoming more verbal or emphatic (if conveying one's conviction is needed)
A firm handshake
Disengaging in a judgmental tone if others don't fall into line: *Well, good luck, then.*
Being the first to act or react
A willingness to approach or engage
A voice that is firm
Speaking one's mind; not beating around the bush
A noticeable lack of fidgeting, touching the face, or fiddling with things
Stating opinions rather than making suggestions
Making grandiose statements on where one stands: *I'm right about this. I'd bet my house on it.*
Moving with confidence (no hesitation, a direct stride, etc.)
Becoming smug and dismissive

INTERNAL SENSATIONS:
An expanding feeling in the chest
A vibration in the mouth, throat, and chest that accompanies humming (if one's certainty allows one to let go of all worries)

MENTAL RESPONSES:

Being willing to commit without knowing all the details
Focusing on information that supports one's belief and dismissing the rest
Forming a mental case (examples to use, information to cite) to convince others to align with one's viewpoint
A mind-over-body mindset, allowing for increased endurance, fortitude, and stamina
Having a strong mental focus
A sensation of being untouchable, as if one is invincible

ACUTE OR LONG-TERM RESPONSES FOR THIS EMOTION:
Increased self-confidence
Choosing a leadership role so one can have influence (if this is important)
A need to warn any who will be negatively impacted if they don't agree
Becoming closed to new information that's contrary (ignoring facts, refusing to converse)
Taking risks without thought
Being comfortable making far-reaching plans and going out on a limb
Increased impatience with those who constantly try to interfere or sway one's convictions
Pushing one's view and even becoming argumentative if the stakes are high

SIGNS THAT THIS EMOTION IS BEING SUPPRESSED:
Asking others for their input or advice
Asking questions that one knows the answers to: *It's a good sign he agreed, right?*
A smile that one quickly masks
Avoiding eye contact, or breaking eye contact by looking down
Backpedaling to make people think that one's mind isn't set: *But you never know, right?*

MAY ESCALATE TO: Confidence (64), Fearlessness (130), Smugness (246), Pride (210)

MAY DE-ESCALATE TO: Surprise (252), Conflicted (66), Confusion (68), Unease (266), Doubt (108), Worry (284)

ASSOCIATED POWER VERBS: Affirm, agree, assert, assure, avow, charge, claim, commit, convert, convince, credit, engage, entrust, express, fixate, forecast, foresee, give, influence, know, lead, magnify, motivate, obey, plan, praise, preach, predict, proclaim, push, reassure, reinforce, rely, secure, serve, sign, state, support, trust, voice, volunteer

> **WRITER'S TIP:** *How a character views their world should always be filtered through their emotions. What they are concerned about, desire, fear, and what impacts their self-identity will steer emotions and change how they perceive each setting.*

CONCERN

DEFINITION: Sincere regard for (or having a personal interest in) someone or something

PHYSICAL SIGNALS AND BEHAVIORS:

Eyebrows drawing together
Tilting the head and making strong eye contact
Opening one's mouth to speak, pausing to collect one's thoughts, then continuing
Looking inward and blinking rapidly
Leaning in while moving closer
Growing still to better observe
Making a micro-movement toward the object of concern, then stopping
Asking pointed questions to better understand the importance of what's unfolding
Nodding and blinking as someone explains in more detail
Raised eyebrows
Pursed lips
Entering the personal space of the person one is concerned about
Asking *Are you okay?* or *What does this mean for you?*
Maintaining an open body posture to include others
Lowering or deepening one's voice
Pinching one's chin while listening or thinking
Touching the face more often
Asking questions and requesting clarifications to understand the situation in full
Covering the mouth or rubbing at the lips in thought
Pulling out a phone to make a note or do further research
Physically touching a person who is the focus—offering a light squeeze, rub, or tap
Pointing the knees toward the speaker (while sitting) and leaning in
Cutting people off or interrupting—not out of rudeness but from a need to know
Prompting another with questions so they'll reveal more detail
Offering platitudes: *We'll get this figured out,* or *I'm sure everything will be fine.*
Giving well-meaning (and possibly unsolicited) advice
Validating another's concerns: *That makes sense. I can see why you're worried.*
Speaking in terms of *we*, not *you*, so others feel supported
Offering comfort in small ways (providing a seat or drink, going for a walk with them, etc.)
Offering to step in, use one's resources, investigate, or run an errand to help
Volunteering one's time to a project or initiative in hopes of resolving a problem
Making promises to offer support, show that one cares, or prove commitment
Using one's connections to try and help another navigate this situation

INTERNAL SENSATIONS:

One's pulse picking up
Muscles tightening
Body tension from strained attentiveness

MENTAL RESPONSES:
A hyper-focus on the person or thing one is interacting with
Forgetting other priorities or responsibilities in the moment
Paying more attention to cues (verbal and physical) to better understand how another feels
Listening intently
Scanning the mannerisms of others for clues as to the stakes involved or possible situational undercurrents
Reading into things; analyzing
A desire to help, encourage someone, or fix the situation
One's mind skipping ahead to possible consequences, fallout, and repercussions
Feeling protective of another
Looking backward to try and understand how things ended up in the current state
Thinking about how this new information will personally impact oneself

ACUTE OR LONG-TERM RESPONSES FOR THIS EMOTION:
Following up (with phone calls, texts, visits, etc.)
Obsessive thoughts about the situation or person
Investigating independently to gain new insight or more information
Crowd-sourcing (asking others to weigh in) in hopes an idea or solution will hit
One's mind going to the worst-case scenarios
Being unable to let go
One's mind constantly turning back to the problem or situation
Needing reassurance that one is viewing things the correct way

SIGNS THAT THIS EMOTION IS BEING SUPPRESSED:
Brushing the situation off as if it isn't important
Changing the topic
Shrugging and nonchalance
Making excuses to leave so one can think about how to help
Talking louder and without hesitation

MAY ESCALATE TO: Anxiety (48), Frustration (134), Impatience (160), Worry (284), Pity (204)

MAY DE-ESCALATE TO: Relief (216), Acceptance (28), Curiosity (74), Hopefulness (148), Gratitude (136)

ASSOCIATED POWER VERBS: Advise, assist, bolster, consider, devote, embrace, empathize, examine, express, focus, help, include, involve, listen, question, reflect, relate, repeat, research, rivet, support, touch, volunteer

WRITER'S TIP: To check if your emotional showing is on point, ask WHY: Why does the character care so much? Why does this moment impact them so deeply? The answers should be

CONFIDENCE

DEFINITION: Having faith in one's influence and ability

PHYSICAL SIGNALS AND BEHAVIORS:
Strong posture (shoulders back, chest out, chin high, etc.)
Walking with wide steps and a steady gait
Strong hygiene and personal grooming
Holding the hands loosely behind the back
Touching one's fingertips together (tapping, forming a steeple, etc.)
A gleam in one's eye
Sharing a smile or playful grin
Winking or giving someone an easy nod
Keeping one's hands out of the pockets
Appearing relaxed (slouching against a wall, humming, etc.)
Taking up space (legs spread wide, arms loose at the sides, etc.)
Approaching people with ease and inviting them into one's personal space
Looking others directly in the eye
Arms swinging while walking
Choosing the middle, not the sides (be it a couch or a room)
Using exaggerated movements to draw attention to oneself
A booming laugh
A tilted-back head
Speaking boisterously
Offering witty commentary
Giving a half-shrug or a grin that conveys secret knowledge
Lighthearted teasing
Flirting
A strong handshake
Leaning back in a chair, hands behind the head
An easygoing manner
Stretching
Showing comfort in the proximity of others
Initiating contact; approaching others directly and without hesitation
Telling jokes
Adding to or steering a conversation
Hosting events (getting the guys together for a football game)
Openness when dealing with people
Appearing unbothered by what others may think
Leaning in to talk or listen
Asking questions to gain knowledge; being able to shelve one's ego
Increased physical contact; becoming touchy-feely
Running one's hands through one's hair or flipping the hair back
Assuming a pose that draws attention to one's best attributes

INTERNAL SENSATIONS:
A downward pull in the shoulder muscles as one's arms hang relaxed and tension-free
Easy breaths
Lightness in the chest

MENTAL RESPONSES:
A sense of calm and ease
A positive outlook
Interest in whatever's going on
A desire to help by using one's skills to improve a situation or fill a need
Aiming for bigger goals that will stretch oneself

ACUTE OR LONG-TERM RESPONSES FOR THIS EMOTION:
Doing or saying things outside of the norm without anxiety or concern
A willingness to try new things and embrace challenges
Adaptability; taking on new roles as needed
Obsessively talking about an achievement or material object
Reacting with anger or jealousy if one's reputation is impugned
Bragging and showing off

SIGNS THAT THIS EMOTION IS BEING SUPPRESSED:
Minimizing compliments
Modesty
Changing the topic to bring others into the spotlight
Downplaying one's own comfort level to make others feel better
Asking for opinions or advice
Sharing the accolades with others: *I couldn't have done it without their help,* or *We make a good team.*

MAY ESCALATE TO: Satisfaction (230), Pride (210), Smugness (246), Contempt (72)

MAY DE-ESCALATE TO: Doubt (108), Reluctance (218), Regret (214), Uncertainty (264)

ASSOCIATED POWER VERBS: Act, aim, assert, assist, avow, beam, believe, boast, bolster, build, command, commit, delegate, empower, encourage, exude, hearten, help, influence, inspire, lead, motivate, persuade, rebel, restore, shape, steer, thrust, wink

> **WRITER'S TIP:** *It is natural to hold back or hide our true scope of emotions in the presence of others. When writing a conflicted protagonist, it is critical to show through action the emotion the character wants to convey to others while also expressing their true feelings to the reader.*

CONFLICTED

DEFINITION: Experiencing opposing emotions

PHYSICAL SIGNALS AND BEHAVIORS:
The lips pressing together in a slight grimace
Increased swallowing or blinking
Wrinkling the nose
A smile that wavers
A gaze that ping-pongs and avoids direct eye contact
Start-and-stop gesturing (reaching then hesitating, changing direction mid-stride, etc.)
Broken dialogue and self-interruptions
Making apologies for one's unfocused responses
Opening and closing the mouth
Struggling to find the right words
Soft head shaking
Voicing support in a tone that lacks enthusiasm
Becoming quieter and less animated
Scratching one's neck or cheek
Rubbing or pulling at an ear
Asking questions to gain more insight
Talking to others about similar experiences or situations
A need to sit down and reflect
Rubbing or pinching the bottom lip
Making a *Hmmm* noise in the throat
Tilting the head in a side-to-side rhythm
Pulling in and then slowly releasing a deep breath
Apologizing for one's lackluster reaction, citing mixed feelings
Requesting some time to digest everything
Tapping one's index finger against the lip
The brows pulling in as one looks downward
Rubbing at the middle of one's forehead while one's eyes are closed
Voicing conflict or surprise: *This is a tough decision,* or *Sorry, you caught me off guard.*
Knees that bend, then straighten
A restless stance
Pacing
Rubbing a hand through the hair
Smoothing one's clothes or touching items to keep the hands busy
Cancelling gestures (smiling while shaking the head, nodding and grimacing, etc.)
Holding one's elbow while the opposite hand makes a fist against the mouth
Blowing one's cheeks out, then swallowing the air or releasing it
Holding one's hands out and "weighing" them in the air
Forcing enthusiasm because it's the right thing to do
Subdued or delayed reactions

INTERNAL SENSATIONS:
Headaches
A heaviness in the body
Tightness in the chest
A sinking feeling in the stomach

MENTAL RESPONSES:
Weighing the pros and cons
Researching or seeking information
Guilt toward those who may be negatively affected by a final decision
Playing *What if?* to understand the repercussion of a situation
A need to verbalize the internal conflict
A desire to retreat and go somewhere quiet to think
An inability to focus on anything but the internal conflict
Drawing on moral beliefs to help one decide

ACUTE OR LONG-TERM RESPONSES FOR THIS EMOTION:
A disheveled look (hair out of place, clothes rumpled, etc.)
Obsessive information gathering; looking for the "key" solution
Stomach upset, poor diet, or a loss of appetite leading to weight loss
Stress headaches
Difficulty sleeping
A loss of self-confidence
Avoiding making any decisions at all
Hair loss

SIGNS THAT THIS EMOTION IS BEING SUPPRESSED:
Citing that one is not the ideal candidate to make the choice
Making excuses to avoid the situation
Suggesting that a break is needed in order to regroup
Making a joke to alleviate tension or lighten the mood
Giving a distracted nod to what's being said

MAY ESCALATE TO: Confusion (68), Overwhelmed (196), Frustration (134), Anxiety (48)

MAY DE-ESCALATE TO: Doubt (108), Reluctance (218), Regret (214), Uncertainty (264)

ASSOCIATED POWER VERBS: Agonize, backpedal, battle, blur, clash, compete, straddle, strain, struggle, undo, vacillate, waffle, wage, waver, weigh, wonder, worry, wrestle

---

WRITER'S TIP: *In scenes where information must be shared, characters should still be moving, acting, and revealing emotion to keep the pace flowing smoothly.*

CONFUSION

DEFINITION: A state of befuddlement or bafflement

PHYSICAL SIGNALS AND BEHAVIORS:
Difficulty completing a task
Fumbling
Using *um* and *uh* hesitations or an uncertain tone
Grimacing or frowning
Excessive swallowing
Scratching at one's cheek or temple
Rubbing the chin
Repeating back what was said as a question
Touching the base of the neck
Showing one's palms and shrugging
Stuttering or having a difficult time finding the right words
Body posture that loosens or collapses
Tilting one's head to the side while pursing the lips
The head flinching back slightly
Trailing off when speaking
Running the hands through the hair
Eyebrows that squish together
Pulling or tugging on an ear
Asking someone to repeat what was said
One's gaze clouding or going distant
Rubbing one's forehead or eyebrows
Asking questions to buy time
Biting the lip
Rapid blinking
Hands touching the lips, mouth, and face
Glancing around as if looking for answers
Wandering a short distance to think, and then returning
Turning away to gather one's thoughts
A slight headshake
Talking around the situation in hopes that clarity might come about
A mouth that opens but nothing comes out
Blowing out the cheeks, then releasing
A blank look; a slack expression
Asking for affirmation: *Are you sure?*
Tapping a fist against the lips
Poking one's tongue into the cheek
Dry washing one's hands

INTERNAL SENSATIONS:
Rising body heat

Fluttering in the stomach
A tightening chest
Feeling overheated

MENTAL RESPONSES:
Thoughts that freeze
Hoping for an interruption to delay answering
The mind racing, searching for answers
Feeling exposed and judged

ACUTE OR LONG-TERM RESPONSES FOR THIS EMOTION:
Flight responses
Failing grades
Not being trusted with responsibility or decision making
Loss of respect from others for unfinished or inaccurate work
Broken or unfulfilled promises
A lack of productivity leading to a loss of self-esteem

SIGNS THAT THIS EMOTION IS BEING SUPPRESSED:
Nodding or agreeing, to avoid attention
False confidence
Assuring others that everything is under control
Smiling and nodding while waving a hand
Physical touches to reassure others (a clap on the back or shoulder, etc.)
Steering the conversation to a different topic
Launching into a flurry of activity
Showing a sudden interest in other things
The face reddening and starting to sweat
Using "word filler" to stall for time

MAY ESCALATE TO: Flustered (132), Frustration (134), Resignation (224), Insecurity (166)

MAY DE-ESCALATE TO: Acceptance (28), Curiosity (74), Relief (216)

ASSOCIATED POWER VERBS: Addle, analyze, baffle, bewilder, confound, consider, frustrate, fumble, heat, lie, misdirect, misinform, misinterpret, perplex, ponder, question, repeat, stall, stutter, think, vacillate, waver, wonder, worry

WRITER'S TIP: *Men and women often experience and express emotions differently. When writing a character of the opposite sex, consider getting a second opinion to ensure a character's reactions, thoughts, and feelings are authentic.*

CONNECTEDNESS

DEFINITION: To experience a meaningful state of closeness with others, the world, or the universe itself

PHYSICAL SIGNALS AND BEHAVIORS:
A genuine smile (that reaches the eyes, lasts a long time, isn't forced, etc.)
Eyes that light up
A face that softens as all tension leaves it
Holding or squeezing the hand of another who feels the same bond
Hugs that last
Touching the face of another (a stroke of the cheek, touching foreheads together, etc.)
Asking questions out of genuine curiosity and interest
Open, welcoming body posture (facing people head on, standing at ease, reaching out, etc.)
Taking deep, cleansing breaths
Moving closer to those one feels a kinship with (erasing distance)
Sitting cross-legged and leaning back, using one's arms as supports
Turning one's face upward
Spending more time observing, appreciating, and interacting with nature
Closing the eyes and taking in a deep breath before exhaling
Humming or singing (if one is prone to doing so)
Lighter movements and steps (gracefulness)
Leaning towards others
Lighthearted joking or teasing with those one feels connected to
Discussing more personal things in conversations
Sharing deeper thoughts, worries, or fears as it feels natural and safe to do so
Being honest and transparent in conversations
Giddiness or playfulness
Laughing more
Welcoming questions and answering without holding back or feeling self-conscious
Touching (laying a hand on another's arm or shoulder) to enhance the feeling
Interacting with one's immediate surroundings (running one's fingers over the fabric of a hand-stitched pillow on a couch, inhaling a pleasant scent, etc.)
A willingness to help (jumping in to assist, spotting what needs to be done and acting, etc.)
Doing things out of kindness, not obligation (being thoughtful, bringing a gift, etc.)
Making oneself physically vulnerable because one feels completely safe (lying back in the grass, approaching wildlife, standing with the arms thrown wide, etc.)

INTERNAL SENSATIONS:
Goosebumps (from heightened tactile sensitivity)
A pleasurable tingling in the skin (sensitivity to warmth and touch)
A pull in the shoulders as one's upper body slackens into a relaxed state
Tingling in the nasal passages from pulling in deep, contented breaths
An expansive feeling in the chest

MENTAL RESPONSES:
A lack of judgment or desire to judge others
Feeling deep appreciation for all things
Being less attached to physical possessions
Appreciating others and feeling centered in the moment
Engaging in prayer or deep thoughts about the world and one's place in it
Thinking about one's shortcomings and how to be better (a desire to grow)
A lack of self-consciousness

ACUTE OR LONG-TERM RESPONSES FOR THIS EMOTION:
A need to be with those who make one feel complete
Sharing deep, intimate thoughts and ideas that are a core part of one's identity
Increased confidence; feeling more capable
Embracing challenges and bigger tasks in an effort to benefit the wider world
Becoming a deeper thinker
Spending large amounts of time in nature or with other people (depending on who or what one is connecting to)

SIGNS THAT THIS EMOTION IS BEING SUPPRESSED:
Hiding one's hands behind the back or in pockets to avoid reaching out
Avoiding eye contact with those one feels kinship with
Busying oneself with tasks to seem preoccupied or focused elsewhere
Avoiding conversation (to avoid saying something that gives one away)
Being overly polite or formal
Leaving a place that one feels connected to, thereby minimizing its importance to others
Spending time alone rather than with another

MAY ESCALATE TO: Happiness (142), Satisfaction (230), Awe (54), Wanderlust (278)

MAY DE-ESCALATE TO: Peacefulness (202), Valued (270), Happiness (142), Confidence (64), Sappiness (228)

ASSOCIATED POWER VERBS: Accept, affect, appreciate, attach, belong, bind, brush, care, cherish, close, hold, hug, join, link, lock, match, meld, mesh, motivate, need, nurture, revere, seal, sense, serve, sync, touch, transcend, transfix, twin, want, wed, welcome

WRITER'S TIP: *Another way to help readers understand the character's emotion better is to tie it to a universal experience. For example, a character could compare their frustration to a recurring dream where they must make a critical phone call but keep dialing the number wrong.*

CONTEMPT

DEFINITION: A lack of reverence or respect; to hold in disregard

PHYSICAL SIGNALS AND BEHAVIORS:
Crossing one's arms to show a closed body posture
A downturned mouth
One's head tilting away
Sneering
Shaking the head and sighing or muttering
Mocking another through words or derogatory actions
Rolling the eyes
Using sarcasm
Gossiping
Snorting loudly
Buzzing the lips to be rude (blowing a raspberry)
Baiting the other person
Turning the body at an angle instead of facing the other person head-on
Walking away
Waving dismissively while refusing to answer a question because it's not worth the effort
Stiff posture
Fingers curling
Refusing to respond or engage
Lowering the chin to look down on someone
A cold look (devoid of emotion, head tilted down during eye contact, etc.)
A pinched mouth
A hard, distinctive jaw line
Smirking as the person speaks
Ugly laughter
Making jokes at another's expense
Adopting a hard tone and using forceful language
Flashing a cold smile to show insincerity
Spitting in the direction of the one provoking contempt
Holding a wide stance, with the chest thrust out
Talking over someone, ignoring them, or refusing to recognize their input
Revealing someone's mistakes to peers or publicly calling them out
Refusing to acknowledge someone's contribution or position

INTERNAL SENSATIONS:
Rising blood pressure
A tightening in the chest
Stiffness in the neck and jaw
A roiling heat in the belly

MENTAL RESPONSES:
Negative thinking
Unkind observations and mental insults
A hyperawareness of the one causing this feeling (even when pretending to ignore them)
A desire to verbally tear down or hurt another person
Wanting to expose the subject's ignorance

ACUTE OR LONG-TERM RESPONSES FOR THIS EMOTION:
Swearing and offering insults
Yelling and arguing
High blood pressure
A vein throbbing visibly in the forehead
Thoughts of violence
Breaking rules or ignoring processes because one has no respect for those who made them
Angrily dismissing someone from one's presence
Leaving the room (excusing oneself, cutting a meeting short, etc.)

SIGNS THAT THIS EMOTION IS BEING SUPPRESSED:
Flushed skin
Biting at the inside of the cheek
Pressing the lips together to keep from speaking
Purposefully not looking at the source
Turning away to ignore the source
Becoming unresponsive
Pushing on the diaphragm to keep the anger in
Leaning back with one's arms crossed
Moving away and creating more personal distance

MAY ESCALATE TO: Disgust (102), Scorn (234), Anger, (40) Schadenfreude (232)

MAY DE-ESCALATE TO: Agitation (34), Conflicted (66), Indifference (164), Pity (204)

ASSOCIATED POWER VERBS: Belittle, betray, convict, destroy, discard, dismiss, disrespect, expose, eye, glare, ignore, insult, loathe, mistreat, overlook, override, prosecute, provoke, punish, reject, sabotage, scorn, sidestep, sneer, spit, spurn

> **WRITER'S TIP:** *When revising, look for instances where emotions are NAMED. Nine times out of ten, this indicates a lack of confidence that the emotion is shown clearly through thought, sensations and body language. Strong verbal and nonverbal cues negate the need to explain the emotion to the reader.*

CURIOSITY

DEFINITION: Inquisitiveness; a desire for knowledge

PHYSICAL SIGNALS AND BEHAVIORS:
Tilting the head to the side
Raised eyebrows
Body posture that perks up
A slow smile that builds
Repeating a statement as a question
Leaning forward and sliding one's chair closer
Pausing to examine
Eyebrows furrowing and then releasing
Blinking
Gazing at the source with sudden focus
Shifting from casual conversation to pointed questions
A softened voice or tone that may contain wonder
Crossing one's arms while observing
Prying or snooping
Nose-wrinkling
Posing hypothetical questions
Lingering touches
Stopping to pay attention (halting a current activity, like a fork pausing halfway to the mouth)
Straining to hear; shushing others to be quiet
Eavesdropping
Cupping an elbow with one hand while tapping the lips with the other
Squinting or pushing one's glasses up
Bending, kneeling, or squatting to get closer
Tilting one's body toward the source
Shuffling, creeping, or edging closer
Exploring the senses (e.g., smelling something new for the sake of knowing)
Verbally expressing interest: *Oh, look at that!* or *Isn't that amazing?*
Pulling on someone's sleeve to get them to join or follow
A still demeanor to aid in observation
Lips that are slightly parted
Nodding slowly
Poking or prodding at something
Talking to oneself to work through new ideas and thoughts

INTERNAL SENSATIONS:
Breaths that hitch or briefly stop
An increased pulse
Tingling at the base of the neck

MENTAL RESPONSES:
A need to know, touch, or understand
Forgetting what one was about to say or do
A compulsion to detour toward something new
Temporary cessation of worries, stress, or actions
A desire to investigate or experiment
Increased awareness of sensory information
Wonder or interest at how something works or why it's there
Impatience with people who protect the status quo and don't want to learn or grow

ACUTE OR LONG-TERM RESPONSES FOR THIS EMOTION:
Fidgeting or tics
Hypersensitivity to the source of interest
Obsessive thoughts
Pointed or even rude questions
Snooping or sneaking about to satisfy the need to know
Blowing people off through one's single-minded pursuit of knowledge or information
Becoming frustrated when one's efforts are thwarted, or one can't find answers

SIGNS THAT THIS EMOTION IS BEING SUPPRESSED:
Keeping one's eyes down
Holding one's hands in the lap
A lack of eye contact
Providing an excuse to linger or move toward the source
Pretending to ignore or be unaware of the source
A sidelong look
Using one's hair to hide an interested glance
Feigning boredom

MAY ESCALATE TO: Eagerness (112), Amazement (36), Awe (54), Conflicted (66), Intimidation (170)

MAY DE-ESCALATE TO: Disappointment (96), Discouragement (100), Indifference (164)

ASSOCIATED POWER VERBS: Approach, ask, attract, creep, desire, examine, explore, fascinate, follow, inquire, interest, intrigue, investigate, invite, lean, listen, marvel, peer, poke, prod, pursue, question, reach, test, touch, wonder

WRITER'S TIP: *Smell triggers memory. Take advantage of this sense and build olfactory description into the scene. This will draw readers in and make them feel part of the action.*

DEFEAT

DEFINITION: The feeling of having been mastered, conquered, or bested

PHYSICAL SIGNALS AND BEHAVIORS:
The chin lowering to one's chest
Hands that go limp
Holding one's palms up and out
Slowly shaking the head
A lack of eye contact
Staring down at one's hands or feet
Going quiet, muttering, or being unresponsive
Unsteadiness; a lack of balance
Agreeing to hurry things along to end the agony of this moment
Arms hanging at one's sides
A long, low sigh
A thick, emotion-choked voice
Stumbling
Rubbing at the eyes to hide redness or tears from others
Backing away and creating a bubble of personal space
Cheeks that burn
A bobbing Adam's apple (thick swallows)
Hunched or rounded shoulders
Sagging posture, the back bowed
Hands hidden behind the back or in pockets
Chin tremors
Arms clutching one's body as if to hold it together
Lackluster movements; being devoid of energy
Toneless responses
Vacant eyes
Slumping into a chair
Holding one's head with the hands
Covering the mouth and nose with one's hand

INTERNAL SENSATIONS:
Feeling a pulse in one's throat
One's heart thudding dully in the chest
Wheezing breaths
Feeling like one's head is spinning
Chest pain or numbness
A sour taste in one's mouth
A lack of energy
Tears or heat behind the eyelids
A painful lump in one's throat
Limbs that feel too heavy to lift or move

MENTAL RESPONSES:
A desire to flee or be alone
Shame
Worrying that others will feel let down or disappointed
Mental fatigue
Wanting time to pass quickly but feeling trapped in this moment

ACUTE OR LONG-TERM RESPONSES FOR THIS EMOTION:
A quaking or trembling body
Uncontrollable tears
Pleading or begging
Collapsing; the knees giving out
Self-loathing

SIGNS THAT THIS EMOTION IS BEING SUPPRESSED:
Shaking the head
False bravado
Demanding a rematch
Repeating the word *No*
Shouting or cursing
Laying the blame on others
Making accusations of cheating or underhandedness
A chin that juts sharply
The lips pressed flat
A flinty gaze
Using anger to feed strength

MAY ESCALATE TO: Resignation (224), Powerlessness (208), Vulnerability (276), Shame (240), Humiliation (154)

MAY DE-ESCALATE TO: Shock (242), Hopefulness (148), Gratitude (136), Relief (216)

ASSOCIATED POWER VERBS: Ache, beat, bleed, blindside, cave, collapse, crumple, displace, drag, knock, master, oust, outsmart, overcome, overpower, overthrow, pummel, sap, smash, steamroll, strangle, stun, subdue, suffer, surrender, topple, whip, yield

WRITER'S TIP: *To reveal quieter emotions, try using contrast. For example, pairing an easygoing character with someone who is highly volatile will help their own milder body cues stand out clearly.*

DEFENSIVENESS

DEFINITION: Resisting attack; defending against a perceived danger or threat

PHYSICAL SIGNALS AND BEHAVIORS:
Stepping back to increase the distance between oneself and the perceived danger
Leaning away
Crossing the arms over one's chest
Rigid body posture
Squinting, the brow lowering
Sucking the cheeks in
Shaking the head as if to remove any mental fogginess
Sputtering, gaping, or shouting
Holding an object as a shield (a book, a folded jacket, etc.)
A darting gaze (gauging the distance to an exit, looking for a weapon, etc.)
Licking one's lips
Rapid blinking that leads to a wide-eyed look
Hands up, palms toward the aggressor
Fixedly staring at the person while talking in a low, firm voice
False bravado (flipping one's hair, a snort of dismissive laughter, etc.)
Raising one's voice to encourage the other to back down
Crossing the legs (if one is seated and feeling vulnerable)
Body shielding (turning at an angle)
Interrupting or talking over a rival to gain the upper hand
Looking to others for backup
Blowing out a noisy breath
Going on the offensive and verbally attacking the accuser
Deflecting blame
Flinching or jerking back
Speaking quickly while struggling to be articulate
A hand splaying across one's upper chest in a sign of innocence
A stiff neck, cords standing out, and a bobbing Adam's apple
The chin lowering and pulling back against the neck
Wagging a finger or berating another for their accusations
Rising color in one's cheeks
Visible sweating
Dragging others into the situation for support
Verbalizing disappointment or denial
A voice that hardens over the course of an argument
Jerky movements; a loss of fluidity to one's actions
Excessive swallowing

INTERNAL SENSATIONS:
Feeling the thrum of one's own pulse due to raised blood pressure
Dry mouth and an intense thirst
A body that feels hot
The stomach tightening and hardening

MENTAL RESPONSES:
Scrambling thoughts as one tries to diffuse the situation
Anger, shock, and feelings of betrayal
Sifting memories for evidence (to support innocence or challenge accusations)

ACUTE OR LONG-TERM RESPONSES FOR THIS EMOTION:
Eyes darting for an exit or escape (flight response)
Shouting
Bringing up past examples when one supported the accuser or saved the day
Citing an opponent's shortcomings
Increasing one's personal space
Storming away

SIGNS THAT THIS EMOTION IS BEING SUPPRESSED:
Maintaining an even tone
Offering a fake smile
A forcibly calm demeanor
Changing the subject
Denial (shrugging, forcing a laugh, etc.)
Calmly stating that one doesn't need to prove anything
Not leaving or walking away, despite discomfort
Attempting to reason through facts, not emotion

MAY ESCALATE TO: Resentment (222), Suspicion (254), Anger (40), Fear (128), Vulnerability (276), Self-Pity (238)

MAY DE-ESCALATE TO: Unappreciated (262), Confusion (68), Skepticism (244), Relief (216)

ASSOCIATED POWER VERBS: Avoid, balk, bristle, confront, counter, cover, criticize, deflect, deny, disagree, dismiss, dispute, dodge, downplay, guard, insist, lie, oppose, plead, proclaim, push, react, reject, resist, screen, shield, sidestep, stall, stammer, threaten, yell

WRITER'S TIP: *When writing a character's emotional response, consider their comfort level. Characters are more themselves in the company of people they feel safe with. But if they feel vulnerable or uncertain, their reactions will change.*

DEFIANCE

DEFINITION: Boldly resisting an opposing force, even in the face of defeat

PHYSICAL SIGNALS AND BEHAVIORS:
Drawing oneself up to full height (erect posture, tense muscles, etc.)
A sharp chin thrust or lift
Crossing the arms
A gaze or stare that is challenging and full of judgment
A curled lip; smirking
Refusing to obey (or behaving the opposite way one is expected to)
Shoulders pushing back and the chest jutting out
Refusing to be the first to break eye contact
Jerking one's head sharply ("tossing" the head)
Inhaling deeply, the nostrils flaring
Visible tightness in the jaw and neck
Flexing the fingers and drawing them into fists
Stepping into the personal space of others
Placing one's hands on one's hips
Attempting to appear larger by taking up more space—e.g., widening one's stance
Using personal knowledge to attack a rival's position or statement
Forceful movements (slamming a door, pushing a chair in harder than is needed, throwing things, etc.) to vent one's anger
Purposeful actions to incite an opponent (rejecting a gift, ignoring directions, etc.)
Being unable to sit or remain still
Sassiness or rudeness; verbal sparring
Deploying sarcasm (in one's tone, the words uses, in one's smile, etc.)
Heated arguing, which may escalate to yelling and swearing
Refusing to apologize
Refusing to be dissuaded or placated
Communicating one's fixed position, belief, or view in absolutes: *I'll never back down.*
A straight-backed stride when walking away

INTERNAL SENSATIONS:
A throbbing in the chest or throat (the heart beating faster due to increased blood pressure)
Ribs that tighten, creating pressure in one's core
A flush of heat in the face and neck
Tension in one's muscles
Narrowed vision

MENTAL RESPONSES:
Thoughts being clouded by frustration and anger
Reacting before thinking, thereby escalating a situation or burning a bridge
Struggling with focus and concentration, or shifting mental gears to something else
Being unable or unwilling to see things from another's view

Analyzing an opponent for weaknesses that can strengthen one's position
Refusing to negotiate unless one's core demands are met
Mentally justifying actions that break rules or create fallout
Hanging onto anger and being unable to forgive
Needing to have the last word
Using anger to mask fear or uncertainty

ACUTE OR LONG-TERM RESPONSES FOR THIS EMOTION:
Speaking in a hostile tone
Making threats
Refusing to set disagreements aside (becoming fixated on undermining or besting an opponent, starting a feud, seeking revenge, etc.)
Blatant disobedience regardless of the consequences
Allowing one's anger to escalate to violence
Cutting ties with people who disagree: *You're either with me or against me.*
Lunging toward someone
Hurling insults and gestures (giving someone the finger, mooning someone, etc.)

SIGNS THAT THIS EMOTION IS BEING SUPPRESSED:
Body tension (tightness in the muscles, sharp posture, etc.)
Clenching the jaw
Lips that are clamped tight, appearing bloodless and flat
Speaking in an uneven voice, the words sounding strained or forced
Quiet acts of subversion (doing small things that will damage or undermine a foe)

MAY ESCALATE TO: Anger (40), Rage (212), Schadenfreude (232), Fearlessness (130)

MAY DE-ESCALATE TO: Unappreciated (262), Conflicted (66), Confusion (68), Regret (214)

ASSOCIATED POWER VERBS: Arch, argue, bash, belittle, brandish, bristle, call, challenge, confront, criticize, dare, defy, demand, dispute, embarrass, fight, flaunt, fling, glare, hit, hurl, ignore, jerk, jut, lunge, mock, offend, oppose, provoke, punish, push, rebel, reject, resist, seethe, shout, shriek, slam, snarl, spit, stare, subvert, test, threaten, undermine

> **WRITER'S TIP:** *When drafting, if you are unsure of how to show an emotion, use a telling placeholder like* She shivered in fear. *Then, look for the named emotion when revising, remove it, and write something fresh to show. This way, you will not be pulled out of the creative flow.*

DENIAL

DEFINITION: A refusal to acknowledge truth or reality

PHYSICAL SIGNALS AND BEHAVIORS:
Engaging in verbal disagreements
Backing away
Vigorous head shaking
Waving someone off
Dialogue in the negative: *Don't blame me,* or *I had nothing to do with it.*
Speaking emphatically with finger pointing or other hard gestures
Raising one's palms
Shrugging
Tucking in the upper lip
Arms crossing one's chest
Placing a hand against the breastbone
A slackened mouth
Speaking rapidly and not letting others get a word in
Rationalizing or justifying
Shuffling backward
Speaking slowly and stretching out one's words: *What? No way!*
Leaning back and creating space
Warding someone or something off
Raised eyebrows
Widening eyes
The pitch of one's voice rising
Emphatically saying *No*
Slanting the body away from an accuser
Rubbing at the ears, covering them, or pulling on an earlobe
Questioning someone's source or the facts
Constant interrupting to prevent the other person from speaking
Smiling and shaking the head as if the other party is completely deluded
Questioning someone's motives; reacting as if being attacked
Making an "X" motion with one's hands
Eye contact dropping (if one is unsure or lying)
Responding in short, choppy sentences
Sweating
Staring down at one's hands
Stroking one's sleeve in self-comfort
Making demands (for someone to leave, to stop talking, etc.)

INTERNAL SENSATIONS:
The mouth going dry
A lump forming in one's throat
Feeling heavy or numb
Heat rising behind the eyelids
Tingling in the stomach

MENTAL RESPONSES:
Replaying past events in order to understand them
Thoughts centering on the facts of the situation
The brain scrambling to find a logical excuse
Anger or hurt at being put in this situation

ACUTE OR LONG-TERM RESPONSES FOR THIS EMOTION:
Blaming others
Supplying alternative facts to prove one's position
Pleading, crying, or begging to be believed
Becoming closed-minded; refusing to listen
Wanting to be left alone
Needing to escape

SIGNS THAT THIS EMOTION IS BEING SUPPRESSED:
Refusing to argue or respond to an accusation
Steady eye contact
Explaining calmly that one is not in denial
Voicing *We'll see* comments
Supplying reasons to convey that a viewpoint is invalid
Repeating the truth as one sees it and sticking to it
Using a steady, even tone

MAY ESCALATE TO: Defensiveness (78), Hurt (156), Guilt (140), Anger (40), Conflicted (66)

MAY DE-ESCALATE TO: Shock (242), Vulnerability (276), Disillusionment (104)

ASSOCIATED POWER VERBS: Abandon, beg, blame, block, challenge, decline, deflect, disavow, dismiss, dispute, evade, feign, flee, hide, ignore, negate, pretend, quash, refuse, refute, reject, resist, reverse, shift, shrug, shun, sidestep, snub, withdraw

WRITER'S TIP: *Make a list of your body language crutches (frowning, smiling, shrugging, head shaking, etc.). Use your word processor's search and replace feature to highlight these so you can pinpoint where the emotional description needs some freshening up.*

DEPRESSED

DEFINITION: A state of withdrawal; extreme sadness and reduced vitality

PHYSICAL SIGNALS AND BEHAVIORS:
A gaunt appearance
Notable weight loss or gain
Eyes that blink infrequently
Wet or red eyes from crying
Staring down at one's hands
Lying in bed with no motivation to get up
Saggy posture (a bent neck, drooping shoulders, etc.)
Resting the head on one's hand
Tangled hair, overlong nails, and other signs of letting oneself go
Wearing the same clothes day after day
Shuffling steps and lethargic hand movements
Obsession with an object that represents loss (a photo or trinket)
A vacant stare
Making excuses
Poor conversation skills
Stating outright that one doesn't care about one's own well-being
A downturned mouth
Lines in the face
A slack expression
Dark circles under one's eyes
An inability to sleep, or sleeping too much
Poor eating habits
Illness
A tone that lacks strength or vitality
An unclean home, room, or office space
Ignoring phone calls or visitors
Premature aging (wrinkles, tired eyes, gray or white hair, etc.)
Giving up one's interest in hobbies
Failing grades at school or a lack of success at work
Choosing isolation
Dropping out of activities and moving away from friendships
Picking at food or finding food tasteless
Being unable to focus on tasks (work, school, home life, etc.)
Forgetting appointments, conversations, and meetings
Bulky or dull clothing choices
Non-responsiveness to others, even family

INTERNAL SENSATIONS:
A hollowness in one's chest that somehow feels heavy
A slow pulse

Shallow breathing
Aches and pains
Constant fatigue

MENTAL RESPONSES:
Feeling unmotivated
Struggling with a self-critical mindset
Desiring to live in the past or be alone
Poor observation skills
Obsessive thoughts (a focus on the negative, expecting bad things to happen, etc.)
A negative outlook in general; bleak observations about the world and the people in it
Losing track of time
Thoughts of self-harm
An aversion to noise, crowds, and stressful situations

ACUTE OR LONG-TERM RESPONSES FOR THIS EMOTION:
Eating disorders
Manic behavior (hair pulling, OCD, paranoia, etc.)
Wishing life was over; attempting or thinking about suicide
Embracing danger and risk
Addiction to medication
Hoarding

SIGNS THAT THIS EMOTION IS BEING SUPPRESSED:
Slight pauses before reacting
Emotional displays that seem forced or false
Heavy self-medicating or drinking
Wearing false, overly bright smiles
Pretending to be ill to avoid social situations and people
Lying in general

MAY ESCALATE TO: Self-Loathing (236), Worthlessness (286), Homesickness (146), Regret (214)

MAY DE-ESCALATE TO: Loneliness (176), Conflicted (66), Vulnerability (276), Hopefulness (148)

ASSOCIATED POWER VERBS: Ache, collapse, cut, deepen, doubt, endure, engulf, give up, hurt, overcome, overwhelm, sink, slow, struggle, succumb, suffer, weep, worsen

WRITER'S TIP: *It isn't enough to show emotion; a writer needs to make the reader feel it. Think about the core visceral sensations you experience when feeling strong emotion, and if appropriate, utilize them to convey a similar experience to the reader.*

DESIRE

DEFINITION: A yearning to initiate or strengthen a relationship with another person

NOTES: Desire is a strong emotion, particularly as it relates to other people. While desire is often associated with romantic relationships, it can be applied to other people, such as a character who wants a more satisfying relationship with their children, parents, a sibling, or a friend. For information on desire as it relates to things or intangibles, see the LONGING entry (177).

PHYSICAL SIGNALS AND BEHAVIORS:
Firm, intense eye contact
Hands moistening
Stroking one's arm as a surrogate for the person
Mirroring the person's movements
Trembling
Lowering one's voice when speaking
Leaning in or forward
Moving closer to the person to erase the distance
Relaxing one's posture; muscles losing tension
Facing the person straight on
Eyes shining, becoming glossy, and softening
Frequent touching of the face and lips
Hands clenching briefly, then releasing
Becoming tongue-tied or inarticulate; stuttering or stammering
A slight flush of the skin in the face and neck
Knees loosening and feeling weak
Responding immediately when called upon
Casting furtive glances at the person
Positioning oneself near the person one desires
Touching or holding the person close
Holding in a breath
A slow smile that builds
Moving carefully, to set the person at ease and keep from scaring them off
Subconsciously thrusting out one's chest
Lifting one's chin to expose the neck
A lingering touch; brushing up against the object
Touching or stroking one's own throat
Lips parting
Slightly parting the legs
The tongue darting out to touch or lick the lips

INTERNAL SENSATIONS:
A strong awareness of one's own heartbeat
The sensation of being flooded with warmth
The mouth becoming moist with increased saliva

Feeling one's hair rise on the arms and nape of the neck
Fingers aching or tingling with the need to touch
Quickening breath or breathlessness
Hypersensitivity to touch and texture
Fluttering or even mild pain in the chest
Light-headedness
A shiver that brings pleasure; nerve endings that stir and tingle
Bodily cravings of being touched by the person

MENTAL RESPONSES:
A desire to erase all distance; actively looking for a way to get closer
Impatience
Taking opportunities or meeting challenges to prove one's worth
Wanting to care for and put the person's needs first
A loss of inhibitions; becoming more spontaneous
A need to touch and explore
Preoccupation with the person's scent
Focusing on the person's positive qualities

ACUTE OR LONG-TERM RESPONSES FOR THIS EMOTION:
A willingness to endure suffering or hardship to get closer to the person
Obsessive thoughts
Centering all aspects of one's life on being with the person
Neglecting friends, family, work, and other interests
Fixation on self-improvement, education, or goals leading to achievement
Shedding bad habits or flaws to appease or impress the person

SIGNS THAT THIS EMOTION IS BEING SUPPRESSED:
Glancing away for a brief time; feigning interest in something else
Making a display of engaging in conversation with others
Forcing a slow gait rather than rushing to be with the person
Not touching or being alone with the person
Being 100% "up" in public, then falling apart in private

MAY ESCALATE TO: Adoration (32), Love (180), Lust (182), Determination (92)

MAY DE-ESCALATE TO: Disappointment (96), Devastation (94), Inadequacy (162)

ASSOCIATED POWER VERBS: Ache, aspire, burn, caress, chase, covet, crave, devote, express, focus, follow, motivate, need, possess, pursue, quest, reach, seek, seize, touch, want

WRITER'S TIP: *Emotion should always lead to decision making, either good or bad, that will propel the story forward.*

DESPAIR

DEFINITION: Losing all hope; becoming despondent

PHYSICAL SIGNALS AND BEHAVIORS:
Shoulders dragging low, the arms losing all tension
A caved-in chest
A slack expression
A hanging head
Letting out a hard sigh and closing one's eyes
Eyebrows that pinch together
A pained expression
The mouth opening but no words coming forth
Slumping where one stands or sits
Weakly throwing up one's hands
Hands that slide loosely into one's lap
Leaning forward, with the hands draping limply over one's knees
Taking shallow yet audible breaths
Sagging back in one's seat, hands falling to one's sides
Tipping one's head back to look heavenward, then letting it flop forward
Hair that hangs in one's face
Stumbling—one's feet dragging and catching with each step
Reddening eyes
Making no attempt to wipe loose tears away
Placing one's hands over the face
Kneading one's chest with the heel of one's hand as if to stop the pain
Grabbing fistfuls of hair while propping up the head with one's hands
Knees that weaken and then catch (while standing)
A hitching chest or open sobbing
An uncontrollable cry or moan
Lacking the strength to support oneself (falling into a seat or against a table or wall)
Whispering *Oh God*, or *No, it can't be.*
Shaking one's head slowly with one's eyes closed
Lips that pinch together or grimace
Laying one's head down on the arms (at a table)
Weakly slinging an arm around someone in comfort
A body that appears to shrink
Retreating inside oneself (not responding to people's questions or reacting to touch)
Saying things without a filter and not caring who is listening: *We're all doomed.*

INTERNAL SENSATIONS:
A sudden heaviness or numbness
Dizziness
A head that pounds
A heart that aches

Limbs that tingle with fatigue
A thickening in one's throat
Feeling one's heartbeat in one's throat
Eyes growing wet, the vision blurring
A mouth that feels gummy with excess saliva

MENTAL RESPONSES:
Losing track of time
Recycling bleak thoughts: *That's it, she's gone. I'm alone. I can't do this without her.*
Feeling as though things are happening too quickly to process them
Numb emotions; ceasing to care about who is watching or observing
Distorted observations (reacting slowly to movement, not processing what someone says, failing to recognize someone immediately, etc.)
Mentally shutting down

ACUTE OR LONG-TERM RESPONSES FOR THIS EMOTION:
Falling into a depressive state
Turning to alcohol or drugs for comfort
Thoughts of suicide or attempting suicide
Bluntness; saying hurtful things and not caring

SIGNS THAT THIS EMOTION IS BEING SUPPRESSED:
Trying to put on a brave face (smiles that flicker and go out, false enthusiasm, etc.)
Throwing oneself into a task to keep one's mind off what has happened
Keeping secrets so others maintain their hope
Lying to others; telling them that things are fine when they are not

MAY ESCALATE TO: Bitterness (58), Devastation (94), Grief (138), Depressed (84), Defeat (76)

MAY DE-ESCALATE TO: Powerlessness (208), Sadness (226), Vulnerability (276), Hopefulness (148)

ASSOCIATED POWER VERBS: Cave, crumble, cry, cut, defeat, demoralize, drain, dread, droop, fall, lose, numb, pain, rail, sag, shrink, slacken, stumble, surrender, weaken

> **WRITER'S TIP:** *Visceral sensations are powerful, but if used too often, they can lose their strength. Save them for when you really want to make a big emotional impact in a scene.*

DESPERATION

DEFINITION: A state of hopelessness that leads to rashness

PHYSICAL SIGNALS AND BEHAVIORS:
Feverish, over-bright eyes
A darting gaze
Quick movements
Pacing
An inability to sleep or eat
Finger twitches and other compulsive, repetitive movements
A herky-jerky walk
Reaching or touching in hopes of gaining help or favor
Facing danger head-on
Acting in ways that push the limits of endurance
Anxiously muttering to oneself
Grabbing fistfuls of one's hair and pulling (using pain to focus on action)
An emotion-choked voice
Fluttery hand movements
Moaning
A voice that shakes
Rocking in place and rubbing the hands along one's crossed arms
Trying to bargain, ignoring another's cues of disinterest or anger
Shaking and trembling
Curling the arms over the head
Hugging one's shoulders, the chin resting against one's chest
A neck that appears stiff, cords visible
Strained forearms
Eyes that appear wet, darting and not settling
Teeth biting down on the bottom lip
Wringing one's hands or repeatedly flexing the fingers and making fists
Shoulders curling, a bent spine
Shaking one's head in denial
Protective posture (chin to chest, arms holding the body tightly, etc.)
Dragging nails down the cheeks, leaving marks
Squeezing one's biceps while the arms are crossed
Sweating profusely
Swearing in a voice that gets progressively louder

INTERNAL SENSATIONS:
A racing heartbeat
A dry mouth
A sore throat from pleading, crying, or begging
A heightened level of pain resistance
Tightness or pain in the chest

Excessive or manic energy

MENTAL RESPONSES:
Constant planning and obsessing
Irrational thinking and poor judgment
A willingness to do anything
Ignoring the law or society's values
Casting morality and good judgment aside
Sacrificing others or lesser goals, desires, and needs if necessary
Disregarding another's feelings if they conflict with one's goal

ACUTE OR LONG-TERM RESPONSES FOR THIS EMOTION:
Crying, sobbing, wailing, or screaming
Beating one's fists against something to the point of injury
Pleading, abasing, or disregarding personal worth or pride
Extreme risk taking
Offering an exchange: *Take me instead,* or *I'll go, you stay.*
Pushing past one's limits to find needed strength
Refusing to be persuaded

SIGNS THAT THIS EMOTION IS BEING SUPPRESSED:
Holding oneself tight
Believing a lie if it offers hope
Retreating internally to cope; shutting the world out
Difficulty sitting still
Clock-watching
Reassuring others
Fixing one's hair and clothes to appear unaffected
Taking advantage of a distraction (e.g., watching a movie or TV show)
Curling the hands into tight fists

MAY ESCALATE TO: Anguish (42), Dread (110), Anger (40), Determination (92)

MAY DE-ESCALATE TO: Overwhelmed (196), Hopefulness (148), Gratitude (136)

ASSOCIATED POWER VERBS: Beg, betray, cling, clutch, corner, cry, dare, deny, drive, fight, flee, force, gamble, grab, grasp, grope, harass, implore, plead, plunge, pray, promise, resort, risk, scramble, search, steal, strain, strive, take, threaten, wail

WRITER'S TIP: *Clothing choices are individual and project an image of one's personality. When creating unique emotional body language, think about how a character's clothing can be utilized to reveal their insecurities or vanities and show feelings of self-worth.*

DETERMINATION

DEFINITION: Firm intention on achieving a goal; decisiveness

PHYSICAL SIGNALS AND BEHAVIORS:
Being the first to speak
Moving into someone's personal space
Using articulate words and short, strong sentences
A steady, lower-pitched voice
A furrowing brow
Tight muscles
An alert gaze
A set jaw
Strong eye contact
A curt nod
Forming the hands into a steeple
Mirroring the leader's movements
Using affirmative words: *Yes,* and *I will.*
Pressing the lips together
Tightening fists
Organizing one's things; being prepared
Standing solidly, at the ready
Planting one's feet in a wide stance
Leaning in, hand on one knee
Holding one's chin high, with the neck exposed
Pushing up one's sleeves
Shoulders pushing back, displaying a strong posture
Precise movements
Sharp hand movements (jabbing a finger for emphasis, etc.)
A fast-paced stride
Asking pointed questions
Holding one's legs straight out, with the knees uncrossed
Thrusting the chest out
Offering a firm handshake
Inhaling deeply through the nose, then exhaling through the mouth
Exuding calm and focus
Practicing a skill
Making preparations or conditioning the body
Studying or gathering information
Accepting criticism so one can improve

INTERNAL SENSATIONS:
A fluttery feeling in the chest
Increased internal temperature and heartbeat
Muscles tightening in readiness

MENTAL RESPONSES:
Planning for obstacles and strategizing ways to overcome them
Mentally encouraging oneself to succeed
Active listening
Having an acute sense of purpose; setting goals
Ignoring distractions or discomforts
Extreme mental focus on the objective
Running through what one must say or do
Dismissing negative thoughts

ACUTE OR LONG-TERM RESPONSES FOR THIS EMOTION:
Conditioning for the task in advance
A muscle clenching along the jaw line
Headaches and muscle strain
Ignoring pain, stress, or any outside elements
Sacrificing what is needed to achieve the desired result

SIGNS THAT THIS EMOTION IS BEING SUPPRESSED:
Purposely adopting a languid pose
Feigning disinterest (yawning, shrugging, etc.)
Meaningless gestures (scrutinizing cuticles, checking for split ends, etc.)
Placing one's hands in one's pockets
Engaging in banter or non-threatening conversation
Asking benign questions
Laughing or making jokes meant to disarm
A lack of eye contact
Closing one's eyes as if one is relaxed or dozing

MAY ESCALATE TO: Hopefulness (148), Confidence (64), Satisfaction (230)

MAY DE-ESCALATE TO: Frustration (134), Disappointment (96), Insecurity (166), Acceptance (28)

ASSOCIATED POWER VERBS: Anticipate, battle, compete, condition, confront, counter, dedicate, defend, deliver, devote, dive, fight, focus, harden, persevere, plan, prevent, prioritize, push, resist, sharpen, strengthen, strive, tackle, target, withstand

WRITER'S TIP: *Never underestimate the power of texture. The way an object feels against the skin can create a powerful reaction (positive or negative) and add to the reader's emotional experience.*

DEVASTATION

DEFINITION: Overwhelming shock and sorrow

PHYSICAL SIGNALS AND BEHAVIORS:
Asking someone to repeat the news out of utter disbelief
Laying a splayed-out hand against one's chest
Needing to sit or be supported
Covering one's face with both hands and collapsing
Stopping what one was doing mid-task
A pained expression, with eyes that cloud or focus inward
Brows that pull together and down
A gape that widens
Slow shakes of the head that become wider and faster as the news sinks in
Not knowing where to look or what to do
Expelling an audible breath
One's chest caving, the spine curling forward
Using a hand to support one's head or rub at the forehead
Being at a loss for words (speaking in fragmented sentences, starting and stopping, etc.)
Pressing a palm over one's mouth and then letting it fall away or pull down
Arms that drag at one's shoulders, with the limbs going loose
Sagging back into a chair
A voice that goes weak or cracks
Eyes that fill with tears
A shaking hand reaching to cover the mouth
Repeating negatives: *It just can't be,* or *I don't believe this is happening.*
Receiving a hug but being too numb to return it
Not responding to questions
Not knowing what to do with one's hands
Staring down, with the neck bent forward
Shuffling steps
A strangled sob
Letting out a grief-choked wail or scream
Swaying slightly on one's feet
Sinking to one's knees
Leaving without explanation (flight)
Loosening one's grip, which leads to dropping an item or letting something go

INTERNAL SENSATIONS:
A sudden weakness in one's limbs
Pressure building in the chest from forgetting to breathe
Dizziness
Tingling in the chest and stomach that signals dread
A heart that hurts

MENTAL RESPONSES:
Being unable to believe what one is seeing (if one is experiencing the cause firsthand)
Imagining the event unfolding as it is described (if one is hearing the news secondhand)
Immediately remembering the last time one was in contact with the affected person, people group, or place
Thinking of the people most deeply affected and how they are taking the news
Sudden regret: *Why didn't I visit more often?* and *I should have told her what she meant to me.*
Feeling relief, followed by guilt: *Thank goodness Joe stayed home, or he'd be dead too.*
Struggling with even the small things; feeling overwhelmed

ACUTE OR LONG-TERM RESPONSES FOR THIS EMOTION:
Being unable to eat, sleep, or engage in normal activities
Cutting the source of pain from one's life (giving up a passion, quitting a job, etc.)
Progressing into grief but never moving past it
Becoming a hollowed-out version of oneself (lacking vitality, drive, or personality)
Emotional numbness that prevents connection with people or the world outside
Losing the will to live

SIGNS THAT THIS EMOTION IS BEING SUPPRESSED:
Withdrawing from the situation to be alone (flight)
Saying nothing and retreating inside oneself
Self-medicating to numb the emotional pain
A chin that quakes with one's effort to keep in tears
Throwing oneself at a task (e.g., funeral arrangements) to avoid the pain of grief

MAY ESCALATE TO: Powerlessness (208), Grief (138), Despair (88), Depressed (84)

MAY DE-ESCALATE TO: Loneliness (176), Neglected (188), Wistfulness (282), Acceptance (28)

ASSOCIATED POWER VERBS: Ache, beg, buckle, clutch, collapse, console, cry, cut, destroy, disbelieve, gasp, grieve, hold, hurt, moan, mourn, pray, quiver, rock, sag, shake, slacken, slouch, stare, sting, stutter, suffer, tear, tremble, twist, undo, weep, wheeze

WRITER'S TIP: *Opening up about difficult feelings signals an important breakthrough for a character on their journey of change. To be realistic, it won't be easy; emotional pain is hard to face and harder to talk about. Show this stress and struggle using vocal cues and body language.*

DISAPPOINTMENT

DEFINITION: A state of dismay due to being let down

PHYSICAL SIGNALS AND BEHAVIORS:
Lowering one's head
Lips pressing tight into a grimace
Shoulders dropping or slumping slightly
A hunched posture
Looking up with hands raised in the *Why me?* position
Collapsing onto a chair or bench
A frustrated shake of the head
A bitter smile
A heavy sigh
Briefly covering one's face with one's hands
Breaking eye contact
Bending the neck forward
Slowly shaking one's head
Tilting the chin down and frowning
Muttering or making a noise in one's throat
Swallowing hard
Sagging against a door or wall
Reaching out to steady oneself
Dropping the head, eyes closed
Stumbling mid-stride
One's face going slack and paling slightly
Pressing hands to one's temples
Weaving hands into the hair and pulling
Frowning or wearing a stony expression
Watering eyes, an inward focus
Wincing
The mouth falling open slightly
Looking around in confusion or shock
Attempting to hide (covering the head, ducking one's chin, turning away, etc.)
Hands that hang, lifeless and loose
Hands fluttering like they've lost track of what they should be doing
Feet shuffling or kicking at the ground
Rubbing at the back of one's neck
A voice that drops or goes quiet
Whispering *No* or cursing under the breath
Biting or chewing at the lip
Clutching oneself (gripping the elbows, rubbing the arms, etc.)
Pressing a hand to the abdomen
Slinking away (flight response)

INTERNAL SENSATIONS:
A heart that feels like it's shrinking
A clenching stomach followed by the sudden onset of nausea
Ribs that grow tight, restricting one's breath
Breaths that hitch, or momentarily forgetting to breathe
A heaviness in the body

MENTAL RESPONSES:
A feeling of dread or hopelessness
Defeatist thoughts and negative self-talk
Wanting to be alone
Feeling worthless

ACUTE OR LONG-TERM RESPONSES FOR THIS EMOTION:
Flushed cheeks (embarrassment)
Berating oneself
Wallowing (drinking too much, listening to depressing songs, etc.)
Obsessing over why things happened the way they did
An inability to move on
Avoiding future goals that are not a sure thing

SIGNS THAT THIS EMOTION IS BEING SUPPRESSED:
A slight lip press
Dropping the shoulders, then hitching them up again
Offering false cheer, a weak smile
Making a joke as if it doesn't matter
Citing a backup plan or listing more options
Making promises
Clasping one's hands in one's lap
Congratulating the victor

MAY ESCALATE TO: Depressed (84), Defeat (76), Resentment (222), Anger (40), Inadequacy (162)

MAY DE-ESCALATE TO: Resignation (224), Acceptance (28)

ASSOCIATED POWER VERBS: Break, cloud, cope, crush, dampen, defeat, deplete, derail, dismay, drag, droop, fail, falter, forfeit, frustrate, mourn, pummel, sigh, slacken

> **WRITER'S TIP:** *Characters experiencing raw emotion often react without thinking—either through dialogue or action. Rash behavior creates the perfect storm for increased tension and conflict.*

DISBELIEF

DEFINITION: Withholding belief; a refusal to see the truth

PHYSICAL SIGNALS AND BEHAVIORS:
The mouth slackening
Eyes widening
Looking down or away, or doing a double-take
Rubbing at an eyelid or brow
Being at a loss for words
Turning away and covering the mouth
One's expression blanching, going pale
Asking *Are you sure?* type questions
Scratching one's jaw
A shake of the head
Rubbing absently at the arms
Verbalizing shock: *Are you kidding?* or *Impossible!*
Moving back slightly, increasing one's personal space
Showing one's palms
Lifting a single eyebrow and cocking the head
An unfocused gaze
Rapid blinking
Running the hands through one's hair
Gaping or stuttering
One's mouth opening and closing
Hands dropping to one's sides
The posture slumping slightly
The neck bending forward, then stiffening back up
Hands carving through one's hair, holding it back and then releasing it
Pulling glasses down and looking over the rims
Openly staring
Covering one's ears
Repeating *No* and other negatives: *It's not true!*
Folding the arms over the stomach and bending forward slightly
Staring at one's palms as if they hold the answers
Jiggling, tugging, or tapping the earlobe
Waving something off
Making accusations: *You're lying.*
Refusing to listen to the people sharing the bad news

INTERNAL SENSATIONS:
A tingling in one's chest
A hardening or clenching stomach
A small intake of breath (gasp)

Light-headedness
Restricted breathing

MENTAL RESPONSES:
Making an immediate moral judgment (either good or bad, wrong or right)
Thoughts scrambling to understand
Attempting to reason or glean more information
Pretending to have misheard
Growing angry but not knowing where to direct it
Thinking back to the last time one was with the person being discussed

ACUTE OR LONG-TERM RESPONSES FOR THIS EMOTION:
A restless stance
Arguing; trying to poke holes in the information one is being given
Walking away—refusing to listen or discuss it further
Voicing the emotion over and over: *I just can't believe this*
Difficulty speaking; giving choppy responses
Holding a hand up to ward off the truth
Demanding those with influence do something to change the outcome
Closed body posture (the arms creating a barrier across the chest)

SIGNS THAT THIS EMOTION IS BEING SUPPRESSED:
Changing the topic
Making excuses for one's behavior: *Sorry, I've not been sleeping well.*
Supporting the outcome; acting like one was "in the know" all along
Reassuring others of one's belief, commitment, etc.
Asking questions to glean information without giving away disbelief
Clearing one's throat, pinching at one's Adam's apple, or laughing nervously
Coughing, then pretending a drink went down wrong
Offering fake platitudes: *Interesting,* or *Well, that's good then.*

MAY ESCALATE TO: Denial (82), Anger (40), Overwhelmed (196), Resignation (224)

MAY DE-ESCALATE TO: Doubt (108), Uncertainty (264), Resignation (224), Acceptance (28)

ASSOCIATED POWER VERBS: Bulge, deny, freeze, frown, fumble, gape, gasp, grunt, question, recoil, reel, refuse, retreat, shake, shock, slacken, splutter, sputter, stammer, stare

WRITER'S TIP: *While melodrama is usually a bad idea in fiction, it can be used effectively to characterize an over-the-top character.*

DISCOURAGEMENT

DEFINITION: Deprived of courage, spirit, or confidence

PHYSICAL SIGNALS AND BEHAVIORS:
Displaying low interest in one's surroundings
Slumped shoulders
Hands lying still in one's lap
Trudging; walking with a slow, heavy step
A bowed head
Holding one's head
Sitting bent over, with one's hands or elbows on one's knees
Rubbing or covering one's face with the hands
A vacant stare, slackness in the face
A voice that is quieter and lower in pitch than normal
Sitting limply (the head back against a wall, arms beside one's body, legs outstretched, etc.)
Leaning against supports instead of standing tall on one's own
Not participating in conversations
Eyes that look tired
A partial smile offered out of habit or because it's expected
Speaking in monosyllables
A body that curls in on itself
Getting drunk or high
Going quiet for long periods of time
Sleeping a lot
Shutting down others who try to encourage: *What's the point? Just accept it.*
Always being on the verge of tears
Becoming emotionally volatile (lashing out, jumping quickly to anger, etc.)
Frequent sighing
A downward gaze
Being very still
An overall decrease in one's energy and enthusiasm levels
Agreeing because it's easier than arguing or it just doesn't matter anymore
Avoiding conversations that touch on the source of one's discouragement
Becoming confrontational about other things as a way of regaining some level of power

INTERNAL SENSATIONS:
Lacking mental and physical energy
A sense of heaviness in one's limbs
A constricted throat

MENTAL RESPONSES:
Thinking poorly of oneself or the cause of the discouragement
Giving up on one's dreams or goals
Emotional numbness

Berating oneself for wanting this goal (instead of settling for the status quo)
Sluggish or slow-moving thoughts
Feeling an overall lack of urgency, as if nothing is important
Pessimistic thinking that makes it difficult to make future plans

ACUTE OR LONG-TERM RESPONSES FOR THIS EMOTION:

Depression
Becoming risk-averse
Losing faith in the people, beliefs, or organizations one used to count on
Becoming negative, skeptical, cynical, or bitter
Discouraging others from trying to succeed or be happy
A lack of interest in hobbies and passions
Major changes in one's appearance (gaining or losing weight, looking years older, etc.)
Being easily frustrated and quick to anger
Giving in to apathy
Throwing caution to the wind; becoming reckless
Lacking the motivation to make a change or try again

SIGNS THAT THIS EMOTION IS BEING SUPPRESSED:

Over-the-top exuberance meant to mask one's true feelings
Exhibiting positive emotions (happiness, joy, contentment, etc.) in a way that seems forced
Hiding or denying one's tears
Surreptitiously avoiding the topic of one's discouragement (not going certain places, steering conversations away from the subject, etc.)
Feigning disinterest; pretending one wasn't really invested in the goal anyway
Putting on a happy face in front of others, then falling apart when one is alone
Self-medicating in private

MAY ESCALATE TO: Anger (40), Defeat (76), Self-Loathing (236), Indifference (164), Disillusionment (104)

MAY DE-ESCALATE TO: Acceptance (28), Hopefulness (148), Self-Pity (238), Bitterness (58)

ASSOCIATED POWER VERBS: Abandon, alienate, cave, choke, daunt, deny, disengage, distract, droop, drowse, exhaust, flop, forfeit, frown, give up, hide, laze, lost, lumber, mumble, ostracize, pass, punish, sag, shun, slack, slouch, slump, trudge, weaken, wither

WRITER'S TIP: *Disappointments will happen throughout a story to your characters, creating an opportunity to showcase different behaviors. What will each do if things don't go their way: talk it out, get angry, wallow in self-pity, something else? Pull from their personalities, and experiment!*

DISGUST

DEFINITION: An aversion, usually to something distasteful; revulsion

PHYSICAL SIGNALS AND BEHAVIORS:
A curling lip
An open mouth with the tongue pushing slightly forward
Wrinkling one's nose
Flinching, recoiling, or shuddering
Swallowing hard, then pinching the lips shut
Leaning back, the neck disappearing
Stroking the throat and grimacing
Turning one's back to the source
Eyes that appear cold, dead, or flat
Refusing to look
Shaking one's head and muttering
Walking away to regain one's composure
The toes curling up
Pulling up a collar to cover the mouth and nose
Spitting, coughing, dry heaving, or throwing up
Putting a hand up and backing away
Repeating what someone has said, purposely devoid of all emotion
Dry washing the hands
Pressing a fist against the mouth and puffing out the cheeks
Rubbing at one's exposed forearms
Covering the mouth
Making a choking noise in the throat
Jerking away from contact, or even the suggestion of contact
Pressing hands against the stomach
Demanding that someone stop speaking or desist what they are doing
Violently rolling the shoulders as if one's clothing is creating discomfort
Using a purse or jacket to create a shield
Offering evasive answers
Eyebrows lowering and pinching together
Pressing one's knees together
Narrowing one's stance (e.g., bringing the feet together)
A face that blanches
Rubbing at one's nose or mouth
Speaking in an unsteady voice
Losing track of one's words
Cringing away from the source
An expression that appears pained, the eyebrows furrowing

INTERNAL SENSATIONS:
Having trouble swallowing, or feeling like one is choking
Excessive saliva; a need to spit
A sour or bitter tang in the mouth
Nausea or a heaving stomach
A burning in the throat
The skin tightening (crawling flesh sensation)

MENTAL RESPONSES:
A compulsion to flee
Feeling unclean
Wishing to be somewhere else
The mind replaying what was seen in agonizing detail
Being unable to concentrate properly
A sensitivity to smell and touch

ACUTE OR LONG-TERM RESPONSES FOR THIS EMOTION:
Focusing on cleanliness (showering, rubbing skin raw, etc.)
Hyper-protectiveness of personal space
Acting jumpy or jittery when one is near the source
Becoming unresponsive or less verbal
An intense need to flee the source

SIGNS THAT THIS EMOTION IS BEING SUPPRESSED:
Offering a watery smile while maintaining a safe distance
Hesitating while forcing oneself to come closer
Maintaining eye contact, no matter how difficult
Waving a hand as if something doesn't matter
Slowly walking closer, but keeping the arms close to the body
Standing away and reaching in with one hand
Heavy, jerky movements

MAY ESCALATE TO: Scorn (234), Fear (128), Anger (40), Horror (150)

MAY DE-ESCALATE TO: Shock (242), Reluctance (218), Unease (266), Wariness (280)

ASSOCIATED POWER VERBS: Churn, curdle, faint, flee, grimace, heave, nauseate, purge, recoil, reject, repel, retch, roil, shake, shrink, shudder, sicken, spit, spurn, swallow

WRITER'S TIP: *With extreme emotions that trigger an immediate fight-or-flight response, it's important to know which "side" fits best with your character's personality. All actions should line up with this choice.*

DISILLUSIONMENT

DEFINITION: Hurt and disappointment upon discovering that one's belief is false or trust in someone has been misplaced

PHYSICAL SIGNALS AND BEHAVIORS:
Rapid blinking while the rest of the face goes slack
Cocking the head and displaying a fixed look as one wrestles with a sudden discovery
Posture that stiffens, then droops
Stumbling slightly as realization kicks in
Laying a hand against one's chest, then pulling the front of one's shirt into a fist
Stuttering; trying to form sentences but failing
Breaths coming faster and deeper, with the chest visibly rising and falling
Looking at the source, then away, and then back in utter disbelief
Holding one's head in one's hands
Uttering *No*, or *It can't be.*
Arms wrapping around oneself in a self-soothing manner
The eyes widening while one's head moves forward
Being open-mouthed and incapable of speech
Citing evidence that supports old beliefs: *But you promised you'd quit!*
Putting one's hand up in a warding off gesture
Rapid breathing while glancing upward
A mouth that trembles
A visible shudder that goes through the entire body
Pinching one's lips with tented hands while shaking the head
Stepping back to increase one's personal space
Clutching at a totem that symbolizes one's belief (a cross, a gift from the subject, etc.)
Backing up and stumbling because one is not attentive to one's surroundings
Recoiling from those who offer comfort
Doubting the messenger: *You must be wrong. He'd never do that.*
Voicing shock
Openly staring at the subject with a pained look that contains hurt and anger
Weaving one's hands into the hair and pulling slightly to try and anchor one's emotions
Color bleeding from one's face (shock) or suddenly flushing (anger)
Offering excuses to cling to previously held beliefs: *But they forced you, right?*
Leaning forward to catch signs of guilt (when one is with the individual involved)
Staggering away from the person or thing representing one's disillusionment
Shaking the head and cutting the person off so one can process the information

INTERNAL SENSATIONS:
Feeling cold all over
An unsettling heaviness or ache in the chest
The stomach hardening
Ribs tightening
A shudder that shakes one's core

MENTAL RESPONSES:
The mind flashing to events or moments that first made one believe
Experiencing epiphanies in the form of signs one didn't pick up on at the time
The mind racing for explanations due to an extreme desire to disbelieve the evidence
Thoughts jumping from memory to memory as one wonders if the accusations could be true
Feeling so disoriented one begins to question related beliefs

ACUTE OR LONG-TERM RESPONSES FOR THIS EMOTION:
Growing unsteady—needing to support oneself or sit down
Sarcasm and the need to hurt with words
Spilling secrets to cause the subject pain
Yelling, pointing fingers, moving aggressively, and other signs of anger taking over
Lashing out with violence (running at someone, trying to hurt them, etc.)
Running away out of an inability to cope (flight)
Becoming embittered toward the person, organization, or idea one was once loyal to

SIGNS THAT THIS EMOTION IS BEING SUPPRESSED:
Denial (shaking one's head, making excuses, arguing, etc.)
Excessive anger at people revealing the deception
Clinging to and verbalizing one's reasons why other people are wrong about this
Walking out in anger; refusing to listen

MAY ESCALATE TO: Anger (40), Bitterness (58), Humiliation (154), Disgust (102), Betrayed (56)

MAY DE-ESCALATE TO: Skepticism (244), Disappointment (96), Neglected (188), Inadequacy (162), Embarrassment (118), Shame (240)

ASSOCIATED POWER VERBS: Abandon, ache, blame, break, bruise, confuse, damage, denounce, distress, ditch, forsake, humiliate, hurt, injure, insult, paralyze, question, quit, rattle, renounce, shock, shout, spit, stun, stymie, tremble, wound

> **WRITER'S TIP:** *Make sure to show how a character's emotions escalate or shift in a tense scene. This causes anticipation for what is to come.*

DISSATISFACTION

DEFINITION: Being unsatisfied and discontent

PHYSICAL SIGNALS AND BEHAVIORS:
Eyebrows that pull close and down, creating a forehead crease
Grimacing and shaking the head
Becoming more vocal and contrary
Crossing the arms and looking down
Rubbing at the back of the neck
Twisting or crushing an empty water bottle to relieve frustration
Rubbing the legs while seated
Breaking eye contact with others
A pinched, unhappy expression
Muttering something unkind under the breath
Rolling the eyes, sighing, or letting out a derisive snort
The stride slowing when one approaches the source of dissatisfaction (a person, a job, etc.)
Growing more insistent or emphatic in conversation
Demanding someone "do it again" until it's right
Perfectionistic tendencies
Complaining or grousing
Shifting position (turning the torso, moving the arms frequently, etc.)
Feet that point away from the people one is engaged with
Staying out late to avoid going home (if one's home life is the source of dissatisfaction)
Restless sleeping
Replaying the day's events with a focus on the negative
Waking before the alarm clock and dreading it going off
Finding it hard to relax
Pacing or moving about frequently rather than remaining in one place
Asking revelatory questions: *You ever wish you could just hit the reset button and try again?*
Going through the motions rather than participating (at work, in relationships, at church, etc.)
Having no patience for small talk
Pulling away from others to be alone
Holding grudges
Growing angry quickly; letting small things get under one's skin
Always wanting more or something better
Talking about the past and better times
Self-medicating—drinking, gambling, smoking weed, or taking pills to escape
Playing hooky to get out of obligations, then lying about it

INTERNAL SENSATIONS:
Headaches (increased blood pressure)
Hardness in the gut
An overall feeling of jitteriness due to exhaustion from poor sleeping habits

MENTAL RESPONSES:
Feeling lost and directionless
Feeling trapped (in a bad marriage, in an unfulfilling job, by an illness, etc.)
Frequent thoughts about the unfairness of life or how others are to blame
Focusing on the negative; having a pessimistic outlook
Resenting people who seem happy and content
Mentally comparing oneself to others
Daydreaming about one's problems being solved (winning the lottery, a bad boss being transferred, etc.)
Becoming obsessed with finding a way out of one's situation

ACUTE OR LONG-TERM RESPONSES FOR THIS EMOTION:
Taking risks (to improve one's situation or to feel excitement and vitality)
Going through a mid-life crisis
Chasing the wrong things, such as investing in get-rich-quick schemes
Having an affair
Insomnia
Depression
Stress-induced maladies (ulcers, hypertension, etc.)
Being unable to feel gratitude
Becoming bitter and jaded towards others or the world in general
Flight (leaving one's job, one's family, etc.)
Appearing older than one is (frown lines, broken blood vessels in the nose and cheeks, etc.)

SIGNS THAT THIS EMOTION IS BEING SUPPRESSED:
Busying oneself with work or family to avoid thinking about one's needs or wants
Deferring a yearning: *Someday I'll travel like my sister*, or *I'll learn to paint next year.*
Encouraging others so one can live through their successes
Playing the martyr: *Just because I was cheated out of my dreams doesn't mean you have to be.*
Manically trying new things in hopes of finding the "magic" that will change one's life
Buying things to get a brief burst of happiness (retail therapy)

MAY ESCALATE TO: Depressed (84), Contempt (72), Anger (40), Bitterness (58), Resentment (222)

MAY DE-ESCALATE TO: Frustration (134), Resignation (224), Wistfulness (282), Acceptance (28)

ASSOCIATED POWER VERBS: Agonize, belabor, clench, clutch, complain, covet, interrupt, irk, irritate, miff, moan, mutter, resent, rouse, spurn, sulk, thwart, worry, yearn

WRITER'S TIP: *To show a character's emotional growth and maturity, provide a situation early on that will cause them to overreact. Then, when a similar circumstance arises later, they*

DOUBT

DEFINITION: To lack confidence in or consider unlikely

PHYSICAL SIGNALS AND BEHAVIORS:
One's brows drawing closer, the face tightening
Looking down or away
Avoiding eye contact
Pressing the lips together
Shuffling one's feet
Shoving one's hands into pockets
Throat-clearing
Thumbing the ear
Asking questions without clear answers to imply that more thought is needed
Checking and rechecking one's appearance (self-doubt)
Delaying tactics (suggesting time to review options, etc.)
Pauses, *ums*, or other conversation fillers
Taking a slight step back
Lingering at the edge of a group or event
Biting one's cheek
Declining an offer of support
Running hands through the hair (and other signs of restlessness)
Pulling or tugging at one's clothes
A smile that appears tight
A hesitating nod
Rocking on one's heels and pretending to study the floor
Cocking the head while raising an eyebrow
Swallowing more than usual
Tipping one's head side to side, weighing an idea or choice
Tapping the fingers together while steepled
Slightly clenched fists
A deep, weighted sigh
Pursing the lips
Shrugging
Shaking the head
Asking for assurances or clarification
Arguing or questioning
Citing possible repercussions
Rubbing the back of the neck
Fiddling with a ring or button to avoid eye contact
Putting a hand over the face and closing the eyes
Drawing in breath and holding it for a time before releasing it
Tactfully offering alternative suggestions
Hesitation (accepting a leaflet with reluctance, etc.)

Asking a third party to weigh in, hoping to sway someone's decision

INTERNAL SENSATIONS:
Ribs that tighten slightly
A light quiver in the stomach

MENTAL RESPONSES:
Worrying over the current path
Looking ahead to possible collateral damage
Second-guessing a prior decision (in choosing someone for the job, supporting an idea, etc.)
Searching for ideas on how to circumvent the situation
Dredging up evidence to sway opinions
Hoping or praying it will work out

ACUTE OR LONG-TERM RESPONSES FOR THIS EMOTION:
Avoiding speaking or agreeing openly
Looking for ways to distance oneself from the situation
Sharing a look with an ally; raising the eyebrows to convey a message
Wincing as others rally behind a weak solution
Fearmongering: *This could really blow up if you're wrong. Remember how George got fired last year?*

SIGNS THAT THIS EMOTION IS BEING SUPPRESSED:
Coughing as one agrees or supports a doubtful decision or stance
Mimicking confidence (straightening, speaking in a booming voice, etc.)
Lying or misleading others
Making excuses for not agreeing immediately
Reassuring others of loyalty, commitment, etc.
Offering to handle the problem

MAY ESCALATE TO: Worry (284), Disbelief (98), Unease (266), Suspicion (254), Insecurity (166)

MAY DE-ESCALATE TO: Skepticism (244), Conflicted (66), Curiosity (74)

ASSOCIATED POWER VERBS: Backpedal, challenge, counter, delay, discredit, dismiss, dispute, dwindle, exit, fade, falter, fidget, flounder, hang back, hesitate, procrastinate, question, regret, reject, research, scoff, stumble, stutter, tank, vanish, waffle, waver

> **WRITER'S TIP:** *When steering your character through scenes that allow for emotional growth, don't forget to also provide setbacks. The path to enlightenment isn't smooth for anyone, including our characters.*

DREAD

DEFINITION: A deep fear of a future event or circumstance that leads to a strong desire to avoid it

PHYSICAL SIGNALS AND BEHAVIORS:
Clutching arms to one's chest
Shoulders curling forward, caving the chest in
A bent neck
Leaning back or away from the source of discomfort
Dragging footsteps
Hanging back
Making excuses to leave
Speaking in a quiet voice
Offering one-word responses
A hunched posture and a drooping head
Clasping one's knees tightly together
Avoiding eye contact
Turning the torso (shielding it from the source of one's discomfort)
Lifting the shoulders as if to hide one's neck
Sweating
Rocking slightly
Hands that tremble
Moving to the back of a room
Following the main group, leaving a buffer of space so one can retreat or flee if necessary
Seeking the safety of darkness, an exit, etc.
Hesitating before entering a room
Holding one's elbows tightly against one's sides
Making oneself appear smaller
Flinching or cringing at loud noises
Increased swallowing
Arms crossing the stomach in a protective huddle
Fidgety movements (twisting one's wrists, rubbing hands on one's pants, etc.)
Clutching comfort items (a necklace charm, phone, etc.)
Repeatedly dragging the palms down one's pant legs
Chewing at one's lips or inner cheeks and making them bleed
A pale or sickly complexion

INTERNAL SENSATIONS:
A roiling stomach or a dropping sensation
A heavy or sluggish heartbeat
Chills
Cold fingers
Tingling in the chest
A weighted chest

Difficulty breathing
A sour taste in the mouth
An ache in the back of the throat
Difficulty swallowing
Dizziness
Shakiness in the limbs

MENTAL RESPONSES:
Thoughts of escape; wanting to hide
Wishing time would speed up
An inability to see a positive outcome
Imagining the worst-case scenario and wishing for rescue
Sensitivity to sound and movement

ACUTE OR LONG-TERM RESPONSES FOR THIS EMOTION:
Shaking or shuddering
Jumping at sounds
Flinching if touched
Seeking any excuse to avoid what is to come
Hyperventilating
Bargaining and pleading

SIGNS THAT THIS EMOTION IS BEING SUPPRESSED:
Acting like one is simply feeling under the weather
Attempting to escape via distraction (with TV, a book, or music)
Focusing one's thoughts to keep fear from taking over
Keeping still

MAY ESCALATE TO: Anguish (42), Powerlessness (208), Terror (258)

MAY DE-ESCALATE TO: Nervousness (190), Uncertainty (264), Wariness (280), Insecurity (166), Hopefulness (148)

ASSOCIATED POWER VERBS: Brace, collapse, cringe, crumple, fear, grip, imagine, obsess, panic, relive, retreat, shake, shiver, shrink, shrivel, suffer, sweat, tremble, worry

> **WRITER'S TIP:** *Maintain an overall perspective of the character's emotional range. A strong manuscript will always expose the reader to several contrasting emotional experiences that fit within the context of the protagonist's growth.*

EAGERNESS

DEFINITION: Enthusiasm for what is to come

PHYSICAL SIGNALS AND BEHAVIORS:
Leaning forward
Eyes that glow
Rushing one's words
Speaking in a bubbly or loud tone
Rapt attention
Rapidly nodding the head
Using excitable language
Agreeability to whatever is suggested
Fiddling with an object to keep the hands busy
Squeezing the hands at one's sides
Strong eye contact
Talking over others or interjecting to add to the conversation
Offering suggestions to ensure the event is successful or runs more smoothly
Raising a hand immediately to be called on
Asking questions to get information
Rubbing the hands together
Leaning forward with a hand on the knee
Sitting at the edge of a chair
Allowing others into one's personal space
Licking one's lips and smiling
Feet pointing forward
Shoulders straight and back
Using animated gestures
Bouncing on one's toes
Moving, fidgeting, or pacing
Blowing out a long breath and smiling
Eyes that are wide and rounded, with very few blinks
Hands clutched together
Head up, alert
A fast walk, jog, or run
Sharing a look or wink with another
Clambering closer to a group or event
Whispering in hushed, excitable tones
Scuffing a chair closer to the table
Arriving early
Volunteering one's time to help make the event better
Quirking an eyebrow and smiling
Friendliness, even with those not in one's social circle
Pulling or prodding others to hurry up
Moving toward others who share one's mindset (and even from those who don't)

INTERNAL SENSATIONS:
A fluttery stomach
Increased heartbeat
An expanding feeling in the chest
Breathlessness
Adrenaline that causes hyper-alertness

MENTAL RESPONSES:
Focused listening
Strong organization and preparedness
An inability to concentrate on anything else
Desiring to share and include others
Losing all inhibitions
A positive outlook and thinking pattern
A willingness to take on responsibility, help, or lead
Making quick decisions due to being completely committed to one's path

ACUTE OR LONG-TERM RESPONSES FOR THIS EMOTION:
Preparing early, often hours or days before needed
Planning or obsessing over every detail
Seeking perfection
Hurrying or rushing to make things happen quicker
Daydreaming and imagining what the future experience will be like

SIGNS THAT THIS EMOTION IS BEING SUPPRESSED:
Clamping the hands in the lap, forcing oneself to sit still
Tight muscles
Slowing one's speech; concentrating on being articulate
A series of deep breaths
Taking up a task or chore to pass the time
Feigning disinterest by adopting a loose and relaxed posture
Making a slight detour as a ruse

MAY ESCALATE TO: Excitement (126), Schadenfreude (232), Impatience (160)

MAY DE-ESCALATE TO: Satisfaction (230), Disappointment (96)

ASSOCIATED POWER VERBS: Advance, agree, animate, approach, babble, flock, hasten, help, join, jump, lean, pounce, pursue, run, rush, snatch, urge, volunteer, wish

WRITER'S TIP: *To generate friction in dialogue, give the participants opposing goals. A heightened emotional response is the natural result of not getting what one wants.*

ELATION

DEFINITION: In high spirits; a state of exhilaration

PHYSICAL SIGNALS AND BEHAVIORS:
High color, a flushed appearance
A smile or grin that cannot be contained
Laughing
Squealing, screaming, shouting, or hollering
Falling to one's knees
Jumping up and down
Talking over one another
Holding the arms up in a "Victory V"
The head tipped back, one's face turned to the sky
Running a victory lap
A beaming face, with strong color and sheen
Embracing others
Dancing in place
Whooping loudly
Not caring what others think; a lack of self-consciousness
Enjoying communal happiness; feeling part of the crowd
Repeating words over and over: *Wow!* or *This is amazing!*
Flinging out the arms and legs, taking a wide stance
Thrusting the chest out
The eyes wide and glowing
Grabbing at the sides of the head in an *I can't believe it* gesture
High energy (a bouncing walk or run, skipping, etc.)
Hugging, kissing, or other displays of affection
Breaking into a run
Happy tears and shining cheeks
Throwing something into the air—a hat, books, confetti, a helmet, etc.
Sweating
Drawing in deep breaths
Thrusting a fist into the sky
Spinning in place, the arms flung out
Welcoming others into one's personal space (arms out, open posture, etc.)
Tapping a fist against the chest and thrusting it at others involved (teammates, etc.)
Becoming highly talkative and expressive

INTERNAL SENSATIONS:
Warmth radiating throughout the body
Racing heartbeat
A drumming in the chest
Feeling ultra-awake, rejuvenated by adrenaline

MENTAL RESPONSES:
Thoughts scattering; being too excited to think straight
Wanting to be surrounded by family and friends
Feeling vindicated for the effort, sacrifice, or hard work
Revisiting the hurdles leading to this moment
Gratitude to those who helped make this possible
A desire to thank or acknowledge those who contributed to this moment
A need to touch a symbol tied to this moment (a trophy, the grass on a field of victory, etc.)

ACUTE OR LONG-TERM RESPONSES FOR THIS EMOTION:
Tears streaming down the face
Loss of motor control; becoming clumsy as all tension leaves one's body
Trembling muscles
Sinking to the ground, exhausted
Breathlessness
Losing one's voice from screaming or shouting
Speechlessness

SIGNS THAT THIS EMOTION IS BEING SUPPRESSED:
A grin that can't be contained, no matter how hard one tries
Bottling up one's breaths to try and calm down
Self-hugging to contain the feeling
Closing the eyes and covering the mouth
Quivering with the effort of controlling oneself
Looking down to hide a grin

MAY ESCALATE TO: Euphoria (124), Pride (210), Schadenfreude (232), Gratitude (136)

MAY DE-ESCALATE TO: Satisfaction (230), Happiness (142), Peacefulness (202)

ASSOCIATED POWER VERBS: Beam, boast, cheer, clasp, crow, cry, dance, dazzle, explode, express, flood, flush, glow, grin, grip, hug, inflate, intoxicate, laugh, mesmerize, pump, rejoice, shout, soar, surge, swell, thank, thrill, vault, wave, whoop

WRITER'S TIP: *Make a list of the body parts you incorporate when expressing emotion. Are there ones you don't use at all? Challenge yourself to come up with a unique cue by using one of those parts and substituting it for a gesture that is overused.*

EMASCULATION

DEFINITION: A weakened state due to a perception of being stripped of power, authority, or a role tied to one's identity

NOTES: Emasculation is traditionally attributed to males, but in the right circumstances, it can be experienced by any gender.

PHYSICAL SIGNALS AND BEHAVIORS:
Dropping the shoulders and ducking the chin
The chest caving slightly
Maintaining fleeting eye contact, or avoiding it all together
Rubbing at the back of the neck
Pulling at an earlobe
Directing a burning stare at the ground or away from the person stealing one's power
A visible flush in the face and neck
A sudden stillness in the face but visible tension in the jawline
Hiding one's hands (in pockets, etc.) and looking down
Not speaking up, even when one has important ideas to share
Swallowing more often
Sweating
Touching the face more than usual
Shrinking slightly as the shoulders hunch
Visible tension, especially in the forearms
Slanting away from the person who is judging and stealing one's power
Glancing toward the exit
Growing quiet or appearing to zone out
Rocking stiffly and almost imperceptibly
Engaging in small, self-soothing motions (e.g., rubbing an arm)
Disengaging from the conversation
Making excuses to leave: *Well, I must go. Lots to do.*
Agreeing, in hopes of shortcutting the painful experience and heartache
Apologizing or mumbling a response
Smiling along with jokes at one's expense in hopes the situation will end quicker
Hidden hands (in pockets, behind one's back, etc.) that fist and shake
Lashing out: *You have no idea what you're talking about!* or *Lay off, I'm doing the best I can!*

INTERNAL SENSATIONS:
Heat in one's core, neck, and face
An unpleasant tingling across the back of the neck
Tension in the jaw from clenching one's teeth
Difficulty swallowing (feeling a lump)
One's pulse rushing in the ears
Chest pain
Hardness in the gut

MENTAL RESPONSES:

Keeping quiet to keep the peace, and resenting it
Negative self-talk that lowers one's self-worth
A distorted sense of time (painful moments seeming to out)
Being caught in a mental loop of second-guessing oneself
Asking others for advice and opinions so one will feel validated
Thinking of comebacks afterward and getting mad for not coming up with them sooner
Fantasizing about revenge or giving an aggressor their comeuppance
Feeling small and insignificant, like one's actions and thoughts don't matter
Experiencing jealousy around people one views as "better", such as those who are successful, well respected, in great physical shape, or amazing parents or spouses

ACUTE OR LONG-TERM RESPONSES FOR THIS EMOTION:

Underachieving to avoid disappointing others and oneself
Becoming more of a follower than a leader (even if one desires to lead)
Unhappiness and dissatisfaction with one's life
Depression
Keeping secrets (a private bank account, guilty pleasures, interests no one knows about, etc.)
Acting out (engaging in violence or adopting behaviors that embrace risk or danger)
Pessimism about the future

SIGNS THAT THIS EMOTION IS BEING SUPPRESSED:

Projecting insecurity by disempowering others and cutting them down
Boasting, controlling conversations, and being overly opinionated when it's safe to do so
Inserting oneself when it isn't appropriate (taking over, giving unsolicited advice, etc.)
Becoming a people-pleaser
Overcompensating (with material possessions, one's physique, one's hobbies, etc.)
"Falling in line" to negate the need for the aggressor to publicly display control, avoiding personal humiliation

MAY ESCALATE TO: Humiliation (154), Insecurity (166), Shame (240), Anger (40), Self-Loathing (236), Vengefulness (272)

MAY DE-ESCALATE TO: Stunned (250), Uncertainty (264), Relief (216), Gratitude (136)

ASSOCIATED POWER VERBS: Break, crumble, cull, cut, dampen, decline, dim, drain, fade, falter, flag, hurt, isolate, lose, muffle, pain, redden, reduce, retreat, sap, shame, shrink, sink, steal, stumble, stutter, subdue, totter, weaken, wilt, wither, wound

> **WRITER'S TIP:** When emotionally charged, does your character think before acting, or act without thinking? Whatever their default is, put them in a situation that causes them to do the opposite.

EMBARRASSMENT

DEFINITION: A lack of composure due to self-conscious discomfort

PHYSICAL SIGNALS AND BEHAVIORS:
A flush that creeps across the cheeks
Visible sweating
The body freezing in place
Grimacing or swallowing
Ears that turn red
The chin dipping down
The chest caving, the spine bent
Hands curling around one's middle
Feet shuffling
Clearing the throat and coughing
Covering oneself (crossing the arms, closing a jacket, etc.)
Pulling at one's collar
Rubbing the back of the neck
Wincing
Covering the face with one's hands
Cringing or shaking
Fidgeting and squirming
Touching the forehead
Slanting one's body away from onlookers or an aggressor
Stuttering and stammering, growing more frustrated as words refuse to come
Flinching away from touches
Speechlessness or a weakened voice
The toes curling up
Knees pulling together
Arms tucking in at the sides
Sliding down in a chair
Looking down, unable to meet someone's eyes
Shoulders slumping or curling forward
Responding with anger (shoving, punching, etc.)
Gritting one's teeth, pressing the lips tight
Shoving one's hands in one's pockets
Fiddling with shirtsleeves
Hiding behind a book
Shielding oneself (having a death grip on a purse, etc.)
A walk that accelerates into a sprint
Using the hair to hide one's face
Glancing about for help, an exit, or escape
Tugging a hat down low or pulling a hood over the head
A trembling chin

INTERNAL SENSATIONS:
Excessive swallowing (a lump in the throat)
Light-headedness
A tingling that sweeps up the back of the neck and across the face
A tightening chest
The stomach hardening or dropping with a manifestation of dread
The face, neck, and ears feeling impossibly hot
Rushed breathing and a rapid heartbeat

MENTAL RESPONSES:
A compulsion to flee (fight-or-flight)
Muddied or panicked thoughts
A disconnect where the mind struggles with belief: *This can't be happening!*
Thoughts searching for a solution

ACUTE OR LONG-TERM RESPONSES FOR THIS EMOTION:
Bursting into tears
Running from the room or situation
Plummeting self-esteem
Fear of public speaking or being on display
Withdrawing from groups, activities, and social interaction
Loss of appetite and resulting weight loss
Obsessing about the embarrassing event; reliving it

SIGNS THAT THIS EMOTION IS BEING SUPPRESSED:
Pretending to not have heard or seen
Intensely concentrating on something else; actively ignoring others
A fake smile as one tries to laugh it off
Changing the topic in any way possible
Lying or deflecting attention by assigning blame to another

MAY ESCALATE TO: Humiliation (154), Depressed (84), Regret (214), Shame (240), Anger (40)

MAY DE-ESCALATE TO: Insecurity (166), Relief (216), Gratitude (136)

ASSOCIATED POWER VERBS: Blush, bolt, burn, cringe, cry, curl, duck, escape, flee, flush, gasp, hide, pain, retreat, run, scurry, shame, shrink, squirm, stammer, suffer, sweat

WRITER'S TIP: *Be wary of showing emotion too readily through the act of crying. In real life, it takes a lot to reach a tearful state, so it should be the same for our characters.*

EMPATHY

DEFINITION: To intimately identify with (and possibly experience) another's feelings through the ability to place oneself in their emotional shoes

NOTES: Sympathy and empathy are close in nature but aren't the same. Empathy occurs when a character feels connected to someone through a meaningful shared emotional experience. Sympathy is more surface-level, prompting one to provide comfort and support without necessarily becoming personally attached. For ideas on the latter, please view the SYMPATHY entry (255).

PHYSICAL SIGNALS AND BEHAVIORS:
A softening of the features
Eyebrows drawing together
A pained look (if one is sharing another's negative feelings)
Steady eye contact that is comforting, not invasive
Offering a small smile that communicates acceptance
Reaching out to touch (to show connectedness)
Choosing words with care (to show understanding, be inclusive, or raise someone up)
Leaning in to listen without interrupting (no judgment)
Moving closer; closing the distance
One's body facing the other person straight on
Cupping a shoulder or placing a hand on the other's back to provide comfort while wishing someone would offer this comfort in return
Rubbing at one's own chest and the pain or tightness one feels there
Adopting a soft tone, rich with understanding and acceptance
Asking questions to allow the other to experience the relief of answering as it will help them better understand their own narrative
Crying with the other person
Physical contact (knees or legs touching, pulling the other in, etc.)
Mirroring the posture and body language of whomever one is connecting with
Going to someone and offering to talk or just sit with them
Cancelling plans or appointments to be fully present in the moment
Using empathetic foresight to lessen another's burdens (safeguarding their privacy, offering care, handling tasks for them, etc.)
Acknowledging a shared burden: *This is so hard, isn't it?*
Verbalizing and sharing happy feelings: *Today couldn't be better, could it?*
Increased touchy-feely behaviors (holding hands for an extended time, drawing the other in so shoulders touch, etc.) when the experience is joyful
Consoling the person verbally: *I know it's difficult,* or *We'll get through this together.*
Offering truth (e.g., sharing a personal experience to provide the other person comfort)

INTERNAL SENSATIONS:
A sharp pain in the chest
Tightness in the throat
A feeling of overall heaviness

Difficulty swallowing due to having a lump in the throat and holding back tears
Shakiness or weakness (if one's emotions are overwhelming)
The sensation of phantom pain
A light, floaty feeling in the chest (if the situation is pleasing)

MENTAL RESPONSES:
A need to help or fix (if the situation is negative) or a desire to enjoy the moment (if the circumstances are positive)
Feeling frustration when others don't understand the situation as one does
The ability to forgive quickly by attributing any wrongdoings to stress and circumstances
Disconnecting from personal concerns to take on the emotions and concerns of another
A desire to escape before one's painful emotions become visible
Feeling discomfort at witnessing another's physical pain
Being mindful and tactful when others are in emotional stress
Letting go of prejudice or pre-conceived notions and focusing on connection

ACUTE OR LONG-TERM RESPONSES FOR THIS EMOTION:
Being despondent because the pain is too much
Feeling emotionally drained or depressed
A need to be alone to sort out one's feelings after the crisis has passed
Showing kindness and compassion whatever the situation
Pessimism or disillusionment brought on by an inability to see a reason for suffering
Feeling light, a renewed sense of optimism when the moment of empathy is positive

SIGNS THAT THIS EMOTION IS BEING SUPPRESSED:
A voice that sounds "off" (choked with emotion, gravelly, etc.)
Words that don't match behavior (saying something gruff while showing compassion)
Backing down from a tough stance: *You can stay the night. Or…a few nights if you need to.*

MAY ESCALATE TO: Admiration (30), Humbled (152), Valued (270), Love (180)

MAY DE-ESCALATE TO: Connectedness (70), Hopefulness (148), Peacefulness (202)

ASSOCIATED POWER VERBS: Accept, awaken, brush, care, clasp, connect, develop, echo, encourage, endure, entrust, entwine, evoke, express, feel, hold, hug, link, listen, love, need, nurture, relive, respond, seek, sense, squeeze, stir, touch, undergo, weave together

> **WRITER'S TIP:** *In some situations, your character will be emotionally steady while in others, they will be a hot mess. For the latter, ask yourself why this is. If it is the result of an unresolved emotional wound, how can you can use this to further the inner conflict of the story?*

ENVY

DEFINITION: Resentful awareness of an advantage enjoyed by another, paired with a longing to acquire that advantage

NOTES: The advantage can be a person, an object, or an intangible (popularity, lifestyle, career, accomplishments, etc.)

PHYSICAL SIGNALS AND BEHAVIORS:
Staring or glowering
The mouth turning down
The lips parting slightly
A tightening under the eyes
A thinning mouth
The chin poking forward
Squinting
A slight baring of the teeth
A pouty bottom lip
Crossing the arms over the chest
Rounding the shoulders and curling inward
Leaning closer
Reaching for the thing one desires
Flaring nostrils
A coveting gaze that drifts to the symbol of envy (the advantage)
Being snarky or rude, seemingly without cause
Shoving one's hands into one's pockets
Twitching hands
Hands tightening into fists
Muscles bunching
Turning away from the advantage and stalking off
Swallowing frequently
Rubbing the hands over one's clothing
Muttering about the unfairness under one's breath
Positioning oneself so the feet and torso are facing the advantage
Licking or sucking on the bottom lip
Sweaty hands
A reddening of the face
Rubbing at or massaging one's chest
Stroking or pinching one's throat
Taking a step toward the person or object one wants
Obsessive behavior (stalking, making a plan to acquire the advantage, etc.)

INTERNAL SENSATIONS:
A quick heartbeat

Rising body temperature
A pulling sensation in the gut
The mouth drying as one sucks in breath through clenched teeth

MENTAL RESPONSES:
A strong desire to touch, hold, and own
Anger at the unfairness or injustice of the situation
Unkind thoughts about the other person
Frustration
Scheming ways to acquire what another has
Self-loathing
Fantasizing about the advantage
An inability to commit to or focus on anything else
Dissatisfaction with what one does have
A feeling of entitlement: *I deserve it,* or *That should be mine!*

ACUTE OR LONG-TERM RESPONSES FOR THIS EMOTION:
Feeling that life isn't worth living without the advantage
Grabbing or stealing the coveted object
Fighting or arguing with the envied one to release frustration
Falsely belittling or minimizing the attributes of the desired advantage or object
Irrational thinking
Anger at the advantage itself (if a person) for choosing someone else
Making demands: *Give it to me.*

SIGNS THAT THIS EMOTION IS BEING SUPPRESSED:
Congratulating the person or offering them praise
Forcing a smile
Acknowledging the object and complimenting it
Attempting not to stare
Watching from a distance

MAY ESCALATE TO: Determination (92), Resentment (222), Anger (40), Depressed (84), Jealousy (174)

MAY DE-ESCALATE TO: Defeat (76), Insecurity (166), Embarrassment (118)

ASSOCIATED POWER VERBS: Admire, arouse, burn, confess, consume, covet, desire, devour, elicit, gaze, gnaw, provoke, resent, rouse, stir, suffer, tempt, tinge, vex, want, wish

WRITER'S TIP: *When crafting the details of a fight scene, remember that less is more. Too many details create a play-by-play feel which can come across as mechanical.*

EUPHORIA

DEFINITION: A transcendent state of intense pleasure, happiness, and well-being

PHYSICAL SIGNALS AND BEHAVIORS:
Unrestrained smiling or laughter
One's head tipping back and the eyes closing
The mouth opening in wonder
Eyes going as wide as they can
Thrusting the chest out and up
Letting out a gasp
All tension leaving the body
Repeatedly laying a hand on the chest and lightly pressing down
Pulling in deep breaths and holding them before releasing them
Becoming more affectionate (hugging, touching, etc.)
Happy tears and laughter
Arms held high above the head in a "Victory V"
Jumping and pumping the fists
Dropping to one's knees with the head tipped back
Celebrating (flag waving, crushing others in a bear hug, shouting and whooping, etc.)
Temporary breathlessness
Slurring slightly or drawing out one's words
Spinning around to take everything in
Visible gooseflesh; rubbing at the arms and shivering with pleasure
Stretching out—lying on the grass with one's limbs spread wide, for example
Rapid speech and declining articulation
An instant release of stress (the body going slack)
The face and neck flushing with color
Grabbing onto the sides of one's head and tipping it back
Changes in the voice (growing higher, taking on a breathless quality, etc.)
Holding the arms out to the side, palms up
Wrapping one's arms around oneself and squeezing, to hold the feeling in
Interacting more with one's sensory environment (especially through touch)

INTERNAL SENSATIONS:
Weightlessness
Warmth infusing the body
A tingling surge that starts in one's head or chest and spreads outward
The stomach fluttering
A racing heart
An expansive feeling in the chest
Light-headedness
Sunbursts or spots in one's vision

MENTAL RESPONSES:
The mind emptying of all concerns and worries
Engaging in mental exploration and daydreaming
Stimulated senses (colors, smells, textures, etc. becoming more intense)
A feeling of "being carried away" or experiencing a higher state of being
The cessation of pain or discomfort
Feeling powerful and capable of anything (invincibility)
Viewing the world through a lens of serenity and connection

ACUTE OR LONG-TERM RESPONSES FOR THIS EMOTION:
Heightened creativity and a sudden desire to express it (via writing, art, etc.)
Taking risks due to feeling invincible and powerful
Feeling energized and at peace
Hallucinations
A pleasant sensation of dizziness
The belief that everything in one's life has aligned, and one will be taken care of
Seeking to share the experience with others and feel more deeply connected
An increased capacity for empathy, compassion, and altruism
Being more likely to take time to notice beauty in all forms

SIGNS THAT THIS EMOTION IS BEING SUPPRESSED:
Flinching or jumping slightly
A sharp intake of breath
Losing track of what one was doing or saying
Turning away to hide one's joyful smile
A smile that keeps creeping back onto one's face
Losing track of the conversation
Making excuses: *Sorry, I felt light-headed for a minute,* or *Can you repeat what you just said?*

MAY ESCALATE TO: Awe (54)

MAY DE-ESCALATE TO: Elation (114), Satisfaction (230), Connectedness (70), Moved (186)

ASSOCIATED POWER VERBS: Bask, bathe, captivate, climb, comfort, dazzle, drift, elate, enthrall, fill, float, flood, infuse, inhale, intoxicate, leap, mesmerize, overflow, peak, radiate, rapture, reap, seep, share, shine, soak, soar, sweep, tremble, weep, welcome

> **WRITER'S TIP:** *Whenever you are using thoughts to show the character reflecting on what they feel, make sure the language you use fits their voice, age, worldview, education, and life experience.*

EXCITEMENT

DEFINITION: The state of being energized or stimulated and provoked to act

PHYSICAL SIGNALS AND BEHAVIORS:
A wide grin
Eyes that sparkle and gleam
Bouncing from foot to foot
Squealing, hooting, yelling, and laughing
Telling jokes
Chest bumping with others
A loud voice
Singing, humming, or chanting
Slam-dunking trash into a barrel after a game or event
Babbling or talking over one another in a group setting
Fanning oneself
Clutching one's fists to the chest and squeezing the body tight, then releasing
Pretending to faint
Clutching at oneself for comedic effect to amuse others
Verbalizing thoughts and feelings without hesitation
Lifting someone up or swinging them around
Acting hyper, immature, or foolish out of a sense of fun
A ruddy complexion
Moving about, being unable to stay still
Good-natured shoving and pushing
Waving the arms and being demonstrative
Drumming one's feet against the floor
Hugging others
Grabbing onto someone's arm and holding it
Bumping shoulders with others in one's group
Raising up or bouncing on tiptoe
Phoning or texting to share news or pass on the excitement
Speed-talking with others, heads close together
Throaty laughter
Getting the giggles
Friendly demands: *Tell me! Show me! Let's go!*
A body that's constantly in motion (nodding, bobbing, weaving, pacing, etc.)
Walking with a fast-paced strut
Making eye contact with others; showing confidence
Displaying affection with friends or loved ones

INTERNAL SENSATIONS:
A lightness in the chest
A fast pulse

Dry mouth
Heightened senses
Breathlessness
Feeling energized and awake due to an adrenaline rush

MENTAL RESPONSES:
Camaraderie with others
Imagining what could happen
Enjoyment of the communal energy
Impatience
Being agreeable to ideas and suggestions that align with the energy one feels

ACUTE OR LONG-TERM RESPONSES FOR THIS EMOTION:
A need to run, jump, scream, or whoop it up
An intense desire to share the feeling with others
A beaming face
A racing heartbeat
Sweating
A hoarse voice from screaming, yelling, or shouting
A loss of inhibitions

SIGNS THAT THIS EMOTION IS BEING SUPPRESSED:
Controlling one's movement with intent
Biting down on a smile
Swallowing a laugh or shout of glee
Smoothing down clothing as a way of releasing one's energy
Eyes that glow with an inner light
Nodding rather than speaking

MAY ESCALATE TO: Amazement (36), Happiness (142), Elation (114)

MAY DE-ESCALATE TO: Satisfaction (230), Disappointment (96)

ASSOCIATED POWER VERBS: Bounce, bubble, build, buzz, drum, fill, glow, grip, gyrate, intensify, jiggle, jump, laugh, leap, mount, pound, pump, quicken, quiver, race, squeal, stir, suppress, surge, swell, tingle, tremble, vibrate, whirl, whoop, yell

WRITER'S TIP: *If you're stuck on how to show an emotion, form a strong image of the scene in your mind. Let the scene unfold, and watch the character to see how they move and behave.*

FEAR

DEFINITION: To be afraid of; to expect a threat or danger

PHYSICAL SIGNALS AND BEHAVIORS:
The face turning ashen, white, or pallid
Body odor and cold sweats
Wiping clammy hands on one's clothing to rid them of sweat
Trembling lips and chin
Tendons standing out in the neck
Veins beating a visible pulse beneath the skin
Elbows pressing into the sides, making one's body as small as possible
Freezing, feeling rooted to the spot
An inability to speak
Rapid blinking
Tight shoulders
Staring but not seeing
Eyes that are shut or crying
Hands jammed into armpits or self-hugging
One's breaths bursting in and out
Leg muscles tightening as the body gets ready to run
Looking all around, especially behind oneself
A shrill voice that one cannot control
Keeping one's back to a wall or corner
Shaking uncontrollably
Flinching at noises
Gripping something so hard one's knuckles turn white
Stiff walking, the knees locking
Beads of sweat on the lip or forehead
Grabbing onto someone to feel protected
Eyes appearing damp and overly bright
Stuttering and mispronouncing words
Tremors in the voice
Jerky movements, squirming, cringing, and bumping into things
Licking the lips and gulping down water
Sweeping a shaky hand across the forehead to get rid of sweat
Gasping and expelling one's breath
Slapping a hand over the mouth to silence one's uncontrolled whimpering
Pleading with or talking to oneself

INTERNAL SENSATIONS:
Shakiness in the limbs (causing increased clumsiness)
A racing heartbeat that causes pains in the chest
The sensation of one's hair lifting on the arms and nape of the neck

A loosening of the bladder
Holding one's breath, or gulping down breaths to stay quiet
A stomach that feels rock hard
Hypersensitivity to touch and sound

MENTAL REACTIONS:
Wanting to flee or hide due to a sense of impending doom
The sensation of things moving too quickly to process
Images of what-could-be flashing through the mind
Flawed reasoning
Jumping to a course of action without thinking things through
A skewed sense of time
Mistrusting one's own judgment (when it comes to safety and security)

ACUTE OR LONG-TERM RESPONSES FOR THIS EMOTION:
Uncontrollable trembling
Fainting
Exhaustion or insomnia
Panic attacks, phobias, or depression
Substance abuse
Withdrawing from others
Tics (a repetitive grimace, a head twitch, talking to oneself, etc.)
Resistance to pain from rushing adrenaline

SIGNS THAT THIS EMOTION IS BEING SUPPRESSED:
Turning away from the cause of the fear
Attempting to keep one's voice light
A watery smile that's forced into place
Masking fear with a reactive emotion (anger or frustration) or showing false bravado
Overindulgence in a habit (nail biting, lip biting, scratching the skin raw, etc.)
Telling jokes in a voice that cracks

MAY ESCALATE TO: Anger (40), Terror (258), Paranoia (200), Dread (110)

MAY DE-ESCALATE TO: Agitation (34), Overwhelmed (196), Wariness (280), Relief (216)

ASSOCIATED POWER VERBS: Cast, creep, cry, flee, flutter, force, freeze, gasp, gouge, grab, gulp, hiss, jar, jump, overcome, panic, paralyze, pierce, quiver, rush, seize, shake

WRITER'S TIP: *Prime readers for an emotional experience by describing the mood of a scene as your character enters it. If your character is antsy, the reader will be too.*

FEARLESSNESS

DEFINITION: Feeling dauntless in the face of intimidation, fear, and challenge

PHYSICAL SIGNALS AND BEHAVIORS:
A calm exterior (strong eye contact, a neutral expression, the head steady, etc.)
Good posture, legs spread slightly, arms at the sides in a state of readiness
Leaning in to pay closer attention
Shoulders back and the chest out
Observing and asking questions to better understand the situation
Rubbing hands against one's pants so they are free of sweat
Shaking out one's hands or arms to enter a state of readiness
Closing and opening the fists to prepare for action
Engaging in positive self-talk: *Okay, you can do this.*
Moving forward and closing the distance to others, to danger, etc.
A curt nod
Lifting the chin
A purposeful stride with no hesitation
Moving to the front of a crowd
Being direct (e.g., calling someone out for being rude or wasting time)
Blowing out a deep breath, the mouth forming an "O"
Speaking economically; using less words (staying mentally focused)
Using an even, serious tone
Choosing words with care (to neutralize a situation, avoid being viewed as a threat, calm people down, or provoke the other party into making a mistake, etc.)
Impatience at long-winded answers or inaction
Falling only to get right back up
Walking forward without looking back
Flexing one's fingers
Making one's own decisions rather than leaving them up to others
Engaging in meditation practices (to become centered and hone one's focus)
Showing a lack of self-consciousness—changing clothes in front of others when time is of the essence, for example
Being self-sufficient yet unafraid to ask for help when it is needed
Making bold claims: *I know I can do it*, or *It's a matter of when, not if.*
Making plans for the future regardless of one's circumstances
Quoting statistics, facts, and historical successes that support one's endeavor
Going toe-to-toe with an adversary that others would avoid

INTERNAL SENSATIONS:
A tightness in the chest that one mentally forces to loosen
Tingling and light-headedness (adrenaline)
A rushing sound in the ears (rapid heartbeat)
Muscles tightening in the torso

MENTAL RESPONSES:
Being self-aware and self-accepting (of flaws, limitations, strengths, etc.)
Observing before reacting
Imagining the worst-case scenario so one can proactively think past it
A willingness to experiment and try new things
Embracing struggle rather than running from it
Seeking out mentors and experiences to help one become more capable
Adopting a mind-over-matter mentality
Determining to deal with the problem right away instead of putting it off
Hypersensitivity to sound and movement

ACUTE OR LONG-TERM RESPONSES FOR THIS EMOTION:
Refusing to put on an act to impress others
Learning to compartmentalize in emotion-driven situations
Challenging one's fears (climbing a building if one is afraid of heights, for example)
Pushing past one's limits—e.g., ignoring pain and other distractions
Being highly logical (reasoning things out in one's mind)
Being goal-oriented
Doing what's right rather than what's easy
Working out, strength-training, eating well, etc. to stay in top condition

SIGNS THAT THIS EMOTION IS BEING SUPPRESSED:
Voicing common worries to make oneself seem unsure
Forcing oneself to hesitate before jumping into a new situation
Asking for permission
Hunching the shoulders and avoiding eye contact with others
Letting others go first (into a new situation, into danger, etc.)
Debating the pros and cons of action as if one is uncertain

MAY ESCALATE TO: Confidence (64), Vindication (274), Smugness (246), Anticipation (46)

MAY DE-ESCALATE TO: Conflicted (66), Reluctance (218), Acceptance (28)

ASSOCIATED POWER VERBS: Act, buck, challenge, charge, conquer, dare, defy, discipline, eliminate, endure, exert, explode, expose, grip, join, kick, manipulate, meet organize, plunge, press, propel, prove, pull, research, risk, rush, seize, shove, strain, stride

WRITER'S TIP: *A character's emotional responses reflect their deepest self. Take the time to explore their past and understand how their backstory will steer specific behaviors and actions.*

FLUSTERED

DEFINITION: Feeling overwrought and self-conscious due to confusion, uncertainty, or frustration

PHYSICAL SIGNALS AND BEHAVIORS:
Breaking eye contact with someone
Blinking rapidly
A sharp intake of breath
A flush appearing in the face and neck
Using speech disfluencies (*ums, ahs*) to stall while trying to salvage a conversation
Stumbling over one's sentences
Sputtering and struggling to find the right words
A nervous smile
Scraping a hand through one's hair or tucking it behind an ear
The mouth opening and closing without speaking
Touching the face repeatedly
Making excuses that sound scattered or hastily put together
Lying to cover up perceived weaknesses or goof-ups
Clumsiness and jerky movements
Giving a quick shake of the head
Tapping or rubbing the forehead with one's fingertips
Self-deprecation: *Well, that was a stupid thing to say, wasn't it?*
Shielding or turning the body to the side rather than facing someone directly
Changing direction multiple times
An inability to stay still
Second-guessing oneself
Retreating from the conversation
Being unable to move on until a mistake is corrected (when giving a speech, teaching, etc.)
A strangled-sounding laugh
Throat-clearing
Making a joke to alleviate the situation or save face
Apologizing or talking rapidly
Pressing a fist against one's thigh
Squeezing or pinching oneself (an arm, wrist, the skin between the thumb and forefinger, etc.) to try and regain focus
Turning to a physical task to busy one's hands (clearing a table, straightening pillows, etc.)
Briefly cupping the back of the neck with one's hand
Heat entering one's tone
Deflecting (blaming another, arguing, changing the focus to something else, etc.)
Becoming emphatic to regain control: *No, I'm fine. I've got it. I'll have it to you Monday, really.*
Glancing around for a rescue
Refusing help that is offered
Diverting attention: *It's too warm in here, don't you think? Let's open a window.*

Stepping back to increase personal space if the cause is negative (being criticized in the presence of one's peers, for example)

INTERNAL SENSATIONS:
An increase in internal temperature
Heat in the face (blushing)
Tingling or tightness in the chest from not getting enough oxygen (holding one's breath, not taking enough breaths, etc.)
A prickling along the back of the neck

MENTAL RESPONSES:
Feeling insecure or vulnerable
A loud, critical inner voice (for reacting this way)
Heightened awareness of being in the spotlight
Feeling as though time has stopped or slowed
A desire to flee that one must fight to overcome
Racing thoughts bent on regaining control of the situation

ACUTE OR LONG-TERM RESPONSES FOR THIS EMOTION:
Clamping the mouth shut to avoid exacerbating the situation
Uncontrolled blushing and visible sweating
Allowing someone else to take over
Making an exit regardless of the consequences

SIGNS THAT THIS EMOTION IS BEING SUPPRESSED:
Feigning disinterest to minimize the importance of the current moment
Asking a question that will cause a reaction and put the spotlight elsewhere
Denying being flustered: *No, you just caught me off guard, that's all.*
Manipulating the situation: *You two introduce yourselves while I get us drinks.*

MAY ESCALATE TO: Frustration (134), Agitation (34), Embarrassment (118), Self-Loathing (236)

MAY DE-ESCALATE TO: Annoyance (44), Uncertainty (264)

ASSOCIATED POWER VERBS: Addle, agitate, annoy, babble, blurt, blush, dart, dazzle, drop, fidget, flush, frustrate, gape, hamper, hesitate, hinder, joke, panic, rattle, squeeze, stare, struggle, stumble, torment, twitch, unbalance, undermine, upset, waffle, wobble

WRITER'S TIP: *Sometimes a character will fight the emotion they are feeling. If this is the case, think about how their body language and dialogue may be at odds, and show that struggle.*

FRUSTRATION

DEFINITION: Vexation caused by unresolved problems or unmet needs; the feeling of being hindered

PHYSICAL SIGNALS AND BEHAVIORS:
Pinching the lips together
Placing the arms behind the back, gripping one wrist with the other hand
Rushed speech
Tapping one's fingers to release energy
Pointing with an index finger
Scratching or rubbing the back of the neck
Shaking the head
Jerky movements (talking with the hands, changing direction mid-stride, etc.)
Signs of restlessness, such as pacing in short spans
Stiff posture and rigid muscles
Speaking through the teeth with forced restraint
An impatient snort or sneer
Cursing under the breath
Drawing breath and releasing it before speaking
Stretching the hands out wide, then relaxing them
Baring one's teeth
Throwing the hands up in an *I give up* gesture
Stalking away from someone; leaving in a huff
Lashing out; attempting to hurt someone through name-calling and personal jabs
Speaking without thought in a way that could lead to regret
Slamming a door
A heavy sigh
Laying one's head down on the table
Stilted speaking
Tension in one's voice
Running the hands through the hair
Fists tight, fingernails biting into the palms
A pinched, tension-filled expression
Pounding a fist against the tabletop
Scrunching up the face and then relaxing it, trying to regain calm
Holding one's head in one's hands
A high chin (exposing one's neck without fear)
Arms crossing in front of the chest
Clumsiness due to rushing (slopping coffee, knocking something over, etc.)
Theatrical groaning

INTERNAL SENSATIONS:
The throat closing up

Tightness in the chest
Signs of high blood pressure (a headache or pounding in one's ears)
Jaw pain from clenching the teeth

MENTAL RESPONSES:
Extreme focus on problem solving
Replaying a scene or event over and over in one's mind, obsessing over it
Self-talking to calm down and think straight
A need to ask questions and rehash information
Forcibly trying to rein in one's emotions before it damages relationships

ACUTE OR LONG-TERM RESPONSES FOR THIS EMOTION:
Shouting, yelling, ranting, screaming, or criticizing
Pleading or bargaining: *Please stop!*
Storming out of a room
An inability to sleep or relax
Profuse sweating
Using more force than is necessary (a stomping type of walk, throwing an item instead of handing it off, etc.)
A display of violence (kicking, grabbing, shaking, or destroying something in release)

SIGNS THAT THIS EMOTION IS BEING SUPPRESSED:
Swiping at tears, trying to hide them
Silence or minimal responses
Briefly closing one's eyes and taking a deep breath
Scraping a hand over the face as if to wash away emotion
Excusing oneself and leaving
Trying to shake or roll tension from the shoulders

MAY ESCALATE TO: Contempt (72), Anger (40), Impatience (160)

MAY DE-ESCALATE TO: Annoyance (44), Conflicted (66), Regret (214), Indifference (164)

ASSOCIATED POWER VERBS: Bottle, burst, crush, grip, grit, growl, incite, infuriate, inhibit, mutter, pace, push, shake, simmer, steam, stew, stifle, torment, twitch, unleash, vent

WRITER'S TIP: *Use a character's intuition to draw the reader more fully into the scene. If you show what has primed it clearly, the reader's own gut will respond, and they will pay extra close attention. Remember that the flash of intuition must pay off in some way to complete the circle.*

GRATITUDE

DEFINITION: Thankfulness; feeling grateful or appreciative

PHYSICAL SIGNALS AND BEHAVIORS:
Eyes that are soft and filled with an inner glow
Clasping another's hand or forearm
Tapping a loose fist against the chest
Placing a hand on the chest
Tearing up
Laying a hand on one's heart, then gesturing to a person or group
Pressing fingers to smiling lips
Repeating one's thanks and appreciation
Holding onto someone's hand for longer than necessary
Hugging and showing affection
A light squeeze during a handshake
A smile that has a genuine build and lights up the face
Steady eye contact
Saying *Thank you*
Moving into another's personal space, or welcoming others into one's own
Forming a steeple with the hands and pressing them to one's lips
Offering praise for others
An emotion-rich voice
Offering small touches to connect with others
Laying a hand on someone's back or shoulder
Nodding, the eyes glowing
Offering a gift, favor, or boon of appreciation
Raising one's palms to the sky and looking up
Complimenting others
Clapping vigorously
The body and feet pointing forward
Offering a wave or two-fingered salute
Tipping the head back for a moment and closing the eyes
Bowing or curtseying
Blowing a kiss
Offering a wave of thanks
Needing to pause or swallow to rein in one's emotion before speaking
Vowing to repay the responsible party in time

INTERNAL SENSATIONS:
Tingling warmth in the limbs
A release of all bodily tension
A feeling of expansion in the chest
A heart that feels full

A comfortable warmth in the face
Weakness in the knees

MENTAL RESPONSES:
Desiring to repay another's kindness and support
Feeling overwhelmed in a good way
Wanting to drink in the moment, to remember this feeling forever
A desire to celebrate others and make them feel special, too

ACUTE OR LONG-TERM RESPONSES FOR THIS EMOTION:
Worship
Falling to one's knees
A desire to do anything to repay the responsible party
Joyful tears
A feeling of connection and love

SIGNS THAT THIS EMOTION IS BEING SUPPRESSED:
Closing the eyes
Ducking the head to hide one's expression
Avoiding eye contact with others
Quick, darting glances to express a hidden thanks
Offering a distraction or changing the subject
Clearing the throat before speaking (to steady one's tone)

MAY ESCALATE TO: Satisfaction (230), Peacefulness (202), Happiness (142), Elation (114), Connectedness (70)

MAY DE-ESCALATE TO: Overwhelmed (196), Uncertainty (264), Vulnerability (276), Confusion (68)

ASSOCIATED POWER VERBS: Appreciate, beam, bow, cherish, clasp, envelop, evoke, express, extend, hug, include, meet, nod, offer, overflow, profess, promise, radiate, reach, rise, select, share, shine, squeeze, swallow, tap, thank, touch, voice, warm, whisper

> **WRITER'S TIP:** *Make it a goal to offer the reader something unexpected in every scene, be it an emotional reaction, a roadblock to trip the character up, or a snippet of dialogue that sheds new light on the events unfolding.*

GRIEF

DEFINITION: A deep and painful sorrow over a personal loss, which is often a loved one

PHYSICAL SIGNALS AND BEHAVIORS:
Shaky hands
Movements that lack strength
A vacant look and slack facial expression
A sudden loss of breath, or struggling to find one's breath
Rubbing at one's chest
Lashing out at others
A loss of appetite
Lips that tremble and press together
Holding or wearing a cherished item or gift belonging to the one who died
Forgetting to change clothing or attend to one's hygiene
Wanting to be left alone
Barely speaking, or speaking in a voice that cracks or lacks strength
Breaking things to vent one's emotions
Losing track of conversations and time
A collapsed body posture (appearing small or frail)
Feeling heavy (bowed shoulders, arms that drag, having no desire to move, etc.)
Uncontrollable crying or screaming
Praying for strength (if one is religious)
Writing in a journal to the person who passed on
Attending counseling
Losing track of time
Pacing from room to room, touching objects and mementos
Refusing to sleep, or sleeping to escape
Self-medicating
Clinging to loved ones out of a need to have them close
Rubbing at one's wrists, shoulders, knees, etc. to try and relieve body pain
A sensitivity to noise (flinching, rubbing at one's ears, etc.)
Avoiding people and social functions
Eyes that appear red and raw

INTERNAL SENSATIONS:
An overall feeling of weakness or numbness
Low energy
Irregular heartbeats and dizziness
A tightness in the chest that will not loosen
The sensation of one's heart being heavy
Stabbing stomach pain, nausea, and digestive sensitivity
Body pains and headaches
Frequent swallowing due to a feeling of constriction in the throat

MENTAL RESPONSES:
Mental fog, forgetfulness, and losing track of time
Frequently dreaming of one's loss
Irrational thoughts and anxiety
Guilt for being alive
Sad thoughts that come and go
Painful longings to touch and hold who or what one has lost
Anger at others who have moved on quickly
A renewed interest in spirituality
Anger at God; doubting one's faith
Profound loneliness
A lack of motivation
Apathy for others and their needs (impatience with small talk, etc.)
Feeling that one is going crazy and fearing this state of grief will last forever

ACUTE OR LONG-TERM RESPONSES FOR THIS EMOTION:
Depression and possible suicide attempts
Premature aging
A significant weight loss or gain
Paranoia and obsession regarding the well-being of loved ones
A loss of control when self-medicating (drinking too much, overdosing, etc.)

SIGNS THAT THIS EMOTION IS BEING SUPPRESSED:
Not wanting to talk about the person who is gone
Getting rid of the person's personal items (boxing them up, donating them, etc.)
Adhering to a strict and often busy routine
Throwing oneself into work or a project to avoid dealing with one's pain
Pulling away from others who are reminders of one's loss
Moving to a new home or city
Extreme behavior shifts (e.g., engaging in promiscuity to avoid getting attached again)

MAY ESCALATE TO: Anger (40), Bitterness (58), Guilt (140), Despair (88), Depressed (84), Vengefulness (272)

MAY DE-ESCALATE TO: Devastation (94), Overwhelmed (196), Loneliness (176), Acceptance (28)

ASSOCIATED POWER VERBS: Buckle, cave, clutch, collapse, cry, despair, mourn, pain, pucker, shake, shudder, shuffle, slump, sob, tremble, weave, weep, whisper, wilt

WRITER'S TIP: *When showing emotion, spend more airtime on describing whatever the POV character is most focused on. What has their attention will have the reader's attention, too.*

GUILT

DEFINITION: A feeling of culpability over an offense (either real or imagined)

PHYSICAL SIGNALS AND BEHAVIORS:
Averting or lowering one's gaze
Turning away or shifting about
The chin dipping to the chest as one's posture slumps
Blushing
Scratching at the face
Reacting defensively; short-temperedness
Consuming antacids
Repetitive swallowing
Lying
Sweating
Grimacing and lip biting
Avoiding a person or place
Talking too much or too fast
Keeping at a distance
Rubbing the nose or tugging at a collar
One's shoulders drawing up, the elbows tucking into the sides
Closing or curling one's hands inward
Stuttering, growing flustered, a voice that cracks
Joking to lighten the mood or distract others from the truth
Pinning the arms against the stomach
Becoming unnaturally quiet or still
A quivering chin
Muttering tearfully to oneself
Taking a deep, pained breath and closing the eyes
Staring down at one's feet and focusing on one's knees (if sitting)
Palms hidden (stuffed into pockets, held behind the back, etc.)
Darting glances at the person who was wronged
Following the one who was wronged, trying to convince oneself to confess
Inflicting pain on oneself as a penance
Destroying one's own possessions
An inability to join in fun activities or be with friends
Looking pale; having a harried or haunted look
Not showing up for work or school
Avoiding the people one believes have been wronged
Cutting oneself down in front of others; vicious self-deprecation

INTERNAL SENSATIONS:
Tightness in the chest
Skin sensitivity, or skin that feels more itchy than normal

Upset stomach and a loss of appetite

MENTAL RESPONSES:
Replaying what happened, making it bigger in one's mind
Thoughts filled with self-loathing
Wishing one could go back and change what happened
Feeling anxious and desiring to confess or share the pain or burden with another
Brooding, retreating inward, and withdrawing from others
Paranoia that others know and are passing judgment
An inability to concentrate on anything else

ACUTE OR LONG-TERM RESPONSES FOR THIS EMOTION:
A lack of interest in one's own appearance or wellness
Drinking until passing out (to forget)
Exhaustion or even insomnia
Depression
Nightmares
Crying, sobbing, and hitching breaths
Flight responses—running away, unable to deal with the consequences
Growing reclusive and cutting oneself off from others
Self-mutilation
Self-loathing
Wanting to take one's own life as a way out (or even attempting suicide)

SIGNS THAT THIS EMOTION IS BEING SUPPRESSED:
Becoming excessively resourceful or helpful to make up for earlier failures
Fidgeting and throat-clearing
Hiding one's mouth behind a hand
Changing the subject and deflecting attention
Verbally denying having anything to do with the event

MAY ESCALATE TO: Conflicted (66), Regret (214), Shame (240), Remorse (220)

MAY DE-ESCALATE TO: Doubt (108), Reluctance (218), Regret (214), Uncertainty (264)

ASSOCIATED POWER VERBS: Absolve, admit, burden, conceal, confess, deny, escape, haunt, imply, lessen, project, prove, punish, purge, riddle, suffer, tinge, torment, torture

WRITER'S TIP: *Character bibles can help you keep track of hair, eye and clothing choices for each character, keeping the continuity from the first page to the last.*

HAPPINESS

DEFINITION: A state of well-being or joyful contentment

PHYSICAL SIGNALS AND BEHAVIORS:
An upturned face
Smiling
Humming, whistling, or singing
A relaxed appearance
Telling jokes and laughing frequently
Raised, prominent cheekbones (from smiling)
Eyes that dance, sparkle, or shine
A bubbly or light voice
Rapid speaking
Buying gifts for others or offering tokens of kindness
Stretching out the legs and adopting a wide, open stance
Giving someone the thumbs-up
Sitting up, straight and alert
Fluid movements
A polite manner
Offering compliments
Swinging the arms while walking
Stepping lightly, skipping, or swaying in place
Initiating physical contact with others
Infusing one's speech with positive words
Showing a talkative nature and courtesy with strangers
Spontaneity
Lightly rapping one's fingers (as if to internal music) on a leg or other surface
Swinging or tapping one's foot to an easy beat
Satisfied, catlike stretches
Expressing enjoyment of the senses (swaying to music, savoring food, etc.)
Nodding or leaning in and enjoying the act of listening (actively showing interest)
Bouncing on the toes and waving enthusiastically
Offering encouragement and support
Quick movements, with no hesitation
An overall visage that glows or radiates
Holding the arms out wide as if to hug the world
Initiating random acts of kindness
Becoming more talkative

INTERNAL SENSATIONS:
Heat that radiates through the chest
Tingling hands
Lightness in the limbs and an overall feeling of weightlessness

MENTAL RESPONSES:
Positive thinking
Desiring to spread joy and make others feel good
Noticing the small things (smelling the roses, so to speak)
Helpfulness and patience with others
Being at ease with the world; content
A bright outlook (glass half full)
A desire to be with loved ones or friends
Fearlessness
Benign risk-taking for fun

ACUTE OR LONG-TERM RESPONSES FOR THIS EMOTION:
Joyful tears
Shaking with excitement
Big movements (leaping, pumping a fist, running, dancing, etc.)
Shows of affection and happy bursts of screaming, shouting, laughter, or giggles
Laugh lines
Generosity, compassion, and the desire to improve the lives of others

SIGNS THAT THIS EMOTION IS BEING SUPPRESSED:
Pressing the lips tightly together to keep from smiling
Bouncing lightly in place
Taking deep, calming breaths
Grabbing onto something to anchor oneself rather than move toward the source
Carefully masked features but with eyes that betray the true emotion
Putting away happy thoughts to savor later
Intense concentration on something or someone else
Hiding a joyous expression with one's hair
Holding a hand over the mouth to cover a smile
Pinching oneself and using the pain to help contain the emotion

MAY ESCALATE TO: Elation (114), Gratitude (136), Satisfaction (230)

MAY DE-ESCALATE TO: Inspired (168), Valued (270), Pleased (206)

ASSOCIATED POWER VERBS: Animate, appreciate, beam, brighten, caress, cheer, clap, embrace, encircle, energize, express, extend, fill, gather, glow, greet, help, host, include, jump, laugh, radiate, rejoice, relish, savor, share, smile, thrill, toast, wave, welcome

WRITER'S TIP: *To increase tension in a scene, think about what is motivating your character, and which emotions could get in the way. Introduce an event that creates the very emotions the character wishes to avoid.*

HATRED

DEFINITION: To loathe or detest; to feel animosity toward

PHYSICAL SIGNALS AND BEHAVIORS:
Fists that shake
An intense, fevered stare
A clenched jaw and grinding teeth
Rigid and defined forearm muscles
Uttering dark, hurtful words meant to provoke someone
Stiff posture, square shoulders, and a lurching walk
Shoving, pushing, or tripping
Baring the teeth
Fingers retracting, turning claw-like
Shouting, screaming, or swearing
Lunging at an enemy
Spittle flying while one is yelling
A red face and neck
Sweating
A visible vein throb
A corded neck
Leaving an event or situation; refusing to be in the same place if the other person arrives
Switching shifts or altering a schedule to avoid an enemy
Tightness in the face, one's skin stretched into a snarl
An animalistic growl in the throat
Flaring nostrils
A grip that unintentionally crushes or breaks (snapping a pen, etc.)
A tense body, on the verge of springing
Bullying—both online and off
A mouth that curls with dislike; sneering
Spitting at someone or in their direction
Reaching out to throttle, hit, or cause pain
Shoving people aside to reach the enemy
Angry tears
Cursing and swearing
A scathing tone
A shaking voice
Using friends to help ostracize or bring the enemy low
Initiating hateful gossip, setting the enemy up, or starting rumors
Wrenching an enemy's arm to stop them from leaving
Acting on violent urges (throwing a chair, destroying property, etc.)
A heaving chest

INTERNAL SENSATIONS:

Pain in the jaw or head from clenching and grinding one's teeth
A pounding heartbeat
Rising body temperature
Strain or soreness from tense muscles
Roaring in the ears (high blood pressure)

MENTAL RESPONSES:
A dark mood that no one can reach through or dispel
Rash decisions and impaired judgment
Irrational thoughts—taking risks to get even
A desire to carry out a vendetta (via vandalism, theft, etc.)
A single-minded focus on how to destroy another
Humiliation fantasies featuring the enemy
A desire to break, crush, or destroy something

ACUTE OR LONG-TERM RESPONSES FOR THIS EMOTION:
An inability to enjoy positive things or happiness
Difficulty eating and sleeping
Isolating oneself
Fixating on an enemy—stalking, committing crimes against them, etc.
Gravitating to people who feel the same way about the person or entity
Making plans to sabotage an enemy or reveal their ugliness to others
Deriving pleasure from violent fantasies involving an enemy
Assault or murder

SIGNS THAT THIS EMOTION IS BEING SUPPRESSED:
Clamping the teeth shut to contain hard words
Taking deep breaths to calm oneself
Seeking out a distraction or diversion
Leaving the situation or presence of an enemy
Surrounding oneself with supportive friends

MAY ESCALATE TO: Paranoia (200), Rage (212), Obsession (194), Vengefulness (272)

MAY DE-ESCALATE TO: Bitterness (58), Resentment (222), Scorn (234), Jealousy (174)

ASSOCIATED POWER VERBS: Attack, bash, bite, blacken, blaze, burn, consume, despise, fantasize, fuel, glare, harbor, incite, loathe, obsess, rant, ravage, sabotage, scorch, scream, seethe, shatter, shout, simmer, slander, smash, swear, tear, threaten, wreak

WRITER'S TIP: *One way to create emotional intensity is to have the character remember the stakes on the cusp of taking action. Worry over the outcome can add a slice of desperation to any scene and create a compelling emotional pull for the reader.*

HOMESICKNESS

DEFINITION: Grief at being separated from the people or places that represent belonging and comfort

PHYSICAL SIGNALS AND BEHAVIORS:
Lethargy, moping about—movements that lack energy
Sleeping a lot
Aimless wandering
Slouching in one's chair (slumped posture)
Crying easily
Reddened, puffy eyes
A nose red from crying
Dull eyes lacking any sparkle
Facial features being downturned
A dropped-down chin; not holding one's head up proud and high
Sighing often
Rubbing a palm against one's breastbone, massaging a constant ache
Wrapping arms around one's torso (self-hugging for comfort)
A face devoid of emotion
Lying on a couch, watching TV for hours on end
Frequently being startled out of a reverie
An inward, thoughtful expression, as if one is thinking of other things
Comforting oneself with memorabilia (pictures, old videos, keepsakes, etc.)
Reminiscing with anyone who will listen
A voice that wavers or breaks when speaking of home
Calling the people one is missing
Grilling them about what's happening at home
Counting the days to a trip home
Distracting oneself with activities
Reading books, watching movies, or listening to music associated with one's past
Comparing one's new surroundings with the old place and finding them lacking
Stalking loved ones on social media to stay informed about what's going on back home
Overindulging (in food, drink, exercise, shopping, video games, etc.) as a way of coping
Spending a lot of time alone or with other people, depending on how one copes
Desperately trying to fit in within the new environment (to get past the homesickness)
Haunting the mailbox or constantly checking one's phone, hoping for correspondence

INTERNAL SENSATIONS:
Eyes stinging with tears
A hollow feeling in the chest
A thick lump in the throat that never seems to go away
A sensation of emptiness or sinking
Ribs growing tight, restricting one's breath

A sharp twinge in the chest upon hearing about activities one is missing back home
An adrenaline jolt when the phone rings or a care package arrives

MENTAL RESPONSES:
Recalling the good about one's old home and forgetting about the bad
Trying not to think about home
Striving to find any positives in one's new environment
Struggling with feelings of disloyalty as one begins to integrate into the new surroundings
The sensation of time passing very slowly
Constantly wondering what loved ones are doing right now
Experiencing longing and sadness when one is missing out on notable events back home (family dinners, a birthday, putting the kids to bed, etc.)
Becoming angry at friends and family who seem to have "moved on"

ACUTE OR LONG-TERM RESPONSES FOR THIS EMOTION:
Depression
Excessive weight loss or gain
Clinging desperately to the old way of life; being unable to move forward
Spending all of one's time traveling so one can return home as much as possible
Being unable to integrate into one's new environment, even after an extended time
Reluctance to attach to anyone in the new situation so one can avoid experiencing the same hurt again

SIGNS THAT THIS EMOTION IS BEING SUPPRESSED:
Feigned happiness
Drinking or overeating in private
Disparaging the old home verbally (despite really loving and missing it)
Speaking to loved ones in an overly bright tone of voice
Mementos being placed in prominent positions or showing signs of overuse and wear

MAY ESCALATE TO: Nostalgia (192), Sadness (226), Depressed (84), Anxiety (48)

MAY DE-ESCALATE TO: Indifference (164), Resignation (224), Satisfaction (230)

ASSOCIATED POWER VERBS: Ache, complain, covet, crave, cry, grieve, languish, long for, miss, mope, mourn, oversleep, pine away, sigh, suffer, uproot, weep, yearn

> **WRITER'S TIP:** *Character emotion can be shown to great effect through how they view the world. What attitudes, observations, and judgments can be tied to what they are currently feeling?*

HOPEFULNESS

DEFINITION: A bright, promising outlook; optimism

PHYSICAL SIGNALS AND BEHAVIORS:
Holding one's breath
Raising the eyebrows and offering a questioning gaze
Leaning in
Clutching at the chest or belly
Muttering *please* repeatedly under the breath
Clasping the hands under the chin (in a prayer gesture)
A face that seems to shine
Gently biting the lip
Covering the mouth with a hand, eyes wide and shining
Taking deep breaths
Wiggling or squirming
Verbalizing the pros, not the cons
Strong eye contact
Smiling
Stiff posture, an air of readiness
Smoothing one's clothing to appear collected or worthy
Nodding along as another speaks
Holding still in expectation
Rapid swallowing and nodding
Chattiness and babbling
The lips parting slightly
Asking others to reaffirm the chances of success
Shifting back and forth
Making promises to convince others of one's worthiness
Offering commitment, to show one's ability to meet expectations
Attentiveness to the tasks or people connected with one's goal
Restlessness
Licking the lips with cautious hope
Exhaling while the eyes look up
A gaze that darts to a symbol of hope (a friend in the know, a table of judges, etc.)

INTERNAL SENSATIONS:
A flutter in the belly
A lighthearted feeling
Tingling limbs
A jolt through the body (an adrenaline spike)
A floating sensation, like all one's burdens have been removed
Breath that temporarily bottles up in the chest

MENTAL RESPONSES:
A willingness to believe that everything will be all right
A strong awareness of one's surroundings
Thinking positive thoughts
A sense of calm
Focusing on improvement (studying, working extra hard, etc.)
Refusing to consider, speak of, or listen to negatives
Preparing for the best-case scenario

ACUTE OR LONG-TERM RESPONSES FOR THIS EMOTION:
Hands clasped in prayer, pressed to the lips, eyes closed
Quivering breaths
Shakiness
Tears
A trembling voice
Whimpering

SIGNS THAT THIS EMOTION IS BEING SUPPRESSED:
Locking one's hands together to force them into stillness
Mentally reducing high expectations
Reminding oneself of obstacles or competition
Pressing the palms downward to stave off overconfidence
Keeping one's face blank
Looking down or away

MAY ESCALATE TO: Eagerness (112), Excitement (126), Uncertainty (264), Disappointment (96)

MAY DE-ESCALATE TO: Powerlessness (208), Discouragement (100), Doubt (108), Anticipation (46)

ASSOCIATED POWER VERBS: Anticipate, aspire, await, babble, beam, beg, build, chatter, cheer, desire, dream, jabber, pledge, quiver, radiate, smile, sparkle, strive, tremble

> **WRITER'S TIP:** *Force your characters to make choices between bad and worse. Readers will empathize with your character, remembering their own past when they faced a similar dilemma.*

HORROR

DEFINITION: A mixture of repugnance and fear arising from a negative experience beyond one's comprehension or imagining

PHYSICAL SIGNALS AND BEHAVIORS:
The body freezing mid-movement
One's mouth falling open, the upper lip curling back
Grimacing and wanting to look away but being unable to
The head recoiling from the source, eyes wide and staring
One's words drying up mid-sentence
Opening the mouth to speak but being unable to find words
Trying to make sense of what one is experiencing by reading other people's reactions
Speaking in fragments: *This...He...Why...*
Shaking the head in a slow, back-and-forth sweep of denial
The neck disappearing as shoulders rise and pull forward
Placing trembling fingertips against one's open mouth
Eyebrows folding inward, the nose crinkling
Gripping one's own throat or pressing a hand against the breastbone
Swallowing rapidly
Retreating; putting distance between oneself and the source
A slow intake of uneven breath (shuddery or shaky)
Turning the head to the side with the eyes tightly closed
Shielding the body (turning the torso to the side, crossing one's arms over one's chest, etc.)
Clamping a hand across one's mouth and applying pressure
Stumbling back a step or two
Tripping and falling as one tries to create some distance
Pushing the back of the hand against one's nose and looking away
Holding a shaking hand up between oneself and the source
Eyes that are unable to close
Cringing and rubbing one's palm against the chest (above one's heart)
The body contorting (knees drawing up, the torso twisting, arms pulling in, etc.)
Scraping one's palms against clothing as if to rid them of something
Rubbing or pulling at the ears (if a sound is part of the experience)
Clapping the hands over the sides of one's head to block out a specific noise
Forcing oneself to look down or to the side, breaking eye contact
Taking a deep breath to try and regain control of one's emotions
Trying to verbally diffuse the moment (reasoning, bargaining, or placating) by talking slowly and enunciating one's words
Moving slowly, using no sudden movements
Pulling loved ones close (gathering children, drawing a spouse near) to protect them

INTERNAL SENSATIONS:
Internal chest pressure from forgetting to breathe
Body tension (e.g., the stomach hardening)
The burn of bile in the back of the throat
An uncontrollable shudder that sweeps through one's entire body
A sudden drop in body temperature
A hard thudding in the chest from an increased heart rate

MENTAL RESPONSES:
Losing track of spatial awareness (fumbling, clumsiness, stumbling, etc.)
Focusing on something small (like breathing) to feel more in control
Sudden revelations (putting together pieces of information that would have foreshadowed the negative experience, if one had only realized their significance)
A hyper-focus on the possible dangers associated with this moment (survival instinct)

ACUTE OR LONG-TERM RESPONSES FOR THIS EMOTION:
Breaths coming in short bursts once the initial shock passes
A loosening of the bladder
Shutting down and freezing on the spot
Uncontrolled tears sliding down one's cheeks and onto trembling lips
Looking for an escape
Turning and fleeing
A heart attack

SIGNS THAT THIS EMOTION IS BEING SUPPRESSED:
A hard, visible swallow as one's lips press tight
A slight tremor in the fingertips
A voice that warbles before it steadies
Adopting a strained smile that twitches as it widens, fighting for mind over body
Nervous laughter

MAY ESCALATE TO: Terror (258), Powerlessness (208)

MAY DE-ESCALATE TO: Fear (128), Disgust (102), Hatred (144), Desperation (90)

ASSOCIATED POWER VERBS: Clench, conceal, convulse, cringe, flee, freeze, gag, gasp, grip, nauseate, quiver, recoil, reject, repress, retreat, seize, shake, shrink, shudder, stare

WRITER'S TIP: *Too much self-awareness can hurt emotional descriptions. Rarely do people think about the mechanics of what their bodies are doing (I felt my lungs swell with unspent breath), so weigh description more on showing a character's reactions and behaviors naturally as they happen.*

HUMBLED

DEFINITION: An awareness of one's lowly or modest status

PHYSICAL SIGNALS AND BEHAVIORS:
Ducking one's head
Dropping the chin to the chest
Squeezing the eyes shut
Taking a step back
Standing behind others
Covering the eyes with one's hands
Standing with hands on hips and the head bowed
Giving a slow nod, as if acknowledging the truth of the situation
Running the hands through one's hair and turning away
Steepling the fingers in front of one's mouth
Speaking in a quieter voice than normal
Getting choked up
Tilting the head back and blinking quickly to keep from crying
Not defending oneself
Letting others be in the spotlight; not calling attention to oneself
Shaking the head and exhaling loudly through the nose
Mashing the lips together in frustration
Going very still
Pacing in the background, away from others
Making one's body small
Crossing the arms
Fidgeting and fiddling with things, such as buttons, coins, hair, or earrings
Wincing
Not looking other people in the eye
Tense jaw muscles
Clenched teeth
Walking in slow, small circles

INTERNAL SENSATIONS:
Tightness in the chest
A dropping sensation in the belly
The throat squeezing shut
Prickling eyes
Nausea roiling in the pit of the stomach
Tense muscles

MENTAL RESPONSES:
The mind racing as one tries to come to grips with what has happened
The mind going blank as new information changes the perception of oneself and one's path forward
Suspended disbelief
Self-berating thoughts
Wanting to hide
Replaying the humbling moment on a loop in one's mind

ACUTE OR LONG-TERM RESPONSES FOR THIS EMOTION:
Doubting oneself
Self-isolation (if shame is a factor)
Avoiding the place where the humbling situation occurred
No longer participating in that activity, even if it was one's passion
Letting one's physical appearance go
Risk-aversion
Avoiding the spotlight
Being overly critical of oneself
Perfectionism (to avoid being humbled again)
Hyper-focusing on the humbling activity to prove one's worth in that area
Renewed determination and an evolved outlook

SIGNS THAT THIS EMOTION IS BEING SUPPRESSED:
Denying the truth of what happened
Hatred or rage toward the person doing the humbling
Making excuses for what happened
Laughing off what happened as if it was no big deal
Overcompensating
Striving to prove oneself repeatedly to others
Having a cocky attitude

MAY ESCALATE TO: Resentment (222), Defensiveness (78), Denial (82), Humiliation (154), Devastation (94), Regret (214), Shame (240), Self-Loathing (236)

MAY DE-ESCALATE TO: Resignation (224), Gratitude (136), Determination (92)

ASSOCIATED POWER VERBS: Abase, acknowledge, admit, apologize, astound, aver, awe, blunder, botch, bungle, chasten, concede, confess, congratulate, deflate, fall short, flop, flub, fumble, lapse, misstep, own up, recant, recognize, screw up, slip, stoop, wallow

WRITER'S TIP: *Does your character have a bad habit, mannerism, or tic that occurs when they're trying to hide emotion from others? If so, show this when they're working to hold back their true feelings.*

HUMILIATION

DEFINITION: Feeling degraded or mortified, worthless or cheap

PHYSICAL SIGNALS AND BEHAVIORS:
The body collapsing in on itself
A bowed head
Shoulders curling over the chest
Angling one's torso away from others
Uncontrollable shuddering or shivering
Hair hanging in the face, hiding the eyes
A downward gaze
A flushed face
A hitching chest
Dull and lifeless eyes
Pulling down a shirt hem (covering gesture)
Body shielding (if one is holding onto an object)
Hands clutching at the stomach
Covering the face with the hands
The bottom lip or chin trembling
Whimpering
A bobbing Adam's apple
Arms falling to the sides, lifeless
Uncontrolled tears
Flinching at noises or from being touched
Huddling or crouching
Trying to cover one's body with one's hands
The neck bending forward
Slow and jerky movements; walking stiffly
Knees that are locked tightly together
A loss of coordination
Cold sweat
Stumbling and staggering
Backing up against a wall, sliding into a corner, or hiding
Visible tremors coursing through the body
Hands gripping the elbows
Pigeon toes (standing with the toes tilted inward)
Sobs trapped in the throat
Drawing the knees up to the body's core
Wrapping one's arms around oneself
A runny nose

INTERNAL SENSATIONS:
Weakness in the legs

Pain in the chest and throat
Rapid swallowing
Dizziness; a sense of vertigo
A squeezing sensation in the ribs
Loose muscles, the body feeling broken
The skin tightening (a "crawling" sensation)
Hot eyes and cheeks
Nausea

MENTAL RESPONSES:
Self-loathing
Shattered thoughts; feeling disillusioned by a lack of human decency
A feeling of nakedness, of being on display
A need to hide or flee that supersedes all else
Thoughts desperately racing for a way to end the experience

ACUTE OR LONG-TERM RESPONSES FOR THIS EMOTION:
Curling up on the floor
Hiding behind or against something
Crying, blubbering, hitching sobs
Wanting to escape by any means
A desire to die, for the emotional pain to end

SIGNS THAT THIS EMOTION IS BEING SUPPRESSED:
Numbness in the mind and body
Becoming passive and disengaged
Closing off all thoughts of what is happening
Not speaking or making any sound
Sending the mind "somewhere else"

MAY ESCALATE TO: Depressed (84), Regret (214), Shame (240), Rage (212), Hatred (144), Vengefulness (272)

MAY DE-ESCALATE TO: Apprehension (52), Nervousness (190), Confusion (68), Embarrassment (118)

ASSOCIATED POWER VERBS: Cower, cringe, dissemble, escape, flee, flinch, hide, lurch, retreat, shake, shrink, stammer, stoop, stumble, stutter, topple, wince, wither

> **WRITER'S TIP:** *Add conflicting emotions for a richer experience. A character might feel excitement and pride at purchasing their first car, yet worry that they might be extending themselves too far financially. This inner conflict helps to humanize a character to the reader.*

HURT

DEFINITION: Suffering mental pain; feeling wounded or aggrieved

PHYSICAL SIGNALS AND BEHAVIORS:
Eyes widening, yet the brows are furrowed
Swallowing hard
Lowering the head, the neck appearing to shrink
A slow, disbelieving headshake
A trembling chin
The mouth falling open
Flinching, starting
Color draining from the face
Saying *How could you?* as an accusation
Verbalizing betrayal in a strangled tone: *Leave me alone!*
Hunching over, as if choking down a sob
Pressing a fist to the lips
Biting down on one's bottom lip
Gripping a fistful of one's shirt at the chest level
Holding a hand up, warding others off
Clutching the stomach
The body crumpling in on itself
A hitching chest
Drooping shoulders
Weakness in the knees
An uneven step
Displaying poor balance and coordination
A hand pressing against the throat or breastbone
Stuttering, choking out words
Letting out a whimper
Eyes that water
The mouth opening but no words forming
Sending someone a long, pained look and then breaking eye contact
A hanging head
Retracting the arms, bringing them close to the torso
Stumbling back a step
Retreating or spinning away
A grimace that lingers
Offering a cutting remark: *Wow. Family doesn't mean much these days, does it?*
Clutching at oneself, elbows pressed to the sides

INTERNAL SENSATIONS:
Dizziness
The stomach hardening

A painful tightness in one's throat
Constricting lungs, making it hard to breathe
One's heartbeat seeming to slow or stop momentarily
Weakening muscles
A trembling in the limbs
Spots flashing in one's vision

MENTAL RESPONSES:
The sense that time has stopped
Thoughts spinning, focusing inward
Shock and disbelief
Dredging up history, trying to understand how it led here
Questioning one's beliefs and relationships (disillusionment)

ACUTE OR LONG-TERM RESPONSES FOR THIS EMOTION:
A sense of betrayal that rocks the mind to the very core
A collapse in body posture
Tears, sobbing
Running away
Reacting with anger (screaming, slapping, hitting, hurling insults, etc.)

SIGNS THAT THIS EMOTION IS BEING SUPPRESSED:
Visible swallowing
Unnatural stiffness
Pinching the lips tight to keep them from trembling
Tensing the body to ward off shaking
Lifting the chin
Forcing oneself to maintain eye contact or offer a frozen smile

MAY ESCALATE TO: Depressed (84), Anguish (42), Betrayed (56), Anger (40), Rage (212)

MAY DE-ESCALATE TO: Confusion (68), Stunned (250), Insecurity (166), Self-Pity (238)

ASSOCIATED POWER VERBS: Argue, attack, collapse, crumple, defend, dissolve, fight, flinch, reject, shout, shrink, sob, squabble, tremble, whimper, withdraw, yell

WRITER'S TIP: *A natural way to describe a character's appearance is to show them interacting with their environment. A sense of movement also allows this type of description to flow with the scene as it progresses.*

HYSTERIA

DEFINITION: An excess of emotion resulting in extreme responses and a loss of control

NOTES: This entry refers to the emotion rather than the hysteria associated with psychological disorders.

PHYSICAL SIGNALS AND BEHAVIORS:
Screaming or yelling
Uncontrollable sobbing
Heavy breathing
Flared nostrils
Flushed skin
Sweat breaking out on the skin
Eyes wide open, with the white showing all around the iris
Closing the eyes and covering the ears to block out all stimuli
Vehement head shaking
Hands clenching into fists
Stamping one's feet
Pounding one's fists against one's thighs
Pulling at one's hair
Muttering or screaming the same words over and over: *It's not true, This isn't happening, He's all right*, etc.
Screaming oneself hoarse
Thrashing about in a way that could cause harm
Veins standing out in the face or neck
Flapping the hands
Falling to the ground
Throwing oneself down (on a couch, bed, the ground, etc.)
A bent posture, as if protecting oneself
Jerking away from nearby people or surfaces
Clinging to or hanging onto people
Passing out
Attacking the bearer of bad news (if bad news triggered the hysteria)
Verbally denying the bad news
Curling into the fetal position
Hugging one's knees and rocking back and forth
Hyperventilating and being unable to speak coherently

INTERNAL SENSATIONS:
Elevated heart rate and pulse
Muscles going limp
Seeing spots
Feeling like one can't get enough oxygen; shortness of breath

The sensation of being squeezed; feeling physical pressure

MENTAL RESPONSES:
An inability to listen to reason
A complete lack of regard for what others think (loss of inhibition)
Not noticing what's going on in the immediate environment (not hearing people calling one's name or touching one's arm, etc.)
Recognizing the loss of control but not knowing how to rein it in
The mind jumping from one thought immediately to another
Feeling separated from one's body and viewing oneself from an external vantagepoint

ACUTE OR LONG-TERM RESPONSES FOR THIS EMOTION:
Exhaustion that could lead to a physical collapse
Experiencing a mental break
Losing one's voice
Sleeping for a long period of time
Muscle soreness
Bruising and body aches from having to be physically restrained by others
Burst blood vessels in the eyes
Suffering a heart attack

SIGNS THAT THIS EMOTION IS BEING SUPPRESSED:
By its definition, hysteria cannot be controlled; therefore, it cannot be suppressed.

MAY ESCALATE TO: Rage (212), Denial (82), Overwhelmed (196)

MAY DE-ESCALATE TO: Anxiety (48), Fear (128), Sadness (226), Agitation (34), Unease (266), Confusion (68)

ASSOCIATED POWER VERBS: Accuse, beat, bruise, claw, cling, clutch, collapse, crack up, crumple, cry, curl, drop, faint, flail, flinch, gasp, go to pieces, grab, grip, huddle, jerk, keel over, lose it, lunge, sag, scream, shout, shriek, sob, spit, startle, thrash, wail, yell

WRITER'S TIP: Characters in a heightened emotional state have their senses dialed up. Describing an awareness of a sound, smell, taste, etc. they may not otherwise notice is a good way to show this.

IMPATIENCE

DEFINITION: Feeling restless or short-tempered; having a desire for immediate change, relief, or gratification

PHYSICAL SIGNALS AND BEHAVIORS:
Raising one's eyebrows
Placing the hands on the hips
Scowling
Tilting the head back and looking upward
Crossing the arms
Standing or sitting stiffly
A tapping foot
Folding the hands
Pursing one's lips
Fiddling with cuffs or jewelry
Glancing repeatedly at the clock
Pacing
A hard jaw line (clenched teeth)
A jutting chin
Clicking one's fingernails against a table
Fidgeting instead of sitting or standing still
Narrowing the eyes; having an intense focus
Talking over others
Compressing the lips while someone else speaks
Being unnerved by annoying stimuli, such as loud breathing or the clicking of a pen
Frowning
A sharp tone
Massaging the temples, as if weary
Pinching the bridge of the nose and squeezing the eyes tight
Attention that snaps toward sound or movement
Door-watching (or clock-watching, email-watching, etc.)
Complaining under the breath: *Where is he?* or *This is taking too long!*
Whining, grumbling, or pouting (small children)
Letting out a loud breath
Moving about (sitting and then standing, choosing a different chair, etc.)
Toying with items (turning a cup, mangling a paperclip, etc.)
Shaking the head and muttering
Pushing sleeves up or down (and repeating)
Tilting the head to the ceiling and letting out a heavy sigh
Uncrossing and re-crossing the legs
Tension in the face, shoulders, and neck
Using the body to nudge, push, or block (line jumpers)
Repeatedly running the hands through the hair
Veiled anger or light sarcasm

INTERNAL SENSATIONS:
Breathing that grows heavier, louder
Rising body temperature
Feeling exhausted or strained to the limits
Headaches

MENTAL RESPONSES:
Mentally berating a time-waster
Wishing time would speed up
Running through how to do something faster or more efficiently
One's attention straying to other things
Asserting mental restraint to avoid snapping

ACUTE OR LONG-TERM RESPONSES FOR THIS EMOTION:
Slapping a hand against the table
Yelling or barking orders
Cutting people off
Taking over a project or duty
Telling the speaker to move on and get to the point
Redirecting the focus to allow things to proceed better
Setting a time limit
Making demands
Resorting to the physical (pushing, shoving, etc.)

SIGNS THAT THIS EMOTION IS BEING SUPPRESSED:
A frozen smile
Going for a walk
Using the time to run an errand or complete a task
Attempting to distract oneself to maintain patience
Rooting in a purse or pocket as a distraction
Checking and rechecking a phone for messages
Fussing with one's appearance (brushing away lint, checking one's fingernails, etc.)

MAY ESCALATE TO: Irritation (172), Frustration (134), Anger (40), Scorn (234)

MAY DE-ESCALATE TO: Resignation (224), Acceptance (28), Satisfaction (230)

ASSOCIATED POWER VERBS: Bemoan, complain, distract, fiddle, fidget, fret, gripe, grumble, hover, interrupt, jiggle, manipulate, mumble, pace, sigh, start, take over, wince

WRITER'S TIP: *Never let the reader notice the writing. Overusing metaphors, similes, descriptive terms, and repeated body language can pull the reader out of the story.*

INADEQUACY

DEFINITION: A persistent feeling of shame and self-doubt due to the perception that one is inferior to others

PHYSICAL SIGNALS AND BEHAVIORS:
A lack of eye contact; often looking down or to the side when being spoken to
Hiding one's hands in one's pockets
Avoiding the spotlight (staying on the fringes, supporting rather than leading, etc.)
Not contributing to conversation (out of a fear of revealing one's inferiority)
Hesitating before speaking
Stumbling over one's words
Blushing
A caved-in chest and overall poor posture
Acting to impress others, seeking flattery and validation
Overpreparing (practicing a speech to death, studying every angle, over-packing, etc.)
Asking others for advice and opinions because one doesn't trust one's own
Giving in (or giving up) when challenged by another
Fidgeting at the feeling that all one's flaws are on display (shifting position, tugging at one's clothing, crossing and uncrossing the legs)
Apologizing when it is not necessary or expected
Words drying up because one feels inferior to others in the conversation
Folding the arms in front of oneself; forming a barrier
Hands that shake slightly (especially when others are watching)
Standing with a narrow stance and hunched shoulders, taking up less space
Slouching and rubbing the back of the neck
Holding the hands in front of the body in a shielding position
Covering one's lap with the hands
A too-brief or weak handshake
Verbalizing one's stupidity over miniscule mistakes: *I can't believe it—I'm such an idiot!*
Crossing the arms and the legs
Dressing carefully and obsessing over details to mask one's inferiority within the group
Deflecting compliments by pointing out what one should have done better
Procrastinating on things that could determine one's sense of worth
Avoiding confrontation by backing down even if one believes one is in the right
Trying to hide one's flaws (styling one's hair to cover a birthmark, for example)

INTERNAL SENSATIONS:
Nausea
A racing heartbeat (anxiety-induced)
Raised body temperature that leads to sweating
A dry mouth
Light-headedness

MENTAL RESPONSES:
Feeling like an impostor

Fleeting thoughts of unhappiness when the inner focus on one's failings kicks in
Mentally running oneself down; having a critical inner voice
Holding oneself to impossibly high standards that one would never place on another
Having a hard time sharing one's ideas (due to the assumption that they're flawed)
Constantly comparing oneself to others (over wealth, success, beauty, talents, the ability to fill a specific role properly, etc.) and feeling shame at coming up short
Never enjoying personal wins, instead focusing on what one should have done better
Not pursuing a meaningful goal by labeling it as out of reach for "someone like me"
Craving praise yet feeling unworthy of it when it happens

ACUTE OR LONG-TERM RESPONSES FOR THIS EMOTION:
Becoming tongue-tied
Second guessing one's choices, actions, and decisions
Growing upset at even the lightest amount of criticism (sensitivity)
Punishing oneself for a perceived poor performance
Self-isolation
A brain that won't turn off (obsessing about small things), causing insomnia
Ulcers and other stress-caused illnesses
Performance anxiety; avoiding social situations
Setting one's sights low (underachieving at work) to avoid revealing the inadequacy
Accepting mistreatment because one believes it is deserved (toxic relationships)
Wanting to hide or flee and then mentally ridiculing oneself for being weak

SIGNS THAT THIS EMOTION IS BEING SUPPRESSED:
Perfectionistic tendencies (working long hours, trying to excel at everything, etc.)
Pushing oneself to keep up with peers and competition
Collecting accomplishments and accolades but not enjoying them
Judging worth by results rather than effort
Unnecessarily pointing out one's importance or level of prestige to others
False bravado; overcompensating through dominance or loudness

MAY ESCALATE TO: Worthlessness (286), Depressed (84), Self-Pity (238)

MAY DE-ESCALATE TO: Conflicted (66), Longing (178), Determination (92), Acceptance (28)

ASSOCIATED POWER VERBS: Compare, cower, criticize, crouch, discard, distort, dwell, fail, fixate, judge, lack, limit, mumble, reject, shrug, slump, stumble, subjugate, worry

WRITER'S TIP: *Restraint is something characters shed when their emotions are fired up. Showing a character's progression as they lose control of their behavior and words makes for great reading.*

INDIFFERENCE

DEFINITION: A state of apathy, casualness, or disinterest

PHYSICAL SIGNALS AND BEHAVIORS:
Shoulders are lowered and loose
A slow, steady gait
Arms hanging limply at the sides
Shrugging half-heartedly
Long pauses before responding
Staring blankly or emotionlessly
Lifting a hand loosely, palm up, in a *Who cares?* gesture
Placing hands in one's pockets
Leaning back or away
Looking sleepy or glazed
Speaking in a flat voice
Smiling politely, not genuinely
The body sagging while seated, lacking tension
A wandering gaze
Picking at lint, scratching at cuticles, etc., to show that interest is lacking
Closing one's eyes to shut everything out
Texting during an event or while someone speaks
Not bothering to answer someone's questions
Being unresponsive during a group discussion or debate
Ignoring something being handed over (a file, business card, etc.)
Turning away
A nonchalant attitude
Speaking only when one is spoken to
Not responding to jokes or personal exchanges
Pointedly ignoring another person or situation that draws others in
Relaxed posture
An unhurried exit
Focusing on one's shoe, scuffing at the ground, etc., rather than giving due attention
Responding with *Whatever* or *So?*
Randomly changing the topic
Yawning
Mimicking boredom (slumping in one's seat, tapping a pencil, etc.)
Half-lidded eyes
Muttering *Uh-huh* or *Yeah* when it seems appropriate
Being easily distracted by other things (TV, a girl walking past, etc.)
Choosing brainless activities to pass the time (TV bingeing, scrolling through memes, etc.)

INTERNAL SENSATIONS:
A lack of energy
Slow, even breaths

MENTAL RESPONSES:
Zoning or tuning others out to concentrate on other things
Wandering thoughts
A lack of empathy
Thinking about the time or future events

ACUTE OR LONG-TERM RESPONSES FOR THIS EMOTION:
A disconnect with one's life or society
A fading sense of empathy
Falling into a routine
Meaningless interaction with others
Finding little day-to-day joy
Ignoring the pain or suffering of others

SIGNS THAT THIS EMOTION IS BEING SUPPRESSED:
Smiling and pretending to pay attention
Nodding along as someone speaks but not actively listening
Asking a few token questions
Making an excuse to leave

MAY ESCALATE TO: Irritation (172), Annoyance (44), Contempt (72), Resignation (224), Curiosity (74), Concern (62), Discouragement (100)

MAY DE-ESCALATE TO: Validation (268)

ASSOCIATED POWER VERBS: Detach, dismiss, disregard, drift, flop, forget, glaze, hunch, ignore, loll, neglect, plod, sag, shrug, slack, slouch, slump, snub, stare, wander

> **WRITER'S TIP:** *To create a fluid, emotional arc in your story, make sure your character's feelings build in intensity and complexity as the novel progresses.*

INSECURITY

DEFINITION: Feeling unsure of oneself or displaying a lack of confidence

PHYSICAL SIGNALS AND BEHAVIORS:
Smoothing down clothing
A self-deprecating laugh
Breaking eye contact and shrugging
Keeping one's hands in one's pockets
Fidgeting
Checking one's breath
Visible blushing
Speaking in a too-quiet voice
Licking or biting the bottom lip
Petting or stroking one's hair (comforting gestures)
Covering up (pulling a jacket tighter, holding one's elbows, etc.)
Holding the knees and legs tightly together
Awkwardly mirroring the behavior of others to try and fit in
Choosing loose clothes over tight, revealing ones
Asking for reassurance from others
Brushing off compliments or putting oneself down (self-deprecation)
Looking down while walking
Staying at the edge of a group or seeking the corner of a busy room
Tucking the hands behind the elbows
Twisting one's wrists
Not smiling, or offering a smile that fades quickly
Visible tension in the muscles
Rubbing one's forearms
Needing advice or instruction on what to say or do
Laughing too loudly, or at odd times
Clutching an item, such as a book, binder, or purse, to the chest
Tapping the leg to settle one's nerves
Hiding behind one's hair
Biting one's nails
Staying at a distance, keeping a wide personal buffer of space
Holding a hand close to the face while speaking
Difficulty speaking or offering opinions
Rubbing at one's lips
Wearing too much makeup
Rushing one's speech or speaking in a stammer
Increased sweat output during uncomfortable moments

INTERNAL SENSATIONS:
A heartbeat that races when one feels confronted
A roiling stomach
Uncontrollable flushes of heat

An uncomfortable, dry throat

MENTAL RESPONSES:
Difficulty making decisions; overthinking problems
Obsessing over one's flaws and shortcomings
Agreeing only to avoid a confrontation or be accepted
Fixating on the talents and strengths of others
Comparing oneself to others and finding oneself lacking

ACUTE OR LONG-TERM RESPONSES FOR THIS EMOTION:
Holding onto a comfort item (a special piece of jewelry, a picture, etc.)
A bent spine and hunched shoulders
Blushing when one is noticed or spoken to
Avoiding social situations
Acting skittish around people
Panic symptoms when one is put on the spot
Wearing plain clothing to reinforce invisibility
Difficulty making friends
Choosing a seat in the back of the room or away from others
Seeking interaction online rather than in person

SIGNS THAT THIS EMOTION IS BEING SUPPRESSED:
Tossing the hair
Standing taller, squaring one's shoulders
Forcing oneself to maintain eye contact
Deflecting questions or concern
Rushing into decisions to prove one's decisiveness
Taking risks
Lying
Inserting oneself into conversations

MAY ESCALATE TO: Unease (266), Wariness (280), Defensiveness (78), Worry (284), Doubt (108), Intimidation (170), Embarrassment (118), Loneliness (176), Paranoia (200)

MAY DE-ESCALATE TO: Uncertainty (264), Nervousness (190), Unappreciated (262)

ASSOCIATED POWER VERBS: Blend in, blush, conform, doubt, falter, fidget, fret, fuss, hesitate, overcompensate, second-guess, shuffle, stammer, stumble, stutter, waffle, waver, withdraw, worry

WRITER'S TIP: *Scenes do not happen in a vacuum. Don't forget to include setting, thoughts or verbal cues that allude to the passage of time.*

INSPIRED

DEFINITION: Wanting to do or be better—usually because of an external stimulus, such as another person, a work of art, a saying or mantra, etc.

PHYSICAL SIGNALS AND BEHAVIORS:
The features suddenly going still as the *aha* moment hits
The mouth hanging open
A brightening of the countenance
Wide-open eyes
An inward gaze as one tries to grasp a fleeting idea
Leaping into motion
Extended periods of frenzied activity
Forgetting to eat or sleep
Being highly productive
Breathing quickly
Talking about one's ideas or the source of inspiration to anyone who will listen
Waving the hands around
Pacing while thinking or talking through ideas
Smiling frequently
Leaning in close when talking to others
Having a serious or intense expression
Not responding when one is addressed
Missing appointments
Expressing frustration or impatience with interruptions
Speaking quickly or louder than usual
Drawing diagrams, illustrations, and plans
Making a mess while working (due to not wanting to stop to clean)
An unkempt appearance (wrinkled clothes, a shirt buttoned wrong, hair sticking up, etc.)
Disappearing for long stretches of time
Using stimulants (coffee, energy drinks, etc.) to increase one's productivity
Bouncing on the soles of the feet
Running to discuss one's idea with someone else
Talking to oneself to hash out ideas
Making excuses to get out of obligations and responsibilities one views as less important
Quickly becoming impatient with people who can't see one's vision

INTERNAL SENSATIONS:
Feeling highly energized
Feeling jittery (from stimulants, a lack of sleep, etc.)
A buoyant sensation; lightness
The heart speeding up as small epiphanies hit

MENTAL RESPONSES:
Mental clarity

Being hyper-focused
Turning inward (to avoid distraction)
The mind constantly churning, cycling through ideas
Frustration at not being able to work fast enough to keep up with one's ideas
Losing track of time
Forgetfulness
Relief when personal obligations are lifted (e.g., when a spouse is asleep, one can work late)

ACUTE OR LONG-TERM RESPONSES FOR THIS EMOTION:
Neglecting one's health
Neglected personal hygiene taken to an extreme (overgrown fingernails, wearing just underwear because one has no clean clothing, etc.)
Sallow skin from not getting enough sunlight
Reddened eyes from lack of sleep
Weight loss
Being unaware of dramatic events going on in the world

SIGNS THAT THIS EMOTION IS BEING SUPPRESSED:
An unnaturally still countenance and posture
Animated eyes (a darting gaze, frequent blinking, brightness, etc.)
Jittery extremities
Making excuses so one can get back to work on one's ideas
Being easily distracted (as one's mind keeps going to the source of the inspiration)
The lips twitching as though trying to hide a smile

MAY ESCALATE TO: Euphoria (124), Obsession (194)

MAY DE-ESCALATE TO: Disappointment (96), Remorse (220), Self-Pity (238)

ASSOCIATED POWER VERBS: Achieve, admire, arouse, birth, build, challenge, create, develop, devote, drive, emulate, energize, galvanize, generate, incite, invigorate, kindle, motivate, produce, prompt, push, root, rouse, spark, stimulate, stoke, trigger, wonder

WRITER'S TIP: Common gestures and expressions such as shrugging or frowning are easy to interpret but can lead to lackluster description if they're written "as-is" too often. Customize responses based on the character's personality and comfort zone to paint a fresh image for readers.

INTIMIDATION

DEFINITION: Feeling afraid or timid due to a real or perceived threat

NOTES: When someone is feeling intimidated, their responses will vary depending on whether they lean toward a fight-flight-or-freeze-type response to threats. This entry contains some of each of these reactions.

PHYSICAL SIGNALS AND BEHAVIORS:
The body shrinking in on itself
The posture sagging
Stepping back from the perceived threat
A darting gaze; not looking people in the eye
A brittle laugh
Hands jammed in the pockets
Arms crossed, hands clenching the upper arms
Hiding behind one's hair, a hoodie, another person, etc.
Shuffling one's feet
Crossing and re-crossing the legs
Becoming very still (to avoid attention)
A furrowed brow as one tries to figure out what to do or say
Biting the lips or nails
Standing back from the group
Not engaging in conversation
The skin flushing or sweating
Stuttering or stammering as one tries to respond
The voice dropping to a mutter or murmur
Fast-blinking eyes
Hands up, in a placating or surrendering gesture
Backpedaling: *Oh, I was just kidding,* or *I didn't mean anything by it.*
Passing a job or responsibility to someone else instead of taking it on oneself
Taking deep breaths to try and settle one's nerves
Making a quick escape; physically leaving the area
Speaking to others privately afterward to get their take on what happened
Becoming argumentative
Making passive-aggressive comments
Making oneself look larger: squaring the shoulders, standing as tall as possible, etc.
False bravado (getting louder, making empty threats, etc.)
Hands tightening into fists
Flinching but holding one's ground
A muscle tic developing along the jawline
A flinty or hard gaze

INTERNAL SENSATIONS:
The mouth going dry
Weakness in the muscles

A tightness in the chest
An increased heartrate
A spike of adrenaline
One's focus narrowing in on the threat
The senses becoming more acute

MENTAL RESPONSES:
A desire to either escape or go on the defensive
Thoughts racing as one tries to make sense of what's happening
The mind cycling through possible responses
Frantically trying to think of something to say to prove one's credibility or capability
Cataloguing possible escape routes or plans

ACUTE OR LONG-TERM RESPONSES FOR THIS EMOTION:
Sucking up to the threat
Not taking risks; sticking with what's safe
Keeping one's opinions or ideas to oneself
Not speaking when the threat is near
Agreeing with the threat on everything; losing one's sense of self
Self-loathing
Co-dependency

SIGNS THAT THIS EMOTION IS BEING SUPPRESSED:
Becoming defensive when the threat is present or mentioned
Overcompensating
Regaining a sense of power by belittling someone else
Avoiding the threat
Surrounding oneself with "yes" men or people who will provide affirmation
A marked change in behavior when one is around the threat

MAY ESCALATE TO: Insecurity (166), Emasculation (116), Fear (128), Humiliation (154), Resignation (224), Anxiety (48), Bitterness (58), Contempt (72), Defensiveness (78), Denial (82), Anger (40), Paranoia (200), Powerlessness (208), Self-Loathing (236)

MAY DE-ESCALATE TO: Indifference (164), Hurt (156), Regret (214)

ASSOCIATED POWER VERBS: Abandon, abase, avoid, backpedal, brownnose, bumble, challenge, cower, doubt, evade, faze, flee, fluster, grovel, hem and haw, hesitate, kowtow, pressure, quail, repress, retreat, shrink, stammer, stumble, surrender, withdraw

WRITER'S TIP: *If you need to show a wide personality divide between clashing characters, try to show them responding with vastly different emotions to the same situation or event.*

IRRITATION

DEFINITION: Impatience and displeasure; the sense of being bothered

PHYSICAL SIGNALS AND BEHAVIORS:
The lips pressing together, pursing, or flattening
Features tightening
Narrowing the eyes; squinting or tilting the head down while making eye contact
Rubbing the back of the neck
Watching the source furtively
Frowning
Crossing one's arms
Pulling or plucking at clothing as if it chafes
Fidgety movements (scraping the hair back, curling one's fingers, etc.)
Adopting a challenging tone
A hard smile
Poking a tongue lightly into the cheek and inhaling a long breath
Asking pointed questions
Changing the subject
Forcing a laugh
Raising the voice
Opening the mouth to say something, then thinking better of it
Biting the inside of the cheek
Restless legs (crossing and uncrossing, unable to stand still, etc.)
Going silent; disengaging from conversation
Feigning interest in other things to buy time and regain control
Making small, jittery movements with the fingers
Breathing through the nose (audibly to others)
Curling one's toes
Clasping the hands tightly so the knuckles turn white
Interrupting people
Repeating a mannerism (scratching an eyebrow, adjusting glasses, etc.)
Spots of color entering the cheeks
Clenching one's teeth

INTERNAL SENSATIONS:
Tightness in the chest
Tense muscles
Sensitive skin
A quickened pulse
A twitchy feeling in the extremities
Raised body temperature
Tightness in the jaw and facial muscles, causing discomfort

MENTAL RESPONSES:
Dismissing the source as unworthy
Trying to put the upsetting information out of one's mind
A desire to talk the situation over with someone else
Wishing someone would stop or shut up
Stubbornly sticking to one's belief, even if it doesn't make sense
Clouded judgment
Judging others and their performance or contribution

ACUTE OR LONG-TERM RESPONSES FOR THIS EMOTION:
Openly challenging another's logic or standpoint
Swearing
Negative language: *You don't know what you're talking about!*
Sarcasm
Name-calling or side insults: *Can you stop that? It's like working with a two-year-old!*
Facial tics
Rising blood pressure
Snapping and saying something that offends others or damages a relationship

SIGNS THAT THIS EMOTION IS BEING SUPPRESSED:
Avoiding the source
Two-faced behavior
Nitpicking
Passive-aggressive comments
Forcing oneself to not look at or acknowledge the source
Leaving the room or situation to clear one's thoughts
Seeking to discredit the source so one won't have to believe him or her

MAY ESCALATE TO: Resentment (222), Frustration (134), Anger (40)

MAY DE-ESCALATE TO: Annoyance (44), Indifference (164), Relief (216)

ASSOCIATED POWER VERBS: Bark, call out, chafe, clench, exhale, frown, glare, gripe, grit, grumble, huff, judge, mutter, snap, squeeze, squirm, stiffen, swear, tense, twitch

WRITER'S TIP: *Make body language unique to the character. Do they lift themselves up in their shoes as they wait in line? Do they run a finger along the seam of their jeans when they're deep in thought? Creative emotional mannerisms help characters leap off the page.*

JEALOUSY

DEFINITION: Hostility toward a rival or one suspected of enjoying an advantage

NOTES: The advantage can be a person, an object, or an intangible (love, success, etc.)

PHYSICAL SIGNALS AND BEHAVIORS:
Adopting a sullen look
Making a slight growl or noise in the throat
Bitterness at seeing others respond positively to the rival
Quick, sharp movements (swiping tears from the cheeks, shoving hair out of the eyes, etc.)
Pursing or pressing one's lips flat
Crossing the arms in front of the chest
Clenching one's teeth
Muttering unkind things under one's breath
Starting rumors; acting catty
Picking on someone weaker to gain a sense of power and control
Sneering and ugly laughter
Shouting insults and calling names
Taking a step closer, fists clenched
A visible flush in the cheeks
A pinched expression
Tight muscles
One's body mimicking that of the rival
Trying to "one-up" the other person
Issuing a challenge to the rival that contains an element of risk
Criticism
Spitting in the direction of the rival
Swearing
Kicking at nearby objects
Showing off
Pulling stunts or pranks to regain attention
Rudeness; saying something that is a low blow
Reckless behavior
Gloating when the rival falters or shows weakness

INTERNAL SENSATIONS:
A burning sensation in the chest or stomach
The stomach hardening
Breaths coming coarser, faster
Spots or flashes in one's vision
A pain in the jaw from clenching one's teeth

MENTAL RESPONSES:
A desire to vent and voice the rival's unworthiness to others
Rash decision making (quitting a team, storming out of a party, etc.)

A flash of anger when the rival is mentioned
A desire to discredit the rival or take away their power
Wishing harm or desiring revenge
Turmoil at having negative feelings
Focusing solely on the rival's negative attributes
Imagining how others view oneself in comparison to the rival

ACUTE OR LONG-TERM RESPONSES FOR THIS EMOTION:
Picking fights
An unhealthy obsession with the rival
Indulging in petty crime (keying the rival's car, etc.)
Engaging in self-mutilation as a release
Negativity spilling into other parts of one's life
Self-doubt; a lack of confidence
Feeling fake from wearing two faces for so long
Dishonesty with oneself and others
A pattern of subversively trying to undermine the rival, thereby lowering them in the eyes of others

SIGNS THAT THIS EMOTION IS BEING SUPPRESSED:
Acting normal to the rival's face but talking negatively behind their back
Watching the rival furtively, privately
Grouping with others who also lack whatever is desired
Kissing up to gain approval through association
Trying not to focus on the rival
Telling oneself that it doesn't matter
Attempting to think positive thoughts about the rival

MAY ESCALATE TO: Envy (122), Determination (92), Contempt (72), Desperation (90), Anger (40), Vengefulness (272), Hatred (144)

MAY DE-ESCALATE TO: Dissatisfaction (106), Self-Pity (238), Resignation (224), Remorse (220), Shame (240)

ASSOCIATED POWER VERBS: Avoid, burn, conceal, covet, crave, damage, disparage, entrap, fantasize, gloat, hack, insult, leer, lure, mock, obsess, pine, provoke, pursue, resent, sabotage, scorn, seduce, slander, snap, snarl, spoil, subvert, undermine, want, yearn

WRITER'S TIP: *In each scene, think about the lighting. Full sunlight, muddy clouds washing everything in grey, the onset of sunset or even darkness...light and shadow can affect a character's mood, amp their stress level or even work against their goals.*

LONELINESS

DEFINITION: The feeling of being isolated or cut off

PHYSICAL SIGNALS AND BEHAVIORS:
A longing gaze
Disinterest in one's appearance (bland clothing, lackluster hair, etc.)
Being meticulous with one's appearance in hopes of attracting interest
Slumped shoulders
Limp posture
A monotone voice
Looking down when walking in public
Watching people furtively
An expressionless, unsmiling face
Sullenness
Being generous in hopes of currying favor
Spying or eavesdropping on others to feel a part of something
Filling one's schedule with work or volunteering to avoid downtime
Using books, the Internet, and TV to escape
An expression that crumples at other people's affection displays
Hugging oneself
A lack of eye contact
False bravado
Tears, sadness
A heavy sigh
Talking to oneself
Feeling a sense of comfort from a full mailbox—even if it's full of junk mail
Stroking oneself (e.g., rubbing an arm absently for contact)
Using bright or eccentric clothing choices to get attention or to stay upbeat
Doting on someone or something (a neighbor, a pet, etc.)
Talking to strangers to feel connected
Asking questions out of a desire to converse rather than because of curiosity
Relishing opportunities to talk or engage (e.g., when the mail is delivered)
Rambling when conversing with others
Trying out dating apps and the like
Adhering to a routine (eating the same meals, visiting the same park, etc.)
Buying oneself gifts or small indulgences to boost one's mood
Living vicariously through an alter ego or avatar (via social networking, gaming, etc.)

INTERNAL SENSATIONS:
A thickness in the throat, signaling the onset of tears
A longing so intense it manifests itself as an ache or pain
Insomnia
Fatigue

MENTAL RESPONSES:
Avoiding crowds, large events, or social situations
A desire to be included or wanted
Anger and bitterness
Daydreaming about people one would like to have relationships with
A feeling of unworthiness

ACUTE OR LONG-TERM RESPONSES FOR THIS EMOTION:
Doubting oneself; a lack of confidence
Weight gain
Believing that one is unattractive or has a boring personality
Uncontrollable crying bouts
Despairing of ever being able to change
High blood pressure
Workaholic tendencies
Bingeing to compensate (eating, drinking, shopping, gambling, etc.)
Hoarding pets
Suicidal thoughts

SIGNS THAT THIS EMOTION IS BEING SUPPRESSED:
Committing too quickly to anyone who shows interest
Choosing negative relationships over being alone
Being too friendly and coming across as desperate
Frequently calling family or friends
Solitary activities that show a craving for contact (e.g., people-watching from the porch)

MAY ESCALATE TO: Resignation (224), Sadness (226), Hurt (156), Depressed (84), Anger (40)

MAY DE-ESCALATE TO: Insecurity (166), Unappreciated (262), Neglected (188)

ASSOCIATED POWER VERBS: Ache, avoid, binge, cling, cope, cry, deflect, dodge, dote, drag, droop, eavesdrop, emulate, endure, fake, fantasize, hide, indulge, languish, laze, long, mirror, mope, numb, plod, pretend, sidestep, slouch, slump, stoop, weep, wish, yearn

> **WRITER'S TIP:** *Body movements should never be random. Everything a character does should have a specific intent: to achieve an end, reveal emotion, or to characterize.*

LONGING

DEFINITION: Urgently wanting something that one has yet to obtain

NOTES: While the object of a character's longing is often another person, it can also be anything else, even something intangible. For instance, they might long to escape a boring job, mend something broken in society, or learn more about their culture. For detailed information on the longing associated with people, please see the DESIRE entry (85).

PHYSICAL SIGNALS AND BEHAVIORS:

Closing one's eyes
Taking deep breaths
Staring out the window
Daydreaming
Smiling wistfully
The lips parting
An inward gaze
Absently toying with a necklace, ring, or other comfort item
Running a finger along the edge of a shirt collar
Long periods of stillness and quiet, as one's thoughts turn inward
Speaking in a soft voice about the subject of one's longing
The voice taking on a wistful tone
Rubbing a palm over one's heart
Throwing oneself into hobbies or work to distract oneself
Frequently losing the thread of conversations
Not noticing the things in one's environment
A waning interest in passions and interests one used to enjoy
Spending time alone
Researching the area of longing (e.g., visiting travel sites, looking into educational courses, frequenting forums where like-minded people are discussing a topic, etc.)
Talking to others about how to set a course that will lead to eventual fufillment
Being in a group but not really engaging; the mind being elsewhere
Insomnia
Loss of appetite (or forgetting to eat)
Facial features brightening when the longed-for subject is broached
Making plans to acquire what one longs for
Talking often about the thing one wants
Looking at pictures, videos, or other mementos that represent what one longs for

INTERNAL SENSATIONS:

A weight in the chest
Heavy limbs
Heartache
A dulling of the senses

MENTAL RESPONSES:
Tuning out distractions in order to concentrate on one's goals
Frustration with any barriers keeping one from one's desire
Daydreaming or fantasizing about what one wants
Desperation, as if one's dreams will never come true
The sense that time is passing very slowly
Difficulty focusing on other things
Thinking obsessively about the thing one wants
Deliberately cutting off thoughts about one's desire; trying not to think about it

ACUTE OR LONG-TERM RESPONSES FOR THIS EMOTION:
Isolation
Depression
Excessive weight loss or gain
Making big changes, such as moving or quitting school, so one can pursue the object
Obsessively pursuing the desire regardless of how futile it is
Sacrificing everything in the pursuit (one's savings, job, self-respect, etc.)
Being unable to enjoy one's blessings
Bitterness and resentment
One's longing turning to contempt and disdain

SIGNS THAT THIS EMOTION IS BEING SUPPRESSED:
Denying one's interest
Avoiding the object of one's desire
Feigning interest in something else to throw people off
Ignoring or scorning what one secretly desires
Forced laughter

MAY ESCALATE TO: Discouragement (100), Desperation (90), Bitterness (58), Anguish (42), Excitement (126), Obsession (194), Elation (114), Satisfaction (230), Resignation (224)

MAY DE-ESCALATE TO: Indifference (164), Curiosity (74), Admiration (30)

ASSOCIATED POWER VERBS: Ache, aspire, calculate, contrive, covet, crave, desire, hunt, need, notice, pine for, plan, plot, pursue, stalk, strive for, want, watch, woo, yearn

WRITER'S TIP: *When characters are distracted, they miss the obvious, creating perfect pathways to conflict and disaster. Think about how overlooked aspects of a setting, the behavior of others, and important bits of dialogue can lead to complications down the road.*

LOVE

DEFINITION: Deep affection, attachment, or devotion for another

PHYSICAL SIGNALS AND BEHAVIORS:
Moving to get closer or touch the person
Smiling at nothing
A beaming expression, glowing cheeks
Strong eye contact, with very little blinking
Taking large, deep, savoring breaths
A yearning look
Unconsciously parting the lips
A light, bouncing step
A silly grin
Laughing and talking nonstop
Leaning against one another
Lying in the other's lap
Using pet names or terms of endearment
Mooning over photos or representations of a love interest
Listening to and connecting with love songs
Adopting a silly love-struck tone when communicating
Nervous behaviors (fiddling with the hands, moistening one's lips, etc.)
Getting tongue-tangled
Saying *I love you*
Pointing one's torso and feet toward the loved one
Playful shoving and grabbing
Sharing secrets and desires
Sitting together so the legs touch
Realigning hobbies or interests to match the other person's
Hooking a hand in the other person's belt or pocket
Ignoring or neglecting other friends to be with the significant other
Writing notes or poetry to the other person
Offering gifts of time, value, or thoughtfulness
Talking to friends about the special person, asking for advice
Obsessively checking the phone to see if the love interest has called
Constant texting back and forth
Doodling hearts and names
Trying to improve one's appearance in some way, by coloring one's hair, working out, etc.
Watching romantic movies

INTERNAL SENSATIONS:
A fluttering in the stomach, a feeling of emptiness
A racing pulse
The heart beating, banging, or hammering
A hyper-awareness of the body
Weak knees or legs

A tingling or electrical jolt at accidental touches

MENTAL RESPONSES:
Euphoria; pleasure at touching and closeness
Appreciating the world and everything in it
Losing track of time when one is with the other person
Mental fuzziness, distraction, and daydreaming
Seeking ways to make a loved one proud
Worrying when too much time has passed without contact
A feeling of possessiveness and jealousy
Feeing safe and whole when one is with the other person
A tendency to notice things the love interest would enjoy, even in their absence

ACUTE OR LONG-TERM RESPONSES FOR THIS EMOTION:
Exchanging personal effects (clothing, jewelry, keys, etc.)
Embracing the love interest's friends as one's own
Sharing finances and possessions
Enduring hardship to be with the love interest or make them happy
Sharing hopes and dreams; becoming emotionally vulnerable
Future planning that centers around the love interest
Entering into a committed relationship (living together, getting married, etc.)

SIGNS THAT THIS EMOTION IS BEING SUPPRESSED:
Flushed skin
A high-pitched voice
Nervous laughter or giggling
Standing close, yet not touching
Darting glances
Watching from a safe distance
An increased interest in the other person's personal life
Forcibly declaring that nothing's going on: *We're just friends*
An overall brightening of one's mood when the other person enters the room

MAY ESCALATE TO: Peacefulness (202), Satisfaction (230), Desire (86), Adoration (32)

MAY DE-ESCALATE TO: Acceptance (28), Connectedness (70), Gratitude (136), Longing (178)

ASSOCIATED POWER VERBS: Beam, canoodle, caress, confide, embrace, encourage, flirt, gaze, grin, kiss, laugh, nurture, nuzzle, ogle, stare, stroke, tease, tingle, touch, trust

WRITER'S TIP: *Sentence structure is especially important when writing descriptions. Varied sentence length keeps the pace moving and makes the flow of sensory detail feel more natural, avoiding a "dry report" feel.*

LUST

DEFINITION: An intense sexual craving or longing

NOTES: Some displays of lust may be more masculine or feminine in nature, so choose descriptors that best fit your character's personality and preferred sexual expression.

PHYSICAL SIGNALS AND BEHAVIORS:
Deep and prolonged eye contact
Arching the back
Thrusting out one's chest and exposing the neck
Trailing a finger toward one's cleavage or open collar while maintaining eye contact
A gaze that explores and suggests
Self-petting gestures (slowly running a hand down a thigh, caressing a forearm, etc.)
Opening one's legs slightly while seated
Pressing oneself against the other person, or allowing oneself to be pulled close
Touching the other's face with the back of the hand and drawing it downward
Running one's palms over the other's sleeves, squeezing the forearms
Leaning in and tilting one's head
Pushing one's lips against another's in a soft stroke or brush, testing the connection
Deepening the kiss (tasting, pushing, quickening, a gentle stroke of the tongue, etc.)
Firmly pulling closer, conveying one's desire and need
Anchoring one's hand on the other's belt, then slipping a finger beneath the waistline fabric
Reaching past a gap between buttons to touch warm skin
Breathing that grows faster and more audible
Fingers that rub and tweak, stroking and squeezing each curve
One's gaze being drawn to the lips
Entwining limbs
Opening one's mouth, panting, or gasping
Closing the eyes to better focus on the intensifying sensations
A grip that grows possessive and more intense
Lips touching and sampling the neck and shoulders, leaving moist prints and trails
Heads that tip back
Pulling at restrictive clothing to loosen it
Hands that fumble with buttons and zippers, trembling in urgency
Skin tightening or hardening
Lips visiting sensitive places to tease (nipples, earlobes, forearms, the stomach, etc.)
Teeth playfully dragging at the lower lip during a kiss
Vocalizing (soft sighs, moans, whispered directions or suggestions, etc.)
Bodies pressing against one another to become one

INTERNAL SENSATIONS:
Growing hot or feverish
Fluttery sensations in the chest and stomach

Tingling and pleasure aches flooding the body
A pounding heartbeat
Shivering from pleasure or desire
Growing wet (women) and more sensitive, desiring pressure and friction
Hands that ache with the need to touch and explore
Sexual throbbing and tingling
A sudden flush of warmth that spreads from the groin outward
Shudders of pleasure, and the need to bear down

MENTAL RESPONSES:
Hypersensitivity to smell and touch
Fantasizing about past sexual encounters or imagining new ones
Concentrating one's focus on pleasure centers of the body
An overwhelming desire to join and become one
Thoughts that disappear in the moment of release
Euphoric satisfaction and completeness

ACUTE OR LONG-TERM RESPONSES FOR THIS EMOTION:
Sexual aggressiveness
Being unable to concentrate on anything but obtaining sexual release
A need to satisfy one's urgings regardless of who one is with, the timing, or location

SIGNS THAT THIS EMOTION IS BEING SUPPRESSED:
Playing out fantasies in one's head
Squirming in one's seat; feeling antsy
Having difficulty concentrating, staying on task, or sleeping
Finding one's gaze being drawn to attractive attributes of suitable partners
Arguing, getting angry over nothing, and other signs of extreme irritability

MAY ESCALATE TO: Elation (114), Love (180), Frustration (134), Disappointment (96), Jealousy (174), Scorn (234), Bitterness (58), Shame (240)

MAY DE-ESCALATE TO: Satisfaction (230), Desire (86)

ASSOCIATED POWER VERBS: Arouse, bathe, brush, buck, burn, caress, cradle, curl, drift, erupt, explore, flick, flicker, graze, grip, lick, lunge, massage, need, nibble, nip, please, press, pulse, quiver, rock, rub, seize, shiver, shudder, skim, soothe, spiral, squeeze, stroke, suck, sweep, throb, thrust, tilt, tingle, trail, tremble, twist, warm, whisper

WRITER'S TIP: *Curiosity is perfect for revealing deeper layers. What draws one character in may be different for others, so use this feeling to shed light on their personality, interests, and desires.*

MOODINESS

DEFINITION: Experiencing unexpected mood swings; feeling emotionally sensitive or temperamental

NOTES: Moodiness can cause either volatile or reserved behavior, so choose the best fit for your character's personality and temperament.

PHYSICAL SIGNALS AND BEHAVIORS:

Crossing one's arms over the chest
Body tenseness (e.g., tightly gripping a backpack strap or one's car keys)
Rubbing one's temples
Restless movements (shuffling one's feet, biting one's nails, twisting a lock of hair, etc.)
Pacing or walking in circles
Crossed legs, with the foot bouncing up and down
Biting the lip
Being highly negative
Glaring at people or staring them down
Taking things wrong (e.g., misreading something that's said) and snapping at people
Raising one's voice
Interrupting others
Rolling the eyes
Blowing out breath in an exaggerated huff
Making annoyed noises in the back of one's throat
Muttering under the breath
Exploding in an angry outburst (yelling or swearing)
Becoming argumentative or picking a fight
Speaking tactlessly and saying things that hurt others
Storming out of the room
Squeezing one's eyes shut to regain control of one's emotions
Blinking back tears or crying at little provocation
A voice that breaks or cracks
Slack posture and an inward look
Refusing to engage in conversation
Trying to release one's emotions (via going for a run or heading to the beach)
Taking big breaths
Sighing
Distracting oneself (with a cell phone or book, by going for a drive, etc.)
Avoiding the people one expects to be frustrating or infuriating
Withdrawing from others

INTERNAL SENSATIONS:

Eyes prickling with tears
Tightness in the chest

An ache in the jaw from clenching one's teeth

MENTAL RESPONSES:

Being easily startled; feeling jumpy or jittery
Expecting people to be annoying before they actually are (predicting what people will say, anticipating an irritating habit or gesture, etc.)
Being impatient; getting upset by small setbacks that normally wouldn't be a problem
Being easily frustrated
Difficulty finding things that one wants to do
Being easily hurt by playful or teasing comments (feeling attacked)
An inability to think clearly or see the situation accurately
Being unable to admit wrongdoing; believing that everyone else is to blame
Feeling out of control and responding poorly but not knowing how to stop

ACUTE OR LONG-TERM RESPONSES FOR THIS EMOTION:

Headaches or migraines
Stomach pains and ulcers
Insomnia
Driving loved ones away, leading to isolation
Turning to medical aids, drugs, or alcohol as a way of coping
One's school or work performance suffering
Becoming more and more negative in one's thinking
Migrating toward other negative people

SIGNS THAT THIS EMOTION IS BEING SUPPRESSED:

Being passive-aggressive
Putting on a happy face
Exiting a room or situation to avoid becoming angry or bursting into tears
Clamming up
Taking a background role; letting others be in charge

MAY ESCALATE TO: Irritation (172), Anger (40), Self-Pity (238), Sadness (226), Hurt (156)

MAY DE-ESCALATE TO: Agitation (34), Conflicted (66), Indifference (164)

ASSOCIATED POWER VERBS: Argue, belittle, confront, cry, disrespect, dissolve, explode, flee, flinch, groan, hide, insult, mutter, provoke, sigh, sulk, tear up, tremble, yell

> **WRITER'S TIP:** *If a character is pretending to feel something to fit in or because it is expected, make sure to show hesitation, initial awkwardness, or internal thoughts to emphasize this forced emotion.*

MOVED

DEFINITION: Being deeply stirred emotionally

PHYSICAL SIGNALS AND BEHAVIORS:
One's hand covering the heart
Eyes glistening
Smiling broadly
Moving slowly
Covering one's eyes
One's chin dropping to the chest
Turning away or stepping outside to get oneself together
Closing the eyes and pulling in an expansive breath
The bottom lip pressing into the upper one and the chin quivering slightly
Pressing one's fingers to the lips
Laying a hand against the breastbone
Speaking in a trembling voice
A voice that cracks with emotion
Letting out an involuntary moan or cry
Expressing gratitude (via a letter, with a gift of appreciation, verbally, etc.)
Swiping at tears on one's cheeks
Sweeping someone into a hug
Sharing a nod and meaningful eye contact with the person causing the feeling
A brief loosening of the posture as muscles give out and then "catch"
Grabbing onto someone for support
Collapsing into a chair
Shaking the head in disbelief
Steepling the fingers in front of one's mouth
Sniffling
Wiping one's nose or eyes with a tissue
Difficulty speaking
Hands that tremble slightly
Pressing the lips together, as if trying to contain one's emotion
Rising shakily to one's feet
The skin reddening or turning blotchy
Reaching out to touch someone who is part of the experience
Becoming verbose while expressing gratitude

INTERNAL SENSATIONS:
A prickle in the nose or behind the eyes
A thickness in the throat
A lightening sensation; feeling as if a load has been lifted
The extremities going numb
Warmth expanding through one's chest

MENTAL RESPONSES:
An overwhelming sense of relief
Scattered thoughts or an overall foggy mental state
Tunnel vision; not noticing the peripheral things
Being hyper-focused on the person or circumstance responsible for one's emotion
Not caring what other people think about one's emotional response
Experiencing a mixture of emotions (joy, relief, gratitude, surprise, etc.) and not knowing how to express them

ACUTE OR LONG-TERM RESPONSES FOR THIS EMOTION:
Passing out
Hyperventilating
Getting hiccups from prolonged crying
Being so energized that one can't sleep
Being so determined to show appreciation that one neglects one's basic needs
Becoming clingy or needy; smothering the recipient of one's gratitude

SIGNS THAT THIS EMOTION IS BEING SUPPRESSED:
The body going very still
The eyes furiously blinking
Turning away
Biting on the lips
Expressing thanks in a gruff tone of voice
Clearing the throat
Speaking as few words as possible to avoid revealing one's true feelings
Putting space between oneself and the person responsible
Giving a curt nod
One's expression growing stony and hard to read

MAY ESCALATE TO: Happiness (142), Gratitude (136), Overwhelmed (196), Elation (114), Euphoria (124)

MAY DE-ESCALATE TO: Disbelief (98), Stunned (250), Relief (216), Pleased (206)

ASSOCIATED POWER VERBS: Bawl, clasp, collapse, cry, drop, fall, gasp, give out, grasp, hold, hug, ignite, nod, press, quiver, reach, shake, sob, stir, touch, tremble, weep

WRITER'S TIP: *Is your character more introverted or extroverted? Knowing where they are on the spectrum can help indicate how expressive they will be, especially when they're with other characters.*

NEGLECTED

DEFINITION: Feeling ignored, overlooked, or unloved

NOTES: This entry will focus on the effects of emotional neglect, such as being ignored, marginalized, devalued, and sidelined by the important people in one's life.

PHYSICAL SIGNALS AND BEHAVIORS:
An expression that indicates hurt or confusion
A furrowed brow
Frowning
Wincing
Flinching away from the offending party
An inward gaze
A downcast countenance
Rounded shoulders
Leaning away from the person; keeping one's distance
Not speaking up for oneself
Withdrawing from others
Crying
Standing behind others; keeping to the background
Sniffling
Turning away to hide one's hurt
Hugging oneself
Seeking comfort (with another person, with food, by retreating to a safe place, etc.)
Voicing one's dissatisfaction to the one withholding affection or attention
The voice rising or breaking
Nagging, cajoling, or wheedling to get the other person to do what one wants
Placating the other person to win them over
Casting darting glances at the person
Jumping at the first sign of attention
Gazing with longing at people who are receiving what one is missing
Looking askance at the person withholding affection; wanting attention but fearing further rejection
Treading carefully with the other person; not wanting to rock the boat
Speaking loudly or more excitedly (even subconsciously) as a way to gain attention
Doing anything to gain attention or favor from the person
Making excuses for the other party
Being highly attentive to others to avoid causing anyone else the same pain

INTERNAL SENSATIONS:
A dropping sensation in the midsection
A strong yearning for what is being withheld
The heart fluttering hollowly

A surge of adrenaline when the person shows attention

MENTAL RESPONSES:
Confusion
Believing that one is responsible for the neglect
Mentally searching for what one did wrong to cause the problem
Practicing what one will say or do next time an opportunity arises
Wanting to avoid the person but being pushed by one's unmet need to fill the void

ACUTE OR LONG-TERM RESPONSES FOR THIS EMOTION:
Fawning over the neglectful party
Becoming clingy
Acting out in unusual or negative ways to get what one wants (pursuing someone else to get the person's attention, engaging in harmful behaviors, etc.)
Entering into toxic or dangerous relationships as a way of meeting one's need
Rejecting others before they can do the rejecting
Consistently initiating drama
Being fiercely independent and determined to care for oneself
One's affection turning to scorn, bitterness, or anger
Hardening oneself against the other person

SIGNS THAT THIS EMOTION IS BEING SUPPRESSED:
Holding one's chin high
Maintaining a steady voice
Acting as if the neglect is no big deal
Withdrawing from the person but still pursuing them in subtle ways (asking friends about the person, stalking them on social media, etc.)

MAY ESCALATE TO: Unappreciated (262), Intimidation (170), Longing (178), Anger (40), Confusion (68), Discouragement (100), Anxiety (48), Defiance (80), Depressed (84), Hurt (156), Resentment (222), Scorn (234)

MAY DE-ESCALATE TO: Indifference (164)

ASSOCIATED POWER VERBS: Blanch, cling, contract, cringe, crumple, cry, doubt, flinch, hesitate, manipulate, nag, quail, rebel, recoil, shrink, shrivel, tremble, wince, wither, wonder

WRITER'S TIP: *Do you know your character's emotional wound? Whatever difficult trauma is in their past, the emotion surrounding it will act as a trigger, awakening their pain and causing them to overreact.*

NERVOUSNESS

DEFINITION: Feeling unsettled and being easily agitated

PHYSICAL SIGNALS AND BEHAVIORS:
Short, jerky movements
Pacing
Rapid blinking; a tightness around the eyes
Rubbing the back of the neck
Unfastening the top button of a shirt
Scratching or rubbing one's skin
Biting at the lips
Jumpiness
Flighty hand movements
Clumsiness
Rubbing one's hands down one's pant legs
A lack of eye contact
Scraping a hand through the hair
Quick breaths
Crossing and uncrossing one's arms or legs
Eyeing the exits
Bouncing a knee (while sitting)
Repeated gestures (straightening one's tie, touching an ear, etc.)
Increased sweat, particularly on the hands
Tingling fingers and toes
Pupils that appear dilated
Biting or picking at one's fingernails
Shaking out the hands
Clearing the throat
Facial tics
Stuttering and stumbling over one's words
Quick, high-pitched laughter
Restlessness (e.g., sitting, then standing)
Laughter that goes on for longer than normal
Closing the eyes and taking a calming breath
Rapid speaking, babbling, revealing things one didn't intend to, etc.
A change in the pitch, tone, or volume of the voice
Tackling a task (cleaning, waxing the car, etc.) to distract oneself

INTERNAL SENSATIONS:
Sensitive skin
Faintness
An empty feeling in the pit of the stomach
Quivery, twitchy muscles

Loss of appetite
Dry mouth
Heart palpitations
Headache

MENTAL RESPONSES:
Acute senses (especially regarding sound and movement)
The desire to flee
Erratic thought processes and irrational fears
Second-guessing oneself
The mind going to the worst-case scenario
Wishing time would speed up

ACUTE OR LONG-TERM RESPONSES FOR THIS EMOTION:
Vomiting
Fatigue or insomnia
Panic attacks
Withdrawal
Irritability
Ulcers and other digestive disorders
Weight loss or gain
Negative thought patterns
Indulging in alcohol, drugs, or chain smoking to take the edge off

SIGNS THAT THIS EMOTION IS BEING SUPPRESSED:
A pasted-on smile
Clasping one's hands together
An unnatural stillness
Eyes that blink too much or don't blink enough
Not meeting anyone's gaze
Changing the topic
Avoiding conversation

MAY ESCALATE TO: Flustered (132), Insecurity (166), Anxiety (48), Fear (128), Dread (110), Doubt (110)

MAY DE-ESCALATE TO: Uncertainty (264), Apprehension (52), Relief (216)

ASSOCIATED POWER VERBS: Babble, chafe, chatter, dart, fiddle, fidget, fool with, giggle, interrupt, jerk, jump, overreact, panic, startle, stifle, swallow, tap, twitch, worry

WRITER'S TIP: *Body movement and external reactions alone will not create an emotional experience for the reader. Pairing action with a light use of internal sensations and/or thoughts creates a deeper emotional pull.*

NOSTALGIA

DEFINITION: Fondly recalling a past period or situation one would like to revisit

NOTES: While nostalgia and homesickness are often seen as the same thing, there are subtle differences between the two. The former is typically a fond remembering, while the latter is a deeper feeling that's often coupled with a strong sense of sadness or even grief. If your character is feeling HOMESICK, see that entry (141) for ideas on how it might be expressed.

PHYSICAL SIGNALS AND BEHAVIORS:
An unfocused gaze
A slight smile
Slowly flipping through old pictures, stroking the pages
A relaxed posture
Eyes that fill with happy tears
Using a quiet voice
Cocking one's head to the side while remembering
Subdued laughter
A shallow sigh
An unhurried walk
Slouching on a sofa, watching old movies from the time period one fondly remembers
Slow, languid movements
Growing animated when memory is triggered (an old song playing on the radio, etc.)
Eyes brightening as memories are recalled
Keeping mementos from the happy time
Telling and retelling stories about the past
Seeking out those who share one's memories
Gently touching memorable items (a baby blanket, wedding invitations, etc.)
Closing one's eyes to more clearly recall the memories
Trying to recreate a past event (burning the same scented candle, wearing the old clothes, etc.)
Seeing similarities in the present: *You look just like him,* or *This is the same color as our first car.*
Increased tenderness (sitting close, a quick kiss, etc.) for those who shared in the event
Talking frequently about the past
Baking an old dessert that was a favorite of the person one is remembering
Visiting special places (the kids' favorite playground, a favorite restaurant, etc.)
Using social networks to find old friends and family
Remembering only the good about the time or person; forgetting the negative associations
Seeking to reconnect (phoning out of the blue, arranging a visit, etc.)

INTERNAL SENSATIONS:
Eyes prickling with tears
An excited flutter in the belly
An overall relaxation of the body
The breaths slowing as a memory takes over

Dulled awareness—e.g., sitting in an uncomfortable position without feeling it
Experiencing (to a lesser degree) the same physical sensations felt during the past event

MENTAL RESPONSES:
Losing track of the time while remembering
A desire to go back and visit the past
Mentally replaying past events
Pushing oneself to recall small details (the color of a friend's jacket, the name of a child's best friend who often stayed for dinner, etc.) to make the memory more vivid
Satisfaction at having experienced the event despite any pain or loss resulting from it

ACUTE OR LONG-TERM RESPONSES FOR THIS EMOTION:
Discontentment with the way things presently are
Choosing to reconnect with someone, even if it means working past a challenge (e.g., a past falling-out, dealing with problematic family members, a fear of flying, etc.)
Expressing more emotion about the past than the present
Spending large periods of time in the past
Hoarding tendencies
Neglecting current duties or relationships
An inability to move on

SIGNS THAT THIS EMOTION IS BEING SUPPRESSED:
An austere lack of mementos from the past
Sniffing back tears
Rejecting opportunities to revisit the past (reunions, trips to the old hometown, etc.)
Not engaging in conversations about the past
Refusing to speak about someone, or changing the topic when their name comes up
Masking nostalgia with practicality: *I kept his toys so he could give them to his kids.*

MAY ESCALATE TO: Longing (178), Dissatisfaction (106), Sadness (226), Happiness (142), Sappiness (228)

MAY DE-ESCALATE TO: Wistfulness (282), Gratitude (136), Satisfaction (230), Connectedness (70)

ASSOCIATED POWER VERBS: Call, caress, celebrate, cradle, cry, grasp, graze, grieve, grin, hold, honor, hug, joke, kiss, laugh, meditate, memorialize, peruse, ponder, pore over, recall, reflect, relive, remember, reminisce, retell, share, sigh, smooth, stroke, voice

> **WRITER'S TIP:** *When introducing and describing characters, parcel out personal details in small bits. Anything that isn't pivotal to plot or characterization can be left to the reader's imagination.*

OBSESSION

DEFINITION: Being excessively concerned about or interested in someone or something

NOTES: The character's obsession could be a person or group of people (a love interest or sports team), a goal (being elected class president, escaping from a captor), a hobby (a specific exercise regime, scrapbooking), or anything else that holds their attention for an extended period of time.

PHYSICAL SIGNALS AND BEHAVIORS:
Listening with rapt attention (leaning forward, eyes wide, vigorously nodding the head, etc.)
The pitch of one's voice rising
An over-bright, fanatic shine in the eyes
A laser-focused gaze
An unkempt appearance (uncombed hair, wrinkled clothing, bags under the eyes, etc.)
One's words running together as one talks about the obsession
Speaking animatedly (flapping the hands, bouncing on the heels, fingers jittering, etc.)
Monopolizing conversations; talking over other people to voice one's opinions
Staring longingly at the focus of one's obsession
Quickening breaths
Moving closer or rising up on one's toes to see the person through a crowd
Wearing clothing, accessories, jewelry, etc. that are associated with one's obsession
Moving to a location that makes it easier to pursue the focus of one's interest
Choosing clothing and hairstyles to emulate the person one is focused on or to specifically draw their attention
Talking about the obsession with anyone who will listen
Collecting the object in its many forms—buttons, bobbleheads, cards, whatever applies
Joining a fan club
Attending events (conferences, book signings, etc.) where the subject is being honored
Seeking out others who share this same obsession
Growing angry when the subject is belittled
Allowing one's conversation and focus to be distracted
Stalking the subject
Learning everything one can about one's obsession
Blowing off friends and family in favor of the obsession
Crossing moral boundaries in one's pursuit
Pursuing the person or goal despite rejection or failure
Spending excessive time, money, or energy on activities tied to the obsession
Turning conversations back to the object of one's obsession

INTERNAL SENSATIONS:
A rush of adrenaline when the subject appears or is mentioned
A taut feeling in the midsection when one is unable to pursue the obsession
The heart beating frantically when the subject appears

MENTAL RESPONSES:
Having a single-minded focus
A compulsive need to pursue or own the object of desire
The mind constantly turning back to the obsession
The mind replaying the same events over and over
Fantasizing about one's obsession
Believing that life is less fulfilling without the object of one's desire
Mood swings that are driven by one's perceived success or failure

ACUTE OR LONG-TERM RESPONSES FOR THIS EMOTION:
Fatigue
High blood pressure
An inability to fully function when one isn't near or pursuing the subject
Muscle tics
Lack of hygiene and self-care
Going long stretches without engaging with others; becoming isolated
Obsessive-compulsive behaviors
A loss of self as the preoccupation with the obsession takes priority over other needs
Losing touch with one's emotions; becoming numb to them
Becoming angry and defensive when confronted about having an unhealthy obsession

SIGNS THAT THIS EMOTION IS BEING SUPPRESSED:
Attempting to play it cool around others
Avoiding mention of the subject in an attempt to throw others off
Denying any interest at all in the object of one's desire
Inattentiveness; trying to pay attention but not always being able to do so
Joining groups or going out with friends but not truly engaging
Escalating worry over what people would think if they found out
Trying to hide one's displeasure if the subject is disparaged (mashing the lips together, crossing the arms, turning away, etc.)

MAY ESCALATE TO: Betrayed (56), Despair (88)

MAY DE-ESCALATE TO: Indifference (164), Adoration (32), Awe (54), Desire (86), Eagerness (112), Excitement (126)

ASSOCIATED POWER VERBS: Consume, engross, enthrall, fixate, focus, grip, haunt, preoccupy, pursue, stalk, strive, target, torment

WRITER'S TIP: *When it comes to emotion, humor can have many uses. For some, it is a way to work past a situation with optimism intact. Others use it to deflect or distract. What purpose does humor serve your character's state of mind?*

OVERWHELMED

DEFINITION: To be overpowered or overcome by feelings or circumstances

PHYSICAL SIGNALS AND BEHAVIORS:
Bringing a shaky hand to the forehead
Holding a palm up to stop someone from dumping on more worry
Waving people away
Shoulders that drop or curl
A chest that caves in
Clutching at one's arms or stomach
Touching a temple while closing the eyes
A voice choked with tears
A chest that hitches
A quaking voice
Poor balance
Mumbling, muttering
Letting out an uncontrollable cry, sob, or whimper
Uncertain (almost drunken) steps
Sagging into a chair or leaning against a doorframe or wall
Pulling the knees up to the chest and circling them with the arms
Falling against another person
Teary eyes
Difficulty forming responses
Holing up in a corner and placing one's back against the wall
Dropping or spilling things
Shaking the head repeatedly
A glassy stare; a glazed look
Staring down at one's empty palms
Putting one's hands over one's ears
Rocking back and forth
Closing the eyes
Inappropriate responses (laughing, screaming, etc.)
Leaning over with the hands on the knees
Hyperventilating
Loosening a belt, collar, or other confining article of clothing
Touching one's fingertips to the lips

INTERNAL SENSATIONS:
Weakness in the legs; a sudden need to sit down
A wave of heat or cold
Light-headedness
Difficulty breathing
Stomach discomfort (pain or nausea) and being unable to eat

Tunnel vision

MENTAL RESPONSES:
Noise sensitivity
Mental numbness and an inability to focus
Becoming unresponsive to others, almost catatonic
Wishing for comfort
Irritability; desiring to be alone
Indecisiveness
Negative self-talk; feeling like one is dropping the ball, inept, or incapable

ACUTE OR LONG-TERM RESPONSES FOR THIS EMOTION:
Flight
Snapping under pressure (screaming, yelling, hitting others, etc.)
Fainting or swooning
Weeping
Hysteria
Headaches or hypertension
Muscle fatigue and soreness
Seeking comfort in unhealthy ways
Heart attack or stroke
Chronic fatigue or insomnia
Decaying physical health
Hospitalization

SIGNS THAT THIS EMOTION IS BEING SUPPRESSED:
Verbal denial: *I'm fine, really.*
False smiles and confidence
Agreeability or false enthusiasm
Masking weakness with excuses: *Sorry, I stood up too fast.*
Feigning a headache or other malady rather than admitting one's limits

MAY ESCALATE TO: Anxiety (48), Hysteria (158), Depressed (84), Powerlessness (208)

MAY DE-ESCALATE TO: Determination (92), Gratitude (136), Relief (216)

ASSOCIATED POWER VERBS: Collapse, crumple, hyperventilate, mumble, overreact, panic, paralyze, quit, retreat, shake, shut down, snap, stare, stumble, sweat, tremble, withdraw, yell

WRITER'S TIP: *When delivering emotional description, it's easy to rely too much on facial expressions. Instead, look down and describe what the arms, hands, legs, and feet are doing.*

PANIC

DEFINITION: A sudden and incapacitating fear that produces neurotic or illogical behavior

PHYSICAL SIGNALS AND BEHAVIORS:
Quick, shallow breathing
Eyes that are wide, with white showing around the whole iris
Hyperventilating
Squeezing the eyes shut
Clenching and unclenching the fists
Folding the body over and making oneself small
Veins standing out in one's neck
Involuntary moans or whimpers
Being on edge (jumping at sounds, difficulty concentrating, etc.)
Sitting upright
Grasping the sides of one's head to try and regain control
Hands that shake and flutter
Muscles that look tight and clenched
Sweaty, flushed skin
Gasping to control one's breath
Pressing a palm against one's chest to the point of pain
A voice that elevates in pitch and volume
Speaking quickly; using choppy sentences
Backing against a wall or corner
Crying
Holding one's own shoulders tight to try and still one's quaking
Repeating the same thing over and over: *No, no, no, this isn't happening!*
Calling for help
Desperately holding onto a source of stability, such as a person or comfort item
A darting gaze that attempts to absorb everything in one's environment
Passing out
Fleeing

INTERNAL SENSATIONS:
Adrenaline shooting through one's system
Heart palpitations and tingling in the chest
Elevated blood pressure
Feeling as if one is choking or smothering
The sensation of not being able to get enough oxygen (chest tightness)
Tingling in the extremities, the fingers and toes going numb
Nausea
Vertigo
Seeing spots in one's vision
Feeling faint or dizzy
A temperature increase (profuse sweating) or decrease (uncontrollable shivering)

MENTAL RESPONSES:
A sudden and overwhelming sensation of dread
Believing that one is going crazy or is going to die
Trying to make sense of one's situation but being unable to think coherently
Focusing on subduing the symptoms (calming down)
Repeating to oneself that everything is going to be okay
Searching for a trigger or cause for one's panic
Becoming disoriented
Fixating on worst-case scenarios
Becoming hyper-reactive to sounds, movement, touch, etc.

ACUTE OR LONG-TERM RESPONSES FOR THIS EMOTION:
Developing a panic or anxiety disorder
Depression
Reliance upon prescription medications
Drug or alcohol abuse
Phobias
Becoming homebound
Avoiding situations that trigger one's panic
Avoiding places where one can't escape if a panic attack comes on
Constantly worrying about when the next attack will hit
Sleeping more than usual

SIGNS THAT THIS EMOTION IS BEING SUPPRESSED:
Closing the eyes
Taking deep, controlled breaths
Leaving the room or turning aside to regain control
Practicing relaxation techniques
Avoiding eye contact with others
Talking oneself down using logic and reasoning

MAY ESCALATE TO: Hysteria (158), Paranoia (200), Terror (258)

MAY DE-ESCALATE TO: Anxiety (48), Dread (110), Fear (128), Sadness (226), Unease (266), Worry (284)

ASSOCIATED POWER VERBS: Choke, cling, collapse, faint, flee, flinch, freak out, gasp, grab, hide, hyperventilate, jerk, scrape, shake, shudder, sob, sweat, tremble, whimper

WRITER'S TIP: *To dig deeper into a character, think about shame. What makes them feel this painful emotion? Drill down to important backstory to understand what happened, and then make them face their shame on the page.*

PARANOIA

DEFINITION: Excessive or illogical suspicion and/or distrust of others

PHYSICAL SIGNALS AND BEHAVIORS:
Flinching and startling easily
Clenching the jaw
Darting eye movements; a wide-eyed look
Adopting excessive safety precautions (extra locks, guard dogs, video surveillance, etc.)
Fidgety hands that won't settle
Restless sleep or insomnia
Backing away with raised hands
Eyes that don't seem to blink often enough
Crossing the arms tightly over the chest
Muttering under one's breath; talking to oneself
Sweating
Bloodshot eyes
Scouting for exits when entering a room
A heightened need for personal distance
Dependency on caffeinated beverages or drugs to stay alert
A rumpled appearance
Accusing innocent people of planning or carrying out mischief
Facial tics; muscles that jump
A quick, erratic pace
Always looking over the shoulder or around the next corner
Plucking at clothing as if it chafes
Aligning with fringe groups and conspiracy theorists
Espousing far-out beliefs and opinions
Becoming easily offended; jumping to the defensive
Verbally attacking any perceived opponents
Spouting inane or irrational arguments
Citing unreliable sources
Stubbornly adhering to one's beliefs no matter how outlandish they are
Perfectionist tendencies
Compulsive behaviors
Refusing food or drink prepared by others

INTERNAL SENSATIONS:
Fatigue
Muscles that are always tense, ready to fight or run
Sensitivity to touch and sound
A racing heartbeat
Raw nerves and skin
A high adrenaline level; jumpiness

MENTAL RESPONSES:
Seeing danger symbols in everything
Judging too quickly
Believing that others always have a hidden agenda or motive
A heightened sense of self-importance
Irrational responses; jumping to illogical conclusions
Mental fatigue from not getting enough sleep
An inability to connect with others due to a lack of trust
Negative thought patterns
Feeling watched or followed
The belief that everyone else is deluded
Adhering to superstitious beliefs to stay safe

ACUTE OR LONG-TERM RESPONSES FOR THIS EMOTION:
Contacting the authorities for help against suspected assailants
An inability to maintain long-term relationships
Isolation
Living off the grid
The belief that one is no longer required to live by the laws of society
A complete break with reality
Hallucinations and delusions
Rage
Anxiety attacks, phobias, and/or psychosis

SIGNS THAT THIS EMOTION IS BEING SUPPRESSED:
Avoidance of social situations
Attempting to engage socially but with wary and darting eyes
Agreeing with everything to seem part of the group
Watching others and mimicking them as a way of appearing normal
A smile that is frozen or manic
A high voice or odd laugh
Using medicine or seeking therapy

MAY ESCALATE TO: Fear (128), Obsession (194), Anger (40), Rage (212), Hatred (144), Desperation (90)

MAY DE-ESCALATE TO: Skepticism (244), Scorn (234), Unease (266), Wariness (280)

ASSOCIATED POWER VERBS: Analyze, argue, bolt, challenge, contradict, dart, fixate, flinch, jerk, jump, obsess, peer, pry, race, scuttle, shudder, snap, snoop, sprint, start, twitch

WRITER'S TIP: *In dialogue, it's not always what a character says that's important, it's how they say it. (And sometimes it's what they are trying hard not to say!)*

PEACEFULNESS

DEFINITION: A state of calm that is devoid of strife, agitation, or commotion

PHYSICAL SIGNALS AND BEHAVIORS:
A relaxed posture (slack muscles, loose limbs, etc.)
Smiling or grinning
Fingers loosely clasped in one's lap
Closed eyes, with the head tipped back
Softened features that imply calm
Nodding to others in greeting
Leaning back, an arm hooked over the back of a chair
Taking a deep, satisfied breath
Using a friend's shoulder as a shelf to rest one's elbow
An unforced laugh
Whistling or humming
Being honest and transparent—doing what feels right in the moment
Sparkling eyes and a weightless gaze
Enjoying an event (a movie, a concert in the park, a picnic, etc.)
Lying on the grass to soak up the sun
Catlike stretches
A warm voice with a caring tone
Taking slow, easy breaths
Half-closed eyes; a lidded look of satisfaction
Lacing the fingers behind the head
A wide stance and open demeanor
Languid movements
Rolling the neck back and forth
Looping the thumbs in the front pockets while standing
An easy, unhurried walk
A wandering gaze, taking in random things
Noticing and enjoying the small things (stopping to smell the roses)
A satisfied sigh
Unhurried speech
Contentedly taking more time to complete tasks
Helping others out of a desire to lift some of their burdens also
Expressing a greater interest in the happiness of others
Engaging in meaningful conversations

INTERNAL SENSATIONS:
Drowsiness
A lack of tension and stress that almost equates to a feeling of nothingness
A steady, calm pulse and heartbeat

MENTAL RESPONSES:
Being with others with no need to fill the silence
Satisfaction with the world at large
A feeling of connection to life
Appreciating beauty more, in all forms
Having no desire to be anywhere else
Enjoying listening to others
Living in the moment, not acknowledging the past or future
Avoiding topics of conversation that will kill the mood
Delighting in even mundane, everyday tasks
A desire for everyone to experience such peace

ACUTE OR LONG-TERM RESPONSES FOR THIS EMOTION:
A lessened need for worldly goods
Choosing to spend time with positive or like-minded people
A growing interest in spiritual or religious philosophy
A desire to maintain a positive status quo
Changing one's lifestyle to accommodate new beliefs, such as recycling or moving to the country
Impatience with corporate greed and capitalism
A desire for more natural living
An increased awareness of one's body and what goes into it
Engaging in new and satisfying hobbies and interests

SIGNS THAT THIS EMOTION IS BEING SUPPRESSED:
Claiming that one's calm demeanor is simply tiredness
Forcing oneself to maintain a slight stiffness in posture
Pretending to disengage because of boredom
Asking expected questions so others assume one is of the same mindset

MAY ESCALATE TO: Happiness (142), Satisfaction (230), Connectedness (70)

MAY DE-ESCALATE TO: Curiosity (74), Wistfulness (282)

ASSOCIATED POWER VERBS: Amble, appreciate, chat, discuss, enfold, experience, hum, lean, linger, loiter, lounge, meander, relax, rest, share, smile, stretch, stroll, whistle

WRITER'S TIP: *Choose verbs carefully. The meaning of a sentence can be altered through the words used to describe action. Readers will see a character who trudges up the stairs as being in a different emotional state than one that bounds up them, two at a time.*

PITY

DEFINITION: Feeling discomfort at the distress of others while being grateful one doesn't have to experience it oneself

PHYSICAL SIGNALS AND BEHAVIORS:
Giving a clenched half-smile
Sighing
A sagging body posture
Head tilted slightly to the side
Looking at the person sideways rather than straight on
Sharing a pained glance with someone else
Facial cues that show disdain (a curling lip, the nose wrinkling, etc.)
Laying a hand over one's heart before quickly lowering it
Looking at the person as they talk but being unable to meet their eyes
Carefully weighing one's words before speaking
Leaning back and shaking the head at the person's misfortune
Wincing
Making a *tsk* sound
The face wrinkling up
One's gaze dropping to the ground
Narrowing one's eyes as one tries to listen without judgment
Wringing one's hands
Holding a fist to one's mouth
Shuffling backward
Turning away, unable to look any more
Overall awkwardness, such as not knowing what to do with one's hands
Looking around, as if for someone to do something
Reaching out to the person but not touching them
Stepping closer while providing the person adequate personal space
Offering clichéd platitudes: *You'll get through this,* or *It's always darkest before the storm.*
Clearing the throat
Offering to say a prayer for the person
Fidgeting (with a button, cell phone, jewelry, etc.)
Asking questions about what happened instead of simply listening and offering comfort
Making comments hinting that the person is somehow to blame for their misfortune
Speaking in a falsely sympathetic tone
Talking it over with others later, in private
Offering false hope: *Maybe this will lead to something better,* or *I'm sure he'll forgive you in time.*
Offering superficial comforting gestures (such as clapping the person on the back) but not doing anything that would really help
Clutching whatever one is holding, such as a set of keys or a binder
Blocking a child's view of the sight
Making excuses to others as to why one didn't get involved

INTERNAL SENSATIONS:
An uncomfortable sensation in the belly
A flutter of guilt, as if one should do something to help
A squeezing in the chest
An uncomfortable lump in the throat

MENTAL RESPONSES:
Wanting to help but not knowing what to say or do
Fearing that one might suffer the same hardship
Subconsciously making plans to keep the hardship from befalling oneself
Seeking a way to exit graciously
Thoughts turning to loved ones (if the misfortune involves the person's family)
Guilt, because the situation requires more aid than one is willing to offer
Being grateful one has never had to suffer in the same way

ACUTE OR LONG-TERM RESPONSES FOR THIS EMOTION:
Distancing oneself from the party because the situation is just too awkward
Blaming the person for their misfortune so one doesn't have to feel sorry for them
One's pity turning to contempt or scorn
Helping in ways that doesn't require emotional involvement, such as giving financial gifts
Becoming two-faced
Realizing one can help in a tangible way and choosing to step up and do it

SIGNS THAT THIS EMOTION IS BEING SUPPRESSED:
No one likes to be pitied, since there's often an element of condescension or patronization involved. Because of this, people feeling pity will try to make it look like true EMPATHY or CONCERN. For ideas on what suppressed pity might look like, please see those entries.

MAY ESCALATE TO: Contempt (72), Smugness (246), Guilt (140), Empathy (120), Determination (92)

MAY DE-ESCALATE TO: Indifference (164), Concern (62)

ASSOCIATED POWER VERBS: Ache, act, agonize, comfort, commiserate, consider, console, cry, deplore, empathize, enable, encourage, feel, give, gossip, grieve, help, hurt, judge, lament, mourn, nod, offer, pat, pray, soothe, suffer, sympathize, warn, weep

> **WRITER'S TIP:** *No matter how resilient your character is, some things will get under their skin. Look for emotions that force them to be vulnerable so they'll seem more realistic to readers.*

PLEASED

DEFINITION: Experiencing a pleasurable sense of satisfaction

PHYSICAL SIGNALS AND BEHAVIORS:
A relaxed smile crossing the face
An overall lifting of the facial countenance
The head tilting slightly to the side
The cheeks going lightly pink with pleasure
Rubbing a hand self-consciously through one's hair
Lifting the chin
The chest puffing out
Leaning back in one's seat
Maintaining an open body posture (not tense or defended)
Sighing in satisfaction
Placing the palm of a hand over one's heart
One's voice going soft and gentle
Giving a thumbs up
Covering one's smile with a hand
Offering a conspiratorial gesture to someone involved (winking, giving a high five, etc.)
Nodding the head
Shaking the head slightly while smiling in happy disbelief
Laughing to oneself
Clapping the hands
Making strong eye contact with others
Making physical contact with those nearby—hugging, squeezing a shoulder, etc.
Sharing a happy glance with someone
Bouncing lightly in place (trying to contain a sudden boost in energy)
Verbalizing one's pleasure: *I couldn't be more proud*, or *Isn't this great?*
Offering encouragement or kind words to others; passing the feeling along
Eagerly discussing the event that has caused one's pleasure
Celebrating in some way—indulging in a special treat or going out with friends, for example

INTERNAL SENSATIONS:
Warmth spreading throughout the chest
One's face feeling stretched from so much smiling
Relaxed muscles
Warmth in the cheeks
The chest-swelling sensation that accompanies pride in a job well done

MENTAL RESPONSES:
A sense of contentment; a lack of stress or worry
Wanting the feeling to last
Being more tolerant and patient with others

Capitalizing on the situation by continuing whatever brought on the pleased feeling
Looking more fondly on others and wishing to pass on the feelings of goodwill

ACUTE OR LONG-TERM RESPONSES FOR THIS EMOTION:
An increased sense of pride and self-confidence (if the pleasure was caused by one's actions)
Improved productivity
Improved relationships due to one's expansive feeling and a desire to keep it going
A positive shift in priorities; realizing that certain "problems" aren't as important as one once thought
Lost productivity in other areas due to one's attention being fractured
People in one's life feeling marginalized (if the pleasure is associated with another person)
Ignoring one's problems out of a desire to hold onto the pleased feeling

SIGNS THAT THIS EMOTION IS BEING SUPPRESSED:
The corners of the lips twitching
The lips pursing or mashing together
Covering the mouth with one's hand
The eyes becoming more animated
Drawing in a big, settling breath
Turning one's attention away from the cause of one's pleasure
Holding unnaturally still
Maintaining a tall, stiff posture
Leaning back or turning one's body away, as if to show a lack of interest
Acting unconcerned while one's eyes dart to the cause of the pleasure
Not talking about the cause but keeping a memento nearby to remind one of it

MAY ESCALATE TO: Satisfaction (230), Confidence (64), Happiness (142), Validation (268), Pride (210), Inspired (168), Elation (114)

MAY DE-ESCALATE TO: Amusement (38), Surprise (252)

ASSOCIATED POWER VERBS: Beam, chuckle, grin, high-five, hug, laugh, nod, relax, smile, tease, wink

WRITER'S TIP: *Gratitude is a powerful emotion for self-protective characters, since it lowers their emotional shield. Think about including an event that causes them to experience gratitude so they can see that not everyone is an enemy. This will help them grow and move past their own fears.*

POWERLESSNESS

DEFINITION: Feeling that that one lacks the authority, skills, or resources to act

PHYSICAL SIGNALS AND BEHAVIORS:
Making oneself small (legs close together, slouching, a caved-in chest, etc.)
Dressing in a way that doesn't attract attention
Maintaining a vacant look while staring off into space
Hiding one's hands in pockets or behind the back
A lack of coordination (bumping into things, fumbling or dropping objects, etc.)
Movements that lack energy
Poor posture
A bent neck
Avoiding eye contact
Starting sentences but not finishing them
Giving one-word answers
Speaking in a monotone voice that lacks emotion or interest
Verbalizing self-blame: *I should have stopped her*, or *I deserve this.*
Giving a single nod rather than speaking an affirmation
Sagging back in a chair as if needing support
Arms that hang at one's sides
Asking for instructions or seeking approval before acting
A weak handshake or grasp
Avoiding people or bodily contact
Slack facial features
Shaking one's head while looking at the floor
Shrugging weakly
Pressing one's fist to the lips and closing the eyes
Rubbing one's legs or squeezing the knees while sitting
Placing one's hand against the forehead to support the head
Feet that point away from the person one is talking to (and toward an exit or source of safety)
Looking down at one's hands
Not asking for what one needs or wants
Difficulty making independent choices
Avoiding conflict and risk; choosing what is safe or known
Self-deprecation: *I'm useless,* or *You need someone better to do this job.*
Not asking questions
Following instructions blindly
Erratic pacing (when frustrated)
Twisting one's hands
A voice that cracks with emotion when one is pressured

INTERNAL SENSATIONS:
A heavy stomach
Ribs that seem too tight
Body fatigue
Feeling hollowed out

MENTAL RESPONSES:
Time seeming to slow down
A desire to be alone
Escaping into one's thoughts rather than engaging with the real world
Frustration with oneself
Thoughts of self-loathing and inadequacy

ACUTE OR LONG-TERM RESPONSES FOR THIS EMOTION:
Desiring guidance even with the smallest things
Blindly doing what one is told
Increased self-loathing, which may progress to self-harming
Being taken advantage of by those who notice one's weakness
Not attending to personal needs or pursuing meaningful personal goals

SIGNS THAT THIS EMOTION IS BEING SUPPRESSED:
Putting on a happy face
Referencing times when one was strong or victorious
Making empty threats: *He'd never say that to my face!*
Fighting back in small, though unsuccessful, ways
Fantasizing about sabotage or giving someone their comeuppance

MAY ESCALATE TO: Defeat (76), Resignation (224), Shame (240), Self-Loathing (236), Inadequacy (162)

MAY DE-ESCALATE TO: Uncertainty (264), Hopefulness (148), Determination (92), Satisfaction (230), Peacefulness (202)

ASSOCIATED POWER VERBS: Avoid, bend, bow, break, cave, cower, cringe, defer, deflate, drain, drift, droop, drop, fetch, follow, grovel, hide, mumble, obey, paralyze, report, resign, sag, scuff, serve, shrink, shrug, shuffle, slump, submit, surrender, weaken, yield

WRITER'S TIP: *If you want readers to connect with a point-of-view character's emotions, make him or her likeable, relatable, or vulnerable. This allows for empathy bonds to form.*

PRIDE

DEFINITION: Proper self-respect arising from a significant achievement, possession of an item, or involvement in a relationship

PHYSICAL SIGNALS AND BEHAVIORS:
A high chin
Shoulders held back
The chest thrust out
Standing tall with good posture, the legs spread wide
A gleam in one's eye
A knowing grin
Perfectionism
Watching others to see their reactions
Verbalizing the ups and downs that led to this point
Calling friends and loved ones to tell them about an accomplishment
Direct or intense eye contact
A booming laugh
A huge smile that shows a lot of teeth
Becoming talkative
Being generous with compliments
Using one's success to encourage others: *If I can do it, so can you.*
Lifting the heels and rising slightly to emphasize one's words
Steering or dominating the conversation
Becoming more animated when there's an audience
A grin that conveys secret knowledge
Thrusting oneself into the middle of an event or debate
A satisfied smile
Expansive movements
Hooking the thumbs into one's belt loops and thrusting the pelvis forward
Pulling in a deep breath
Ignoring or overlooking any flaws associated with the pride item
A preoccupation with one's appearance
Standing with the hands tucked into one's armpits, thumbs visible and pointing up
Flipping the hair back
Assuming a pose that's sexy or draws attention to one's best attributes
Appearing unaffected by what others think
Speaking first and thinking second (if at all)

INTERNAL SENSATIONS:
The feeling of being taller, bigger, and stronger
The lungs expanding to their fullest through deep, satisfied breaths

MENTAL RESPONSES:
Positive self-thoughts
Preoccupation with one's achievements or successes
A feeling of being able to conquer the world
Wanting to be surrounded by supportive loved ones
A desire to share achievements with others
A tendency to judge people according to one's personal measuring stick
Overestimating one's capabilities
Underestimating others
A sense of entitlement
Planning and seeking advantages
Being terrified of failure (if one is used to succeeding)
Thinking about how to exceed the expectations of others

ACUTE OR LONG-TERM RESPONSES FOR THIS EMOTION:
Enjoyment at proving others wrong
Bragging; obsessively talking about an achievement or material object
Praising group accomplishments to remind people of one's involvement
Reacting with anger or jealousy if one's reputation is impugned
Making radical statements or promises about future goals
Revisiting the source or place of accomplishment to feel empowered

SIGNS THAT THIS EMOTION IS BEING SUPPRESSED:
Waving off a compliment
Passing the credit to someone else
Turning attention away from oneself
Seeking others' opinions as a form of validation
False modesty

MAY ESCALATE TO: Smugness (246), Contempt (72), Confidence (64)

MAY DE-ESCALATE TO: Pleased (206), Uncertainty (264), Insecurity (166)

ASSOCIATED POWER VERBS: Bask, boast, brag, confide, confront, defend, deliver, disdain, dismiss, flaunt, laugh, preen, puff up, regale, smirk, sneer, strut, swagger, swell

WRITER'S TIP: *How comfortable is your character with the full range of emotions? Are there certain feelings they're afraid to show? Explore this possibility to add nuance to your character's emotional responses.*

RAGE

DEFINITION: Violent and uncontrolled anger

PHYSICAL SIGNALS AND BEHAVIORS:
Flushed or mottled skin
Shaking extremities
Hands that clench and unclench
Wide eyes, showing the whites
Spittle building up in the corners of the mouth
Biting criticism and belittlement
Jabbing a finger in someone's face
Nostrils flaring
Lips pulling back, baring the teeth
Cracking the neck from side to side
Muscles and veins straining against the skin
A guttural roar
Planting the feet wide apart
Sudden explosions over seemingly little things
Pushing and shoving
Limbering up the shoulders and neck as if readying to fight
Squeezing someone's arm to the point of bruising
Using insults to pick a fight
Pulling out a weapon, or finding something nearby to use as one
Moving slowly and deliberately toward another person
Barreling toward someone and uttering a scream or war cry
Fighting with no thought for one's safety
Throwing or kicking things, causing damage
Screaming
Threatening violence
Uttering death threats: *I'll kill you!*
Staring someone down to frighten them
Getting into someone's personal space
Manipulation

INTERNAL SENSATIONS:
A pounding in the ears
Increased blood flow to the extremities
Elevated pulse
A dry throat from rushed breathing
Pain that is suspended until later
Adrenaline rushing through the body
A sensation of increased strength
An edgy, twitchy feeling
Tunnel vision or flashes in one's vision

MENTAL RESPONSES:
Being driven by the belief that one has been mistreated or done wrong
A desire for vengeance
Looking for a fight
Wanting to hurt someone, to see blood
A sense of release when violence is expressed
Not thinking or caring about consequences
A need to dominate or control
Difficulty focusing or concentrating

ACUTE OR LONG-TERM RESPONSES FOR THIS EMOTION:
Beating someone senseless
Committing assault or murder
Seeking out opportunities to react violently
Self-destructive addictions
Depression
Heart disease and stroke
Ulcers
An inability to cope with smaller problems over time
Insomnia
Fatigue
Destroying property

SIGNS THAT THIS EMOTION IS BEING SUPPRESSED:
Unnatural silence
Uncontrollable body tremors
Pain in the jaw from clenched teeth
A tight smile that doesn't reach the eyes
Grabbing onto something secure (like a steering wheel) and shaking it violently
Punching or ripping apart something soft
Aggressive workouts

MAY ESCALATE TO: Vengefulness (272), Paranoia (200), Regret (214)

MAY DE-ESCALATE TO: Anger (40), Guilt (140)

ASSOCIATED POWER VERBS: Attack, bellow, break, charge, clench, clutch, explode, flush, glare, grab, hit, hurl, hurt, jeer, kick, roar, scream, seize, smash, swear, taunt, tense, threaten, throw

WRITER'S TIP: *As your character reacts emotionally to circumstances within the environment, don't underestimate the importance of sensory details. Do textures bother them because of a heightened state? What sounds do they pick up on that they might not otherwise notice?*

REGRET

DEFINITION: Sorrow aroused by circumstances beyond one's ability to control or repair

PHYSICAL SIGNALS AND BEHAVIORS:
Scrubbing a hand over the face
Laying a hand against the breastbone
A heavy sigh
A downturned mouth
Bent posture
Crossing the arms over the stomach
Heavy arms, the shoulders pulled low
Apologizing
Trying to reason or explain
Eyebrows gathering in
A pained expression
Staring down at one's feet
Squeezing one's eyes shut
Lifting the hands up and then letting them fall
Pinching the bridge of the nose, eyes closed
Wincing or grimacing
Rubbing the chest, as if one is feeling pained
Avoiding the victims
Seeking reconciliation; determination to set things right
Berating oneself for one's actions or choices
Losing the thread of conversations
Hiding behind one's hair
Shaking the head
A voice that loses its power
Using broken sentences or trailing off while speaking
Asking questions about the fallout: *How did she take the news?*
Scrambling to reverse what was said or done
Increasing one's distance from others
Trying to fade into the background at social events
Putting oneself down

INTERNAL SENSATIONS:
A knotted belly
Insomnia
An inability to fill the lungs completely
A nervous stomach
Loss of appetite
Dullness in the chest
A feeling of heaviness

MENTAL RESPONSES:
Feelings of inadequacy
Self-loathing
Obsession with the person or event associated with the regret
Reliving past events
Thoughts that turn inward
Trying to forget the event
A desire to go unnoticed
Distractedness

ACUTE OR LONG-TERM RESPONSES FOR THIS EMOTION:
Not taking physical care of oneself
Withdrawing from society
No longer finding joy in hobbies or favorite pastimes
Overcompensation in other relationships
Crying, sobbing
Drug and alcohol abuse
Unsafe sexual practices
A string of broken or abusive relationships
Ulcers
A lack of intimacy with others
An inability to forgive oneself

SIGNS THAT THIS EMOTION IS BEING SUPPRESSED:
Desperately seeking out new relationships
Talking about one's accomplishments as a way of winning people over
Making life-altering decisions (a career change, a move, etc.) as a way of starting over
Acting like the life of the party
Putting on a happy face

MAY ESCALATE TO: Shame (240), Frustration (134), Depressed (84), Self-Pity (238), Self-Loathing (236)

MAY DE-ESCALATE TO: Sadness (226), Embarrassment (118)

ASSOCIATED POWER VERBS: Avert, cry, deny, downplay, elude, evade, flinch, hide, isolate, minimize, murmur, stray, wallow, wander, wince

WRITER'S TIP: Watch for possible description crutches. Is the color green used too much? Does a sensory sound (like wind rustling through the trees) happen in multiple scenes? Keep track of these details to avoid overuse.

RELIEF

DEFINITION: The alleviation or lightening of oppressive stressors

PHYSICAL SIGNALS AND BEHAVIORS:
Covering the mouth with a hand
Shaking the head and closing the eyes
Gasping
Trembling hands
Reaching out to another for comfort
Slumping posture
A slow smile
Using humor to lighten the moment
Shaky laughter
Sagging against a wall or person
Pressing the palms to the eyes
Asking for the good news to be repeated
Wobbly legs
Buckling knees
Stumbling back a step
Flopping back in a chair
A gaping mouth
Struggling to speak, to find the right words
An unsteady walk
Crying or calling out in release
Asking redundant questions to assure that the moment is real
Eyes going up, looking heavenward
Letting out a huge breath
Rocking back and forth
Eyes shining, locked on the source of relief
A slight moan
Lips parting
Showing kinship with the people involved (hugging, reaching for their hands, etc.)
Pressing one's hands to the stomach
A palm pressed to the heart
A bowed head
Starting to fall, then catching oneself
Closed eyes and compulsive nodding
Letting the head fall back
Uttering a soft curse or thanking God
Making the sign of the cross (if one is religious)

INTERNAL SENSATIONS:
Dry mouth
Weak muscles
An unexpected release of all tension
Tears welling up behind the eyelids
A sudden lightness or giddiness

MENTAL RESPONSES:
Wanting to be held
A desire to be still and let the relief sink in
Gratitude
Jumbled thoughts
An inability to formulate an appropriate verbal response
Postponement of residual loss or pain until a later time

ACUTE OR LONG-TERM RESPONSES FOR THIS EMOTION:
Breaking down and crying
Exuberant responses (jumping up and down, shouting, running, hysterical crying, etc.)
Collapsing
An expanding feeling in the chest
Light-headedness
A thick throat

SIGNS THAT THIS EMOTION IS BEING SUPPRESSED:
A deliberately quiet exhale
Briefly closing the eyes
Drawing a deep breath through the nose
Biting the lips to keep from smiling
Swallowing and nodding
Narrowed eyes (when it's necessary to focus on something besides the source of relief)
Not thinking about it; putting it off to savor later
Inattentiveness

MAY ESCALATE TO: Happiness (142), Excitement (126), Gratitude (136)

MAY DE-ESCALATE TO: Uncertainty (264), Confusion (68), Worry (284)

ASSOCIATED POWER VERBS: Beam, cave, clutch, collapse, crumble, crumple, droop, exhale, faint, fall, laugh, shake, sink, slump, smile, sob, squeal, thank, tremble, weaken

WRITER'S TIP: *When a character is hiding an emotion, the cues are not as noticeable. In this circumstance, it's often more effective to show the emotion through change—altering a speech pattern, falling back on habits, posture shifts, etc.*

RELUCTANCE

DEFINITION: Unwillingness; aversion

PHYSICAL SIGNALS AND BEHAVIORS:
Stalling gestures, such as taking time to think or turning away
A hard, obvious swallow
Wetting the lips
Tense arms, shoulders, or face
Hesitant steps
The head pulling back as the shoulders push forward
Responding slowly
Pressing the lips together
Glancing around uneasily
Hands that shake; nervous twitching
The hands almost curling into fists and then straightening
A grimace or pained look
Eyebrows squeezing together
Stuttering and stammering
Making excuses or lying
Tentatively reaching out or touching someone
Holding a hand up, warding someone or something off
Suggesting someone else to help or act instead
Shaking the head
A hand fluttering to the lips or neck
Nervous habits (running hands through the hair, pacing, repetitive gestures, etc.)
A too-quick smile
Glancing at one's watch
Jumpiness
Taking a steeling breath before responding or acting
Moving toward an exit
Putting distance between oneself and the requester
Biting the lip or nails
Pinching the bridge of the nose and tightly squeezing the eyes
Changing the topic or diverting attention
Closed body language (hands up, crossed arms, etc.)
Leaning or turning away from the person making the request
Asking for time to make the decision
Expressing skepticism
Asking questions for clarification
Not meeting the requester's eyes
Making suggestions for a better option: *Tim's so good with clients, though. Why not ask him?*
Answering with a *Maybe* response
Muttering negatives: *No,* or *I don't want to.*

INTERNAL SENSATIONS:
A tightening chest
Slight tenseness in the muscles
A heaviness in the stomach

MENTAL RESPONSES:
A desire to get away from the person making the request
Indecision
A mind that is clearly distracted
Guilt
Searching for ways to get out of whatever is requested
An inability to focus on anything but the decision to be made
A need to justify one's reluctance

ACUTE OR LONG-TERM RESPONSES FOR THIS EMOTION:
Resentment
A tight or roiling stomach
Avoidance of the source
A strained relationship

SIGNS THAT THIS EMOTION IS BEING SUPPRESSED:
Agreeing, then not following through
Hints about being busy or overly stressed
A rising antipathy toward the person responsible for the situation
Passive-aggressive comments
Deflecting (e.g., making jokes)
Acting as if the request is absurd
Revealing one's true feelings to a third party, hoping they'll pass the information along

MAY ESCALATE TO: Skepticism (244), Defensiveness (78), Anger (40), Fear (128), Disgust (102), Resentment (222), Dread (110)

MAY DE-ESCALATE TO: Resignation (224), Satisfaction (230), Relief (216)

ASSOCIATED POWER VERBS: Avoid, balk, dawdle, defer, divert, feign, gulp, hedge, procrastinate, protest, put off, refuse, resist, second-guess, shuffle, squirm, stall, stammer

WRITER'S TIP: *Avoid brand-dropping to characterize. Brand names come and go and can date your writing. Instead, use other clues to convey your character's personality, strengths or shortcomings.*

REMORSE

DEFINITION: Distress resulting from guilt over wrongdoing; a desire to undo or fix

PHYSICAL SIGNALS AND BEHAVIORS:
Heartfelt apologies
Asking to talk
Following the aggrieved party
Repeatedly returning to the scene where a past event took place
Keeping the head down as the eyes look up
Watering eyes
A hand that cups the mouth
Holding one's head in one's hands
Tears that one does not try to hide or control
Silence
Offering restitution or making promises
Using the victim's name in dialogue when they are present
Telling the unvarnished truth
Speaking without hesitation when answering
A quivering chin
Holding the stomach
Shoulders that curl over the chest
Not defending oneself against attack (verbal or physical)
A crumpled body posture
Staring down at the floor
Clasping the hands together in the lap
Shaking
Begging for forgiveness
Shoulders that quake with repressed sobs
A pleading tone
A pale or unhealthy complexion
Dark circles under the eyes
Hollowed cheeks
Reaching out to touch and then pulling back, as if one isn't worthy
Readily agreeing to a punishment or pronouncement
A voice that cracks
Verbalizing responsibility for what happened
Giving quiet answers to questions
Arms hanging at the sides
Still hands and feet
Obedience
Breaking into sobs
Asking others for advice on how to make up for what happened

INTERNAL SENSATIONS:
A stomach that feels hard
A runny nose
Nausea
Gritty or dry eyes from lack of sleep
A lump in the throat

MENTAL RESPONSES:
Mentally berating oneself over an action or poor decision
Wanting to face the consequences
Obsessing over finding a way to repay the debt
Empathy for the other party and what they are going through
Being honest about one's role in the situation
Relief for owning up to wrongdoing

ACUTE OR LONG-TERM RESPONSES FOR THIS EMOTION:
Weight loss
Headaches
Heart problems
Self-destructive behaviors out of the belief that one does not deserve happiness
Desperation to balance the scales or resolve the situation
A complete life change (taking up charity work, finding God, etc.)

SIGNS THAT THIS EMOTION IS BEING SUPPRESSED:
Avoiding friends who are also culpable (if it was a group act)
Lying about one's feelings
Claiming that the victim was partly responsible
Making an excuse to leave
Dropping out of activities, school, or work on false pretenses
Moving away

MAY ESCALATE TO: Shame (240), Regret (214), Desperation (90), Determination (92), Devastation (94), Worthlessness (286)

MAY DE-ESCALATE TO: Shame (240), Regret (214), Desperation (90), Determination (92), Devastation (94), Worthlessness (286)

ASSOCIATED POWER VERBS: Apologize, beg, confess, cower, cringe, cry, grieve, grovel, implore, languish, muddle, pester, plead, seek, shrink, sob, surrender, voice, wish

WRITER'S TIP: *Description is clearest when a writer adheres to the real order of events in a scene. Show the action (stimulus), then the reaction (response), and a reader will clearly see how A leads to B.*

RESENTMENT

DEFINITION: Moral-centered anger arising from disrespect, unjust treatment, or unfairness

PHYSICAL SIGNALS AND BEHAVIORS:
A pinched mouth
Arms crossed over the chest
A flat look, the eyes narrowed
Scowling
Increasing one's personal distance from others
Complaining
Rudeness and sarcasm
Pouting
Catty behavior
Name-calling
A voice that rises in volume or intensity
Arguing
Looking past someone rather than at them
A hard expression
Arms straight, hands locked into fists
Refusing to be bought off through kindness or thoughtfulness
Shunning the source
A stiff stance
Purposely ignoring someone's conciliatory efforts
Muttering or cursing under the breath
Twisting the mouth; a soured expression
Belittling another's status or accomplishment
Tension in the neck and shoulders
Pointing and jabbing the air for emphasis
A curling lip, showing the teeth
A sharp, defined jaw line
The voice taking on a tart tone
Snapping at others
Sabotaging another's projects or actions out of a sense of being wronged
Talking behind someone's back; gossiping
An unkind smile
Shaking the head in disapproval but not saying anything
Balling the hands into fists
Walking out of the room
Spinning away in a huff and stomping up the stairs
Shutting a door with more force than is necessary

INTERNAL SENSATIONS:
Tension headaches

A tight chest
Constricting the throat
High blood pressure
Stomach troubles or ulcers

MENTAL RESPONSES:
Unkind thoughts toward the target
Frustration at unfairness or a lack of justice
Fantasizing harm or the downfall of another
Moodiness
Wanting to be alone
Fixating on a person or situation to the detriment of other relationships
A desire to bring others in and create a mob mentality of resentment
Becoming obsessed with fairness (noticing imbalances, always treating others equally, etc.)

ACUTE OR LONG-TERM RESPONSES FOR THIS EMOTION:
Weight gain
Illness
Insomnia
Arriving late, calling in sick, or refusing work shifts to avoid the source of resentment
High blood pressure
Seeking revenge

SIGNS THAT THIS EMOTION IS BEING SUPPRESSED:
Walking away
Keeping silent
Changing the topic to something safe
Putting on a smile
Pretending to move on while making plans to bring about justice

MAY ESCALATE TO: Bitterness (58), Contempt (72), Anger (40), Hatred (144), Jealousy (174), Defiance (80), Vengefulness (272)

MAY DE-ESCALATE TO: Acceptance (28), Hurt (156), Determination (92)

ASSOCIATED POWER VERBS: Accuse, attack, defend, fester, frown, fume, gossip, gripe, harbor, insult, pout, sabotage, scowl, seethe, snap, stew, sulk, undermine, vent

> **WRITER'S TIP:** *When you're exposing the reader to a new scene, person, or object, it can be useful to have some description or opinion delivered through a secondary character's dialogue. What they notice and how they respond provides an opportunity to characterize.*

RESIGNATION

DEFINITION: The state of surrendering, often with little or no resistance

PHYSICAL SIGNALS AND BEHAVIORS:
Sighing dejectedly
Slumped shoulders
Blank features
Stooped posture
Shuffling footsteps
Taking small steps
Tears
A monotone voice
Becoming less verbal over time
Dull eyes
A chin that trembles
Answering with a small nod
Sagging facial features
Limp hands and arms
Unwashed hair
Wrinkled and disheveled clothes
Disinterest in former hobbies or passions
Making oneself small (hugging oneself, squatting down, curling into the fetal position, etc.)
Avoiding eye contact
Being at a loss for words
Lethargically giving comfort to someone (rubbing their back, patting their shoulder, etc.)
A shake of the head
Tipping one's head back on the neck to look skyward
Agreeing, but without emotion
Leaning forward, elbows on the knees
Staring off at nothing
A hanging head
A loose jaw
A half-hearted shrug
A long exhale
Muttering and mumbling
Holding the head in the hands
Propping a cheek on a fist
Slowed reactions to stimuli
Grunting; giving one-word answers
Purposely closing the eyes, as if to process
Excessive sleeping

INTERNAL SENSATIONS:
A falling or dropping sensation

A sensation of emptiness
Feeling numb and heavy
A lack of emotion
Weakness in the muscles
Pain in the throat (because it's constricted)

MENTAL RESPONSES:
A determination to make the best of the situation (glass half full)
An inability to focus or concentrate
Feeling directionless
Confusion: *How did this happen?* or *What will happen to me now?*
The sense that nothing will ever be the same
Feeling powerless over the present or future
Believing that one has failed

ACUTE OR LONG-TERM RESPONSES FOR THIS EMOTION:
Depression
Retreating inward
Disconnecting from others
Doubting oneself; a decrease in confidence
Apathy
Becoming submissive; giving up control

SIGNS THAT THIS EMOTION IS BEING SUPPRESSED:
Whining and questioning
Offering token weak arguments
Squaring the shoulders but without any real force or strength
Offering a small display of anger
Acting like giving in was a choice, not the only option

MAY ESCALATE TO: Sadness (226), Disappointment (96), Defeat (76), Self-Pity (238)

MAY DE-ESCALATE TO: Acceptance (28)

ASSOCIATED POWER VERBS: Abandon, capitulate, cave, defer, deliver, droop, drop, end, evacuate, fade, forfeit, give up, mumble, murmur, nod, quit, recant, relinquish, sag, shuffle, sigh, slouch, slump, stare, submit, surrender, waste away, whisper, wither, yield

> **WRITER'S TIP:** *Too many emotional internalizations in a scene can slow the pace considerably. If the character's reflections are key to readers understanding what is being felt, try shifting some of these inner thoughts to active, realistic dialogue. It will increase the pace and still reveal the character's feelings.*

SADNESS

DEFINITION: Characterized by unhappiness

PHYSICAL SIGNALS AND BEHAVIORS:
A puffy face or eyes that appear red
Smudged makeup
Splotchy skin
Sniffing and wiping at the nose
Wincing or sighing
Speaking less; seeming too-quiet
A tearful or breaking voice
Staring down at one's hands
Stooped posture—a caved chest, lowered shoulders, etc.
A distant, dull, or empty stare
A flat, monotone voice
Difficulty participating in conversation, as if responding takes a great effort
Downturned facial features
Covering the face with the hands briefly before pulling them away
Arms hanging at the sides, slack
Crossing one's arms and holding onto the shoulders (self-comforting)
Slumping rather than sitting up straight
A heavy-footed walk
Wet, dull eyes
Bending forward, laying the head on the arms
Movements that lack energy
A trembling chin
Digging for tissues
Drawing the limbs close to the body
Staring down at one's empty hands
Making excuses for one's despondency: *I'm just tired,* or *Everything's fine, really.*
Decreased interaction with the world at large

INTERNAL SENSATIONS:
Hot or gummy eyelids
A scratchy throat
A runny nose
Soreness in the throat and lungs
Heaviness or tightness in the chest and limbs
Blurred vision
Lack of energy
The body feeling cold

MENTAL RESPONSES:
Feeling like time is slowing down

Difficulty responding to questions
An inability to see where the future might go
Turning inward; withdrawing
A desire to escape the sadness (through sleep, drink, companionship, etc.)
A need to be alone
Desiring comfort from others but not knowing how to communicate it
Avoiding the painful subject
Denial
Focusing on distractions (work, the problems of others, etc.) to avoid one's pain

ACUTE OR LONG-TERM RESPONSES FOR THIS EMOTION:
Crying
A loss of appetite
Losing all hope that something positive might come
Despondency
Struggling with motivation
Avoiding friends, since their positivity or happiness makes one feel worse

SIGNS THAT THIS EMOTION IS BEING SUPPRESSED:
Turning away
Halting one's speech to gain control
Biting the lip
Blinking
Clearing one's throat
Changing the subject
Sipping a drink or taking a bite to eat (to prove to others that one is stable)
Quivery smiles
A voice that sounds falsely bright
Focusing on alleviating another's pain rather than one's own
Excusing oneself to use the restroom or get a drink so one can be alone

MAY ESCALATE TO: Nostalgia (192), Depressed (84), Loneliness (176), Frustration (134)

MAY DE-ESCALATE TO: Somberness (248), Wistfulness (282)

ASSOCIATED POWER VERBS: Collapse, contract, cry, deflate, double over, drag, fall, internalize, loll, moan, obsess, quiver, recoil, rock, shake, shamble, shuffle, sniffle, stare

WRITER'S TIP: In dialogue, be on the lookout for where your character "thinks" instead of responding verbally. This leads to unnatural, one-sided conversations.

SAPPINESS

DEFINITION: Overly sentimental; feeling an exaggerated sense of happiness, connectedness, or romance

NOTES: Sappiness is similar to nostalgia in the way it manifests. But while the former is typically a result of happier emotions, the latter is more often associated with wistfulness and sadness. If that's the response you're seeking, please see the NOSTALGIA entry (191).

PHYSICAL SIGNALS AND BEHAVIORS:
Languid, contented movements
Showing more patience and tolerance; being more easygoing
Cocking the head to the side
The gaze going distant as one recalls a happy memory
Smiling broadly at the person or thing evoking one's feelings
Clasping the hands against one's chin
Being very touchy-feely
A blush in the cheeks (as one realizes how silly one is being)
Hugging someone often
Trailing one's fingers along favorite mementos
Snuggling or cuddling with someone
Nuzzling someone with one's head or chin
Running a hand up and down the person's arm or back
Tousling the person's hair
Walking with one's head on the other person's shoulder
Watching old videos or playing sentimental music
Sighing happily
Sending someone a letter or text message "just because"
Buying gifts for the person
Creating a personalized gift, such as a poem or playlist of meaningful songs
Cooking foods associated with the happy memory or person
Telling happy stories about the good old days
Verbalizing one's feelings: *Everything is perfect right now*, or *I'm so glad you're here.*
Wearing a silly grin
Eyes sparkling with unshed tears
The face turning rosy
A smile that quavers
A quivering chin, eyes shining with happy tears
Buying a certain kind of cologne, shampoo, or fabric softener because it reminds one of the other person's smell
Complimenting the other person
Having difficulty restraining oneself, even when the other person is not as responsive

INTERNAL SENSATIONS:
An effusion of warmth
An expanding feeling in the chest
Eyes prickling (tearing up)
Feeling energized or twitchy
The heart rate increasing when the person approaches
One's heart feeling as if it's swelling or growing
Restlessness when one is distanced from the other person or thing

MENTAL RESPONSES:
The mind playing a loop of happy memories involving the person or thing
Being in a good mood
A sense of calm and contentment
Being highly focused on that person or thing
Exaggerating one's memories so they're wholly positive

ACUTE OR LONG-TERM RESPONSES FOR THIS EMOTION:
Being clingy or smothering
Going over-the-top for the person (giving hard-to-acquire gifts, throwing elaborate themed dinners, etc.)
Driving the person away with one's ongoing sappiness
Annoying others with one's constant reminiscing
One's feelings turning to sadness, frustration, or anger if one can't be with the other person
One's sappy feeling naturally returning to a more even-keeled emotion over time

SIGNS THAT THIS EMOTION IS BEING SUPPRESSED:
Not touching the other person, despite wanting to do so
Quickly glancing at or touching the thing that reminds one of the happy memory
One's attention drifting frequently; having to be pulled back on task
Always being near the other person
One's true feeling slipping through if the other person offers encouragement

MAY ESCALATE TO: Adoration (32), Longing (178), Euphoria (124), Confusion (68), Frustration (134)

MAY DE-ESCALATE TO: Despair (88), Satisfaction (230), Happiness (142)

ASSOCIATED POWER VERBS: Affirm, beam, clasp, cuddle, grasp, hold, hug, kiss, laugh, massage, smile, snuggle, spoil, spoon, squeeze, stroke, swoon, touch, tousle, twine

WRITER'S TIP: *One emotion to include in every story is hope. Without it, even the most carefully crafted fiction will contain a void that readers will notice and cause them to disengage.*

SATISFACTION

DEFINITION: The state of being content or fulfilled

PHYSICAL SIGNALS AND BEHAVIORS:
A high chin and exposed neck
A crisp nod
Smoothing the front of a shirt or tugging down the sleeves
Offering a thumbs-up
Giving a toast or praise
Clapping someone on the back
A wide stance—fists on hips, elbows wide, etc.
Surveying the finished product with a pleased expression
A raised eyebrow and a *See?* look
A sleek walk that draws the eye (catlike and deliberate)
A shy, confident, radiant, or cocky smile
Apt dialogue that sums up the situation perfectly
Saying *I told you so!*
A puffed-out chest
Shoulders back, straight posture
A fist pump
Clapping
Loud cheering or whooping
Fingers forming a steeple
Including others in the moment
Bragging
A hand casually anchored on the hip
Stretching the arms out wide
Leaning back, at ease and in control
A deep, gratifying sigh
Whistling or humming
A distant, unfocused smile
Taking deep breaths, savoring the moment
Unhurried, relaxed movements
A direct manner (eye contact, strength in the voice, etc.)
Offering congratulations where they are due
Rewarding oneself
Lingering near one's accomplishment (a person, place, event, or object) to bask in the feeling of a job well done

INTERNAL SENSATIONS:
A hyper-awareness of others and their reactions
A lightness in the chest
Warmth spreading through the body

MENTAL RESPONSES:
Happiness over a job well done
Euphoria and exhilaration
Contentment
Gratification
Increased confidence
Looking forward to a well-earned rest
Mentally fixating on the recent success
Not paying attention to one's surroundings
Self-congratulations
Generosity to others as a result of feeling gratified
A desire to tell everyone about the success

ACUTE OR LONG-TERM RESPONSES FOR THIS EMOTION:
Justified possessiveness
An expression of supreme confidence
A glowing countenance
Cockiness

SIGNS THAT THIS EMOTION IS BEING SUPPRESSED:
Twitching lips
Hiding a smile behind a hand
Bouncing lightly on the toes
Getting away at the first opportunity to tell someone the good news
Settling back in a chair in release

MAY ESCALATE TO: Happiness (142), Smugness (246), Pride (210), Gratitude (136)

MAY DE-ESCALATE TO: Unease (266), Indifference (164)

ASSOCIATED POWER VERBS: Applaud, bask, brag, cherish, clap, congratulate, delight, grin, linger, polish, relish, savor, smile, smirk, smooth, strut, swell, swing, toast

WRITER'S TIP: Loners and their lack of social interaction present specific writing challenges. To break up long stretches of introspection, maintain some character relationships. Remember that a person can be lonely even when surrounded by people; use the dialogue, dysfunction, and drama that go along with those relationships to keep the pace moving forward.

SCHADENFREUDE

DEFINITION: Malicious enjoyment from the suffering or unhappiness of others

PHYSICAL SIGNALS AND BEHAVIORS:
A sneer, followed by a bark of laughter
Squinting (from the force of one's grin)
Fingers that alternately flex and curl into fists
The face and neck flushing with pleasure
Having a wild-eyed look
Tipping the head back
An unkind smile spreading slowly over the face
Pumping one's fist at the sky
Chuckling unpleasantly
One's chest rising and falling as breaths come quicker and faster
Rubbing the hands together
Drawing out one's words: *Would you look…at…that!*
Verbally kicking someone when they're down: *You'll never fit in here.*
Nodding one's head rapidly
Wetting the lips
Bouncing in place or shifting from one foot to the other
Seeking to benefit from the situation—e.g., making a bet against the victim
Looking the person up and down with a disgusted expression
Standing back and watching with an intense gaze
Egging on whoever is doing the hurting
Joining in the attack on the victim
Savoring the moment with one's friends (shaking heads scornfully, giving high fives, etc.)
Muscles that quiver and shake
A muscle tic jumping in the cheek, jaw, or neck
Clapping and jeering
Asking questions designed to make the person squirm: *You did prepare for this, right?*
Mumbling or muttering under the breath: *Yeah, do it,* or *Couldn't happen to a nicer guy.*
Crossing the arms so firmly the fingers dig into the biceps
Squatting down to get on the same level with the victim
Watching raptly but silently, the fingers steepled in front of one's mouth
Relishing a secret's reveal: *Mom, did you know it was Jess who backed into your car last week?*
Not responding to requests for help
Toying with the victim—e.g., reaching out a hand as if to help, then jerking it back
Catching the victim's eye and making a fake "pouty" face
Talking about the experience later with friends

INTERNAL SENSATIONS:
A flush of warmth through the body
Feeling light-headed with adrenaline
An expansive feeling in the chest

A heady rush of power; feeling invincible
A buzzing sensation in the extremities
Twitchy muscles
Weakness in the knees as the adrenaline wears off

MENTAL RESPONSES:
One's focus narrowing on the victim; everything else fading away
Fantasizing about participating in the victim's misfortune
Feeling vindicated (if one had been mistreated by the victim in the past)
Wanting to continue the feeling of satisfaction by engaging in other harmful activities
Justifying one's feelings by blaming the victim or recalling their faults

ACUTE OR LONG-TERM RESPONSES FOR THIS EMOTION:
Yelling oneself hoarse
Profuse sweating
Decreased empathy for people in general
Wanting more (and more extreme) pain for the victim
Becoming sexually aroused (sadism)

SIGNS THAT THIS EMOTION IS BEING SUPPRESSED:
A smile that one tries (and fails) to restrain
Making eye contact with the victim and shrugging with a smile
Looking away (breaking eye contact)
Darting glances at others to see their emotional states before reacting
Positioning oneself so one can witness the mistreatment without being seen
Claiming to have no knowledge of the situation
Making passive-aggressive or ambiguous comments: *Oh, you poor thing.*
Watching with a stony face that seems to be devoid of emotion

MAY ESCALATE TO: Elation (114), Hysteria (158), Vengefulness (272), Vindication (274)

MAY DE-ESCALATE TO: Conflicted (66), Doubt (108), Guilt (140), Shame (240)

ASSOCIATED POWER VERBS: Bash, bask, belittle, cackle, castigate, cheer, clap, crow, crucify, declare, delight, enjoy, flaunt, gloat, humiliate, jeer, lambaste, lord, mock, preen, pretend, relish, savor, scoff, shout, simper, smirk, sneer, snicker, taunt, titter, torment

WRITER'S TIP: *When you're trying to write a specific character's emotional reaction to a situation, remember that their core personality traits, past experiences, and deepest fears will steer their actions.*

SCORN

DEFINITION: Extreme contempt or derision; regarding as inferior

PHYSICAL SIGNALS AND BEHAVIORS:
A biting remark
Belittling comments that remind the target who has the upper hand
A smirk
A quick, disgusted snort
Looming over the target
Crossed arms and a wide stance
Sarcasm
A tight jaw
A harsh squint
A deliberate eyebrow raise and head tilt
Pulling down one's glasses and looking over the rims with a flat gaze
Flapping a hand in dismissal
Bullying tactics
An exaggerated eye roll or upward glance
Blowing out a breath that rattles the lips
Insulting the target in front of others
A thrust-out chest
An ugly twist to the mouth
Encouraging others to speak up against the target
Limited verbal responses, as if the target isn't even worth talking to
Laughter at the person's expense
A wrinkled nose
Flicking a hand in front of one's nose as if to get rid of a bad smell
A tight mouth, as if tasting something bad
Narrowed eyes
Staring the target down
Applauding in a deliberately false fashion
Projecting hurtful observations: *I'd be embarrassed if I were you!*
Ridiculing the person's beliefs
Anger at being touched or addressed by the target
Calling attention to the person's weaknesses
Ignoring the target
Speaking slowly to emphasize hurtful words
Leaving to show that the target is not worth one's time
Apologizing to others for having their time wasted by the target

INTERNAL SENSATIONS:
A puffed-up feeling
The rush of adrenaline at taking away another's power

Elevated body temperature
Increased heart rate

MENTAL RESPONSES:
Elation at delivering a blow to an opponent through dialogue or action
Anger
A desire to put the person in their place
Superiority
Arrogance

ACUTE OR LONG-TERM RESPONSES FOR THIS EMOTION:
Asking questions to further incriminate the target
Egging the target on
Picking fights
Forcing the target into circumstances where they're sure to fail
Gathering other like-minded people and encouraging their scorn
Seeking to hurt through a low blow comment

SIGNS THAT THIS EMOTION IS BEING SUPPRESSED:
A blank, emotionless face
Becoming unresponsive to questions or actions
Turning away
Shaking the head
A slight muscle jump in the cheek
A tightened jaw
Clamping one's lips tight to keep from saying anything
Making an excuse to leave
If pressed, stating that one's opinions will not be popular and it's better to stay silent

MAY ESCALATE TO: Anger (40), Hatred (144), Elation (114)

MAY DE-ESCALATE TO: Resentment (222), Pity (204)

ASSOCIATED POWER VERBS: Bark, belittle, bully, corner, demean, dismiss, disparage, expose, glare, goad, humiliate, insinuate, insult, interrupt, mistreat, mock, narrow, offend, pin, press, ridicule, scoff, shame, smirk, snap, sneer, snicker, snort, squint, taunt, trap

WRITER'S TIP: *When describing a character's emotional state, pay attention to their voice. Does it rise or drop in pitch? Get louder or softer? Grow rough or silky smooth? Changes in pitch and tone are great indicators for when a character is trying to hide their feelings from others.*

SELF-LOATHING

DEFINITION: Intense dislike or even hatred for oneself

NOTES: Self-loathing can manifest through seemingly contrasting behaviors. Some characters may seem guilt-ridden and deserving of pain, while others act aggressively to mask their feelings of self-hatred and low worth.

PHYSICAL SIGNALS AND BEHAVIORS:
Crying or often being on the verge of tears
Apologizing for failures and mistakes
Trying too hard to please
Looking to others for reassurance: *Is this right?* or *Should I do this?*
Having impossible expectations for oneself
Accepting punishments without question
Scrutinizing flaws (grabbing at a non-existent roll of fat, obsessing over pimples, etc.)
Believing the cruel words of others
Feeling guilt at experiencing pleasure or a happy moment
Walking with one's head down
Doing small things that hurt (scratching one's arm, pinching, digging a nail into one's flesh, etc.)
Self-sabotage (talking too much but being unable to stop, telling lies no one believes, etc.)
Slumped posture
Keeping one's arms tight to the sides, not taking up space
Avoiding social situations
Keeping a wide personal space barrier
Adhering to a routine
Dismissing compliments: *Someone else would have done a better job*, or *Are you kidding? My project looks terrible!*
Seeking out negative attention (e.g., drinking too much)
Being unresponsive or speaking very little
Wearing clothing that is unflattering or attracts the wrong sort of attention
Gesturing without energy (e.g., nodding toward something rather than pointing at it)
Verbalizing one's flaws: *I break anything I touch*, or *If I try and fix your hair I'll just ruin it.*
An absence of smiles and facial expressions
Taking stupid risks in the hopes of being caught and punished
Adopting destructive habits such as pill popping, smoking, or drinking
Choosing friendships with negative people (who engage in mean gossip, bullying, etc.)
Being argumentative
Avoiding being touched
Using sarcasm to hurt others and keep them away

INTERNAL SENSATIONS:
Body aches and a feeling of heaviness

An upset stomach
Normal pains that one ignores (believing that the pain is deserved)

MENTAL RESPONSES:
Negative thoughts: *I'm so stupid*, or *I mess everything up.*
Envying others, then feeling guilt for wanting what they have
Constant self-critical assessments: *I can't wear this shirt. Look at my scrawny arms!*
Desiring connection but feeling unworthy: *Who am I kidding? She wouldn't look twice at me.*
Having little motivation to make one's life better
Focusing intensely on one's emotional or physical pain
A desire to escape or disappear

ACUTE OR LONG-TERM RESPONSES FOR THIS EMOTION:
Developing an eating disorder
Self-mutilation, such as cutting
Thoughts of suicide
Suicide attempts
Overmedicating with drugs or alcohol
Being trapped in a lifestyle where one is devalued (in the sex industry, with an abusive partner, etc.)

SIGNS THAT THIS EMOTION IS BEING SUPPRESSED:
Overachieving (setting high goals but taking no pleasure in meeting them)
Pushing oneself past reasonable limits as a form of punishment
Avoiding people and relationships
Hoarding behaviors

MAY ESCALATE TO: Depressed (84), Despair (88)

MAY DE-ESCALATE TO: Worthlessness (286), Insecurity (166), Conflicted (66), Hopefulness (148)

ASSOCIATED POWER VERBS: Abuse, belittle, blame, bully, curse, degrade, despise, discredit, hate, humiliate, mock, punish, ridicule, sabotage, scoff, shame, taunt

WRITER'S TIP: *Regret is a difficult emotion, one that is felt both in the moment and in the long-term. What old regrets have power over your character, steering their actions and decisions? Think about how these can become part of the story so your character can learn to let go of them.*

SELF-PITY

DEFINITION: A self-indulgent preoccupation with one's problems or complaints; feeling sorry for oneself

PHYSICAL SIGNALS AND BEHAVIORS:
An overall downcast countenance
Frowning
Flaccid or sagging muscles
Rounded shoulders
Slumped posture
Shuffling footsteps
Plodding or trudging along
Eyes that lack sparkle or shine
Deep sighs
A flat, emotionless voice
Sitting slouched in a chair, the head propped on one's hand
Sleeping too much or not enough
Doodling on paper or sketching shapes with one's finger on a desk
Complaining about one's circumstances
Dissolving into tears over one's situation
Becoming more animated when one is discussing one's problems
Being unable to laugh at oneself; taking oneself too seriously
One-upping others: *Oh, you think that's bad? I'd trade places with you any day.*
Fishing for compliments
Posting cryptic social media messages to encourage sympathy and attention
Not fussing with one's appearance
Withdrawing from others
Seeking comfort from others; needing validation
Melodramatic responses to circumstances
Apathy toward other people and their problems
Trying to pull others into one's drama
Frequently calling friends to "help" one through a difficult situation
Blaming others for one's misfortunes; not taking responsibility for one's own actions
Always turning the conversation back to oneself
Constantly talking about past glory days (before everything went sideways) instead of focusing on the way ahead and improving one's situation
Railing against perceived enemies (a certain person, a group of people, God, etc.)
Self-destructive behaviors, such as drinking excessively or abusing medication
A tendency to overreact and personalize things (e.g., viewing an innocent slight as an attack)
Overindulging to boost one's mood (shopping for a pick-me-up gift, eating treats, etc.)

INTERNAL SENSATIONS:
A feeling of heaviness that won't lift (the physical manifestations of emotional pain)

MENTAL RESPONSES:
Difficulty empathizing with others
Comparing one's situation with other people's
Believing that one is being persecuted or targeted in some way
A sense of despair; believing that things will never get better
Always seeing the bad in situations
Believing that the worst-case scenario will come to be
Not seeing one's reality clearly; being prone to exaggeration
Believing untruths about oneself (that one is incapable, a victim, stupid, etc.)
Craving a happier path but being afraid to pursue it (fear of failure and hurt)

ACUTE OR LONG-TERM RESPONSES FOR THIS EMOTION:
Becoming isolated
Becoming codependent on those who offer sympathy and support
Purposely or subconsciously making choices that ensure a negative outcome (so one can continue to feel sorry for oneself and receive sympathy from others)
Becoming depressed
Losing friends who are drained by one's constant negativity
Giving up on long-term goals or dreams because one believes they're out of reach
Bitterness and resentment
Self-loathing (if one recognizes the unhealthy need for other peoples' validation but feels unable to change)
An inability to move forward because one is so focused on past slights and unfairnesses

SIGNS THAT THIS EMOTION IS BEING SUPPRESSED:
Inquiring about other people's problems and feigning interest in them
Forcing oneself to socialize with others
Not talking (to avoid calling attention to one's problem)
Smiling and laughing a lot
Speaking in a bright and happy voice
Being purposely animated in one's movements and gestures
Not mentioning one's problems but being negative about other things

MAY ESCALATE TO: Worthlessness (286), Defeat (76), Depressed (84), Self-Loathing (236)

MAY DE-ESCALATE TO: Insecurity (166), Powerlessness (208)

ASSOCIATED POWER VERBS: Blame, brood, cling, complain, drown, excuse, falter, forfeit, grieve, gripe, grouse, justify, lament, mope, mourn, pout, stew, sulk, wallow, whine

WRITER'S TIP: *When working to evoke an emotional response from readers, choose words with care. Language choices will color the mood and influence what readers feel as they read.*

SHAME

DEFINITION: The feeling that arises from a dishonorable or improper act; disgrace

NOTES: Not all shame is deserved; many victims of violence and abuse feel shame when they are, in fact, blameless. Even when a feeling of shame is unfounded, it will present the same way.

PHYSICAL SIGNALS AND BEHAVIORS:
Cheeks that burn
Crumpling onto a chair or sofa
Pulling one's arms and legs in toward the core
Muttering *What have I done?* or *How could I let this happen?*
Using the hair or a ball cap to hide the face
Pressing one's hands against the cheeks
Dropping the chin to the chest
Eyes that are wet with tears
An inability to meet another's gaze
Crumpling under scrutiny
Shaking, trembling, and shivering
A perpetual slouch
A closed-off stance (crossing the arms, making oneself small, averting the head, etc.)
Pressing a palm over the lips to hold back a cry
Shaking the head
Letting out an uncontrolled moan
Punching one's fists against one's thighs to release frustration
Lashing out at others to transfer anger or blame
Arms hanging at the sides
Hitching breaths
A trembling chin
Shielding the body
Angling away from those bearing witness to the shame
Pulling and tugging at one's clothes to make one less visible
Vandalism of one's own things (self-punishment)
Loss of interest in one's personal appearance
Seeking out second chances (fawning, begging, following others, etc.) to regain self-worth
Lying or doing whatever it takes to keep a shameful secret

INTERNAL SENSATIONS:
Hypersensitivity to noise, crowds, and activity
Flu-like symptoms (nausea, sweats, tingling in the chest, etc.)
Weak knees
Thickness in the throat
Heat and tingling in the face
Body tremors

MENTAL RESPONSES:
Flight reactions
Pulling away from friends and loved ones
Avoiding familiar places and activities
Self-loathing, berating oneself, anger, and disgust
Risk-taking behaviors; hoping something will happen to balance the scale
An utter lack of self-confidence
A desire to fade into the background and avoid notice
Believing that people are watching and judging (if the shameful event is a close-kept secret)

ACUTE OR LONG-TERM RESPONSES FOR THIS EMOTION:
Self-violence (scratching, cutting, pulling hair, etc.)
Depression
Substance abuse and eating disorders
Increased sexual activity
Panic attacks or anxiety disorders
Perfectionistic tendencies to balance the source of shame
Seeking power as a means of self-validation
Denial; diverting blame to others
Suicide
Abusive relationships
Attempting to change one's appearance
The belief that one deserves pain
Rejecting help out of a desire to do penance

SIGNS THAT THIS EMOTION IS BEING SUPPRESSED:
Engaging with others, yet showing discomfort (avoiding eye contact, fidgeting, etc.)
Holding oneself rigidly tall and upright
Taking deep, steadying breaths
An overly bright smile
Being unreasonably aggressive or confrontational
Overcompensating

MAY ESCALATE TO: Depressed (84), Humiliation (154), Remorse (220), Self-Loathing (236)

MAY DE-ESCALATE TO: Appalled (50), Defensiveness (78), Guilt (140)

ASSOCIATED POWER VERBS: Avert, clutch, cower, cringe, disguise, duck, flinch, hide, mask, quiver, retreat, self-harm, shake, shrink, sob, tremble, withdraw

WRITER'S TIP: *There are dozens of physical, internal, and mental responses to use when conveying a given emotion. Filter possible cues through what you know about your character. "Would my character react this way?" is a great question to ask to stay on the right track.*

SHOCK

DEFINITION: Lingering upset after experiencing a traumatic or fear-inducing event

PHYSICAL SIGNALS AND BEHAVIORS:
Taking a step or two back
Eyes widening or bulging
Body movements that freeze momentarily
Becoming speechless
Rapid blinking as one tries to process what one has seen or heard
The mouth falling open
Raising the eyebrows
One's head drawing back quickly
Covering one's mouth with the palm
A shaky or disbelieving voice
Not knowing where to look; a wandering gaze that doesn't settle
Pressing a fist to the mouth or pinching the lips between the thumb and index finger
Needing to sit down or lean against something for support
Rubbing one's forehead and shaking the head
Asking questions to better understand or cope with the news
Tears welling up at bad news
Turning away and shielding the face
Rubbing at one's eyes as if to reaffirm what one is seeing
Taking shaky breaths
Lightly holding or stroking one's throat in a self-soothing gesture
Rubbing or pressing down on the breastbone
Posture that crumples (shoulders falling and the chest caving in)
Stepping back from others to create space; needing a moment to process the information
Stuttering; struggling to find the right words
Pressing one's hands against one's ears
Shaking the head in denial
Stumbling or shambling
Forgetting what one was doing
Swaying slightly
Folding an arm against one's stomach
One's voice cracking or warbling with emotion
Voicing denial
Squeezing the eyes shut

INTERNAL SENSATIONS:
A sudden feeling of cold or a heaviness that expands in one's core
Muscles that go weak or numb
Feeling dizzy
Skin that tingles with discomfort
Light chest pain or a tightness in the chest

A heavy feeling in the stomach

MENTAL RESPONSES:
Refusing to believe the truth of what one has seen
Tuning out everything other than what has caused the shock
Replaying what one has seen (or imagining what one has heard)
Time seeming to slow down
Wishing something was not true or real
Wishing one could go back to a state of ignorance
Wanting to have a reason for what happened to better understand it

ACUTE OR LONG-TERM RESPONSES FOR THIS EMOTION:
Shutting down; emotional numbness
Fleeing the situation
Collapsing; one's body being unable to bear its own weight
Denial
Sobbing
Rapid swallowing to try and dispel a thick ache in the throat
Seeking comfort or closeness with others who are sharing the experience

SIGNS THAT THIS EMOTION IS BEING SUPPRESSED:
Eyes bulging before one can control one's expression
Muscles that stiffen involuntarily before one forcibly relaxes them
Busying oneself to appear indifferent about what has happened
Seeking a quick exit to avoid the scrutiny of others
Hands that tremble slightly
A sudden onset of clumsiness

MAY ESCALATE TO: Disbelief (98), Disgust (102), Anger (40), Humiliation (154), Anguish (42)

MAY DE-ESCALATE TO: Regret (214), Sadness (226), Resignation (224)

ASSOCIATED POWER VERBS: Ache, appall, back away, collapse, comfort, disbelieve, dread, drop, flinch, gape, grasp, hold, horrify, jerk, lean, numb, question, reach out, regress, regret, retreat, shake, shout, stroke, stumble, stutter, traumatize, tremble, weaken, weave

WRITER'S TIP: *Sometimes an unexpected emotion creates a gateway to a revelation, showing the character a deeper truth about a past event or offering them clarity in a current one. Spend time describing these moments because they often lead to growth and transformation.*

SKEPTICISM

DEFINITION: Feeling doubtful or incredulous

PHYSICAL SIGNALS AND BEHAVIORS:
Pursing the lips in thought
Tilting the head and pausing
Shaking the head
Pressing the lips into a fine line
Raising the eyebrows
Clearing the throat
Shrugging
Nodding, but with a tight expression to show one is not fully committed
A smirk or eye roll
A hand flap that dismisses the person or their idea
Demanding proof or evidence
Polite verbal opposition
A condescending smile
Muttering negatives: *I don't think so,* or *No way that would work.*
Restlessness (pacing, tapping fingers, clock-watching, etc.)
A tightness in the face
Rigid body posture
Rubbing the back of the neck without making eye contact
Narrowed eyes
Biting or chewing on one's lip
Gossiping with others; running a person down for their choices or ideas
Sniping remarks
Licking one's lips
Hemming and hawing
Referencing similar events from the past that did not pan out
Bringing up everything that could go wrong
A purposeful shiver or shudder
A heavy sigh
Walking away
Tapping a finger against the tabletop to drive a point home
Asking *Are you sure?* or *What if?* questions
A jutting chin
A silent look while crossing the arms
Wrinkling the nose like there's a bad smell
A quick exhale through the nose (a snort)

INTERNAL SENSATIONS:
Tightness in the chest
Increased heartbeat and pulse
Tense muscles

A flare of adrenaline, firing the brain to act

MENTAL RESPONSES:
Negative thoughts
Uncertainty
Homing in on flaws, either of logic or of a personal nature
A desire to change the speaker's mind or standpoint
Wanting to be around people with the same opinions

ACUTE OR LONG-TERM RESPONSES FOR THIS EMOTION:
Anger
Frustration and a loss of patience
Passive skepticism becoming more overt: *You're making a mistake.*
Looking for ways to discredit the speaker
A desire to shut the speaker up
The mind racing through possible arguments
Disbelief (that others can't see the truth)
Actively seeking to bring people over to one's way of thinking
Becoming argumentative

SIGNS THAT THIS EMOTION IS BEING SUPPRESSED:
Attempting to keep a neutral facial expression
Footsteps that drag
A quick widening of the eyes before schooling one's expression
Apologizing for not showing immediate support
Sitting still, hands clasped, mimicking interest and attention
Acting noncommittal: *Interesting idea*, or *That's something to think about.*
Suggesting a trial basis as a solution
Requesting more time to reflect
Suggesting that perhaps more thought or study is needed

MAY ESCALATE TO: Suspicion (254), Resignation (224), Fear (128), Scorn (234), Paranoia (200)

MAY DE-ESCALATE TO: Uncertainty (264), Confusion (68)

ASSOCIATED POWER VERBS: Argue, attack, challenge, deny, discredit, disprove, dispute, distrust, doubt, oppose, question, refute, smirk, sneer, snort, suspect, wrestle

WRITER'S TIP: *Don't make it easy for your heroes. Pile on the difficulties. Overwhelm them. Make it seemingly impossible for them to succeed so that when they do overcome, the reader will be properly impressed.*

SMUGNESS

DEFINITION: Supreme confidence in and satisfaction with oneself

PHYSICAL SIGNALS AND BEHAVIORS:
A jutting chin
Crossed arms
A thrust-out chest
Deliberately raised eyebrows
Cocking or tilting the head
A smirk or sneer
Direct, probing eye contact
Squinting and a hard smile
A dismissive nod or glance
Rolling the eyes
Aggressive teasing intended to put another in their place
A sigh conveying annoyance (a huff)
Waving a hand in dismissal
Leaning in aggressively, as if to challenge the other party
Rocking back on one's heels
Mean-spirited talk behind another's back
Projecting the voice to reinforce who has the upper hand
Sarcasm: *Whatever*, or *Sure you are*, or *If you say so!*
A look that radiates superiority
Perfect posture, shoulders back, an exposed neck
A determined walk, strut, or swagger
A loud voice, bragging, full of bluster
Using boisterous movements to draw attention to oneself
A wide stance
Criticism and belittlement
Talking over people and controlling conversations
Looking down one's nose at others
Dominant behavior (invading another's personal space, standing while others sit, etc.)
Lavishing praise on favored ones (children, friends, people in power, etc.)
An arrogant laugh
Preening (fussing with clothing, checking oneself in the mirror, etc.)
Wearing flashy or dramatic clothing
Tossing one's hair back
A shake of the head
Adopting a pondering pose (e.g., clasping the chin and tapping the lips with a finger)
Settling back in a chair with exaggerated casualness
Movements that draw attention (waving a cigar, gesturing with a glass of wine, etc.)
A deliberate crossing of the legs or clasping of the hands
Fidgeting with jewelry to draw attention to it

Name-dropping
Rubbing it in with an *I told you so.*

INTERNAL SENSATIONS:
Warmth radiating throughout the body
A puffed-up feeling
Tingling in the chest
The heart rate rising due to an adrenaline rush

MENTAL RESPONSES:
A firm belief in one's own rightness and superiority
Disdain for those who are unworthy
Overconfidence
A desire to belittle the unworthy and exalt one's own accomplishments
Gratitude at having risen above the rest
The belief that those who have not succeeded are to blame for their failure

ACUTE OR LONG-TERM RESPONSES FOR THIS EMOTION:
Extreme pride in appearance and possessions
Careful consideration of friendships, purchases, places where one is seen, etc.
Reminding someone of a past mistake to rub it in
Choosing to spend time in environments that are a reminder of success
Generosity that displays power (e.g., hosting charity functions)
Acting as if rules do not apply or one is above the law

SIGNS THAT THIS EMOTION IS BEING SUPPRESSED:
Making token acknowledgements to those who played a part in an outcome
Citing that luck was involved but not meaning it
Preachy advice: *Do what I did, and you'll succeed too.*

MAY ESCALATE TO: Contempt (72), Scorn (234)

MAY DE-ESCALATE TO: Disappointment (96), Doubt (108), Insecurity (166)

ASSOCIATED POWER VERBS: Bask, belittle, boast, brag, condescend, deign, demean, dismiss, display, dominate, flaunt, gloat, ignore, insist, jeer, loom, lord, patronize, preen, revel, show off, shun, simper, smirk, sneer, splurge, strut, swagger, taunt, tease, tower

> **WRITER'S TIP:** *When describing a character's feelings, the word "felt" is often a cue for telling emotion, not showing. Run a search for this word and challenge yourself on its use.*

SOMBERNESS

DEFINITION: A feeling of melancholy or gloom

PHYSICAL SIGNALS AND BEHAVIORS:
An unmoving stance
A voice devoid of emotion; deadpan
A grave expression (an inward gaze, lips pressed slightly, eyebrows close together, etc.)
A sad or serious demeanor
Hands folded in one's lap
Sitting quietly
Letting out a heavy sigh
Responding with a slow nod rather than speaking
Flaccid yet unwelcoming (closed) body language
A tendency to look down
Hesitating before speaking, as if weighing one's words
Dark or heavy observations
A bleak mood that affects others, lessens energy, or brings people down
Loose posture, the shoulders dropping
Speaking at the air rather than making eye contact with others
Gazing downward with the hands clasped loosely behind the back
A slow walk
Smooth, expressionless features
Keeping one's arms and legs in close to the body
Functional and precise movements
Unsmiling; humorless
Choosing one's words deliberately
Not reacting to stimuli (laughter, excitement, activities, etc.)
Drab, colorless clothing choices
A grim twist to the mouth
Sedate mannerisms; minimal or economical movement
Eyes that look dark or serious
Opening the mouth to speak and then closing it and shaking one's head
An unnatural stillness
Not responding when someone calls one's name
Using an arm to prop up one's chin, the fingers covering one's mouth
Being less enthusiastic about former enjoyments (food, favorite sports teams, etc.)

INTERNAL SENSATIONS:
Fatigue; lacking energy
Heaviness in the limbs or muscles
A weighed-down feeling
Slow and even breathing

MENTAL RESPONSES:
A subdued personality
A negative outlook
A desire to be alone
Difficulty engaging in conversation
Searching internally for answers rather than asking others
Losing track of time
Finding it hard to pay attention; getting lost in one's thoughts

ACUTE OR LONG-TERM RESPONSES FOR THIS EMOTION:
Accepting a negative outcome or realization
Becoming uninterested in hobbies or entertainments
Melancholy; gloominess
Shunning other people who are not of like mind
Inability to focus on the needs of others (children, family, etc.)
Being apathetic toward goals, desires, or upcoming events

SIGNS THAT THIS EMOTION IS BEING SUPPRESSED:
Forced laughter
A too-frequent smile
Smiles that quickly fade
Agreeing to attend happy social events, then not showing
Smiles that don't reach the eyes
Light words delivered in a serious tone
Adding an adornment (a pin, fancy hat, a bright scarf, etc.) solely for appearances

MAY ESCALATE TO: Depressed (84), Despair (88), Resignation (224)

MAY DE-ESCALATE TO: Indifference (164), Moodiness (184)

ASSOCIATED POWER VERBS: Avoid, brood, commiserate, complain, darken, defeat, deflate, despair, dim, dismiss, dwell, ebb, mope, mumble, mute, shrug, sigh, slack, worry

WRITER'S TIP: *If your scene includes a small dip into the past to retrieve information that has direct bearing on the current action, make sure there is an emotional component. Emotions are triggers to memory and help tie the present to the past.*

STUNNED

DEFINITION: Feeling mentally numbed or paralyzed, usually as a result of a shocking revelation or blow

PHYSICAL SIGNALS AND BEHAVIORS:
Going completely still
Standing with slumped shoulders
Arms hanging loosely at one's sides
Leaning on someone else
The mouth falling open
Absently licking the lips or wiping at one's mouth
Dull eyes
A flat gaze
One's facial muscles going slack
Glancing around without really seeing anything
Moving one's eyes (to take in the surroundings) while the rest of the body is still
One's head slowly swiveling as one glances around
Blinking slowly
Being physically led by others, as if one has lost the ability to move
Shuffling footsteps
Randomly picking up items and putting them back down
Sitting limply
Clutching an object (a purse, stuffed animal, a comfort item, etc.) firmly to the chest
Curling up in the fetal position
Not responding when one's name is called
Delayed reactions to a phone ringing, someone's touch, or other stimuli
Lying down with one's face to the wall
Sitting with elbows on the knees, hands covering one's face
Rubbing one's eyes
Stuttering or stammering
Voicing confusion: *It can't be possible. I don't understand.*
Forgetting what one was doing, mid-action
The eyebrows furrowing as one tries to understand what has happened

INTERNAL SENSATIONS:
A ringing in the ears
Muffled sounds, as if one is wearing earplugs
Dry eyes
A sense of paralysis; one's muscles feeling frozen
A heaviness in the limbs
A knot in the stomach
Nausea
Light-headedness
Seeing spots

MENTAL RESPONSES:
Blank thoughts, as if one's brain has stopped working
Thoughts swirling so quickly it's hard to follow them
Difficulty focusing
Emotional numbness
A sense of vertigo
Questioning what one has just learned or witnessed; feeling disbelief

ACUTE OR LONG-TERM RESPONSES FOR THIS EMOTION:
Falling into a catatonic state
Forgetting appointments, birthdays, and other notable events
Poor hygiene (wearing dirty or rumpled clothes, not bathing, etc.)
Not leaving home for long periods of time
Feeling out of it, as if one never quite knows what's going on
Missing work or school
An inability to focus on anything
Apathy about the future

SIGNS THAT THIS EMOTION IS BEING SUPPRESSED:
Fierce and deliberate blinking
Looking around (as if surveying the area) but not actually looking at anything
Breathing deeply through the nose
Fidgety hands and feet
Leaning against a wall or table (instead of collapsing to a sitting position)
Turning away from the source
Biting one's lip
Pressing the lips together
Asking a question completely unrelated to the cause of the emotion

MAY ESCALATE TO: Denial (82), Despair (88), Anguish (42), Panic (198), Hysteria (158)

MAY DE-ESCALATE TO: Disillusionment (104), Disbelief (98), Resignation (224), Sadness (226), Grief (138)

ASSOCIATED POWER VERBS: Blank, blink, collapse, crumple, drop, falter, forget, freeze, gape, hesitate, hunch, slacken, stammer, stare, stiffen, stumble, stutter, tense, topple

> **WRITER'S TIP:** *To make a villain relatable and layered, have them experience an emotion that shakes apart their hard exterior and briefly causes them to see life through an unbiased filter of hope.*

SURPRISE

DEFINITION: Unexpectedly struck with a feeling of wonder, joy, or fear

NOTES: Surprise can be negative or positive.

PHYSICAL SIGNALS AND BEHAVIORS:
The mouth falling open
Fingers touching parted lips
An incredulous stare or dazed look
Jerking the head back
Slapping the hands against the cheeks
A playful swat at a friend for causing the surprise
Shuffling back a step or two
A yelp, gasp, or squeal
Flinching and clutching one's fists to the chest
A sudden stiffening posture; rigid muscles
Stopping mid-stride or stumbling
Giddiness
Widening or bulging eyes
Doing a double take
A rise in vocal pitch
Grabbing a friend's arm
Hiding the face
Gripping the sides of the head as if to cover the ears
Spreading the fingers out in a fan against the breastbone
Touching the throat
A flush of red in the cheeks and neck
Turning away (negative surprise)
Pulling books or packages tightly against one's chest
Raising a hand to ward off others from approaching or speaking
A shaky, soft, halting, or disbelieving voice
A tentative smile that builds as surprise sinks in
A bark of laughter
Breaths that catch or hitch
Tipping or turning the head to the side

INTERNAL SENSATIONS:
Tingling skin
A racing heartbeat
A sudden coldness that hits at the core (if the surprise is negative)
Disorientation, dizziness, or euphoria
A fluttery feeling in the belly
A flush of adrenaline tingling through the body

MENTAL RESPONSES:
Wanting to hide
Fuzzy thoughts; an inability to think
Embarrassment; feeling exposed and on display

ACUTE OR LONG-TERM RESPONSES FOR THIS EMOTION:
Ducking; covering one's head with the arms
Collapsing from a perceived fright
Tears or shakiness
Jerkiness in the legs
Leaping back
Hands rushing toward the mouth to cover it
Letting out a sharp scream
Muscles tightening
Flight reactions (running away, hiding, etc.)
Fight reactions (shoving the initiator, delivering a punch to release anxiety, etc.)
Arms drawing back to the body core in a protective flinch
Stuttering or speechlessness
Swearing or shouting

SIGNS THAT THIS EMOTION IS BEING SUPPRESSED:
One's smile going stiff in an effort not to lose it (negative)
Rapid blinking
Widening eyes
Lifting the eyebrows
A closed-lipped smile
Nodding the head, as if one is not surprised at all
A quick tensing of the body
A split second where breathing is suspended
Tightening the grip on whatever is being held
Shaking out the hands once the initial shock has passed

MAY ESCALATE TO: Amazement (36), Happiness (142), Fear (128), Anger (40), Relief (216), Disappointment (96)

MAY DE-ESCALATE TO: Acceptance (28), Satisfaction (230), Confusion (68), Resentment (222)

ASSOCIATED POWER VERBS: Beam, catch, exclaim, flinch, flounder, gape, gasp, gawp, grab, grasp, jerk, jump, laugh, retreat, smile, squeal, startle, stumble, swear, yelp

WRITER'S TIP: *With emotion, never be afraid to try something new. Individual expressions should be genuine but unique.*

SUSPICION

DEFINITION: Intuitively suspecting that something is wrong

PHYSICAL SIGNALS AND BEHAVIORS:
Narrowing the eyes; squinting
The body angling away from the source
A wrinkled brow
Flushed skin
A deliberate lowering of the head to study or stare
Arms tight to the body
Shooting glances at the suspect or source
Avoiding direct eye contact
A fake smile
Sneaking or spying
Eavesdropping
Following the suspect
Retreating or keeping at a safe distance
Evaluating the subject's manner and appearance
Forced nonchalance to avoid the subject's notice (hands in pockets, etc.)
Crouching or leaning forward to get closer without being seen
Recording the suspect's activity and movement (taking notes, pictures, etc.)
A set jaw
Tilting the head while mentally weighing the evidence
Being confrontational: *What are you doing here?* or *What do you want?*
Openly expressing distrust
Crossing the arms
Legs that are wide apart
A raised voice
Trying to convince others of the suspect's guilt
Big movements (waving the arms while talking, counting arguments on one's fingers, etc.)
Swaying from side to side
Arguing with the suspect
Pacing
Biting the inside of the lip
Asking questions one already knows the answers to
Sarcasm: *So, you just happened to be there when my car's tires were slashed, huh?*
Questioning others as a way of gathering information
Googling the suspect
Avoiding a particular area or choosing a new route

INTERNAL SENSATIONS:
Quickened breaths
An adrenaline rush
A thumping heartbeat

The fight-flight-or-freeze reflex kicking in
A knot in the belly

MENTAL RESPONSES:
Listening intently to catch the suspect in their lie
Mentally running through everything known about the situation
Wanting to shield oneself and others from the person
Second-guessing oneself, fearing others will think one's concerns are irrational
Carefully preparing an argument or plan of attack
Weighing the danger level of the situation

ACUTE OR LONG-TERM RESPONSES FOR THIS EMOTION:
Obsession with the suspect or source
Stalking
Setting up the suspect in the hopes he will reveal his true self
Attempting to openly discredit or blackball the suspect
Contacting the appropriate authorities to express concern
Fantasizing about the day the suspect is finally exposed
Looking for changes to a location that will confirm one's beliefs about possible danger

SIGNS THAT THIS EMOTION IS BEING SUPPRESSED:
A slight nod
Hmms, as opposed to overt agreement
A flat tone of voice
Noncommittal answers
Avoiding the suspected person
Agreeing too quickly, too loudly
Over-the-top support: *I'm with you 100%,* or *I absolutely agree.*
Nervous movements (biting fingernails, twisting a shirt button, rubbing the neck, etc.)
Standing back from the suspect; not stepping into his circle of friends

MAY ESCALATE TO: Unease (266), Fear (128), Agitation (34), Anger (40), Paranoia (200)

MAY DE-ESCALATE TO: Acceptance (28), Uncertainty (264), Doubt (108), Wariness (280)

ASSOCIATED POWER VERBS: Argue, bait, catch, confront, creep, criticize, disprove, eavesdrop, examine, follow, furrow, lurk, narrow, peer, plant, pose, pretend, question, scrutinize, sneak, snoop, spy, squint, stalk, study, trail, trap, trick, undermine, watch

> **WRITER'S TIP:** *While it's tempting to let a character speak openly about their emotions in dialogue, it will raise a red flag for the reader. If you wouldn't say it in real life, don't let your character.*

SYMPATHY

DEFINITION: A sensitivity to the circumstances of others that results in a desire to offer support

NOTES: Sympathy and empathy are close in nature but aren't the same. Sympathy is felt more at a surface level, meaning a person can provide support without feeling personally invested. On the other hand, empathy is a deeper manifestation where a shared emotional experience makes the moment highly personal and meaningful. For ideas on the latter, please view the EMPATHY entry (119).

PHYSICAL SIGNALS AND BEHAVIORS:
Kind words spoken in a soothing tone of voice
Telling someone that it will be okay
Patting someone's back
Swallowing before speaking
Moving closer; entering another's personal space (if they are open to it)
Squeezing a hand and then letting go
Offering a deep sigh and thoughtful expression
An understanding nod
Eyes narrowing, the eyebrows pulling down in concentration
Asking what the person needs and how one can help
Offering the bright side: *At least now we know*, or *It could have been worse.*
Pulling someone against your shoulder (if the relationship is close)
Stroking or smoothing someone's hair
Clumsy attempts to comfort (a weak smile, an awkward hug, etc.)
Fumbling for words
Patting a leg in comfort
Offering a listening ear
Sitting in silence together because one doesn't know what to say
Phrasing questions in a positive way to make the other person feel better
Sitting with one's knees touching the other person's
Bringing a box of tissue or a cup of tea, unasked
Floundering hand movements
Handling distractions (answering the phone, etc.) so the other person won't have to
Apologizing—not out of accountability but to voice the unfairness of the situation
Offering the advice of a relative or friend: *As my uncle used to say…*
Fussing over the person's appearance while speaking in encouraging tones
Listening intently while ignoring discomforts (cold, rain, heat, etc.)
Listening with one's arms crossed over the chest
Leaning in awkwardly with the hands in the pockets, asking if things are okay
Looking elsewhere while listening, so as not to make the other person unduly uncomfortable
Offering to take the other person somewhere—a walk, a car ride, to hang out—as a distraction
Running defense for the person (making excuses on their behalf, telling people that their concerns can wait since the person needs a few moments, etc.)

INTERNAL SENSATIONS:
Feeling emotionally drained
An overall weighted feeling
A slower heartbeat
An ache in the throat

MENTAL RESPONSES:
Wishing one could alleviate the emotional pain
Uncertainty about what to say
Putting diplomacy above honesty
Forcing oneself to listen without judgment
Worrying that this event could happen again, particularly to oneself or loved ones
Seeing the contrast and having a sudden appreciation for one's good fortune
Offering up prayers on their behalf
A narrowed focus that allows one to solely concentrate on the other person
Relief that one is not experiencing the same challenges

ACUTE OR LONG-TERM RESPONSES FOR THIS EMOTION:
Obsessive thoughts on how to fix the situation
The mind turning often to the person
Employing clichés: *This too will pass, Keep your chin up*, etc.
Giving comfort through gifts or plying the person with food or attention
Devoting time, money, or energy into helping the person navigate this situation

SIGNS THAT THIS EMOTION IS BEING SUPPRESSED:
A hand that lifts towards the person, then lowers
Speaking often of the person or situation
Saying nothing overtly but privately praying for the person
Smiling or sharing a look but not offering verbal support
Watching at a distance, hoping for change

MAY ESCALATE TO: Empathy (120), Sadness (226), Love (180), Gratitude (136), Worry (284)

MAY DE-ESCALATE TO: Indifference (164), Denial (82)

ASSOCIATED POWER VERBS: Advise, cheer up, comfort, commiserate, counsel, dote, encourage, fuss, hug, listen, motivate, observe, pat, protect, smile, soothe, squeeze

WRITER'S TIP: *Emotions usually don't jump from mild to extreme in a short period of time. To gain the reader's trust, lay the proper foundation and show how stressors can lead to a greater intensity.*

TERROR

DEFINITION: A state of extreme fear

PHYSICAL SIGNALS AND BEHAVIORS:
Rasping breaths
Bulging eyes; an inability to blink
Full body tremors
Bolting out of hiding and rushing away from the threat
Screaming, crying, or blubbering
Speechlessness or incoherence
Holding oneself tightly (clutching the arms or wrapping the arms around the belly)
Squeezing one's eyes shut
Moaning and whimpering
Trembling chin and lips
Running away with no destination in mind
Shaking one's head, as if in denial
Clapping the hands over the ears
Crumpling to the ground
Retreating into the fetal position or curling up on the knees
Covering the face
Cringing, flinching, or jumping at sounds
Tense muscles and a rigid posture
Flaring nostrils
Grabbing another person, refusing to let go or leave them
Clumsiness (bumping into things, knocking things over, etc.)
Clutching the throat or chest
Clammy skin
A harried, wild appearance
Clawing at the cheeks, dragging the fingers down
Tremors in the hands and fingers
Copious sweating
Risking a lesser danger in order to escape
Causing self-harm (cuts, bruises, etc.) while trying to escape, and not noticing
Spinning around, trying to spot any and all danger
Backing away in quick, jerky steps from something or someone
Fight responses (a rush attack, using anything at hand to hit or destroy, etc.)

INTERNAL SENSATIONS:
Hyperventilation
A racing pulse
The sound of the heartbeat thrashing in the ears
A clenched jaw
High pain tolerance—not feeling or noticing injuries

Claustrophobia (even if one is not usually claustrophobic)
Pain in the chest, lungs, or throat
Weak legs
Increased sensitivity to every sound, touch, or change in the environment
Dizziness; seeing black spots

MENTAL RESPONSES:
A compulsion to look back (when fleeing)
Impaired decision making
A single-minded focus: to save oneself or someone else
Risk-taking
Surrender (if a breaking point is reached)
Hyper-vigilance
Thoughts that keep coming back to the worst possible outcome

ACUTE OR LONG-TERM RESPONSES FOR THIS EMOTION:
Passing out from a stress overload, lack of oxygen, or both
A mental break (humming, rocking, hands over the ears or eyes, etc.)
Heart attack
Post-Traumatic Stress Disorder
Hallucinations
A development of anxiety attacks, phobias, or depression
Nightmares
Substance abuse
Difficulties relating to others
Isolation

SIGNS THAT THIS EMOTION IS BEING SUPPRESSED:
Terror, by nature, is almost impossible to suppress or hide. Any attempt to hide terror would simply display itself as FEAR (128).

MAY ESCALATE TO: Panic (198), Paranoia (200), Anger (40), Rage (212)

MAY DE-ESCALATE TO: Fear (128), Wariness (280), Resignation (224), Satisfaction (230)

ASSOCIATED POWER VERBS: Blubber, bolt, clench, clutch, collapse, crumple, faint, freeze, gasp, hyperventilate, moan, quiver, run, scream, shake, shriek, stammer, startle

> **WRITER'S TIP:** *When conveying high emotion, keep the metaphors to a minimum. No matter how flowery or creative a character might be, in the midst of strong emotion, most people don't think in those terms. Keep it simple to maintain believability.*

TORMENTED

DEFINITION: Experiencing extreme mental distress because of one's closeness to a possible crisis or disaster

PHYSICAL SIGNALS AND BEHAVIORS:
Eyes going wide, being unable to blink, appearing haunted
Eyebrows pulled together, the crease deep and evident
A quivering chin
Dragging one's fingers down the cheeks
Covering the ears and rocking
Pressing the palms hard against the cheeks
The body quaking
Being unable to sit still
A strangled cry of frustration
A voice that breaks and sounds high pitched
Needing to move, pace, or destroy something
Clock-watching (or door-watching, text-watching, etc.)
Taking shallow, rapid breaths or gulping at the air
Rubbing the arms repetitively as if one is cold (a self-soothing gesture)
Gripping one wrist with the other hand and squeezing, using pain to focus
The posture collapsing, being unable to support one's weight
Clasping hands over one's head and bringing the elbows in tight
Pressing a fist against trembling lips
Slamming a hand into a wall; kicking, hitting, or destroying something for release
Wringing or dry washing one's hands
Gripping a symbol for comfort (holding a son's bear while waiting for news about the child's surgery outcome)
Running one's hands through the hair repeatedly
Needing to vocalize one's torment: *Waiting like this is destroying me!*
Grabbing fistfuls of hair and pulling (using physical pain to push back emotional pain)
Holding the stomach and doubling over
Massaging the throat to try and make swallowing and talking easier
Sensitivity to noise and touch (jumping, flinching, etc.)
Hands that shake and fumble
Pressing a fist against the chest and rubbing it as if to dislodge the pain
Lashing out, yelling, or screaming

INTERNAL SENSATIONS:
An upset stomach
Nausea
A restricted throat
Pain in the chest
Feeling cold all over

MENTAL RESPONSES:

Praying, even if one doesn't normally do so

Making mental bargains: *I'll give up whatever I need to for this to be all right.*

Feeling shame and unworthiness for not avoiding this situation or doing something to prevent the terrible outcome that may result

Feeling paralyzed by hopelessness, guilt, and dread

The sensation that time has slowed or stopped

One's mind embracing the worst-case scenario and playing it out

Feeling as if one will never move on from this moment and the pain will be eternal

ACUTE OR LONG-TERM RESPONSES FOR THIS EMOTION:

Being unable to eat or drink

Being unable to form words

Tears that won't stop

An anxiety attack

Arms tense and hands open as if holding a ball, shaking with extreme force

Mentally shutting down; being unable to cope

SIGNS THAT THIS EMOTION IS BEING SUPPRESSED:

Turning away from other people to hide one's emotions

The body quaking with the force of held-in sobs

Being unable to speak

Fingernails biting into the palms so one can focus on the pain

Finding a way to escape the situation so one can be alone to process it (flight)

MAY ESCALATE TO: Terror (258), Hysteria (158), Vulnerability (276)

MAY DE-ESCALATE TO: Stunned (250), Skepticism (244), Relief (216), Gratitude (136)

ASSOCIATED POWER VERBS: Beat, burn, clench, crush, cry, curse, grapple, grieve groan, hit, pummel, punish, quake, seethe, shake, shout, suffer, weep, worry, wring

WRITER'S TIP: *If you want readers to connect with a point-of-view character's emotions, consider how to make them likeable or sympathetic. This allows for empathy bonds to form.*

UNAPPRECIATED

DEFINITION: Feeling undervalued, as if others don't see or acknowledge one's worth or contribution

PHYSICAL SIGNALS AND BEHAVIORS:
Sticking to the background
Standing in corners or against the wall
Staying behind the rest of the people in one's group
An expectant look upon being addressed that fades when no acknowledgement is forthcoming
Not sharing one's ideas or opinions
Only speaking if one is directly addressed
Standing with rounded shoulders
Fingers nervously or absently fiddling—with one's hair, a cuff, a zipper fob, etc.
Taking quiet steps
Keeping one's arms and legs close to one's side
Making oneself small when sitting (crossing one's legs, placing hands in one's lap, etc.)
Responding eagerly when one is given attention or shown gratitude
Speaking in a soft tone
Becoming uncomfortable when others pay one attention
Struggling with compliments
Walking with downcast eyes and a low chin
Pointedly reiterating how hard one has worked or what one has contributed
Taking pains with one's appearance so one can garner attention
Taking on difficult jobs as a way of showing one's capability
Refusing to cooperate (living up to the expectation)
Sabotaging oneself; deliberately doing a job poorly
Seeking quiet vengeance on those who fail to appreciate one's work
Becoming subservient; losing one's sense of self
When slighted, talking about the offender behind his back to others
Developing a martyr complex
Muttering under one's breath
Pouting and sulking
Snapping at someone in anger and then regretting it
Lips pressing tight, the chin trembling in anger
Fishing for compliments or appreciation
Laying guilt trips: *I'm always picking up after everyone and you sit there like it's expected.*
Hitting one's breaking point and refusing to help when it's needed
Hanging around, waiting for someone to express gratitude
Being extra careful to show gratitude to others

INTERNAL SENSATIONS:
A sinking sensation in one's midsection
Shriveling up inside each time one is dismissed
A fluttering in the stomach in the presence of those who make one feel marginalized

Twitchy fingers
Nausea

MENTAL RESPONSES:
Believing that one's actions aren't worth validating
Feeling badly about oneself (negative self-talk)
Placing oneself lower than others on a hierarchy of worth
Thinking like a martyr

ACUTE OR LONG-TERM RESPONSES FOR THIS EMOTION:
Becoming angry and bitter
Being uncooperative at work, home, or school
Becoming a natural target for bullies
Not volunteering oneself for jobs or projects
Keeping secrets from the offender (a boss, a spouse, etc.) and feeling justified about it
Taking the jobs no one else wants to do, since it will allow one to maintain anonymity
Underachieving
Subjugating oneself to the will of others
Becoming a wallflower
Desperately trying to be noticed by others (through one's actions, clothing choices, etc.)
Not expressing appreciation to others

SIGNS THAT THIS EMOTION IS BEING SUPPRESSED:
Shrugging off the lack of gratitude as if one doesn't care
Not doing anything for anyone so one doesn't have to face the lack of appreciation
Clinging to the people who are appreciative
Suppressed signs of bitterness or hurt around those who don't show appreciation (pressing the lips together, exhaling noisily through the nose, rolling the eyes, etc.)

MAY ESCALATE TO: Betrayed (56), Anger (40), Bitterness (58), Defiance (80), Insecurity (166), Worthlessness (286)

MAY DE-ESCALATE TO: Uncertainty (264), Gratitude (136), Relief (216)

ASSOCIATED POWER VERBS: Avenge, avert, begrudge, fiddle, fidget, gossip, grumble, hide, lash out, mope, mumble, mutter, pout, resent, retreat, scowl, stutter, sulk

> **WRITER'S TIP:** *With emotions, a natural reflex is to try and maintain control. See how far you can nudge a character to the edge of restraint. When it's important, shove them beyond it.*

UNCERTAINTY

DEFINITION: The state of being unsure; unable to commit to a course of action

PHYSICAL SIGNALS AND BEHAVIORS:
Frowning
Glancing at others to see what they think
Looking down
Asking others for advice or opinions
Hands that fidget (twisting together, rubbing down the front of one's pants, etc.)
A downcast expression
The forehead wrinkling
Squinting as one looks inward
Pinching or tugging on the bottom lip
Tilting the head from side to side, weighing one's choices
Rubbing the jaw or back of the neck
Pushing the hair out of the face
An impatient huff
Shuffling one's feet
Hesitating mid-action (while reaching for something or pulling out a wallet, etc.)
Pulling back slightly
A grimace and a slight shake of the head
Asking questions to elicit more information
Making a *Hmmm* noise
Clearing one's throat
Swallowing
Stalling gestures, such as cracking the knuckles or sitting back in one's seat
Doodling on paper
Swaying or rocking on one's feet
Rubbing the lips or chin
Biting the inside of the cheek or bottom lip
Sighing
Rolling the neck
Tapping a pencil against a notepad or table
Jotting down notes to delay answering
A slumped posture—rounded shoulders, the head bowed, etc.
Staring at nothing for an overlong moment
Talking through the options aloud
Asking for reassurance

INTERNAL SENSATIONS:
Breaths that catch in the chest
Tenseness in one's stomach
Increased thirst

MENTAL RESPONSES:
Feeling trapped
Unease at one's options or choices
The mind racing through possibilities
A desperate need to find answers
Feeling flustered by a less-than-ideal situation
Making decisions, then second-guessing oneself
Shutting down; refusing to make a decision

ACUTE OR LONG-TERM RESPONSES FOR THIS EMOTION:
Self-doubt
Uncertainty that bleeds into other decisions and situations
Anger and frustration
Dismissing the situation without making a decision
Inability to make any decision on one's own
Researching (searching the web, speaking with professionals, etc.) to find answers
Going for a walk or leaving the situation in hopes of gaining a clear head
Repeatedly postponing or rescheduling events
An increased sense of desperation as time goes by and the situation is unresolved

SIGNS THAT THIS EMOTION IS BEING SUPPRESSED:
A delayed response
A noncommittal answer: *Maybe,* or *We'll see.*
Changing the topic to avoid hurt feelings or an argument
Diversion rather than open support
A hesitant nod
Stalling for time (e.g., pouring a glass of water and drinking it)
Refusing to answer; letting the silence do the talking
Opening one's mouth to argue, then stopping
Suggesting a vote of majority
Offering weak agreement or half-hearted support
Passive-aggressiveness

MAY ESCALATE TO: Denial (82), Doubt (108), Frustration (134), Unease (266), Wariness (280)

MAY DE-ESCALATE TO: Relief (216), Acceptance (28)

ASSOCIATED POWER VERBS: Deflect, dither, drag, fiddle, fidget, frown, pause, procrastinate, reflect, research, second-guess, shuffle, stall, suspend, vacillate, waver

WRITER'S TIP: *Maintain an overall perspective of emotional range as the story progresses from scene to scene. A strong manuscript will always expose the reader to contrasting emotion-*

UNEASE

DEFINITION: A restlessness of the body or mind

PHYSICAL SIGNALS AND BEHAVIORS:
Crossing and uncrossing the arms or legs
Shifting in one's chair
Twisting or pulling at clothing
Slipping one's hands into one's pockets
Sidelong glances while keeping the head still
Tsking or making a noise in the throat
Leaning away from the source
Making oneself smaller
Stopping to listen intently
Glancing quickly at the source of unease, then looking away
Chewing on a fingernail or picking at one's cuticles
Drawing the mouth into a straight line and biting the lip
Excessive swallowing
A shaky voice
Tugging clothes more firmly into place
Flipping the hair or combing one's fingers through it
Being unnaturally quiet
Throat-clearing
Frowning
Pushing food around on a plate
Gulping food down in order to escape more quickly
Trying to evade notice (slumping in a chair, withdrawing from conversation, etc.)
Turning slowly, unwillingly
Clutching an item tightly or holding it as a shield
Reluctantly speaking or approaching someone
Stilted, halting dialogue
Checking a cell for messages or to see the time
A swinging foot that suddenly goes still
Scrunching oneself up on a chair or sofa
Choosing a safe spot to wait
Flicking through a magazine without reading it
Consciously forcing one's limbs to relax
Licking the lips
Hands that won't settle
Crossing and re-crossing one's legs
Tightening the hands into fists, then loosening them
Rigid posture
Nervous habits (picking off nail polish, humming under the breath, etc.)
Rubbing sweaty hands down the front of one's jeans

INTERNAL SENSATIONS:
A slight chill or shiver
Hair lifting on the back of the neck
A prickling of the scalp
A quiver in the stomach

MENTAL RESPONSES:
The feeling of being watched
Denial: *There's nothing wrong,* or *Stop overreacting.*
Impatience
Time feeling like it's slowing down
Heightened watchfulness

ACUTE OR LONG-TERM RESPONSES FOR THIS EMOTION:
Shifting from foot to foot as one struggles to remain still
Pacing
An unshakeable sense of something being wrong
Needing to leave but not understanding why
Feeling physically ill

SIGNS THAT THIS EMOTION IS BEING SUPPRESSED:
Trying to slow one's breathing
Attempting to loosen up by rolling the shoulders
An unfocused gaze as one strives for mental calm
Wide eyes
A quick, false smile
Studiously not looking at the source
Keeping at a distance
Talking too fast
Pretending to be unaware of a loud argument or uncomfortable situation

MAY ESCALATE TO: Nervousness (190), Worry (284), Fear (128), Anxiety (48), Dread (110)

MAY DE-ESCALATE TO: Resignation (224), Acceptance (28), Relief (216)

ASSOCIATED POWER VERBS: Chafe, fidget, hesitate, pace, placate, quell, question, rub, scratch, sense, shift, squirm, stir, stutter, tap, touch, twist, voice, worry, wriggle

WRITER'S TIP: *To create a stronger reader reaction to emotion, remember to focus on showing what triggers the feeling, rather than only showing the character's response to it.*

VALIDATION

DEFINITION: Feeling that one's thoughts or opinions have been accepted or recognized as worthy

PHYSICAL SIGNALS AND BEHAVIORS:

A smile taking over one's face
One's breaths becoming more steady and deep
A brightening countenance
Expounding on the idea that was accepted; going into further detail
Nodding the head vigorously
Listening eagerly to others
Sharing one's ideas more readily
A lifting of the chin and shoulders
The chest puffing out
Standing taller
Looking people in the eye
Facing people squarely when speaking to them
Eyes narrowing as one tries to block out other noises and pay attention to the speaker
Leaning in when talking to others
Relaxing enough to sit or lean back while others are talking
Gesturing more animatedly with one's hands
Leaning on one's elbows while sitting at a table, hands clasped
Becoming still, as if not wanting to draw attention now that one has established oneself; playing it safe
A cessation of nervous gestures
Speaking in a steady, confident voice
Speaking quickly
Becoming more generous (thanking people, gesturing kindly, showing helpfulness, etc.)
An excited or enthusiastic tone
The glance darting upward as one recalls information
Eyes that are focused intently on others
Being honest and earnest when supplying answers
Joining groups as an equal (rather than standing behind or fading into the background)
Being more willing to argue or disagree with others
Hands gripping each other or being held behind the back, as if to keep them still
Replaying the moment of validation to others, or repeating one's words in other conversations
Jumping into conversation when one sees a chance to add something else
Trying to hide signs of excitement and act cool
Being at ease enough to take a sip or bite of something

INTERNAL SENSATIONS:
A jittery feeling of excitement
Adrenaline shooting through one's body
One's senses becoming highly sensitive
A rush of relief at finally having been validated
An expanding feeling in one's chest

MENTAL RESPONSES:
Looking for opportunities to insert one's knowledge into a conversation
Replaying the moment of validation in one's mind
Thinking of other things one could have said
Considering possibilities for pressing one's advantage (instigating more conversations with the same people, researching certain topics to become more knowledgeable, etc.)
Being seemingly focused on others while thinking of what one can say next
Feeling kinship and loyalty toward the one(s) who recognized one's worth
Thinking negatively about the people who have been dismissive in the past

ACUTE OR LONG-TERM RESPONSES FOR THIS EMOTION:
Becoming overly confident
Speaking without thinking and undermining one's credibility
Not pursuing further knowledge (because one has "arrived")
Feeling superior to those whose opinions or ideas don't measure up to one's own
Being motivated to learn and grow so one can repeat the experience

SIGNS THAT THIS EMOTION IS BEING SUPPRESSED:
Putting the hands in the pockets to look more relaxed than one feels
Being distracted due to one secretly going over the moment in one's mind
Disengaging (to avoid saying anything stupid and negating the previous success)
Asking questions (to stay involved while keeping the attention on others)

MAY ESCALATE TO: Relief (216), Satisfaction (230), Valued (270), Pride (210), Smugness (246)

MAY DE-ESCALATE TO: Uncertainty (264), Nervousness (190), Insecurity (166)

ASSOCIATED POWER VERBS: Add, argue, assert, brag, chat, discuss, engage, gesticulate, gesture, help, hobnob, mingle, offer, preen, pursue, strut, talk, wave

WRITER'S TIP: *If a tense situation occurs and your character remains unmoved, you risk causing readers to disengage because it won't feel realistic. Make sure characters always respond—even in a surprising way—to show they feel something. If they don't react, be prepared to adequately show why.*

VALUED

DEFINITION: Feeling worthy and cherished

PHYSICAL SIGNALS AND BEHAVIORS:
Standing strong, with the head held high
A purposeful stride
Taking a deep breath to center oneself and enjoy the moment
Smiling frequently and genuinely
Trying new things (not letting fear or doubt hold one back)
Politeness (saying *thank you* without hesitation, never interrupting others, etc.)
Becoming more talkative with others
Initiating conversations
Maintaining strong eye contact
Making time for people
Laughter
Being positive and upbeat
Taking up more space (the legs firmly planted, a relaxed pose with a hand on one's hip, gesturing while speaking, etc.)
An easygoing, relaxed manner
Transparency (not keeping secrets or holding back)
Not engaging in gossip
Nodding and smiling as people speak
Cheering others on
Touching people to make interactions more personal (hugging, bumping shoulders, holding hands, etc.)
Friendliness
Never asking others for more than one is willing to give
Thoughtfulness (offering compliments, giving gifts, volunteering one's time, etc.)
Being a good listener
Staying on task and being motivated; not procrastinating
Focusing on one's work and family with dedication and vigor (staying late or making good use of one's time)
Following rules without hesitation
Listening intently when others speak
Smiling in response to someone calling out one's name
Being comfortable giving or receiving friendly touches (e.g., a shoulder tap)
Taking pride in one's appearance (dressing neatly, having good hygiene, etc.)
Offering to help often (taking on extra work, running errands, vouching for someone, etc.)
Doing favors with no ulterior motives
Generosity
Standing up for oneself

INTERNAL SENSATIONS:

Easy breathing
A swelling feeling in the chest (lightness, tingling, etc.)

MENTAL RESPONSES:
Thinking about one's company, group, or country (whichever applies) and the good associated with it
Feeling blessed that one's path led to this place in life and the people in it
Wanting to give back and prove that the value is well placed
Feeling that one has found one's tribe
Longing to learn and gain new skills to better oneself
Wanting to give people what they want when they are deserving
A willingness to take more risks since others have one's back

ACUTE OR LONG-TERM RESPONSES FOR THIS EMOTION:
Working hard at a task; going the extra mile
Loyalty to those one serves
Feelings of well-being and satisfaction
Being open with one's ideas and opinions
A desire to get closer to people and build personal relationships
Wanting to pass the feeling on (letting others know they are appreciated and have worth)

SIGNS THAT THIS EMOTION IS BEING SUPPRESSED:
Needing reassurance or reinforcement before feeling secure: *Are you happy with my work?*
Creating situations where one will be praised if one is valued
Asking for feedback to better oneself: *What can I do better next time?* or *How can I help you more?*
Striving for recognition

MAY ESCALATE TO: Satisfaction (230), Pride (210), Confidence (64), Happiness (142), Smugness (246)

MAY DE-ESCALATE TO: Uncertainty (264), Insecurity (166), Hurt (156), Scorn (234)

ASSOCIATED POWER VERBS: Advise, beam, build, care, cherish, collaborate, congratulate, dedicate, empower, exchange, express, gather, help, improve, include, joke, laugh, listen, mentor, open, pat, please, share, smile, socialize, support, touch, trust, validate

WRITER'S TIP: *To engage a reader's emotions, put characters in real-world scenarios they may identify with: sibling rivalries, telling the truth but not being believed, unreturned affections, etc.*

VENGEFULNESS

DEFINITION: Vindictiveness; wanting to make someone pay for a past wrong

PHYSICAL SIGNALS AND BEHAVIORS:
Stiff posture and visible tension in one's muscles
An intense gaze; an unblinking stare
Tension in the jaw
Holding the chin up
Expanding the chest with a full breath, then holding it in
Flexing one's fingers or creating fists
Observing the target and biding one's time
Constantly venting to one's trusted circle about how one was wronged
Faking friendliness to get close to others and find weak points to exploit
Eavesdropping in the hopes of hearing something to use against the target
Discussing the target and possible revenge scenarios with one's supporters
Noting who and what the target cares about most
Creating connections with people around the target to find out information
Verbally criticizing the target when he or she is not around
Being two-faced
Lying easily and convincingly
Reading into what people say and do
Smirking
Rarely (if ever) apologizing for one's actions; viewing them as justified
Answering questions indirectly: *I might show up*, or *Good question. I'll let you know.*
Holding back information when it suits; enjoying the high of control
Taking purposeful strides toward the target
Invading the personal space of the target
Facing one's target directly and attempting to intimidate them (taking a wide stance, hands on the hips, strong gesturing, etc.)
Baring one's teeth slightly when interacting with the target
Offering false smiles and a forced tone
Stalking one's target (either physically or online)
Saying things to encourage self-doubt: *Worried about the meeting tomorrow? I would be.*
Verbally attacking one's target
Sowing dissent among the target's supporters: *She didn't tell you about the party? How odd.*
Making threats
Starting rumors about the target
Eyes that narrow or seem to flash with emotion when one is angered

INTERNAL SENSATIONS:
A rise in body temperature when the target is sighted
Blood rushing in one's ears
A heartbeat that quickens when one is near the target
Tightness or tingling in the chest

Muscles that tense up
Pressure in the jaw from clamping down
A rush of adrenaline when revenge is attained

MENTAL RESPONSES:
Obsessing about the target
Reliving the events that led to being wronged
Fantasizing about how to get even
Imagining the moment when one's target is brought low

ACUTE OR LONG-TERM RESPONSES FOR THIS EMOTION:
Violence
Stalking or following the person to intimidate or terrorize them
Destroying the target's property and cherished possessions
Involving the police (pressing false charges, making accusations—true or false—that will ruin them, etc.)
Taking revenge on innocents close to the target

SIGNS THAT THIS EMOTION IS BEING SUPPRESSED:
False friendliness (smiling, giving compliments, appearing to forgive any slights, etc.)
Adhering to one's normal routine as if nothing is amiss
Continuing to engage with the target as one historically has—spending time together, texting, hanging out, etc.
Strategically laying revenge plans so they can't be traced back to oneself
Patience in waiting for the right moment

MAY ESCALATE TO: Hatred (144), Rage (212)

MAY DE-ESCALATE TO: Doubt (108), Uncertainty (264), Defensiveness (78), Embarrassment (118)

ASSOCIATED POWER VERBS: Creep, damage, destroy, eavesdrop, envy, follow, gather, heave, hurt, infest, infiltrate, malign, plan, plot, prep, prepare, push, rage, retaliate, sabotage, scratch, slap, smash, sneak, squeeze, stage, stalk, terrorize, twist, wait, want

WRITER'S TIP: *To put readers on edge, key into their own fears. A loved one not checking in when they should, finding the front door open and unlocked, an airplane crash on the news when one has to travel…these types of shared fears can impact a reader more deeply.*

VINDICATION

DEFINITION: Being proven right, absolved of guilt, or set free

PHYSICAL SIGNALS AND BEHAVIORS:
Standing tall
Holding one's head high
The chest being thrust out proudly
Drawing big, chest-expanding breaths
Throwing one's head back with the eyes closed, relishing the moment
Smiling easily and broadly
Laying a fist over one's heart and keeping it there for a moment
Using the hands to cover one's smile, as if afraid to let it out
Shedding happy tears
Dancing or jumping in place
Nodding or closing the eyes while pressing together one's trembling lips
Celebrating with loved ones (hugging, grabbing them, spinning them around, etc.)
Whooping and yelling
Clapping one's hands
The posture sagging (tension letting go) before stiffening again to support the body
Speaking in a louder, brighter tone
Having an open body posture (arms flung out wide, legs apart, head thrown back, etc.)
Taunting one's enemies; rubbing the victory in their faces
Bowing one's head in a silent prayer of thanks
Pumping the fists
Taking a victory lap
Squatting down and hugging oneself
Expressing cautious hope (if one is skeptical and has been disappointed before)
Constant smiling
The voice rising in pitch
Speaking out in circumstances where one wasn't previously comfortable doing so

INTERNAL SENSATIONS:
A rush of adrenaline
Heart flutters
Feeling highly energetic; needing to move
A lack of sleepiness
A sense of exhaustion as the realization hits that one can finally rest in safety and peace
Euphoria
Being washed with a wave of peace and contentment
The face feeling stretched from nonstop smiling

MENTAL RESPONSES:
Having an optimistic outlook

Noticing details one missed before
Scattered thoughts
Difficulty focusing on any one thing
A renewed sense of faith in God, humanity, the system, etc.
A cessation of fear at the realization that the future is brighter for oneself and one's children

ACUTE OR LONG-TERM RESPONSES FOR THIS EMOTION:

Becoming braver; taking on opposition or challenges one wouldn't have before
Attempting to help others who might need vindicating
Seeking further reparations
Increased self-confidence
Positive personal changes (eating healthier, taking time for oneself, etc.)
Getting cocky
Becoming an inspiration for others
Thinking about the future when one was previously unable to do so

SIGNS THAT THIS EMOTION IS BEING SUPPRESSED:

A hidden smile that keeps trying to break through
Forcing one's body to be still
Clasping one's hands to keep them from twitching
Keeping the head down to hide any telltale signs
Taking calming breaths
Turning away or making a quick exit
Biting one's lip to keep from speaking
Lessened productivity due to the distraction of this meaningful victory
Sharing darting glances with the people who are on one's side

MAY ESCALATE TO: Confidence (64), Euphoria (124), Satisfaction (230), Fearlessness (130)

MAY DE-ESCALATE TO: Anger (40), Defeat (76), Despair (88), Determination (92), Disappointment (96), Discouragement (100), Disillusionment (104), Emasculation (116), Frustration (134), Hopefulness (148), Powerlessness (208), Resentment (222), Resignation (224), Skepticism (244)

ASSOCIATED POWER VERBS: Beam, celebrate, clasp, congratulate, dance, expand, flourish, give thanks, hug, jump, party, revel, sag, shout, sigh, swell, whirl, whoop

WRITER'S TIP: *Some emotions, like confusion, should be shorter-lived or paired with another feeling. If the POV character is disoriented for too long, readers may struggle to follow what's happening in the scene.*

VULNERABILITY

DEFINITION: Having one's guard lowered; feeling emotionally exposed

NOTES: Vulnerability can be a positive, negative, or mixed experience. A vulnerable person who feels fear may display protective gestures while a hopeful person purposefully making himself vulnerable may express more optimistic or open actions. It is also common for a character to progress from protective to open movements if he feels safe.

PHYSICAL SIGNALS AND BEHAVIORS:
Ducking one's chin to hide the neck
Avoiding eye contact or struggling to maintain it
Clasping one's arms in a self-soothing gesture
Shallow breaths
A quiet voice
Hesitations in speech
Holding the elbows tightly at one's sides
Using small movements
Eyes that widen slightly
Rubbing one's hands against one's clothing to dry them
Toying with one's necklace, watch, etc. to release nervous tension
Avoiding answering certain questions, or answering indirectly
Changing the subject
Visible swallowing
Wetting one's lips
Taking a hesitant step forward
A nervous smile
Tentatively placing a hand on someone's arm or shoulder to test the connection
Making self-deprecating comments in jest to lighten the mood
Increasing one's personal distance by taking a step back
Covering one's wrists
Taking a deep breath before doing or saying something that reveals one's vulnerability
Closing one's eyes for a moment before putting one's shoulders back and engaging
Taking extra care with one's appearance
Hesitating before moving closer; reaching out tentatively
Over-preparing for an event—excessive rehearsing of a speech, for example
Asking a personal question that allows someone an opportunity to be vulnerable in return
Hunching one's shoulders or curling up to take up less space
Clasping the hands in front of the groin or other sensitive area
Slightly turning one's body rather than facing others directly

INTERNAL SENSATIONS:
A tingling in the chest
A fluttering stomach
A dry mouth

The chest tightening
Bodily heaviness
Muscle tension

MENTAL RESPONSES:
Thoughts that flit between trust and worry, creating debate over the best course of action
A desire to trust or give in
Wanting to close the distance or touch another to feel safe or connect on a personal level
A desire to flee
Being open to suggestions
A desire to be honest and transparent but fearing what it will bring

ACUTE OR LONG-TERM RESPONSES FOR THIS EMOTION:
Forming deep, authentic relationships
A deep sense of self-acceptance
Not letting fear limit one's life choices
An ability to be intimate with others
Sharing secrets, ideas, and fears with the people one trusts
Achieving self-acceptance and viewing the ability to be vulnerable as a strength
Opening up too much and putting oneself in emotional danger

SIGNS THAT THIS EMOTION IS BEING SUPPRESSED:
Acting tough (false bravado, bragging, etc.)
Pretending not to care (having a closed body posture, a tight jaw, breaking eye contact, etc.)
Lashing out with insults, picking fights, or hurting others before they can hurt oneself
Verbal denial: *Oh, I'm fine, really. Everything's good.*
Changing the subject to something safer and less personal
Fleeing the situation
Lying and deception

MAY ESCALATE TO: Happiness (142), Satisfaction (230), Powerlessness (208), Defeat (76), Insecurity (166)

MAY DE-ESCALATE TO: Relief (216), Surprise (252), Disappointment (96), Embarrassment (118)

ASSOCIATED POWER VERBS: Accept, acknowledge, admit, allow, care, choose, communicate, confess, connect, contribute, encircle, forgive, foster, gift, give, hesitate, invite, join, lean, link, offer, open, press, reach, reveal, share, touch, trust, welcome

WRITER'S TIP: *If your character holds in emotion, at some point, these pent-up feelings will take a toll. Make sure that you follow-through with an explosive reaction or show the detrimental fallout in other ways (damaged relationships, a health crisis, a mental break, or whatever applies).*

WANDERLUST

DEFINITION: A desire to explore, travel, and experience the unknown

PHYSICAL SIGNALS AND BEHAVIORS:
Eyes that are bright and engaged
The head moving frequently to take in one's surroundings
Good posture (shoulders back, the chest out, etc.)
Having a light step
An upbeat expression and genuine smile
Holding the head high
Taking one's time (stopping to smell the roses)
Struggling with rules and guidelines
Wanting to be outside rather than inside
Spontaneity
Having an easygoing nature
Introducing oneself first
Being resourceful with one's money (frugalness)
A willingness to take risks
Being able to prioritize well
Open-mindedness to almost everything
Taking road trips or excursions whenever the chance presents itself
Avoiding too much planning
Having no patience for fussy people
Trying new things without feeling self-conscious
Being always on the move rather than sitting or standing in place
Spending time in nature (hiking, exploring, practicing photography, etc.)
Reading about other cultures, locations, ways of life, and self-development
Being highly curious: *I wonder what plants would grow at the top of a mountain?*
Frequently bringing travel into one's conversations
Becoming more animated when discussing adventures (moving one's hands, smiling, etc.)
Asking other people about where they've been and what they've experienced
Being unmaterialistic and happily getting by with less
Prizing experiences instead of things
Seeking out like-minded people
Being the first to try things
Having an ever-expanding comfort zone
Downplaying travel-related dangers to loved ones so they won't worry
Being independent (solving one's problems, not worrying about what others think, etc.)
Never second-guessing (because there are no wrong decisions, only experiences)
Building deep and lasting relationships on the road
Being forthright rather than secretive
Encouraging loved ones to take a leap into the unknown
Telling others about one's travel experiences (and sometimes dominating the conversation)

Enjoying trying new foods
Being sexually adventurous

INTERNAL SENSATIONS:
An expansive feeling in the chest (deep breathing)

MENTAL RESPONSES:
Always thinking about the next trip or experience
An unquenchable desire to learn and grow
Feeling antsy when one is stationary for too long (at work, where one lives, etc.)
Heightened senses
Having a strong imagination
Creative problem solving

ACUTE OR LONG-TERM RESPONSES FOR THIS EMOTION:
Becoming highly empathetic
Caring about the planet and becoming involved in advocacy
Confidence that increases with every experience
Feeling part of the world and something larger than oneself
Obtaining wisdom through cultural exposure and experiences
Becoming a globetrotter
Knowing more than one language
Blending the practices and traditions of other cultures into one's own

SIGNS THAT THIS EMOTION IS BEING SUPPRESSED:
Surfing travel blogs and websites
Collecting pictures of the places one wishes to visit in the future
Studying other countries and cultures and sharing one's learning with others
Writing about adventure and discovery to have an outlet
Buying a travel backpack just to have it close

MAY ESCALATE TO: Anticipation (46), Elation (114), Satisfaction (230), Awe (54), Gratitude (136), Connectedness (70)

MAY DE-ESCALATE TO: Disappointment (96), Dissatisfaction (106), Homesickness (146)

ASSOCIATED POWER VERBS: Admire, anticipate, appreciate, behold, celebrate, crave, long, love, marvel, plunge, shine, stir, stun, taste, thrill, trek, uncover, unfold, wander

WRITER'S TIP: *With more subtle emotions, a "tell" can be an effective way to show that your character is uncomfortable or out of their element. Set it up early with a bit more detail so readers will recognize its importance.*

WARINESS

DEFINITION: Mistrust marked by caution and watchfulness; being alert to possible danger

PHYSICAL SIGNALS AND BEHAVIORS:
Cocking the head to the side
Eyes narrowing, as if in confusion
Pursing the lips
Lowering the brows
Cutting the eyes toward the source
Holding up the hands in a defensive stance
Speaking in a soothing, placating voice
Backing away
The posture perking up as awareness increases
Sidestepping while keeping one's gaze on the source
Actively listening for something
Lifting the chin
Keeping one's hands free
Taking note of possible exits
Being aware of what lies behind
Asking questions
Circling; approaching someone or something in a roundabout fashion
Slow, cautious movements
Speaking rapidly, with the intent of maintaining the status quo
Standing back and observing before jumping in
Stiffening and going still
A strained or tense voice
Flinching when touched
Hesitation
Biting one's lip or pressing the lips together
A probing gaze
Careful words
A furrowed brow
An inability to relax or smile
Rubbing at the forehead or temples
Gritting the teeth
A stern or serious expression
A jutting jaw
Being alert to sudden movements

INTERNAL SENSATIONS:
Increased adrenaline
Rapid heartbeat and pulse
Tense muscles

One's breath catching or stopping briefly
An intuitive feeling that something isn't right (hairs standing up, the skin prickling, etc.)

MENTAL RESPONSES:
The mind trying to discern possible danger
Trusting one's gut feelings
Defensiveness
Thoughts that race while one tries to make sense of the situation
Confusion
Difficulty committing fully to any action
A finely tuned sense of observation
Weighing the information one should share and/or choosing to hold back
Trying to see and hear everything at once
Thinking ahead to what might happen

ACUTE OR LONG-TERM RESPONSES FOR THIS EMOTION:
Increasing one's personal space
Positioning oneself to create a barrier (moving behind a table, etc.)
Arguing without aggression, only to provide insight
Scanning for potential weapons
Paying closer attention to other people's body language and tone of voice
Asking questions one knows the answers to in an effort to discern another's intent

SIGNS THAT THIS EMOTION IS BEING SUPPRESSED:
Standoffishness
Looking from lowered lids
Attempting to lighten the mood with a joke
A posture that suggests discomfort
Leaning away
Hesitation

MAY ESCALATE TO: Anxiety (48), Fear (128), Unease (266), Suspicion (254)

MAY DE-ESCALATE TO: Relief (216), Resignation (224)

ASSOCIATED POWER VERBS: Analyze, evade, falter, flinch, hesitate, hold back, inhale, interrogate, pause, prompt, recoil, sidle, stiffen, tense, test, tilt, watch, waver

WRITER'S TIP: When writing emotion, pull from your own past. Even if you haven't experienced what the POV character is going through, chances are you've felt the same emotion about something else. Draw on your personal experience and bring life to the story.

WISTFULNESS

DEFINITION: A yearning (tinged with sadness or regret) for change that one believes is likely out of reach

PHYSICAL SIGNALS AND BEHAVIORS:
A weak, pensive smile
Pressing the lips and glancing down
A far-off look
Growing quiet
Breaths that slow and deepen
The chin dipping slightly
A visible swallow
Letting out a sigh that is a mixture of hope and sadness
Voicing a thoughtful sentiment or yearning: *I wish it could be different, don't you?*
Holding oneself, arms crossed, and rubbing the forearms with one's thumbs
A slow nod while frowning slightly
Reaching out to another in solidarity (clasping their shoulder, taking their hand, etc.)
A voice thickening with emotion
Sharing a sad smile with someone who understands (and has the same yearning)
Laying one hand on top of the other
Talking to oneself (to process complicated feelings or draw comfort from words that one would not feel comfortable voicing around others)
Lightly clasping one's hands together
Light and happiness entering one's expression when remembering a past memory
Closing one's eyes and taking a deep, cleansing breath
Body posture softening, the spine curling slightly
Shoulders that lower or fall slightly
Leaving a task and sitting quietly for a moment
Gently crossing the ankles (while sitting)
Laying a hand on one's breastbone
Discussing what the alternate reality would look like with another
Verbalizing confusion at God's plan but having faith in it (if one is religious)
Lightly stroking the throat while one is lost in thought
Leaning back in a chair, the body relaxing during reflection
Briefly letting go of day-to-day concerns to stop, notice the world, and reflect on something deeper
Sharing a memory of a happier time when it seemed like an option or path was possible
Comforting oneself by applying optimism to the situation: *I would have chosen someone else to lead, but maybe he'll be good for the city.*

INTERNAL SENSATIONS:
A slight heaviness in the chest
Feeling a slight lump in the throat

A tingling sensation on the arms and nape of the neck
An increased sensitivity to temperature

MENTAL RESPONSES:
Briefly becoming lost in the past
Being triggered by symbols, sensory stimuli, etc. that remind one of the yearning
Wishing things were different
Daydreaming about an alternative reality
Feeling that one has settled; experiencing melancholy about the way things turned out
Remembering past difficulties and how things did eventually get easier (staying hopeful)
Thinking about life and one's place in a bigger, more meaningful way
Experiencing regret that one can't change the past

ACUTE OR LONG-TERM RESPONSES FOR THIS EMOTION:
Tears that come, unrestrained
A thickening in the throat that feels painful
Having difficulty reengaging with one's reality after periods of wistful thinking
Increased fantasizing about a life where things are different
A life marked by sadness and unfulfillment
Moving elsewhere to separate oneself from reminders of what could have been
Resolving to live a life unmarked by regret

SIGNS THAT THIS EMOTION IS BEING SUPPRESSED:
Voicing the good in one's life; focusing on what one has rather than what is missing
Clearing the throat to disrupt one's thoughts and return to the real world
Changing the topic or asking an unrelated question
Chastising oneself (or others) for daydreaming
Turning to a task and redoubling one's efforts (to keep the mind from wandering)

MAY ESCALATE TO: Longing (178), Dissatisfaction (106)

MAY DE-ESCALATE TO: Acceptance (28), Sadness (226)

ASSOCIATED POWER VERBS: Ache, bear, cherish, covet, crave, desire, dream, envision, envy, fade, fantasize, grow, imagine, itch, long, mourn, muse, need, pine, regret, remember, seek, speak, stare, struggle, subdue, thirst, wish, withdraw, wonder, yearn

WRITER'S TIP: *Does your character have a trait they take pride in? If so, create an emotional situation that causes them to doubt that trait or skill, leading to internal conflict.*

WORRY

DEFINITION: Mental distress that arises from disturbing thoughts, usually regarding some anticipated event

PHYSICAL SIGNALS AND BEHAVIORS:
Wrinkling the brow
Biting one's lip
Pinching the skin at the throat
Feet that bounce or tap
Pulling or twisting one's hair
Drinking too much coffee or smoking excessively
Circles under the eyes
One's eyebrows drawing together
Tossing and turning in bed; an inability to sleep
Asking too many questions
Stroking or rubbing an eyebrow
Rubbing one's hands on a pant leg
Lank or unwashed hair
Poor communication with others
Repeatedly rubbing the face
A gaze that flits around the room, never settling on a person or object for long
Clinging to loved ones
Taking deep breaths in an effort to calm oneself
Engaging in pointless activities to stay busy
Calling in sick
A stooped posture
Clutching at a sweater, purse, or necklace for comfort
Biting the nails or chewing on a knuckle
Smoothing and re-smoothing one's clothing
Clasping one's hands together
A stiff neck
Strained muscles
A pained or watery gaze
Clearing the throat
Blinking less (as if worried one might miss something)
Sitting, then standing, then sitting again

INTERNAL SENSATIONS:
A loss of appetite
A sensitive stomach
Heartburn or other digestive issues
Dry mouth
A constricted throat

MENTAL RESPONSES:

An unwillingness to leave a place of safety
An inability to focus
A need to control
Regret for a past action
Distancing oneself from others
Reading into things; overanalyzing
Assuming the worst-case scenario
Overprotectiveness
Irritability

ACUTE OR LONG-TERM RESPONSES FOR THIS EMOTION:
Weight loss
Premature gray and new wrinkles
Slipping grades at school or poor performance at work
Ulcers
Anxiety attacks
Panic disorders
High blood pressure
Heart disease
Increased sickness due to a compromised immune system
Insomnia and fatigue
Hypochondria

SIGNS THAT THIS EMOTION IS BEING SUPPRESSED:
Furtively watching the clock or door
Jumpiness
A strained or faked smile
Adopting new hobbies to distract oneself
Putting up a false front as if everything is okay
A shortened attention span
Humming that feels forced or fades quickly after it starts
Going about one's daily activities with the mind somewhere else

MAY ESCALATE TO: Wariness (280), Fear (128), Anxiety (48), Paranoia (200), Dread (110)

MAY DE-ESCALATE TO: Uncertainty (264), Unease (266), Relief (216)

ASSOCIATED POWER VERBS: Agitate, ask, clutch, complain, criticize, demand, droop, fiddle, fret, fuss, hover, investigate, mutter, nag, obsess, pace, pull, repeat, stew, twirl, twist

> **WRITER'S TIP:** *Weather details can add texture and meaning to a scene. Consider how a character's mood can shift because of the weather. It can also stand in the way of their goals, providing tension.*

WORTHLESSNESS

DEFINITION: Feeling devalued, unimportant, and insignificant

PHYSICAL SIGNALS AND BEHAVIORS:
An inward, pained look (eyes drawing closer, brow creased, slackness in the face, etc.)
Avoiding eye contact, looking down
Keeping one's hands hidden (in pockets, jammed into armpits, etc.)
Hesitating when speaking; having difficulty getting words out
Mumbling or talking in a soft-spoken voice
Low energy
Taking up as little space as possible
Collapsed body posture (shoulders that curl forward, the arms hanging limply, etc.)
Being non-reactive (expressing little emotion)
Shielding one's body (crossing the arms or gripping the opposite elbow with a hand, etc.)
Moving slowly (shuffling, dragging one's feet, etc.)
Self-soothing gestures (rubbing the arms, stroking a sleeve, etc.)
Showing surprise when someone engages and responding awkwardly, unsure of how to act
Craving connection yet avoiding social situations and events
Taking insults and bullying rather than challenge them
Flinching at criticisms and needing to escape
Withdrawing; wanting to be alone
Avoiding situations where comparisons are likely (feeling inferior)
Not expressing one's opinions due to the belief that they're invalid
Refusing to speak up or advocate for oneself
Underachieving or avoiding setting any goals
Refusing to ask for help due to the belief that one doesn't deserve it
Not taking care of one's health, hygiene, etc.
Frequently breaking down into tears
Watching oneself cry in the mirror to feel "seen"
Deflecting compliments by citing one's faults or failings instead
Self-deprecation
Feeling alone, even with other people
Giving up easily (expecting failure)
Saying yes to whatever is asked, even if it is unfair or causes hardship

INTERNAL SENSATIONS:
Eyes that grow hot
Heavy, dull pain throughout the body
Experiencing physical pain in the chest or stomach when imagining the future
An almost constant ache in the throat
Difficulty pulling in deeper breaths (tightness in the chest)

MENTAL RESPONSES:

Thoughts that circle failure, creating a self-fulfilling prophecy
Demoralizing self-talk: *Just shut up. No one cares about your ideas anyway.*
Consistently doubting one's abilities
Feeling inadequate in every way; yearning to be someone else
Being prone to envy and jealousy
Viewing any mistake (big or small) as confirmation of one's worthlessness
Feeling that others are judging one negatively (inferiority complex)
Becoming overwhelmed—even moved to tears—by beauty

ACUTE OR LONG-TERM RESPONSES FOR THIS EMOTION:
Constant fatigue
Poor performance at work or school
Seeking out anyone (even toxic people) who provide one with a sense of value
Cutting and other self-harming behaviors
Taking risks with one's life and leaving the outcome up to chance
Engaging in bad habits (drugs, unprotected sex, etc.) to cope and not caring about the effects
Depression
Suicidal thoughts or attempts

SIGNS THAT THIS EMOTION IS BEING SUPPRESSED:
Forming and sustaining dysfunctional or toxic relationships
Lowering one's standards and expectations
Pasting on a fake smile
Lying about one's life, activities, success, etc. to pretend one is someone "better"
Making excuses for the mean or abusive people in one's life
Pretending that one's kindnesses toward others are due to altruism rather than one's low self-worth

MAY ESCALATE TO: Shame (240), Depressed (84), Self-Loathing (236)

MAY DE-ESCALATE TO: Stunned (250), Neglected (188), Hopefulness (148), Insecurity (166)

ASSOCIATED POWER VERBS: Avoid, belittle, blame, cope, cringe, cry, detach, dismiss, disregard, expose, flinch, hate, hide, hunch, hurt, loathe, neglect, recoil, reject, reveal, shield, shrug, slump, sob, stoop, stress, struggle, suffer, undercut, weaken, weep

WRITER'S TIP: *If you aren't happy with an emotional response, change the setting. If the character is alone, put them around people. If they are with others, isolate them or take away their comfort zone.*

ADD COMPLICATIONS FOR YOUR CHARACTER WITH EMOTION AMPLIFIERS

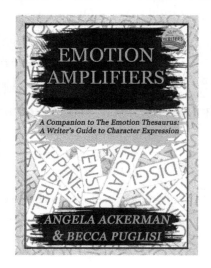

Did you know there's a companion to *The Emotion Thesaurus*?

While *The Emotion Thesaurus* was written to help authors convey character emotions to readers, there are also ways to amplify what a character is feeling, thereby heightening their responses. In *Emotion Amplifiers*, a complementary ebooklet to *The Emotion Thesaurus*, we explore common conditions that naturally galvanize emotion. Exhaustion, boredom, illness, pain, extreme hunger, and the like can push characters to their limits, compromising their decision-making abilities and decreasing the likelihood of them reaching their goals.

Emotion Amplifiers is a great tool for any writer wishing to tighten the screws on their characters and ramp up the tension in their stories. For your convenience, we've provided the following list of the amplifiers that can be found in this book, along with a sample entry so you can see how helpful this resource can be. For more information on all our publications, please visit the Writers Helping Writers' bookstore page (https://writershelpingwriters.net/bookstore/).

Addiction	Exhaustion	Lethargy
Attraction	Hangover	Overstimulation
Boredom	Heat	Pain
Cold	Hunger	Relaxation
Dehydration	Illness	Stress
Distraction	Inebriation	

SAMPLE ENTRY: PAIN

DEFINITION: physical discomfort associated with an injury or illness

Physical Signals:
Clenching or grinding the teeth
Probing, rubbing, or grabbing at the pained area
Wincing
Hobbling about; taking tentative steps
Eyes that water or cry
Flinching when touched
Leaning back and grimacing
Expelling a grunt or pained hiss at exertion
Asking for aid (to move, to get something, to call for help)
Medicating
Breaths that saw in and out
Flaring nostrils
Trying to sleep it off
Gripping people or nearby objects for support
A bent back, hunched shoulders
A stiff walk
Trembling limbs
Blotchy skin
Glassy eyes
Screaming, moaning, or groaning
Biting the lip
Rocking back and forth
Panting
Repeating the same phrase over and over
Distracting gestures (flapping a hand, tapping a foot, nodding the head)
Squeezing the eyes shut, refusing to look
Squirming in discomfort
Arching the back

Internal Sensations:
Shuddering breaths
Hyperventilation
Nausea
Light-headedness at the sight of blood
Starbursts behind the eyelids
Tight muscles
Dizziness
Fainting or blacking out

Feeling cold or feverish
A dry or coppery taste in the mouth
The body shutting down or going into shock

Mental Responses:
Panic
Attempting to calm oneself
Hallucinations
Short-temperedness
Trying to convince oneself that it isn't as bad as it seems
Bargaining with God

Cues of Acute or Long-Term Pain:
Begging for the pain to end
Making final preparations
Depression
A haggard face
Drooping eyelids and mouth
Dark hollows under the eyes
A pale complexion
Excessive sleep
Passing out
Medication dependency or addiction
Personality shifts
Asking for death
Researching, planning, or attempting suicide

Cues of Suppressed Pain:
Clenching the jaw
Whitened lips
Tension throughout one's body
Lying down
Remaining perfectly still
Avoiding talking to others
Sweat gleaming on the face
Hands clenching
Hands bunching up a blanket or clutching at one's clothing

Writer's Tip: *Each person has a different pain tolerance. Your character's personality and (in)ability to withstand pain will determine whether he would show open symptoms of pain or suppress them.*

RECOMMENDED READING

To read further on character emotion and how to convey it well, try these excellent resources.

The Definitive Book of Body Language is meant to help you personally read other people and enrich your communication—necessary information for any author wanting to effectively write body language, attitude, and emotions for readers. (Allan & Barbara Pease)

Characters, Emotion & Viewpoint provides you with the techniques you need to create characters and stories sure to linger in the hearts and minds of agents, editors, and readers long after they've finished your book. (Nancy Kress)

Creating Character Emotion will help you find fresh, creative images, words, and gestures to evoke feelings in your fiction. (Ann Hood)

Telling Lies: Clues to Deceit in the Marketplace, Politics, and Marriage discusses how a person's body language, voice, and facial expressions can give away a lie but still fool others—helpful information when you need to write a character who isn't being honest with others and with readers. (Paul Ekman)

ADD WRITERS HELPING WRITERS®
TO YOUR TOOLKIT!

Over a decade of articles are waiting to help you grow your writing skills, navigate publishing and marketing, and assist you on your career path. Sign up for blog updates to get expert craft advice from resident writing coaches delivered weekly to your inbox, stay informed about forthcoming books, and discover unique resources. You can also access even more practical writing tips by signing up for our Master Storytelling Newsletter at https://writershelpingwriters.net/subscribe-to-our-newsletter/.

PRAISE FOR...

THE EMOTION THESAURUS

"One of the challenges a fiction writer faces, especially when prolific, is coming up with fresh ways to describe emotions. This handy compendium fills that need. It is both a reference and a brainstorming tool, and one of the resources I'll be turning to most often as I write my own books."

~ **James Scott Bell, best-selling author of** *Deceived* **and** *Plot & Structure*

THE POSITIVE AND NEGATIVE TRAIT THESAURUSES

"In these brilliantly conceived, superbly organized and astonishingly thorough volumes, Angela Ackerman and Becca Puglisi have created an invaluable resource for writers and storytellers. Whether you are searching for new and unique ways to add and define characters, or brainstorming methods for revealing those characters without resorting to clichés, it is hard to imagine two more powerful tools for adding depth and dimension to your screenplays, novels or plays."

~ **Michael Hauge, Hollywood script consultant and author of** *Writing Screenplays That Sell*

THE URBAN AND RURAL SETTING THESAURUSES

"The one thing I always appreciate about Ackerman and Puglisi's Thesauri series is how comprehensive they are. They never stop at just the obvious, and they always over-deliver. Their Setting Thesauri are no different, offering not just the obvious notes of the various settings they've covered but going into easy-to-miss details like smells and tastes. They even offer to jumpstart the brainstorming with categories on potential sources of conflict."

~ **K.M. Weiland, best-selling author of** *Creating Character Arcs* **and** *Structuring Your Novel*

THE EMOTIONAL WOUND THESAURUS

"This is far more than a brilliant, thorough, insightful, and unique thesaurus. This is the best primer on story—and what *really* hooks and holds readers—that I have ever read."

~ Lisa Cron, TEDx Speaker and best-selling author of
Wired for Story* and *Story Genius

THE OCCUPATION THESAURUS

"Each and every thesaurus these authors produce is spectacular. *The Occupation Thesaurus* is no different. Full of inspiration, teachings, and knowledge that are guaranteed to take your writing to the next level, it's a must. You need this book on your craft shelf."

~Sacha Black, best-selling author of fantasy and the *Better Writing* series

THE CONFLICT THESAURUS, VOLUMES 1 & 2

"If characters drive the story, then conflict operates as the engine to every tale. Keeping this tenet in mind, writing experts Angela Ackerman and Becca Puglisi return with their most ambitious, hefty thesaurus yet, examining conflict in multiple dimensions and on multiple levels. Every writer should keep this volume handy as they work."

~ Ekta R. Garg, editor and author of *The Truth About Elves*

Curious about our books? Download samples of all the volumes in our special
Show-Don't-Tell Pro Pack, available at Writers Helping Writers®.
(https://writershelpingwriters.net/writers-helping-writers-descriptive-thesaurus-sampler-2/).

EVERYTHING YOU NEED TO CREATE
IN ONE PLACE

Ready for a game-changer?

In today's crowded market, only exceptional fiction gets noticed. So the authors of this book created One Stop for Writers—a go-to web app that will activate your imagination and provide the story support you need to create stronger, fresher stories. It contains:

- The largest show-don't-tell descriptive database available anywhere
- A hyper-intelligent Character Builder tool
- Custom Character Arc Blueprints
- Story Maps, Scene Maps, and Timeline tools
- Idea generators
- Templates, worksheets, tip sheets, and checklists that demystify a variety of storytelling elements
- Craft tutorials and terminology glossaries
- The Storyteller's Roadmap, a step-by-step system for planning, writing, and revising a story or novel

If you've been searching for a resource to shorten the learning curve and help you create authentic characters who are part of well-structured, engaging plots … well, One Stop for Writers will change the way you create fiction. No more staring at the screen, wondering what to write. No more wishing you had an expert to help you navigate story craft. Get ready to write stronger fiction faster.

Visit One Stop for Writers (https://onestopforwriters.com) and test-drive our 2-week FREE TRIAL. If you choose to subscribe, use the **ONESTOPFORWRITERS** code for a one-time discount of 25% off any plan.

PCOS Diet Cookbook

120 Easy and Healthy Recipes That Will Nourish Your Body and Help You Manage Your PCOS Symptoms

Ruby A. Weber

ROSE
TRIFOLIA PRESS

ISBN: Print 978-1-955661-05-8

Ebook 978-1-955661-06-5

SPECIAL BONUS

Want this Bonus Book for <u>FREE</u>?

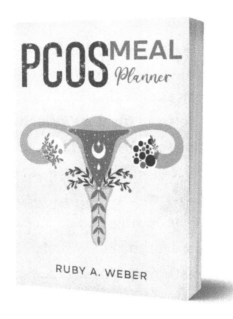

Get <u>FREE</u>, unlimited access to it and all of my new books by joining my Fan Base!

Scan with your camera to join!

Table of Contents

Introduction

I was gaining weight for no apparent reason. I was also losing hair. So I went to see the doctor. After a physical exam, ultrasound, and blood test, the doctor said I had PCOS. Frankly, I had no idea what it was. He said I had cysts in my ovaries... okay... so many girls have them... So I wasn't really worried.

But, he went on to explain that PCOS or Polycystic Ovary Syndrome might affect my ability to become pregnant... that made me really worried... after all, I was only 20. I was married and planning a child.

He also explained that the cysts might rupture causing severe pain... I became really scared. I was ready to do anything to solve the problem.

I started doing research and found that millions of women in the childbearing age suffer from PCOS. But sadly, many of them have very little idea of the condition. Many have undetected PCOS until it turns serious. So I decided to learn as much as I can and spread awareness of the condition.

I was overwhelmed with the response I got. So many women reported having similar symptoms. I urged them to see a doctor and get their PCOS properly diagnosed.

I wanted to reach even more people. So I decided to write a book that would include everything I have learned about the disease... its symptoms, causes, relation with insulin resistance, myths, and most importantly... how to get rid of PCOS by eating the right foods and making lifestyle changes.

Do not take the Polycystic Ovary Syndrome lightly. PCOS can cause many serious health problems like high blood pressure, type-2 diabetes, issues related to heart and blood vessels, and even uterine cancer.

Sadly, we don't yet have a treatment for PCOS. However, a good diet and lifestyle modifications can reduce its symptoms and prevent many of its health complications.

Read my book **PCOS Diet Cookbook**. Here, I have discussed the disease in great detail.

I have also shared 120 yummy PCOS-friendly recipes that you can prepare at home. There are recipes for breakfast, brunch, soups, salads, seafood, meat, desserts, and more. For each recipe, I have provided a detailed list of ingredients and described the making process step-by-step.

I have also provided a 2-weeks meal plan that I have personally followed when I was battling with my PCOS. You can also follow this plan to find relief from the symptoms of PCOS and prevent its health complications.

Happy reading! I am sure you will find this book most useful.

Part 1: All About PCOS

<u>Chapter 1 – Understanding PCOS</u>

PCOS or the Polycystic Ovary Syndrome is a common health condition that affects a large number of women between 15 and 44 years of age, between puberty and the menopause years. A hormonal disorder, PCOS is sometimes also referred to as the Polycystic Ovary Disease or the Stein-Leventhal syndrome.

Up to 26 percent (1) of women in their childbearing years may suffer from PCOS. But many believe that a lot more women may suffer from the condition, as many don't even know that they have it. One study even revealed that 70% of women may have undiagnosed (2) PCOS, making this one of the most common diseases.

When you have PCOS, your ovaries and the process of ovulation will be affected. There will be metabolism issues, which may affect your overall health and how you look. PCOS is also one of the most common causes of female infertility. Hormonal imbalance causes many symptoms at the same time – this is why the condition is called a 'syndrome'.

It can cause many health issues in women like diabetes, insulin resistance, high blood pressure, heart disease, sleep apnea, acne, unwanted facial and body hair, and even stroke. So never take PCOS lightly.

What happens when you have PCOS?

The problem starts when several cysts or small sacs filled with fluid grow in your ovaries. The word 'polycystic', in fact, refers to these many cysts. The sacs will each have an immature egg that doesn't get released, so there is no ovulation.

There are hormonal changes in your body when there is no ovulation. The progesterone and estrogen hormonal levels go down, while the androgen level goes up. The level of LH (Luteinizing Hormone) and FSH (Follicle-Stimulating Hormone) hormones also change.

Your ovaries produce a small number of androgen or the male hormone. This is normal. But, the problem arises only when a lot more androgen is produced. The higher male hormone level disturbs menstruation, which can lead to missed periods.

Symptoms

Here are the common symptoms of PCOS –

- Delayed or missed periods
- Sudden weight gain, especially in the tummy area or abdomen
- Sudden hair loss
- Acne on the upper back, chest, or face
- Problems in becoming pregnant as there is no ovulation
- More body hair because of the higher male hormone levels
- Unwanted facial and body hair
- Skin darkening, especially in the groin, neck, and below the breasts
- High blood pressure
- Diabetes
- Skin tags
- Mood changes

PCOS is not a new problem. Its symptoms were first described in 1721 by the Italian physician Antonio Vallisneri. However, the medical community is still unsure about its exact causes. It is believed that the condition is probably caused by genetics and lifestyle factors. So, you are at a higher risk if it runs in your family.

Many women with PCOS are also insulin resistant, a condition where the body cannot regulate its blood glucose levels efficiently. When you have high insulin levels, your body may also produce more male hormones like testosterone, which can again cause symptoms like acne and unwanted body hair. Obesity is one of the causes of insulin resistance.

Chapter 2 – Connection Between Insulin Resistance and PCOS

30 to 40 percent of women with PCOS are also insulin resistant. This is why it is believed that insulin resistance could be the main cause of PCOS, and it may also worsen its symptoms. Your pancreas produces insulin and allows you to use sugar or glucose extracted from food to give you energy. It will also help you control your blood sugar levels.

When you have insulin resistance (IR), your body cannot manage the glucose quickly or efficiently. So the glucose levels will go up and your energy levels may dip. Over time, your body will need even more insulin to absorb glucose into the tissues. Insulin resistance can eventually cause pre-diabetes and type 2 diabetes.

Insulin resistance will affect everyone differently. Some women with IR develop PCOS, others don't. Some experts have suggested that insulin resistance associated with obesity changes the functions of the pituitary gland and hypothalamus in our brain, which enhances the level of androgen hormones, eventually causing PCOS.

Excessive androgen hormones in your body can cause ovarian dysfunction and female infertility, whether you have PCOS or not.

Australian researchers have collected data from more than 8,000 women and discovered (3) that those with PCOS have a 4 to 8.8 times higher risk of developing Type-2 diabetes. They also observed that obesity was a key risk factor. A second study (4) carried out in Denmark in 2017 found that women with PCOS had a four times higher risk of developing Type-2 diabetes. Also, diabetes was diagnosed in them 4 years earlier than those who didn't have PCOS.

Several studies have also revealed that even those suffering from Type-1 Diabetes show the symptoms of PCOS. So, the experts are suggesting that women who have PCOS should routinely screen themselves for Diabetes.

PCOS and insulin resistance can both cause infertility. Hormonal changes in your body caused by PCOS may interfere with the embryo. IR can cause miscarriage because of inadequate nutrition and lack of support for the growing embryo within your body.

You should seek medical attention quickly if you are insulin resistant, especially if you have PCOS.

Chapter 3 – The Importance of a Healthy Lifestyle

There is no proven or guaranteed way of preventing PCOS. However, good nutrition and lifestyle changes can help you reduce the risk substantially. It is very important that you eat right and lead a healthy life. If you have PCOS, then it is even more important that you do so.

Here are a few tips that may help you –

Eat healthy food – Women having PCOS have higher inflammation levels, which could be the reason for the hormonal imbalance. So the food that reduces inflammation will be good for them. Your anti-inflammatory diet should have a lot of fresh vegetables and fruits, moderate amounts of low glycemic index, and high-fiber grains like quinoa and oats, nuts, avocados, seeds, and foods with a lot of omega-3 fats like tuna, salmon, and trout.

Make sure that you spread your carbohydrate foods throughout the day. Eat carbohydrates moderately in each snack and meal. This will stabilize your blood sugar levels and also reduce any insulin spikes.

Reduce the intake of sugars – Ideally, you should eat food from different food groups – fruits, vegetables, healthy carbohydrates, high fiber grains, fish, and lean meats like poultry. Doctors recommend that you must eat foods with low fat and sugar content. Low glycemic index foods will help your body release insulin steadily and slowly. It will then be easier for you to use the food to generate energy. It won't get stored as fat. High fiber foods will also help you control the sugar levels.

Carbs are converted into sugar. So you should control its intake. Avoid refined carbohydrates that you get from processed foods, particularly rice, potatoes, white flour, and sugar. Stay away from sugary drinks, including juice and soda.

Exercise regularly – Food is certainly a big factor that will help you manage PCOS efficiently. But you will also need to exercise. If you have PCOS, you may see muscle gain because the testosterone levels in your body are higher. If you have more muscle mass, your metabolic rate will increase, which means, you will burn more calories. This will help you use glucose more efficiently.

Weight training for at least 2 days a week will help you build as well as maintain muscle mass. Add more physical activity. Avoid the elevator and take the stairs instead. Park your car further away. Run or jog in the morning for half an hour. Swim or play tennis.

Manage your weight – Many women who have PCOS are also overweight. This can cause many health problems like Type-2 Diabetes, infertility, and even cardiovascular issues. Change your diet to lose weight. Focus on portion sizes. Join a Zumba class.

Get adequate sleep – Lack of sleep can cause many health issues. It can worsen insulin resistance and make it difficult for you to lose weight. Researchers have also linked insufficient sleep with more carbohydrate intake. Studies have also revealed that women having PCOS have a higher risk of OSA or Obstructive Sleep Apnea.

Reduce stress – We are all stressed these days. However, unmanaged prolonged stress can be the cause for many health issues, such as high blood pressure, increased insulin and cortisol levels that can contribute to obesity. Go on a holiday. Meditation, yoga, deep breathing, listening to soft music, the sound of running water, and regular walking can help you combat stress. These activities will also reduce insulin and cortisol levels in women who have PCOS.

Chapter 4 – Myths and Misconceptions

We still don't know a lot of things about PCOS. For instance, modern science is still unsure about its exact causes. There are several myths and misconceptions about PCOS as we are yet to understand the condition well. The misinformation may prevent women from managing PCOS and lowering the intensity of its symptoms.

Here are the most common myths and misconceptions of PCOS.

1. **You have PCOS if you have cysts** – Many women have cysts in their ovaries, but don't have PCOS. For a diagnosis, you have to fulfill two of these three conditions – irregular menstruation, excess levels of the androgen hormone, and multiple follicles.

2. **You have PCOS if your menstruation is irregular** – There are many reasons for an irregular menstrual cycle. The normal cycle is between 21 and 35 days. Over-exercising, extreme dieting, breastfeeding, uterine fibroids, thyroid disorders, and pelvic inflammatory disease can all disturb your cycle. PCOS is just one of the causes. Excessive stress can also cause this. Consult a doctor if your cycle happens in less than 22 days or takes more than 34 days.

3. **You can solve PCOS by losing weight** – We still don't have a cure for PCOS, unfortunately. You can only manage the condition and reduce its symptoms with the right foods and lifestyle changes. Losing weight will only help you manage the condition better. It will help you balance your hormone levels. So you will have a lower risk.

4. **Only overweight women can have PCOS** – It is a fact that many overweight women have PCOS. It is also true that obesity will worsen the symptoms. However, even those who are lean and trim can have the condition. The PCOS and weight relationship relate to your body's inability of using insulin efficiently, which can cause weight gain. This is why you should exercise and eat well.

5. **PCOS is rare** – This is one of the most common conditions that affect women of childbearing age. It is estimated that 5 million women have PCOS only in the US. Many believe this number to be a lot higher as many instances of PCOS remain undiagnosed. It affects women from all backgrounds, from around the world.

Part 2: Getting Started

<u>Chapter 5 – How to Start the Journey</u>

Deciding what to eat and avoid is one of the most important things you can do to effectively manage PCOS and its symptoms. Research has, in fact, shown that lifestyle changes and diet are often more effective (5) than medication for managing PCOS. However, getting started on the right PCOS eating plan can be tricky for many.

What should you eat and avoid to fight PCOS and its symptoms? For this, you have to understand that women who have the condition face problems in processing insulin and carbohydrates. They produce a lot of insulin, which makes the ovaries release too much testosterone, which can trigger the symptoms of PCOS. So it is essential to control your insulin levels.

PCOS and Dairy

There is a protein known as IGF-1 in dairy, which mimics the effect of insulin within us. The main function of IGF-1 is to make the unborn fetus grow. However, IGF-1 from dairy makes the ovaries release testosterone, which ends up worsening (6) the PCOS symptoms. So it is best to avoid or restrict the consumption of dairy products if you already have PCOS or have a higher risk of this condition.

PCOS and Gluten

Gluten will sometimes cause inflammation in the body. The problem is, when you have PCOS, you already have a higher level of inflammation in your body. The even higher level of inflammation will mean that you will become even more resistant to insulin. If we are insulin resistant, we will need more insulin for managing the level of blood sugar. There will be higher production of testosterone from the ovaries. So it is always a good idea to give up gluten-rich foods.

PCOS and Low Glycemic Index Foods

To manage insulin level and PCOS, eat foods that have a low glycemic load. These foods will raise your insulin levels slowly and gradually, which means that fewer testosterone hormones will be produced in the ovaries.

How do you identify low glycemic load foods? Focus on eating unrefined, unprocessed whole foods. The body will metabolize refined and processed foods more quickly, so there will always be a higher need for insulin.

PCOS and Soy

Researchers have discovered that soy products delay ovulation in women trying to have a baby. You may not be trying to become pregnant, but remember, PCOS already causes problems in ovulation (7). There is no point in delaying ovulation any further by eating soy-based products. So restrict their consumption.

Why It Is Important to Have a PCOS Diet Plan

It is always good to have a plan when you are starting something new. Things go wrong when we don't have a plan. Always have a clear idea of what you can eat and what you should avoid. Create a shortlist of foods you can have for your breakfast, lunch, dinner, and snacks. You can even have desserts and drinks, but make sure that they are PCOS-friendly. Prepare your pantry in such a way so that you have everything you need.

Chapter 6 – How to Prepare for the PCOS Diet

Begin with the foundation. Start with whole, real foods. Once done, create a plan for eating balanced meals. Focus on what you have. Half of your plate should have non-starchy vegetables and leafy greens. One-quarter of the plate should have starchy vegetables like sweet potatoes or gluten-free whole grains, such as quinoa. The last quarter should be for lean protein. Also, make sure to include healthy fats like nuts or extra-virgin olive oil.

Such a plate will ensure that you will be having the correct portion sizes. You will also stay satisfied, which will eventually help you stay away from foods that cause inflammation like sugar and processed junk.

How should you divide the calorie intake throughout the day? Many people consider dinner to be the biggest meal in their day. This is the wrong approach. Breakfast should always be the largest meal. Make sure to have light dinners.

A study divided lean women suffering from PCOS into two groups. The first had breakfast with 980 calories, lunch with 640, and dinner with 190 calories. Their BMI was about 24. The second group had 190 calories in their breakfast, 640 for lunch, and 980 for dinner.

It was found after 90 days that the testosterone levels in the firsts group went down by 50 percent. These women had a higher chance of ovulation. The testosterone level did not change in the second group.

Also, eating earlier during the day improved (8) insulin sensitivity and also reduced the androgen levels.

It may not always be possible to have 1000 calories at breakfast. But at least, plan to have a bigger breakfast. You can also plan to have a smaller dinner. This is the right approach.

Avoid Foods That Bother You

We all have foods we cannot tolerate well. Find out your food sensitivities and intolerances (foods that cause gastrointestinal distress like indigestion, gas, and bloating). Avoid eating them. Eat naturally gluten-free whole grains, such as brown rice if you are gluten sensitive. Also, like already mentioned, limit the intake of soy and dairy. However, it is always a good idea to consult a dietician or doctor.

There cannot be any perfect PCOS diet that will work for everyone. That's because we are all different. Also, you can find if you are intolerant to a food through the elimination method, where you remove some foods for a few weeks, and then add them back one at a time. Record if you see any symptoms. This approach will help you identify the foods that are causing problems in your system. You will know what to avoid.

Try to lose weight. A weight-loss diet will help you find relief from the symptoms of PCOS. A 2013 study tried to find the best PCOS diet. The researchers found that weight loss improved (9) many PCOS symptoms like insulin resistance, mood swings, and menstrual irregularity.

When you lose weight, you bring back the balance in your body. However, it should not be the sole focus. Many people have, after all, lost weight by consuming fewer calories, but they don't feel well, because an unhealthy eating plan will lead to poor overall health.

It is always best to focus on nutrient-rich healthy PCOS-friendly foods.

<u>Chapter 7 – Definitions of Terms</u>

1. PCOS – Polycystic Ovarian Syndrome
2. LH – Luteinizing Hormone
3. FSH – Follicle-Stimulating Hormone
4. IR – Insulin Resistance
5. OSA – Obstructive Sleep Apnea
6. Androgenetic Alopecia – Male Pattern Baldness
7. Amenorrhea – When there are no menstruations in the reproductive years
8. Androgens – Male Hormones
9. BMI – Body Mass Index
10. Carbs – Carbohydrates
11. Cyst – A fluid-filled sac
12. GI – Glycemic Index
13. Ovulation – Release of egg from the ovary
14. Testosterone – Steroid hormone made mostly in males by the testes

<u>Chapter 8 – Conversion Table</u>

1 tablespoon	3 teaspoons	15 milliliters
4 tablespoons	1/4 cup	60 milliliters
1 ounce	2 tablespoons	30 milliliters
1 cup	8 oz.	250 milliliters
1/2 cup	4 oz.	125 milliliters
1 gallon	4 quarts	3800 milliliters

The nutrition information in the recipes is approximate and meant as a guideline only.

The servings are also an approximation; they could be more or less, depending on your appetite.

Part 3: Recipes

<u>Breakfast and Brunch</u>

1. **Healthy Chicken Soup**

This chicken soup is very good comfort food. You are sure to love this.

Prep Time: 20 minutes, **Cook Time**: 2 hours, **Servings**: 10

Ingredients:

- 80 oz. roasting chicken
- 4 tablespoons of olive oil
- 2 yellow onions, diced
- 6 carrots, peeled & sliced
- 3 medium potatoes, cut into small pieces
- 8 cups of chicken broth
- 1 rosemary sprig

- 1 garlic head, cut the top off
- 2 sage leaves
- 3 thyme sprigs
- 1 oregano sprig
- 2 bay leaves
- 1 tablespoon of black peppercorn
- 1 tablespoon of salt
- Parsley leaves to garnish

Instructions:

- Preheat your oven to 375 degrees.
- Place the chicken in your oven. Rub the olive oil all over.
- Sprinkle pepper and salt. Coat well.
- Place the sliced carrots, potatoes, onions, garlic, and celery around your chicken. Turn halfway through.
- Roast the chicken uncovered for 90 minutes. Remove the vegetables from the oven after 45 minutes.
- Take out the chicken from the oven. Use two forks to shred the meat apart or chop into cubes.
- Place one large pot over medium heat and add the shredded chicken and the vegetables.
- Then, add the broth.
- Add the thyme, rosemary, bay leaf, sage, and oregano sprigs.
- Boil for 20 minutes.
- Then bring down the heat and simmer for 10 more minutes covered.
- Adjust the pepper and salt.
- Add some fresh parsley leaves to garnish, when serving the soup.

Nutrition Facts Per Serving
Calories 422, Carbohydrates 10.7g, Cholesterol 171mg, Total Fat 27.4g, Protein 36.9g, Fiber 0.7g, Sugars 3.9g, Sodium 2026mg, Potassium 115mg

2. Banana Oatmeal Pancakes

These pancakes are naturally sweetened and made without any flour. You can top them with nuts, fresh fruit, almond butter or date syrup.

Prep Time: 10 minutes, **Cook Time**: 7 minutes, **Servings**: 8

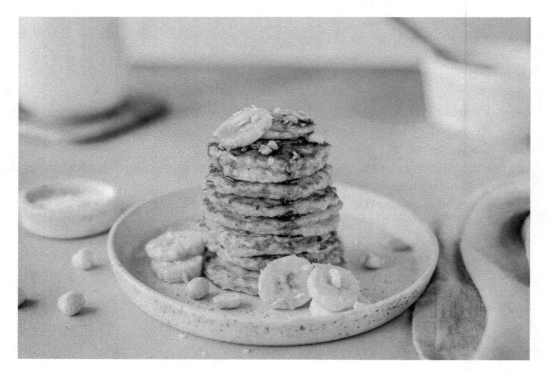

Ingredients:

- 1 cup coconut milk or vanilla almond milk
- 2-1/4 cups of rolled gluten-free oats
- 1 tablespoon of maple syrup or honey
- 2 ripe bananas
- ¼ teaspoon of sea salt
- 1 egg, large
- 1 teaspoon of vanilla extract
- ½ teaspoon cinnamon, ground

- 1-1/2 teaspoons of baking powder
- 1-2 teaspoons of coconut oil for cooking

Instructions:

- Put all the ingredients in your blender, except the coconut oil.
- Blend on high for 1 to 2 minutes. Everything should mix together. The oats should break down.
- Heat a griddle over medium to low heat.
- Melt the coconut oil in your pan.
- Scoop or pour ¼ cup of the batter once the griddle is hot into your pan.
- Cook each side for 2 to 3 minutes.
- You can serve hot with fruits, chopped nuts, extra bananas, date syrup, or nut butter.

Nutrition Facts Per Serving
Calories 170, Carbohydrates 21g, Cholesterol 23mg, Total Fat 9g, Protein 4g, Fiber 3g, Sodium 73mg

3. Low-Carb Biscuits With Jalapeno and Cheddar

These are delicious and healthy biscuits. You will love their crumbly and buttery taste for sure.

Prep Time: 10 minutes, **Cook Time**: 25 minutes, **Servings**: 8

Ingredients:

- 3 jalapeno peppers, diced
- 3.5 oz. cheddar cheese
- 1 teaspoon of baking powder
- ¼ teaspoon of baking soda
- 1.5 cups of almond flour
- ½ teaspoon of salt
- ½ teaspoon thyme
- ½ teaspoon paprika powder

- 1/8 teaspoon cayenne powder
- 1 tablespoon of apple cider vinegar
- 2 eggs
- 6 tablespoons almond milk
- 6 tablespoons of dairy-free butter, melted
- 6 tablespoons of vegan sour cream
- Parsley leaves to garnish

Instructions:

- Preheat your oven to 350 F or 180 C.
- Add all the wet ingredients to a bowl. Mix well.
- Mix all your dry ingredients in another bowl.
- Now, pour your wet ingredients into the dry ones. Use a spatula to mix well.
- Spoon a little bit into your mini tart mold. There should be adequate batter for making around 8 chunky biscuits.
- Keep the biscuits in your oven. Bake for 20 minutes.
- Take out from the oven. Set aside for 5 minutes for cooling.
- Garnish with parsley leaves and serve while still warm.

Nutrition Facts Per Serving

Calories 286, Carbohydrates 6.53g, Cholesterol 78mg, Total Fat 25.8g, Protein 10.52g, Sugar 1.25g, Fiber 3g, Sodium 249mg, Potassium 56mg

4. Breakfast Kolaches

You can have different fillings in this wonderful breakfast recipe.

Prep Time: 15 minutes, **Cook Time**: 15 minutes, **Resting Time**: 1 hour 35 minutes, **Servings**: 12

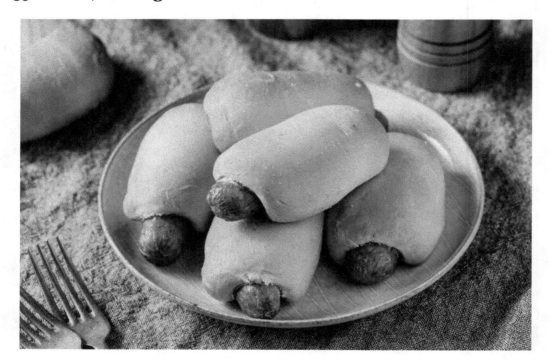

Ingredients:

- 2 large egg, beaten lightly
- 1 beaten egg yolk
- 2 cups of milk, warm
- 4 cups of bread flour
- 6 tablespoons of butter, melted
- ½ tablespoon of salt
- ¼ cup of white sugar
- 3 teaspoons of dry yeast

- 12 sausages, 2-inch each, cut in half
- 6 slices of Cheddar cheese

Instructions:

- Beat the eggs and yolk lightly into a mixing bowl.
- Add the milk, salt, yeast, sugar and melted butter and mix. Let it sit for 5 minutes until foamy.
- Add the flour and whisk thoroughly so that you avoid forming lumps.
- Once the dough can be formed, cover the bowl with a kitchen towel. Let the dough sit and rise for an hour or until it doubles in size.
- Preheat your oven to 190 C or 375 F. Grease a baking sheet.
- Punch down the dough on a floured surface. Divide into 24 pieces.
- Roll into smaller balls and then flatten them.
- Fill one sausage piece into each, and a quarter slice of the cheese. Then roll back the dough and pinch where the dough meets.
- Place them on the baking sheet and let rise again for 30 minutes.
- Bake for 15 minutes until the tops are golden brown.
- Serve while warm.

Nutrition Facts Per Serving
Calories 176.3, Carbohydrates 8.6g, Cholesterol 52mg, Total Fat 13.5g, Protein 8.4g, Sugar 3.8g, Fiber 0.5g, Sodium 543.8mg, Potassium 218.3mg

5. Breakfast Potatoes

Yummy breakfast potatoes you are sure to love. You can serve them with scrambled eggs.

Prep Time: 15 minutes, **Cook Time**: 40 minutes, **Servings**: 4

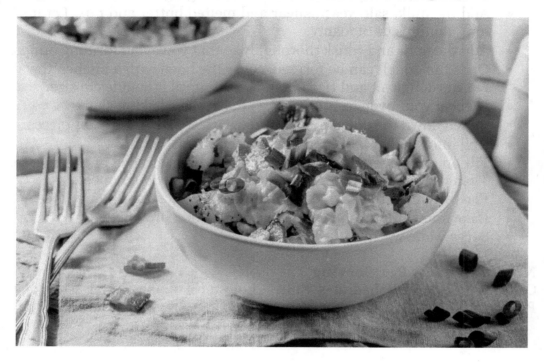

Ingredients:

- 1 onion, chopped
- 4 russet potatoes, medium
- 6 large eggs
- ¼ cup of milk
- 1 tablespoon of cumin, ground
- 2 tablespoons of olive oil
- ¼ cup of butter
- 1 pinch of black pepper (ground) and salt

- ¼ cup of Cheddar cheese, shredded
- 4 bacon slices, chopped
- 1 spring onion, chopped

Instructions:

- Preheat your oven to 175 C or 350 F.
- Cut the potatoes into small pieces. Keep them with onion in a bowl.
- Add the cumin, olive oil, pepper, and salt. Coat well by tossing.
- Spread the onion and potato mix on your baking sheet in an even layer. Place butter on top.
- Bake for 30 minutes. The potatoes should become tender.
- Beat eggs, milk, salt and pepper in a bowl, until well blended.
- Heat a nonstick skillet until hot. Pour in the egg mixture and pull the eggs across the pan with a spatula, so that they form soft curds.
- Continue cooking until the eggs have thickened. Remove from heat when ready.
- Cook the bacon over medium heat for 10 minutes while the potatoes are being baked. Stir frequently.
- Remove and place the bacon on a plate lined with a paper towel.
- Transfer your cooked potatoes to serving bowls.
- Add the eggs and bacon in the bowls and mix them with the potatoes.
- Add the cheese and chopped spring onion on top.

Nutrition Facts Per Serving
Calories 514.7, Carbohydrates 44.7g, Cholesterol 57mg, Total Fat 33.8g, Protein 10.6g, Sugar 3.8g, Fiber 3.9g, Sodium 413.2mg, Potassium 1066.5mg

6. Bacon Patty Cakes

Prepare these patty cakes with any leftover potatoes in your refrigerator.

Prep Time: 10 minutes, **Cook Time**: 20 minutes, **Servings**: 4

Ingredients:

- 4 cups of mashed potatoes
- 3 bacon slices
- 1 teaspoon of onion powder
- 2 eggs
- ½ teaspoon of black pepper, ground
- ½ teaspoon of salt
- 1 cup Cheddar cheese, shredded
- Dill to garnish

Instructions:

- Put the bacon in a nonstick skillet.
- Cook for 10 minutes over medium to high heat. Turn occasionally. It should be crisp and evenly brown.
- Take out the slices of bacon. Crumble. Set aside.
- Let the bacon drippings stay in your skillet.
- Mix the eggs, mashed potatoes, salt, black pepper, and onion powder in your bowl. Stir in the cheese and crumbled bacon.
- Use this mixture to create 8 patties.
- Heat the stored bacon drippings over medium heat.
- Now, pan-fry both sides of your patties in the drippings. 4 minutes for each side. They should be crisp.
- Garnish with dill before serving. You can serve them with a fresh tomato salad.

Nutrition Facts Per Serving
Calories 485.6, Carbohydrates 36.5g, Cholesterol 160mg, Fat 30.2g, Protein 16.6g, Sugar 3.5g, Fiber 3.2g, Sodium 1342.1mg, Potassium 713.8mg

7. Breakfast Casserole

A healthy casserole with your favorite ingredients.

Prep Time: 15 minutes, **Cook Time**: 60 minutes, **Servings**: 6

Ingredients:

- 1 green onion, chopped
- 16 oz. sausage meat
- 2 cups of cheddar cheese, shredded
- 16 oz. hash brown potatoes
- 1 cup of milk
- 6 eggs, beaten
- 1 pinch of paprika
- 3 oz. country gravy mix

Instructions:

- Preheat your oven to 165 C or 325 F. Grease your baking dish.
- Cook the sausage meat over medium heat in your skillet for 10 minutes.
- Keep stirring. It should become crumbly and browned.
- Mix the potatoes with the meat.
- Spread the mixture over the baking dish.
- Add the cheese on top.
- Whisk the milk, eggs, and gravy mix in a bowl. Make it smooth.
- Pour over the casserole. Season using paprika.
- Bake for an hour. A knife should enter into the center of your casserole and come out clean.
- Set aside 10 minutes for firming up.

Nutrition Facts Per Serving

Calories 377.2, Carbohydrates 13.3g, Cholesterol 204.1mg, Fat 29.5g, Protein 21.7g, Sugar 2.2g, Fiber 1g, Sodium 790.3mg, Potassium 528.9mg

8. Chicken Nuggets

The kids will love these chicken nuggets. They are gluten-free and loaded with healthy carbs and protein.

Prep Time: 10 minutes, **Cook Time**: 25 minutes, **Servings**: 4

Ingredients:

- 2 cups of sweet potatoes, finely grated
- 16 oz. chicken, ground
- 1-1/2 teaspoons of onion powder
- 2 tablespoons of tapioca flour
- 1 teaspoon of garlic powder
- 1 teaspoon of paprika
- 1 teaspoon of sea salt

Instructions:

- Preheat your oven to 400 F. Line your baking sheet with parchment paper. Set aside.
- Bring together all the ingredients in your food processor or bowl.
- Blend for 30 seconds on high. The mix should combine.
- Scoop out the mix with a tablespoon and place on the baking sheet.
- Now create the chicken nuggets from the mix with your hands. There should around 20 nuggets.
- The mixture should be sticky and wet. If needed, coat your hands with tapioca flour to prevent sticking.
- Bake the nuggets for 20 minutes in your oven. Turn halfway through.
- Optionally, you can broil them for 3 minutes to get crispy edges.
- Cool and then serve with ketchup or a sauce of your choice.

Nutrition Facts Per Serving
Calories 244, Carbohydrates 6.6g, Cholesterol 101mg, Fat 8.5g, Protein 33.4g, Sugar 2g, Fiber 1g, Sodium 108mg

9. Taco Stuffed Sweet Potatoes

A healthy and easy-to-make breakfast for the family.

Prep Time: 15 minutes, **Cook Time**: 50 minutes, **Servings**: 4

Ingredients:

- 1 tablespoon of olive oil
- 4 sweet potatoes, medium
- 16 oz. turkey, ground
- ½ yellow onion, diced
- ½ teaspoon of paprika
- 1-1/2 tablespoon of cumin
- ½ teaspoon of garlic powder
- 1 teaspoon of chili powder
- 1/2 teaspoon of black pepper

- 1-1/2 teaspoons of salt
- ¼ teaspoon of cayenne pepper
- Diced tomatoes, optional
- Chopped spring onions, optional
- Salsa, optional
- Chopped cilantro, optional

Instructions:

- Preheat your oven to 400 F. Use parchment paper to line your baking sheet.
- Use a fork to pierce the sweet potatoes a few times.
- Put them on the sheet. Bake for 45 minutes.
- Prepare the taco meat while the potatoes are cooking.
- Heat the olive oil over medium heat on a skillet.
- Add the cumin once it is hot. Stir for 2 minutes.
- Now, add the turkey, chili powder, paprika, cayenne pepper, garlic powder, black pepper, and salt.
- Cook until you see the turkey turn brown. Set aside.
- Take out the sweet potatoes from your oven. Create a slit on the top of each.
- Add half a cup of turkey inside each potato.
- Add the chopped spring onions, salsa, cilantro, and tomatoes if using on the top.

Nutrition Facts Per Serving
Calories 445, Carbohydrates 44.6g, Cholesterol 116mg, Fat 16.9g, Protein 34.1g, Sugar 1.2g, Fiber 7g, Sodium 1018mg, Potassium 1608mg

10.   Grilled Teriyaki Burger

You can prepare this teriyaki burger in minutes. It is perfect for the weekday breakfast when you are in a rush.

Prep Time: 10 minutes, **Cook Time**: 20 minutes, **Servings**: 4

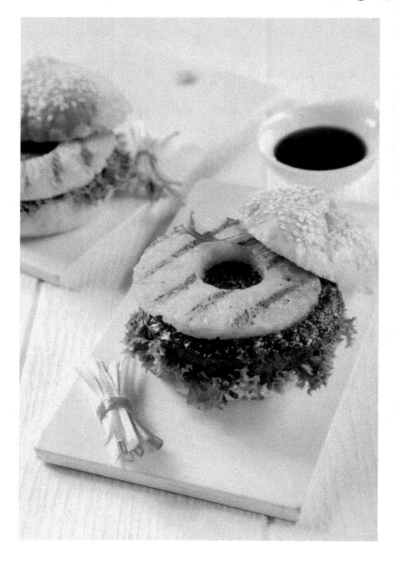

Ingredients:

- 1 lbs. beef, ground
- Coconut oil for brushing the skillet or grill
- 1 teaspoon of paprika
- 2 tablespoons of soy sauce
- 2 garlic cloves, minced
- ¾ teaspoon of chili powder
- 4 slices of fresh pineapple
- 2 teaspoons of ginger, minced
- ½ red onion, cut into slices
- ½ teaspoon of sriracha
- ½ cup of mayo
- 4 Batavia lettuce leaves
- 4 buns

Instructions:

- Mix the beef with soy sauce, chili powder, paprika, ginger, and garlic in a bowl.
- Create 4 equal sized patties.
- Heat your grill to medium. Grill each side for 5 to 7 minutes.
- Add the red onion and pineapple on the grill.
- Cook each side for 4 minutes. They should be caramelized.
- Take out everything from your grill.
- Set aside for 5 minutes.
- Serve on a bun topped with the lettuce, onion, beef burger and pineapple.
- You can add extra soy sauce or teriyaki sauce.

Nutrition Facts Per Serving
Calories 295, Carbohydrates 20g, Cholesterol 101mg, Fat 7.3g, Protein 34.9g, Sugar 14.7g, Fiber 1.8g, Sodium 92mg

11. Vegetable Frittata

You will find some of the best veggies in this frittata recipe. It can be the perfect breakfast option.

Prep Time: 15 minutes, **Cook Time**: 30 minutes, **Servings**: 4

Ingredients:

- ½ yellow onion, sliced
- 2 tablespoons of olive oil
- 1 cup sweet potato, shredded
- 1 garlic clove, minced
- 2 cups of baby spinach
- 2 cups of mushrooms, chopped
- ½ cup coconut milk, canned
- 12 eggs, large

- ½ teaspoon of pepper
- 1-1/2 teaspoons of salt
- 2 tablespoons of chives, chopped
- 2 tablespoons of parsley, chopped
- ½ cup of dairy-free cheese, shredded, optional
- Fresh herbs, arugula or tomatoes for serving

Instructions:

- Preheat your oven to 350 F.
- In the meantime, add 2 teaspoons of oil to your skillet over medium heat.
- Add the onion when hot. Cook for 5 minutes, stirring frequently. The onion should begin to turn golden and become soft.
- Add the mushrooms and sweet potatoes. Cook for 2 more minutes while stirring.
- Whisk the eggs with salt, pepper, coconut milk, cheese, chives, and parsley while the veggies are cooking.
- Now, pour the egg mix over your cooked veggies evenly. Don't stir.
- Cook for 3 minutes over medium heat.
- Transfer your skillet to the oven.
- Bake for 17 minutes.
- Top the remaining half cup of cheese. Broil for a minute on high.
- Serve with arugula, tomatoes, and fresh herbs at room temperature.

Nutrition Facts Per Serving
Calories 151, Carbohydrates 5g, Cholesterol 223mg, Fat 11g, Protein 8.7g, Sugar 1.3g, Fiber 0.8g, Sodium 449mg

12. Sweet Potato Hash

You will get a lot of rich flavors in this healthy breakfast.

Prep Time: 10 minutes, **Cook Time**: 30 minutes, **Servings**: 2

Ingredients:

- 1-3/4 oz. sausage, sliced
- 2 tablespoons of olive oil
- 16 oz. sweet potatoes, cut into cubes
- 1 yellow onion, diced
- 2 bell peppers, diced
- 2 zucchinis, diced
- 1 teaspoon paprika
- 1 teaspoon of garlic powder
- ¼ teaspoon of black pepper

- ½ teaspoon of salt
- Eggs, optional

Instructions:

- Preheat your oven to 425 F. Use parchment paper to line a sheet pan. Set aside.
- Toss together the sausage, olive oil, bell peppers, zucchini, onions, and sweet potatoes with paprika, garlic powder, pepper, and salt in a bowl.
- Place on the baking sheet.
- Bake for 30 minutes in your oven. The potatoes should be tender.
- Stir in the veggies halfway through.
- Remove the sheet pan carefully from your oven.
- Optionally, you can add fried eggs on top of your cooked vegetables.
- Serve while still warm.

Nutrition Facts Per Serving

Calories 328, Carbohydrates 36.1g, Cholesterol 221mg, Fat 14.2g, Protein 14.9g, Sugar 8.4g, Fiber 5.1g, Sodium 487mg

13. Healthy Pumpkin Muffins

Simple to make muffins that are also dairy-free and gluten-free. You can have them for snacks or breakfast.

Prep Time: 10 minutes, **Cook Time**: 20 minutes, **Servings**: 12

Ingredients:

- 3 eggs, large
- 1-1/5 oz. can pumpkin
- ¼ cup of coconut oil, melted
- 1 teaspoon of vanilla extract
- ¼ cup and 2 tablespoons of maple syrup
- ¼ cup of sugar-free almond butter
- ½ cup tapioca flour starch
- 1-3/4 cups of almond flour, blanched

- ¾ teaspoon of baking powder
- 1 teaspoon of baking soda
- ½ teaspoon of sea salt
- 2 teaspoons of pumpkin pie spice
- 1 cup of chocolate chips
- 1 cup walnuts, optional

Instructions:

- Preheat your oven to 350 F. Line a 12-cup muffin pan with paper liners.
- Apply non-stick spray on pan. Set aside.
- Whisk together the eggs, pumpkin, coconut oil, vanilla, maple syrup, and almond butter in a bowl. Combine well.
- Add the tapioca flour, almond flour, baking powder, baking soda, salt, and cinnamon. Combine well by whisking. Do not overmix.
- Fold in the chocolate chips. Optionally, add 1 cup of walnuts to the batter.
- Spoon your batter into the muffin pan evenly.
- Bake for 20 minutes in your oven.
- Set aside for 10 minutes for cooling.
- Serve with almond butter.

Nutrition Facts Per Serving
Calories 239, Carbohydrates 19.3g, Cholesterol 47mg, Fat 11g, Protein 4.6g, Sugar 8.2g, Fiber 1.7g, Sodium 261mg

14. Morning Glory Muffins

These muffins are refined sugar-free, dairy-free, and gluten-free. They are full of fruits and vegetables.

Prep Time: 15 minutes, **Cook Time**: 23 minutes, **Servings**: 12

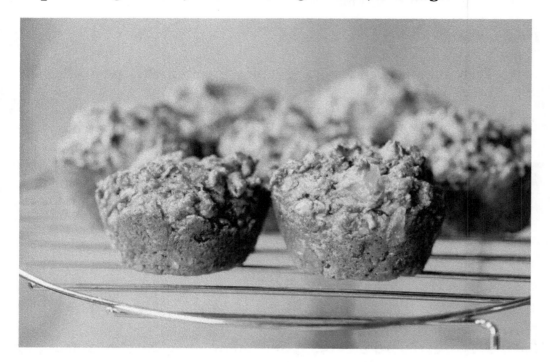

Ingredients:

- 2 teaspoons of baking soda
- 2 cups of gluten-free flour
- ½ teaspoon of salt
- 2 teaspoons of cinnamon, ground
- 3 eggs, large
- ¼ cup of flax, ground, optional
- ¼ cup of raw honey
- ½ cup of coconut sugar

- 1/3 cup of almond milk
- ½ cup of coconut oil, melted
- 2 cups of carrots, shredded
- 1 teaspoon of vanilla extract
- 1 apple, grated
- ½ cup of raisins

Instructions:

- Preheat your oven to 425 F. Line your muffin tin using liners.
- Apply a non-stick spray. Set aside.
- Combine the baking soda, gluten-free flour, salt, flaxseed (optional), and cinnamon in a mixing bowl.
- Whisk together the coconut sugar, eggs, coconut oil, honey, vanilla, almond milk, apple, and carrots in another bowl.
- Now, add your wet ingredients to the dry ingredients.
- Fold together. Add the raisins. Stir to combine well. Don't overmix.
- Divide the batter between the muffin cups evenly.
- Bake for 5 minutes in your oven.
- Bring down the heat to 350 F. Bake for another 18 minutes.
- Set aside for 5 minutes for cooling.

Nutrition Facts Per Serving

Calories 294, Carbohydrates 41.5g, Fat 12.2g, Protein 5.5g, Sugar 20.7g, Fiber 3g

15. Pumpkin Spice Granola

This healthy pumpkin granola is nutty, crunchy, and contains many rich fall flavors. It is also vegan and gluten-free.

Prep Time: 45 minutes, **Cook Time**: 55 minutes, **Servings**: 8

Ingredients:

- 1 cup of almonds, chopped
- 2 cups of hazelnuts, chopped
- 2 cups raw buckwheat groats
- 2 cups of gluten-free rolled oats
- 1-1/2 cups of chopped pecans
- ½ cup of maple syrup
- 1 teaspoon of pumpkin pie spice
- 1 teaspoon of vanilla extract

- ½ cup coconut oil, unrefined
- ¼ cup of pumpkin puree
- ½ teaspoon of sea salt

Instructions:

- Preheat your oven to 300 F.
- Line your baking sheet with parchment paper. Set aside.
- Combine the almonds, hazelnuts, buckwheat groats, pecans, rolled oats, pumpkin pie sauce, and sea salt in a bowl.
- Pour the maple syrup, pumpkin puree, and coconut oil over your dry ingredients. Mix well. The granola should be coated completely.
- Spread the mix over your baking sheet.
- Bake for 40 minutes. Stir halfway through.
- Serve with fresh fruit or dairy-free milk.

Nutrition Facts Per Serving

Calories 293, Carbohydrates 30g, Fat 17.9g, Protein 5.7g, Sugar 8.8g, Fiber 4.3g, Sodium 23mg

<u>Soups and Salads</u>

16.Thai Shrimp Salad

A healthy and creamy low carbohydrate salad for your taste buds. It helps you fight PCOS, high cholesterol, and also fills your cravings.

Prep Time: 10 minutes, **Cook Time**: 5 minutes, **Servings**: 4

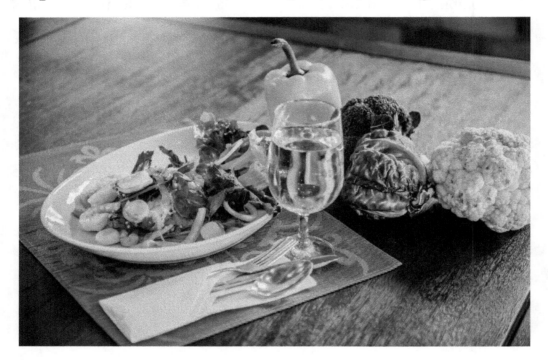

Ingredients:

- 3 cups mix of salad
- 2 cups shredded carrots
- ¼ red onion
- 3 tablespoons lime juice
- 2 tablespoons fish sauce
- ½ teaspoon chili powder

- 1 tablespoon maple syrup
- ½ teaspoon of black pepper
- ½ teaspoon of salt
- 2 teaspoons of olive oil
- 1 lbs. peeled and de-veined shrimps
- 3 garlic cloves, chopped
- ¼ teaspoon ground ginger

Instructions:

- Combine in a large bowl the lime juice, fish sauce, maple syrup, chili powder, black pepper.
- Pour olive oil into your frying pan. Add the garlic, the ground ginger and the salt.
- Cook for 1 minute. Add the shrimps.
- Sauté to cook completely, 2 minutes per side.
- Add the sauce to the shrimps and mix well. Set aside for cooling.
- Mix the red onion, the salad and the shredded carrots in another bowl.
- Transfer the mixture to a plate and top it with the shrimps and the sauce.
- Serve immediately and enjoy the tasty flavor.

Nutrition Facts Per Serving
Calories 289, Carbohydrates 19.6g, Cholesterol 175mg, Total Fat 13.9g, Protein 24.1g, Sugar 5.7g, Fiber 5.3g, Sodium 734mg, Potassium 744mg

17. Vegetable Turkey Low-Carb Soup

Prepare this low-carbohydrate soup with leftover turkey. This is so yummy that you may ask for seconds.

Prep Time: 10 minutes, **Cook Time**: 20 minutes, **Servings**: 6

Ingredients:

- 20 oz. of shredded and cooked turkey
- 1 onion, diced
- 2 tablespoons of olive oil
- 2 stalks of celery, chopped
- 2/3 cup of carrots, chopped
- 2 cloves of garlic, minced
- 2 cups of cauliflower florets, diced
- ½ tablespoon of thyme, minced

- 1 cup of mushrooms, sliced
- 3 cups of chicken or turkey stock
- 1 cup of coconut milk
- 1/3 teaspoon of black pepper, ground
- ½ teaspoon of sea salt
- 1 tablespoon of parsley, minced

Instructions:

- Heat the olive oil over medium heat in your Dutch oven or saucepan.
- Add the carrot, onion, cauliflower, and celery. Cook for 7 minutes.
- Add the mushrooms, garlic, 1 tablespoon of parsley, and thyme.
- Season with pepper and salt.
- Cook for 3 minutes. The mushrooms must start to get brown.
- Add the stock.
- Boil and then bring down to a simmer. Cook for 8 minutes.
- Now, add your cooked turkey.
- Stir in the coconut milk. Simmer for 2 minutes.
- Serve in bowls. Top with the chopped parsley.

Nutrition Facts Per Serving
Calories 254, Carbohydrates 5.1g, Total Fat 19g, Protein 14.3g, Sugar 2.7g, Fiber 1.5g

18. Vegetable Soup

Making this roasted and healthy vegetable soup is really simple. It is family-friendly, filling, and healthy.

Prep Time: 10 minutes, **Cook Time**: 1 hour, **Servings**: 6

Ingredients:

- ½ cauliflower head, cut into large florets

- 1 eggplant, cut & stem removed
- 2 red bell pepper, halved
- 2 quartered onions
- 4 tomatoes, quartered
- 4 garlic cloves, peeled
- 5 carrots, peeled & chopped
- 2 potatoes, cut into large chunks
- 1 cup green beans
- 1 cup red kidney beans
- ½ can tomato sauce
- 5 cups of vegetable soup
- Pepper and salt, to taste
- 2 tablespoons of olive oil

Instructions:

- Preheat your oven to 400 F. Use parchment paper to line your baking sheet.
- Add the cauliflower, eggplant, pepper, onions, tomatoes, garlic, carrots, and potatoes to your baking sheet. They should be in one layer.
- Drizzle some olive oil on top. Sprinkle pepper and salt.
- Roast for 40 minutes at 400 F. The carrots and potatoes should become tender. The vegetables should turn slightly brown.
- Add the roasted vegetables, beans, and tomato sauce to your pot. Add the stock.
- Boil and then reduce the heat to a simmer.
- Let it simmer for 15 minutes. Turn the heat off.
- You can also garnish with herbs.

Nutrition Facts Per Serving
Calories 221, Carbohydrates 24g, Cholesterol 5mg, Total Fat 12g, Protein 8g, Sugar 12g, Fiber 6g, Sodium 269mg, Potassium 937mg

19.Japanese Noodles Salad

This healthy and light salad features delicious Japanese noodles. Enjoy the flavors of Asia.

Prep Time: 15 minutes, **Cook Time**: 10 minutes, **Servings**: 6

Ingredients:

- ½ bell pepper, diced

- 8 oz. tofu shirataki noodles
- 1 cup green beans
- 2 cups peas
- 6 carrots, peeled
- 1 tablespoon of sesame seeds
- 1 teaspoon of chili oil
- 1 tablespoon of sesame oil
- 2 tablespoons of soy sauce, gluten-free
- 1 tablespoon of rice vinegar
- 2 garlic cloves, minced
- 1 teaspoon of agave syrup
- 1 teaspoon ginger, minced

Instructions:

- Boil a pot of water. Place the noodles in it.
- Boil for 5 minutes covered.
- Take out from the heat. Drain and rinse. Set aside for cooling.
- Boil the green beans and peas for 5 about 5 minutes.
- Place the noodles in your salad bowl.
- Mix in the bell pepper, beans, peas, carrots and sesame seeds.
- Whisk together the dressing ingredients (oil, soy sauce, rice vinegar, garlic cloves, agave syrup and ginger) in a dish.
- Now, toss the salad with the dressing. Distribute well.

Nutrition Facts Per Serving
Calories 100, Carbohydrates 15g, Total Fat 4g, Protein 4g, Sugar 2g, Fiber 4g, Sodium 242mg

20. Arugula Salad

You can have this elegant and simple salad anytime you want.

Prep Time: 5 minutes, **Cook Time**: 3 minutes, **Servings**: 4

Ingredients:

- 4 cups of arugula
- 2 tablespoons of Parmesan cheese, shaved
- ½ teaspoon of lemon rind, grated
- 2 tablespoons of extra-virgin olive oil
- 1/8 teaspoon of black pepper, ground
- 2 teaspoons of lemon juice
- 1 garlic clove, minced

Instructions:

- Combine the lemon rind, olive oil, pepper, lemon juice, and garlic, in a bowl.
- Stir to combine well.
- Add the arugula.
- Coat well by tossing.
- Sprinkle the Parmesan cheese

Nutrition Facts Per Serving

Calories 116, Carbohydrates 1.6g, Cholesterol 12mg, Total Fat 10.3g, Protein 5.7g, Sugar 0.5g, Fiber 0.4g, Sodium 209mg, Potassium 92mg

21.Chicken and Spinach Salad

You will have the flavors in each bite in this wonderful salad. Prepare this at home easily whenever you want.

Prep Time: 15 minutes, **Cook Time**: 15 minutes, **Servings**: 4

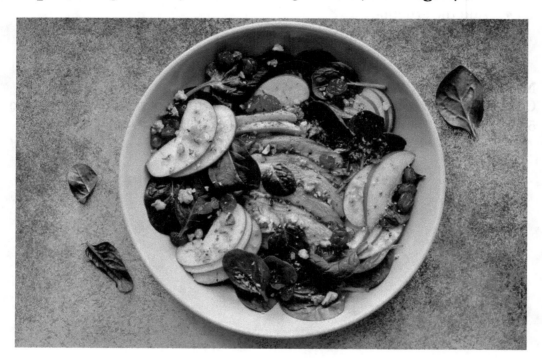

Ingredients:

- 16 oz. chicken breasts, boneless & skinless
- 32 oz. spinach, remove the stems
- 2 red apples, sliced
- ½ cup dried cranberries
- 1 cup walnuts, chopped
- 2 teaspoons of white or red-wine vinegar
- 1 cup orange juice
- ½ teaspoon of salt

- 1/3 cup and 1 tablespoon of cooking oil
- ¼ teaspoon of black pepper, ground

Instructions:

- Toast the walnuts in a pan until they are golden brown, about 5 minutes.
- Combine the vinegar, orange juice, ¼ teaspoon of salt, 1/3 cup of cooking oil.
- Heat the remaining oil in a pan over medium heat.
- Season your chicken breasts with the remaining salt and black pepper. Add to your pan. Keep your pan covered and allow the steam to escape.
- Cook for 5 minutes. Turn. Cook for another 5 minutes.
- Take out the chicken. Add water to the pan over medium heat.
- Cut the chicken breasts when they are cool into bite-size pieces.
- Toss the spinach, apples and cranberries in a bowl.
- Add the chicken breast on top of the salad.
- Serve your salad after spooning the dressing over the top.

Nutrition Facts Per Serving
Calories 542, Carbohydrates 20.5g, Cholesterol 101mg, Total Fat 33.9g, Protein 42.3g, Sugar 2.8g, Fiber 6.9g, Sodium 647mg, Potassium 1662mg

22. Chicken and Rice Soup

Prepare this wild rice and chicken soup with creamy and delicious broth.

Prep Time: 15 minutes, **Cook Time**: 50 minutes, **Servings**: 6

Ingredients:

- 2 yellow or white onion, peeled & diced
- 2 tablespoons of olive oil
- 2 stalks of celery, diced
- 2 carrots, diced
- ¼ cup of all-purpose flour
- 6 garlic cloves, minced
- 16 oz. chicken breasts, boneless & skinless
- 6 cups of chicken stock
- 1 cup of uncooked wild rice, rinsed & drained

- 8 oz. of mushrooms, diced
- 2 bay leaves
- 1 tablespoon of rosemary, chopped
- 2 baby spinach, chopped
- 2 cups of plant-based milk
- Black pepper and sea salt

Instructions:

- Melt the oil over medium heat in a big pot.
- Add the onion. Sauté for 2 minutes. Stir frequently.
- Now, add the celery, garlic, and carrots. Sauté for another 3 minutes, while stirring occasionally.
- Add the flour. Sauté for another minute. Stir frequently.
- Pour the chicken stock gradually. Stir your soup as you are pouring.
- Next, add the mushrooms, chicken breasts, rosemary, rice, and bay leaves. Combine well by stirring.
- Simmer. Bring down the heat to low. Cook for 40 minutes covered. Stir your soup every 5 minutes.
- Take out the chicken, in order to shred it into small bite-sized pieces.
- Stir back into your soup.
- Add your remaining ingredients. Stir in the baby spinach and milk. Combine well.
- Cook for 5 more minutes.
- Season and discard the bay leaves before serving.

Nutrition Facts Per Serving
Calories 339, Carbohydrates 33g, Cholesterol 76mg, Total Fat 11.3g, Protein 27.5g, Sugar 6.4g, Fiber 4.5g, Sodium 832mg, Potassium 637mg

23.   Chicken Tortilla Soup

Prepare this soup with chicken, corn, tomatoes, avocado, black beans, onion and crunchy strips of tortilla. It can be a quick weeknight meal.

Prep Time: 15 minutes, **Cook Time**: 30 minutes, **Servings**: 6

Ingredients:

- 4 tablespoons of olive oil
- 10 corn tortillas, cut into wide strips
- 1 teaspoon of kosher salt
- 1 jalapeno pepper, diced
- 1 cup red onion, peeled & diced
- 4 cups of chicken broth, low-sodium
- 4 cloves of garlic, peeled & minced
- 1 can of black beans, drained & rinsed
- 2 cans of tomatoes + juice, diced

- 1-1/2 cups of corn
- 2 cups of cooked chicken, shredded
- 1 tablespoon of chili powder
- 1 tablespoon of lime juice
- 2 teaspoons of cumin
- Black pepper and salt, to taste
- ¼ teaspoon of cayenne pepper, optional
- 1 teaspoon of smoked paprika
- 1/3 cup of cilantro leaves, minced
- Shredded cheese, avocado, chopped red onion, sour cream, for serving, optional

Instructions:

- Preheat your oven to 375 degrees. Use parchment paper to line your baking sheet.
- Scatter your strips of tortilla chips evenly. Drizzle some olive oil.
- Sprinkle the kosher salt. Coat evenly.
- Bake for 15 minutes. Set aside.
- Pour 2 tablespoons of olive oil into your pot. Heat over medium.
- Add the jalapeno and onion. Sauté for 5 minutes. Stir intermittently.
- Add the garlic. Sauté for another minute. Keep stirring.
- Now, add the tomatoes and juice, chicken broth, corn, black beans, the cooked chicken, chili powder, lime juice, pepper, salt, cumin, smoked paprika, and cayenne pepper if using.
- Boil your mixture for 10 minutes.
- Add the cilantro. Boil for another minute.
- Add more salt if needed. Ladle into your bowls.
- Place the tortilla chips on top.
- Optionally, add avocado, chopped red onion, shredded cheese or sour cream on top, for serving.

Nutrition Facts Per Serving
Calories 737, Carbohydrates 79g, Cholesterol 90mg, Total Fat 33g, Protein 39g, Sugar 21g, Fiber 18g, Sodium 7755mg

24.   Greek Lemon Chicken Soup

A yummy Greek soup with chicken, lemon, orzo and eggs. It is a great soup for a cold winter day.

Prep Time: 10 minutes, **Cook Time**: 1 hour 10 minutes, **Servings**: 6

Ingredients:

- 80 oz. of chicken
- 8 cups of chicken broth
- 2 onions, chopped
- 2 cups orzo
- 4 eggs
- Lemon juice from 1 large lemon
- 1 lemon, halved
- 2 dill sprigs

- 2 rosemary sprigs
- 2 tablespoons of olive oil
- Pepper and salt

Instructions:

- Preheat your oven to 375 F.
- Cook the chicken in your Dutch oven. Rub olive oil all over.
- Sprinkle pepper and salt. Coat well.
- Place the onions, and halved lemon around your chicken.
- Roast for 40 minutes uncovered.
- Take the chicken out from the oven. Set aside for cooling.
- Shred it into small sized pieces. Discard the bones.
- Discard the halved lemon from the oven. Keep the cooked onions.
- Add 6 cups of broth to the oven. Turn up the heat to high.
- Boil. Let it simmer covered for 15 minutes.
- Add the orzo and cook around 10 minutes.
- In the meantime, whisk the eggs into a bowl, about 3 minutes.
- Pour over them the lemon juice and the 2 remaining cups of broth, warmed. Whisk together slowly.
- Add back to the oven the chicken and the eggs mixture. Combine well by whisking.
- Adjust the pepper and salt.
- Cook until the soup thickens, 5 more minutes.
- Serve with lemon slices, rosemary and dill sprigs on top.

Nutrition Facts Per Serving

Calories 305, Carbohydrates 6.7g, Cholesterol 149mg, Total Fat 8.2g, Protein 48.4g, Sugar 2.6g, Fiber 1.8g, Sodium 572mg, Potassium 573mg

25.   Egg, Bacon, Avocado, & Tomato Salad

An easy-to-make salad recipe for the home.

Prep Time: 15 minutes, **Cook Time**: 10 minutes, **Servings**: 2

Ingredients:

- 2 boiled eggs, chopped
- 8 oz rotisserie chicken, chopped
- 1 avocado, chopped
- Juice from a lemon wedge
- 1 tomato, chopped
- 4 slices of salad
- 3 bacon pieces, crumbled
- Pepper and salt to taste

- 5 oz Roquefort cheese, optional

Instructions:

- Place the salad leaves on a big plate.
- Cook the bacon over medium heat for 10 minutes. Stir frequently.
- Remove and place the bacon on a plate lined with a paper towel.
- Cut all the other ingredients and arrange them on the plate. Add the bacon.
- Season with salt and pepper.
- Optionally, you can add crumbled Roquefort cheese on top of the salad.

Nutrition Facts Per Serving
Calories 480, Carbohydrates 18g, Total Fat 37g, Protein 22g, Fiber 10.5g

26. Buffalo Cauliflower Taco Salad

This could be the perfect salad for your dinner. Try making this at home.

Prep Time: 20 minutes, **Cook Time**: 50 minutes, **Servings**: 4

Ingredients:

- 1 cauliflower head, bite-sized florets
- 1 tablespoon olive oil
- 2 tablespoons of flour, gluten-free
- 2 tablespoons of chili powder
- 1 teaspoon of onion powder
- ¼ teaspoon of garlic powder
- ½ cup vinegar sauce
- 4 tablespoons of vegan butter
- 1 tablespoon of milk, dairy-free
- ½ cup of vegan yogurt
- 1 tablespoon of dill, chopped
- 1 tablespoon of chives, chopped
- ¼ teaspoon of agave nectar
- 2 cups of cherry tomatoes
- 6 cups of mixed salad leaves
- 1 avocado, diced
- 4 gluten-free taco-sized tortillas
- 1 teaspoon of salt
- Black pepper to taste
- Optional, 1 cup of shredded cheese of your choice

Instructions:

- Preheat your oven to 425 F. Cut the cauliflower into small florets.
- Toss with olive oil in a mixing bowl.
- Stir together the salt, gluten-free flour, onion powder, chili powder and garlic powder. Toss the cauliflower in your flour mix. Coat well.
- Keep on a sheet pan lined with parchment paper.
- Roast for 20 minutes. Stir a few times.
- Melt the butter in your saucepan. Whisk in the vinegar sauce.
- Remove the florets from your baking sheet. Place in a mixing bowl. Now, pour the sauce mix over it. Toss gently to coat well.

- Transfer the cauliflower back to the oven. Roast for 25 minutes. Rotate the pan halfway through.
- Remove cauliflower from the oven.
- Whisk together all the ingredients for the ranch (dairy-free milk, yogurt, dill, chives, agave). Adjust the seasoning.
- Next, toss the greens in your dressing.
- Assemble the tacos. Load each tortilla with the salad and dressing, cherry tomatoes, avocado and cooked cauliflower.
- Optionally, shred some cheese of your choice on top of the tacos.

Nutrition Facts Per Serving
Calories 345, Carbohydrates 29.2g, Total Fat 24.9g, Protein 8.4g, Sugar 9.3g, Fiber 10.8g, Sodium 763.8mg

27.   Chicken & Kale Salad

Chill this healthy salad before eating so that the flavors can meld together.

Prep Time: 5 minutes, **Cook Time**: 25 minutes, **Servings**: 4

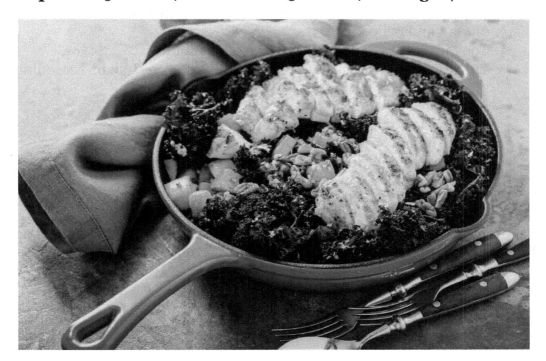

Ingredients:

- ½ red onion, minced
- 3 chicken breasts, cooked and diced
- 5 cups of kale, chopped
- 2 cups of butternut squash, cut into cubes
- 1 cup cooked quinoa
- ¼ cup of white wine vinegar
- 1/3 cup of olive oil
- 1 tablespoon of Italian seasoning
- 4 teaspoons of mustard

- 1 lemon juice
- Pepper and salt, to taste

Instructions:

- Preheat your oven to 425 F. Put the squash in the oven and drizzle oil, salt and pepper over it.
- Cook it for 20 minutes, then cool it for 5 minutes.
- Put all your dressing ingredients (oil, vinegar, Italian seasoning, mustard, lemon juice) in a jar. Mix well by shaking.
- Adjust the seasoning.
- Toss the red onion and kale together.
- Drizzle half of your dressing.
- Add the quinoa, cooled squash and chicken. Combine by tossing.
- Adjust seasoning with more dressing.

Nutrition Facts Per Serving

Calories 405, Carbohydrates 22.9g, Cholesterol 50mg, Total Fat 25.2g, Protein 22.6g, Sugar 5g, Fiber 2.8g, Sodium 1317mg, Potassium 47mg

28.   Romaine & Smoked Salmon Salad

Follow the instructions to prepare an easy but delicious salad recipe.

Prep Time: 10 minutes, **Cook Time**: 3 minutes, **Servings**: 2

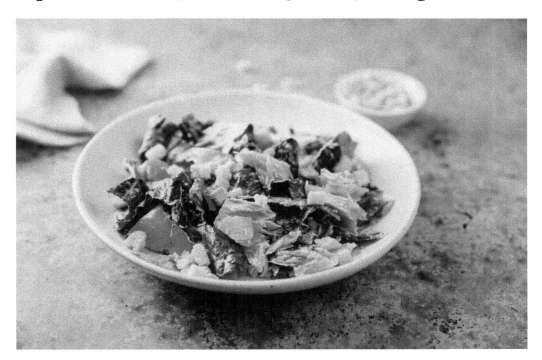

Ingredients:

- 2 teaspoons of capers, drained
- 2 heads of romaine, chopped
- 6 oz. hot smoked salmon
- 1 shallot, thinly sliced
- 1 tablespoon of extra-virgin olive oil
- ½ juice from a lemon
- ½ cup peanuts, chopped
- Salt and pepper

Instructions:

- Combine the shallot, capers, and romaine. Add the salmon on top.
- Squeeze out the lemon over the top.
- Drizzle olive oil. Season with pepper and salt.
- Top with chopped peanuts.

Nutrition Facts Per Serving
Calories 283, Carbohydrates 13.7g, Cholesterol 20mg, Fat 18.7g, Protein 19.9g, Sugar 4.5g, Fiber 1g, Sodium 1894mg, Potassium 971mg

29. Creamy Cauliflower Soup

Try this cauliflower recipe to satisfy your craving for a creamy and warm soup. It is luscious and delightful.

Prep Time: 10 minutes, **Cook Time**: 1 hour, **Servings**: 4

Ingredients:

- 3 tablespoons of extra-virgin olive oil
- 1 cauliflower head, cut into small florets
- 2 garlic cloves, minced
- 1 red onion, chopped
- Sea salt
- 2 tablespoons of unsalted butter
- 4 cups of vegetable broth
- ¼ teaspoon of nutmeg, ground

- 1 tablespoon of lemon juice
- 2 tablespoons of chili flakes, dill or sour cream for garnishing

Instructions:

- Preheat your oven to 425 F. Use parchment paper to line your baking sheet.
- Toss the cauliflower and 2 tablespoons of olive oil on your baking sheet. Coat evenly in oil. Sprinkle salt lightly.
- Bake for 30 minutes. Toss halfway. The edges of your cauliflower should be caramelized.
- Warm the remaining olive oil over medium heat in your Dutch oven. It should be simmering.
- Add ¼ teaspoon of salt and the red onion.
- Cook for 6 minutes, stirring occasionally.
- Now, add the garlic. Cook for 30 seconds while stirring.
- Add the broth.
- Transfer the roasted cauliflower to your Dutch oven. Simmer on medium heat.
- Reduce the heat. Cook for 20 minutes, stirring occasionally.
- Remove everything from the oven. Set aside for cooling.
- Transfer your soup to a blender.
- Add butter. Blend to make it smooth.
- Then, add the nutmeg and lemon juice. Blend again.
- Add more salt if needed and even some lemon juice.
- Top with chili flakes, dill or sour cream when serving.

Nutrition Facts Per Serving

Calories 226, Carbohydrates 18.1g, Cholesterol 15.3mg, Fat 17g, Protein 5g, Sugar 7.7g, Fiber 5.3g, Sodium 1021.2mg

30.   Chicken Tagliatelle Soup

An extremely straightforward chicken soup where you don't need any fancy ingredients. You will love this, especially during the winter.

Prep Time: 15 minutes, **Cook Time**: 40 minutes, **Servings**: 10

Ingredients:

- 2 tablespoons of olive oil
- 3 stalks of celery, sliced
- 1 yellow onion, diced
- 6 garlic cloves, minced
- 2 carrots, sliced
- 4 sprigs of thyme
- 10 cups of chicken broth, low-sodium
- 32 oz. of chicken breasts, skinless

- 2 bay leaves
- ½ teaspoon of black pepper, ground
- 1-1/4 teaspoon of salt
- 30 oz. of tagliatelle, low-carb
- Chopped parsley, for garnishing
- Wedges of lemon, for serving

Instructions:

- Heat the olive oil in a pot over medium heat.
- Add the carrots, celery, and chopped onions.
- Cook for 3 minutes while stirring occasionally.
- Stir the garlic in. Cook for another 30 seconds.
- Now, add the chicken broth.
- Next, add the bay leaf and thyme. Increase the heat. Let your mixture simmer on high.
- Add pepper, salt, and chicken breasts. Stir.
- Simmer covered for 25 minutes over medium heat.
- Remove the chicken breasts from the oven. Transfer to cutting board.
- Shred the chicken.
- Stir the chicken into your soup.
- Add the tagliatelle pasta. Cook for 5 minutes.
- Take out from the heat.
- Discard the bay leaves and thyme sprigs. Adjust the salt.
- Ladle into the bowls. Use parsley for garnishing.
- You can serve with wedges of lemon.

Nutrition Facts Per Serving

Calories 213, Carbohydrates 19g, Cholesterol 35mg, Fat 8g, Protein 16g, Sugar 1g, Fiber 1g, Sodium 323mg, Potassium 326mg

31. Butternut Squash Soup

You are sure to fall in love with this vegan, healthy, and creamy soup. It is rich in fall spices.

Prep Time: 15 minutes, **Cook Time**: 50 minutes, **Servings**: 6

Ingredients:

- 1 butternut squash
- 4 tablespoons of olive oil
- 1 onion, diced
- 3 cups of chicken stock, bone broth, or vegetable stock
- ½ teaspoon of nutmeg, ground
- ¼ cup of maple syrup
- 1 teaspoon of sea salt
- 1 teaspoon of cinnamon, ground
- ¼ teaspoon of black pepper

- Sour cream and pumpkin seeds, to garnish

Instructions:

- Preheat your oven to 400 F. Apply a non-stick spray on your baking pan.
- Peel your butternut squash, cut off the ends of your squash.
- Scoop the seeds out. Cut the squash into small pieces.
- Add the squash in the pan. Toss with pepper, salt, and 2 tablespoons of olive oil. Roast for 35 minutes in your oven.
- Heat the remaining olive oil in a stockpot or Dutch oven while it is roasting. Add the onion over medium heat.
- Cook for 2 minutes. The onion should become translucent.
- Add the squash once done to your pot with the onions.
- Also add the stock. Stir well. Let it simmer at medium heat for 10 minutes.
- Now, mix the soup with your immersion blender. It should be creamy and smooth. You can also mix in a blender.
- Add the nutmeg, cinnamon, and maple syrup. Stir well.
- Top with a spoon of sour cream and pumpkin seeds.

Nutrition Facts Per Serving
Calories 83, Carbohydrates 8.5g, Fat 5.9g, Protein 0.5g, Sugar 5.7g, Fiber 0.7g, Sodium 418mg, Potassium 88mg

32.   Cucumber Tomato Salad

This is a classic salad that is cooling, light, and so refreshing.

Prep Time: 5 minutes, **Cook Time**: 3 minutes, **Servings**: 2

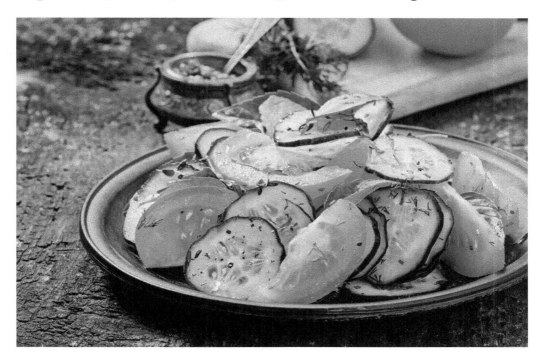

Ingredients:

- 2 tomatoes, diced
- 1 English cucumber, sliced
- 1 tablespoon of chopped dill
- 1 tablespoon of red wine vinegar
- 2 tablespoons of olive oil
- Basil leaves to garnish

Instructions:

- Bring together all the ingredients in a bowl. Toss well.

- Refrigerate for 20 minutes minimum and then serve.

Nutrition Facts Per Serving
Calories 104, Carbohydrates 7g, Fat 8g, Protein 2g, Sugar 4g, Fiber 2g, Sodium 6mg, Potassium 296mg

33. Tomato Avocado Salad

Enjoy the summer harvest with juicy tomatoes and ripe avocados. It is nutty-flavored, creamy, and tangy.

Prep Time: 10 minutes, **Cook Time**: 5 minutes, **Servings**: 2

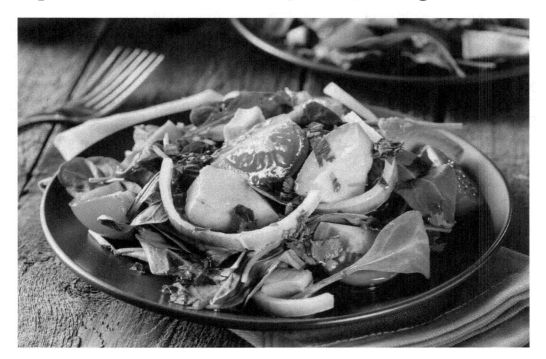

Ingredients:

- 1 lime
- 3 avocados
- ½ cup of red onion, sliced
- 2 cups of cherry tomatoes, halved
- 2 tablespoons of olive oil
- ¼ cup of cilantro or parsley, chopped
- 2 cups of lamb lettuce (or lettuce of your choice)
- 1 garlic clove, minced

- Pepper and salt to taste

Instructions:

- Cut the onions and tomatoes. Set aside.
- Cut your avocados into half. Remove the pits. Dice.
- Squeeze lime over the avocados. Toss well to combine.
- Add the other ingredients. Stir gently.
- Set aside 10 minutes for setting.

Nutrition Facts Per Serving

Calories 331, Carbohydrates 20g, Fat 29g, Protein 4g, Sugar 4g, Fiber 11g, Sodium 21mg, Potassium 940mg

Vegetarian and Vegan Main Dishes

34. **Baked Oatmeal**

This can be the perfect oatmeal breakfast. It is delicious, hearty, and sugar-free.

Prep Time: 10 minutes, **Cook Time**: 35 minutes, **Servings**: 6

Ingredients:

- 1 cup of almonds, sliced
- 1 cup of unsweetened coconut flakes
- 2 cups of whole rolled oats
- 1/3 cup of Swerve Brown sweetener
- ½ teaspoon of cinnamon, ground
- 1 teaspoon of baking powder

- ½ cup of unsalted butter, melted
- ½ teaspoon of salt
- 1 cup of raisins
- 1 cup of dried cranberries
- 1 egg
- 1 teaspoon of vanilla or maple extract
- ½ cup of whipping cream, optional

Instructions:

- Preheat your oven to 325 degrees. Apply grease on your baking dish.
- Grind the almonds and coconut flakes in your food processor. They should look like oatmeal flakes. Transfer to your bowl.
- Whisk in the rolled oats, sweetener, cinnamon, salt, and baking powder.
- Now, add the cream, butter, maple or vanilla extract, egg, raisins and dried cranberries. Combine well by stirring.
- Spread your mixture in the baking pan.
- Bake for 25 minutes.
- Remove. Set aside for 10 minutes to cool.

Nutrition Facts Per Serving
Calories 307, Carbohydrates 5.2g, Fat 26.9g, Protein 10.35g, Fiber 2.5g

35.   Tortilla Wraps

A wholesome and delicious vegetarian tortilla wrap recipe.

Prep Time: 5 minutes, **Cook Time**: 20 minutes, **Servings**: 10

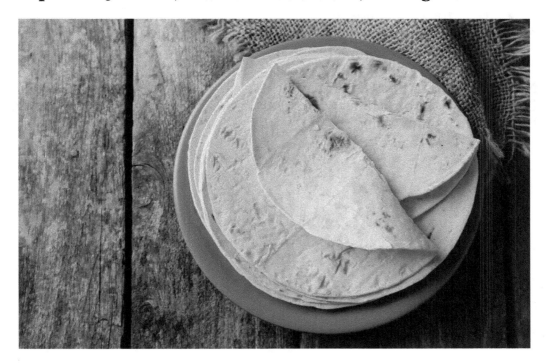

Ingredients:

- 1-1/4 cups of almond flour, blanched
- 3 oz. tapioca flour
- ½ teaspoon of salt
- ¾ cup of almond milk, unsweetened
- 1 tablespoon of olive oil

Instructions:

- Mix the almond milk, almond flour, tapioca, olive oil, and salt in your bowl.

- Heat on medium in your non-stick frying pan.
- Use kitchen paper to absorb some of the oil lightly. Brush this on your pan.
- Place 5 tablespoon of the batter in the pan. Roll it around your pan. You should have a 15 cm diameter circle.
- Heat for 30 seconds. Flip.
- Heat for another 30 seconds. Transfer to a plate.
- Do this for the complete batter.

Nutrition Facts Per Serving
Calories 96, Carbohydrates 8.06g, Fat 6.78g, Protein 1.63g, Sugar 0.25g, Fiber 0.9g, Sodium 25mg

36.   Cauliflower Steaks

An easy and quick recipe you can prepare at home.

Prep Time: 5 minutes, **Cook Time**: 20 minutes, **Servings**: 2

Ingredients:

- 1 teaspoon cumin, ground
- 1 cauliflower head
- ¼ cup of parsley leaves, chopped
- ¼ cup of cilantro, chopped
- 5 tablespoons of canola oil
- 1 garlic clove, crushed
- 3 tablespoons of red wine vinegar
- 1 jalapeno chili, seeded & chopped

Instructions:

- Trim the leaves and excess stem of your cauliflower. Cut off ¼ inch from the stem. Cut two slices from the center.
- Combine a tablespoon of canola oil and cumin.
- Brush over the slices of cauliflower.
- Sprinkle ¼ teaspoon of salt.
- Heat 2 tablespoon of oil in a skillet over medium heat.
- Add the cauliflower. Cook for 3 minutes. Turn the slices over.
- Place the skillet in your oven at 425 F.
- Roast for 15 minutes, then let it cool.
- In the meantime, stir together the parsley, cilantro, garlic, vinegar, jalapeno, ⅛ teaspoon of salt, and the remaining 2 tablespoons of oil.
- Spoon the herb sauce on your cauliflower, when the "steaks" are done.

Nutrition Facts Per Serving
Calories 360, Carbohydrates 4.5g, Fat 37.6g, Protein 2g, Sugar 1.5g, Fiber 1.7g, Sodium 248mg, Potassium 243mg

37. Tofu Pad Thai

This crispy tofu will give you good protein.

Prep Time: 15 minutes, **Cook Time**: 15 minutes, **Servings**: 4

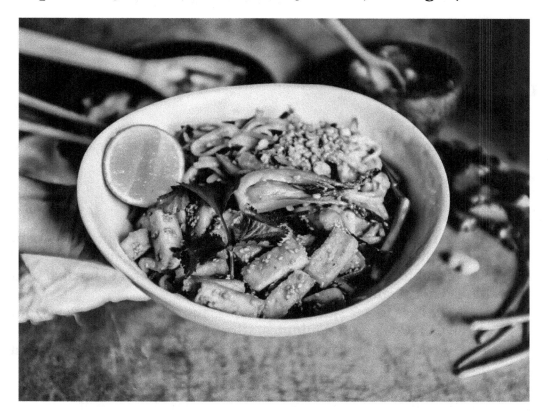

Ingredients:

- 2 teaspoons of salt
- 1 pack rice noodles
- 4 baby Bok Choy
- 1 teaspoon of tamarind paste
- ¾ cup of rice vinegar
- Pinch of cayenne powder or paprika

- 1 cup of granulated sugar
- 16 oz. smoked tofu, drained & cubed
- 1 cup mushrooms
- 10 tablespoons of vegetable or canola oil
- 1/3 cup of peanuts – roasted, unsalted, and chopped
- 4 eggs
- 1 cup of chives
- Cilantro, crushed peanut and sesame seeds topping

Instructions:

- Soak your noodles in cold water in a container.
- Whisk together the vinegar, 2 teaspoons of salt, sugar, and the tamarind in a bowl. Adjust the sauce if needed.
- Add just a pinch of cayenne or paprika for color.
- Boil a large pot of water.
- Divide your ingredients into two batches.
- Add 2 tablespoons of oil to your pan. Crack eggs into your pan. Loosen the yolk gently. Make sure the egg is floating in the oil.
- Shake and flip the egg around your pan. Use a spoon to break it up a bit. Do not scramble.
- Push the eggs to one side so that there is room for the tofu. Place tofu in the pan. Cook it for 5 minutes, stirring it gently.
- Take a handful of the noodles from the water and transfer them to a mesh sieve. Hold it over the water.
- Dip the noodles in and out, up and down of the water.
- Shake off the extra hot water. Ensure your noodles are soft.
- Transfer noodles to your pan. Toss gently.
- Add the mushrooms and Bok Choy to the pan. Add ¼ cup of the sauce to your pan. Toss and flip gently.
- Stir quickly for integrating the sauce.
- Add the chives and peanuts. Toss everything together.
- Cook for 5 minutes. The noodles should look translucent and be soft.
- Turn off the heat.
- Serve with the chopped cilantro, crushed peanuts, and sesame seeds.

Nutrition Facts Per Serving
Calories 870, Carbohydrates 81.3g, Cholesterol 186mg, Fat 51.1g, Protein 21.6g, Sugar 51.9g, Fiber 3.1g, Sodium 1270mg, Potassium 416mg

38.   Veggie Pasta

Fresh and simple pasta that is rich in herbs.

Prep Time: 10 minutes, **Cook Time**: 15 minutes, **Servings**: 4

Ingredients:

- 5 oz. bell peppers, sliced
- 2 teaspoons of butter
- ¾ teaspoon of kosher salt
- 1 cup of water
- 1 cup of zucchini, sliced into thin slices
- 1 cup of eggplant, sliced into thin slices
- 6 cherry tomatoes, halved
- 5 oz. of feta cheese
- 2 teaspoons of lemon rind, shredded

- 1 pack of penne pasta
- ¼ teaspoon of black pepper, ground
- ¼ cup of dill, parsley, or basil, chopped

Instructions:

- Heat the butter over medium heat in your skillet.
- Add the bell pepper and eggplant. Sauté for 3 minutes.
- Next, add half a teaspoon of salt and the water.
- Simmer for 3 minutes.
- Add one teaspoon of lemon rind and the zucchini.
- Simmer for 3 more minutes. The vegetables should be crisp-tender and the liquid should reduce to half cup.
- Bring down the heat to low.
- Add the black pepper, and the remaining ¼ teaspoon of salt to your vegetable mix. Stir to make it smooth.
- Cook pasta as per the package directions.
- Drain in a colander over your bowl. Reserve half a cup of the pasta liquid.
- Add the pasta to your vegetable mix. Coat well by tossing.
- Stir in ¼ cup of the cooking liquid.
- Add the additional cooking liquid.
- Sprinkle the remaining rind, tomatoes and feta over the pasta mix.
- Divide the pasta mix into 4 bowls and sprinkle dill, parsley or basil over it.

Nutrition Facts Per Serving
Calories 351, Carbohydrates 47g, Cholesterol 83mg, Fat 11.8g, Protein 14g, Sugar 51.9g, Fiber 5g, Sodium 587mg

39.   Pasta With Mushrooms and Onions

Mushrooms and caramelized onions make this a flavorful Italian recipe.

Prep Time: 10 minutes, **Cook Time**: 5 minutes, **Servings**: 6

Ingredients:

- 3 cups of mushrooms, sliced
- 1 tablespoon of olive oil
- Cooking spray, olive-oil flavored
- 2 cloves of garlic, minced
- ¼ teaspoon of black pepper
- ½ teaspoon of salt
- ¾ cup of sour cream, low-fat
- 8 cups of tagliatelle pasta
- 1 cup Parmesan cheese, finely grated

- 1 tablespoon of dried oregano

Instructions:

- Heat olive oil in a skillet over medium heat. Apply cooking spray.
- Add the sliced mushrooms.
- Sauté for 5 minutes.
- Add the garlic. Sauté for 30 seconds.
- Add black pepper, salt, onions. Simmer.
- Add the pasta and cook according to instructions (al dente).
- Take out from the heat.
- Stir in the oregano and sour cream.
- Add the finely grated parmesan over the pasta.
- You can garnish with sprigs of oregano if you want.

Nutrition Facts Per Serving
Calories 435, Carbohydrates 75.7g, Cholesterol 12mg, Fat 9.3g, Protein 13.7g, Fiber 8.1g, Sodium 237mg

40.   Asparagus and Pancetta Penne

A healthy recipe with mushrooms, green peas, asparagus, thyme, and parsley.

Prep Time: 15 minutes, **Cook Time**: 25 minutes, **Servings**: 4

Ingredients:

- 2 tablespoons of butter
- 2 tablespoons of all-purpose flour
- 2 oz. pancetta, chopped
- 1 teaspoon of olive oil
- ¼ cup of white wine
- 8 oz. of cremini mushrooms, sliced
- 1 teaspoon of salt
- 12 oz. whole-wheat penne

- 3 cups of milk, low-fat
- 1 tablespoon of thyme, chopped
- 12 oz. asparagus, trimmed & cut into half-inch pieces
- 1 teaspoon of lemon rind, grated
- 3 tablespoons of basil, chopped
- ¾ teaspoon of black pepper

Instructions:

- Combine the butter and flour in your bowl to form a paste.
- Place a sauté pan over medium heat. Pour oil. Coat well.
- Add the pancetta. Cook for 5 minutes while stirring.
- Add the mushrooms. Sauté for 5 minutes. The liquid should evaporate.
- Add the wine and cook for 2 more minutes. Stir to loosen the browned bits. Now, stir in ¼ teaspoon of salt.
- Transfer to a plate.
- Next, add the penne, 2 cups of milk, and the bay leaf to your pan.
- Cook for 8 minutes while stirring occasionally.
- Stir in the asparagus, and half teaspoon salt.
- Cook for 2 minutes while stirring.
- Stir in the remaining salt, thyme, and the remaining milk.
- Cook for 2 more minutes.
- Add the butter-flour paste. Combine by stirring constantly.
- Take out from the heat.
- Stir in the mushroom-pancetta mix, rind, black pepper, and basil.

Nutrition Facts Per Serving
Calories 397, Carbohydrates 54g, Cholesterol 25mg, Fat 11.8g, Sugar 12g, Protein 23g, Fiber 7g, Sodium 721mg

41. Zucchini Noodle Pasta

If you like hot and spicy dishes, this one's for you.

Prep Time: 10 minutes, **Cook Time**: 29 minutes, **Servings**: 2

Ingredients:

- 8 oz. mushrooms, sliced
- 2 zucchini squash, peeled
- 1 cup feta cheese, cut in small cubes
- 2 tomatoes, chopped
- 2 teaspoons of Cajun seasoning
- 1 teaspoon of coconut oil
- Pepper and salt to taste
- Basil for garnish

Instructions:

- Use a peeler or spiral slicer to make noodles from the zucchinis.
- Keep the noodles in a big mesh strainer. Now sprinkle salt.
- Toss noodles well. Set this aside for 30 minutes.
- Melt coconut oil over medium flame. Now add tomatoes and mushrooms. Sauté for 5 minutes.
- Rinse with water after your zucchini noodles are sweated sufficiently. Pat dry using a towel.
- Add noodles to the vegetables and the Cajun seasoning. Stir well and sauté for 2 minutes. Season with pepper and salt to taste.
- Add the noodles, tomatoes, and mushrooms to a plate. Add the feta cheese.
- Sprinkle with basil leaves before serving.

Nutrition Facts Per Serving

Calories 187, Carbohydrates 24g, Fat 8g, Protein 8g, Sugar 15g, Fiber 7g, Sodium 34mg, Potassium 1479mg

42. Spicy Mango Salsa

It is sweet, spicy, and very refreshing. You will also get tangy flavors in this wonderful and easy-to-cook recipe.

Prep Time: 10 minutes, **Cook Time**: 3 minutes, **Servings**: 6

Ingredients:

- 1 red bell pepper, diced
- 3 mangoes, diced
- 3 green onions, chopped
- 2 seedless cucumbers, diced
- ¼ cup of mint, chopped
- 1 jalapeno pepper, chopped
- 2 tablespoons of ginger, minced
- ¼ cup of parsley, chopped
- 2 tablespoons of white balsamic vinegar
- Juice from 1 lime
- ¾ teaspoon of Himalayan salt
- 1 tablespoon of raw honey, melted
- ¼ teaspoon of white pepper, ground

Instructions:

- Put everything in a mixing bowl. Toss to combine well.
- Serve immediately.

Nutrition Facts Per Serving
Calories 83, Carbohydrates 19g, Protein 1g, Sugar 16g, Fiber 2g, Sodium 297mg, Potassium 305mg

43. Vegetarian Gumbo

Tomatoes, roasted peppers, and the smokiness of paprika provide an awesome flavor in this veggie gumbo.

Prep Time: 15 minutes, **Cook Time**: 1 hour, **Servings**: 8

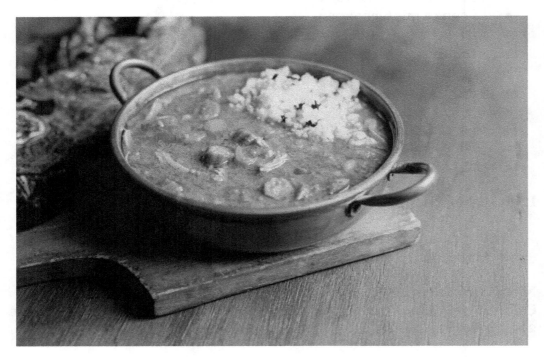

Ingredients:

- 1 banana pepper
- 1 serrano pepper
- ¼ cup + 2 tablespoons of canola oil
- 1 jalapeno chili pepper
- ¼ cup of all-purpose flour
- 1 onion, chopped
- 2 ribs of celery, chopped
- 4 cups of vegetable broth

- 3 bell pepper, chopped
- 2 tablespoons of Cajun seasoning
- 2 garlic cloves, minced
- 1 tablespoon of file powder
- 1 tablespoon of smoked paprika
- 1 sweet potato, peeled & cubed
- 1 cup of roasted tomatoes
- 1 cup of red beans, rinsed & drained
- 1 parsnip, peeled & cubed
- 2 cups of okra, cut
- 1 cup of black-eyed peas, rinsed & drained

Instructions:

- Preheat your oven to broil.
- Arrange the banana, jalapeno chili pepper, and serrano on your baking sheet. Keep in your oven.
- Broil for 5 minutes.
- Take out the peppers from your oven. Keep in a sealed bag for steaming. Take them out after 15 minutes. Peel the crispy skin off.
- Remove the seeds and stems of the peppers.
- Chop them coarsely. Keep in a bowl.
- Heat canola oil over medium heat in a skillet.
- Whisk in the flour. Cook the mix (roux) for 5 minutes, whisking continuously. Remove from the heat.
- Heat 2 tablespoons of canola oil. Stir in the celery with bell peppers and half of the onion.
- Cook for 5 minutes. The veggies should be tender.
- Stir in ¼ cup of the veggie broth. Let it simmer covered for 10 mins.
- Now, stir in the banana, jalapeno, serrano, onions, garlic, bell peppers, paprika powder, and Cajun seasoning into the onions and cooked bell peppers.
- Stir in the roux and a cup of the stock into your veggie mix. The roux should dissolve.
- Simmer for 5 minutes covered.

- Add the sweet potato, tomatoes, red beans, parsnip, okra, peas, and the remaining stock.
- Simmer for 30 more minutes.
- Season with pepper and salt.
- Serve with rice for a more fulfilling meal.

Nutrition Facts Per Serving
Calories 267.8, Carbohydrates 35.7g, Fat 11.8g, Protein 6.8g, Sugar 8.4g, Fiber 8.8g, Sodium 885.8mg, Potassium 679.2mg

44.   Stuffed Potatoes With Beans and Salsa

Prepare this healthy and easy recipe for dinner. It takes only 20 minutes.

Prep Time: 5 minutes, **Cook Time**: 25 minutes, **Servings**: 4

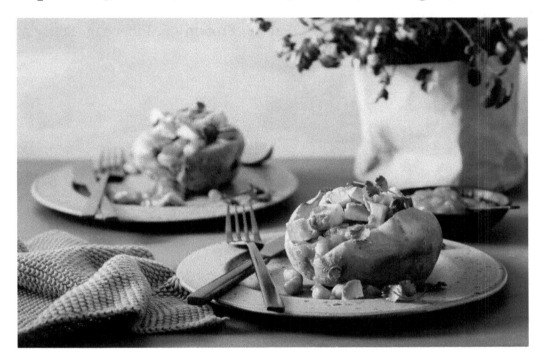

Ingredients:

- ½ cup of salsa
- 4 sweet potatoes
- 1 avocado, sliced
- 4 teaspoons jalapenos, chopped
- 1 can of pinto beans, mashed lightly

Instructions:

- Use a fork to pierce the potatoes.

- Microwave on medium heat for 20 minutes. Turn one, two times.
- Take them out and put them on a cutting board. Let them cool a bit.
- Cut lengthwise to open the potatoes. Pinch the ends.
- Top with avocado, some salsa, jalapenos, and beans.

Nutrition Facts Per Serving
Calories 324, Carbohydrates 57g, Fat 9g, Protein 9g, Fiber 11g, Sugar 5g, Sodium 422mg, Potassium 1415mg

45. Spaghetti Bolognese

A lighter and delicious version of the one from Italy, which is a classic.

Prep Time: 15 minutes, **Cook Time**: 40 minutes, **Servings**: 4

Ingredients:

- ½ yellow onion, diced
- 2 tablespoons of extra-virgin olive oil
- 4 cups of cremini mushrooms, chopped
- ½ cup of walnuts, crushed
- 1 tablespoon of rosemary, chopped
- 1 tablespoon of balsamic vinegar
- 2 cloves of garlic, minced
- 1 can of tomatoes, diced
- 1 tablespoon of tamari

- 1 tablespoon of tomato paste
- 1-1/2 cups of green or brown lentils
- 1 cup of cherry tomatoes
- 1 teaspoon sage, dried
- 8 oz. of spaghetti
- Black pepper and sea salt
- Red pepper flakes
- Pomegranate seeds and chopped spring onion, for serving

Instructions:

- Heat oil over medium heat in your skillet.
- Add the pepper, salt, and yellow onion. Cook for 3 minutes.
- Add mushrooms and a pinch of salt. Cook for 8 minutes. Stir occasionally.
- Stir the rosemary in. Push everything to a side of your pan so that you can include the walnuts.
- Add your walnuts. Toast them for 30 seconds. Stir everything together.
- Now, stir in the garlic. Add the tamari and balsamic vinegar. Stir.
- Add the lentils, tomatoes, sage, cherry tomatoes, and tomato paste. Give it a good stir.
- Bring down the heat. Simmer for 25 minutes. The sauce should thicken. Adjust the seasoning.
- Boil a pot of salted water.
- Prepare the pasta as per the pack instructions.
- Drain. Add your pasta to the pan with the sauce.
- Serve with pomegranate seeds, chopped spring onion, and red pepper flakes.

Nutrition Facts Per Serving
Calories 540, Carbohydrates 54.5g, Cholesterol 41mg, Fat 30g, Protein 18.9g, Fiber 6g, Sugar 8.1g, Sodium 480mg, Potassium 1007mg

46.　　Fajita Veggies

You are sure to fall in love with this rainbow fajita recipe.

Prep Time: 15 minutes, **Cook Time**: 15 minutes, **Servings**: 4

Ingredients:

- 3 portobello mushrooms, stemmed
- 3 multi-colored peppers, stemmed & sliced
- 2 tablespoons of avocado oil
- 1 red onion, sliced
- ½ teaspoon of chili powder
- 2 cloves of garlic, chopped
- ½ teaspoon of sea salt
- ½ teaspoon of cumin
- 2 limes, sliced

- Black pepper, ground
- Splash of balsamic vinegar
- 8 corn or flour tortillas
- Avocado slices
- Jalapenos, sliced
- Diced tomatoes
- Cilantro
- 1 cup sour cream
- Salsa Mexicana, optional

Instructions:

- Heat a grill with a cast-iron skillet inside.
- Keep peppers on a tray. Onion and mushrooms on a separate rimmed plate.
- Whisk together the garlic, avocado oil, cumin, chili powder, pepper, and salt in a bowl.
- Drizzle a tablespoon of the mix over your peppers. Coat well.
- Drizzle the remaining marinade over the onions and mushrooms.
- Add a splash of the balsamic vinegar over the mushrooms.
- Coat both sides of the mushrooms with your hands.
- Now, grill the peppers for 9 minutes. Toss occasionally.
- Grill the onion and mushrooms for 4 minutes per side.
- Take out everything from your grill.
- Squeeze out the juice from half lemon over your peppers.
- Season with chili powder, pepper, and salt.
- Slice mushrooms into strips. Keep on your serving plate.
- Transfer the peppers and onions to your platter.
- Serve with the jalapenos, tortillas, cilantro, tomatoes, salsa, sour cream and the remaining lime wedges.

Nutrition Facts Per Serving
Calories 93, Carbohydrates 17.5g, Fat 1.7g, Protein 4.7g, Fiber 4.9g, Sugar 7g, Sodium 246mg, Potassium 355mg

47.   Mexican Quinoa

Prepare this recipe from Mexico with tomatoes, chilies, black beans, and corn. It is a healthy vegan dinner idea.

Prep Time: 5 minutes, **Cook Time**: 37 minutes, **Servings**: 6

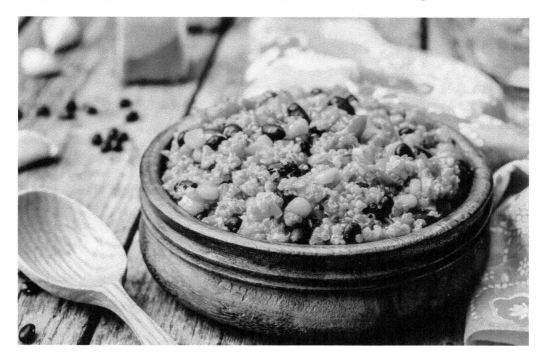

Ingredients:

- 2 cloves of garlic, minced
- 1 tablespoon of olive oil
- 2 cups of quinoa
- 1 can of pinto or black beans, drained & rinsed
- 1 can of tomatoes with green chilies
- ½ teaspoon of cumin
- 1-1/2 cups of corn kernels
- ¼ cup of cilantro, chopped

- ½ teaspoon of salt

Instructions:

- Heat the olive oil on medium in your saucepan or skillet.
- Add garlic. Sauté for 30 seconds.
- Add the other ingredients, except the cilantro. Boil.
- Bring down the heat to low. Simmer for 25 minutes.
- Stir the cilantro in before serving.

Nutrition Facts Per Serving
Calories 125, Carbohydrates 20.7g, Fat 3.3g, Protein 4.6g, Fiber 2.1g, Sugar 0.7g, Sodium 355.2mg

48.   Stuffed Red Peppers

It can be the perfect healthy dinner. It is light, fresh, and easy to prepare.

Prep Time: 15 minutes, **Cook Time**: 35 minutes, **Servings**: 4

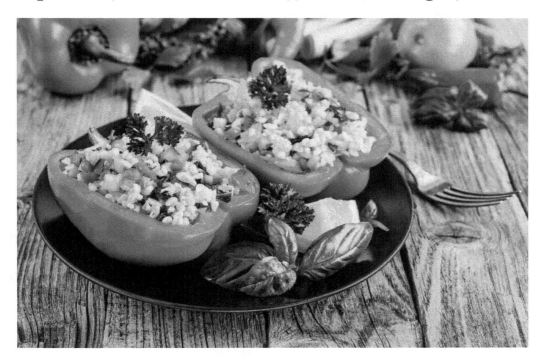

Ingredients:

- 1/3 cup of chopped scallions or diced red onion
- Extra-virgin olive oil
- 4 red peppers
- ½ cup of red bell pepper, diced
- 1 cup of cauliflower florets, break into small pieces
- ½ teaspoon of coriander
- ½ teaspoon of cumin
- 1 clove of garlic, minced
- ½ teaspoon of oregano

- 1 cup of bulgur
- 1 cup cannellini beans, drained & rinsed
- 2 tablespoons of lemon juice, also wedges for serving
- 3 cups of spinach
- Basil leaves, for garnish
- Ground black pepper and sea salt

Instructions:

- Preheat your oven to 400 F.
- Use parchment paper to line your baking sheet.
- Slice your peppers in half. Remove the seeds.
- Keep on the baking sheet. Drizzle olive oil, pepper, and salt.
- Roast for 15 minutes. The cut side should be up.
- Heat a tablespoon of olive oil in your skillet over medium heat.
- Add the cauliflower, onion, cumin, red pepper, oregano, coriander, half teaspoon of salt, pepper, and garlic.
- Cook for 6 minutes. The onion should be soft. The cauliflower should become light brown.
- Take out from the heat. Stir in the bulgur, cannellini beans, tomatillo salsa, lemon juice, and spinach. Adjust the seasoning.
- Place your filling into the peppers.
- Bake for 12 minutes.
- Serve with cilantro, lemon slices, and basil.

Nutrition Facts Per Serving
Calories 413, Carbohydrates 78.4g, Fat 4.9g, Protein 16.4g, Fiber 10.5g, Sugar 5.6g, Sodium 62mg, Potassium 1222mg

49.   Vegan Meatballs

Hearty vegan meatballs are always going to be a hit. You will love its smoky, savory flavor.

Prep Time: 20 minutes, **Cook Time**: 60 minutes, **Servings**: 6

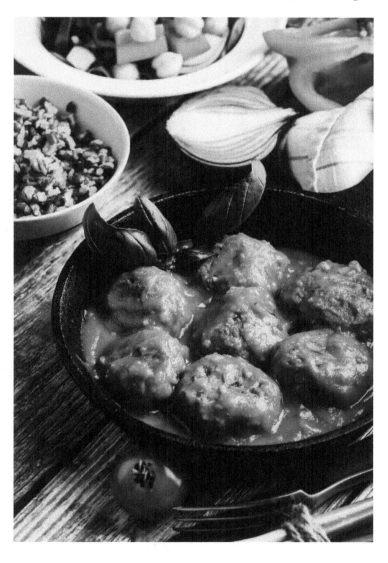

Ingredients:

- ½ yellow onion, chopped
- ½ teaspoon of extra-virgin olive oil
- 1 cup black beans, drained & rinsed
- 8 oz. of mushrooms, de-stemmed & chopped
- 1 tablespoon of balsamic vinegar
- 2 cloves of garlic, chopped
- ½ cup of walnuts
- 1 tablespoon of tamari
- ½ teaspoon of chili powder
- 1-1/2 cups of brown rice
- ½ teaspoon of sea salt
- ½ teaspoon of onion powder
- 1 cup of panko bread crumbs
- ½ teaspoon black pepper, ground
- 2 cups of marinara sauce
- ½ cup of basil, chopped
- Vegan parmesan cheese, optional
- Handfuls of arugula, optional

Instructions:

- Heat half teaspoon of olive oil in a skillet over medium heat.
- Add the onion. Cook for 2 minutes.
- Add some pepper, salt, and mushrooms. Cook for 6 minutes.
- Add half a cup of black beans, balsamic vinegar, tamari sauce, and garlic. Cook for another 2 minutes.
- Take out from the heat. Set aside for cooling.
- Pulse your walnuts in a food processor.
- Add your mushroom mix. Pulse 2-3 times.
- Add the remaining black beans. Pulse briefly.
- Transfer your mixture to a bowl.
- Stir in the chili powder, brown rice, pepper, salt, and chili powder.
- Mix to combine well. Adjust the seasonings.

- Preheat your oven to 400 F.
- Use parchment paper to line your baking sheet.
- Spread the breadcrumbs on a plate. Create 18 balls from your mixture. They should all be 1-1/2 inches in size.
- Roll in the crumbs gently using your breadcrumbs.
- Keep on the baking sheet. Refrigerate for 15 minutes.
- Drizzle olive oil. Bake for 35 minutes. Flip halfway through.
- Heat your marinara sauce in the skillet. Add the meatballs.
- Serve immediately with the basil, arugula, and parmesan cheese.

Nutrition Facts Per Serving
Calories 1136, Carbohydrates 208.5g, Fat 19.8g, Protein 31.8g, Fiber 14.4g, Sugar 7.1g, Sodium 987mg, Potassium 1196mg

50.   Tofu Soba Noodles

Follow this recipe to cook your soba noodles at home. It can be a very good weekday lunch.

Prep Time: 10 minutes, **Cook Time**: 10 minutes, **Servings**: 4

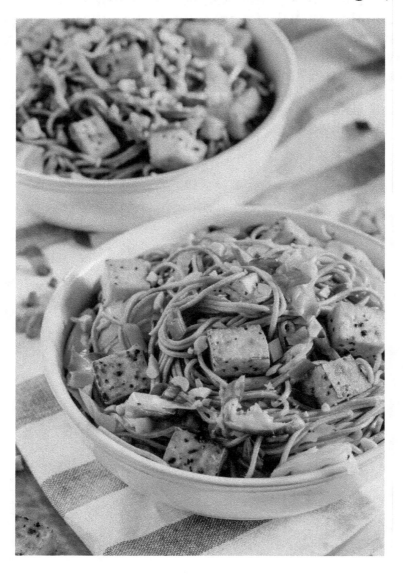

Ingredients:

- 2 tablespoons of tamari
- ¼ cup of rice vinegar
- 1 teaspoon ginger, grated
- ½ teaspoon of sesame oil, toasted
- ½ teaspoon of honey or maple syrup
- 1 clove of garlic, grated
- 1 cup of peanuts, chopped
- 16 oz. smoked tofu, drained & cubed
- 4 spring onions, chopped
- 12 oz. of soba noodles
- Sesame oil for drizzling
- 2 cups of snap peas, blenched
- Sesame seeds, optional

Instructions:

- Combine the tamari, vinegar, ginger, sesame oil, honey, and garlic in a bowl. Set aside.
- Boil a pot of water. Cook your soba noodles as per the pack instructions. Drain, rinse in cold water.
- Place tofu in the pan. Cook it for 5 minutes, stirring it gently.
- Toss your noodles with the dressing. Divide into 4 bowls.
- Add to your bowls the snap peas, cooked tofu, chopped peanuts. Optionally, sprinkle some sesame seeds.
- Drizzle sesame oil.

Nutrition Facts Per Serving

Calories 801, Carbohydrates 100g, Fat 37.9g, Protein 24.7g, Fiber 18.9g, Sugar 15.7g, Sodium 1478mg, Potassium 1235mg

51. Butternut Risotto With Hazelnuts and Cranberries

You cannot get enough of this risotto. It is very good comfort food.

Prep Time: 10 minutes, **Cook Time**: 1 hour, **Servings**: 6

Ingredients:

- 1 butternut squash, halved & seeds removed

- 3 tablespoons of extra-virgin olive oil
- 3 cups of vegetable or chicken broth
- Ground black pepper and kosher salt
- 2 cups hazelnuts, chopped
- 1 cup dried cranberries
- 7 tablespoons of unsalted butter
- 1 cup of Arborio rice
- 1 clove of garlic, minced
- ½ cup of parmesan cheese, grated
- ½ cup of dry white wine

Instructions:

- Put a rack on the lower level of your oven. Preheat to 375 F.
- Add 2 tablespoons of olive oil on your baking sheet. Coat the tray.
- Place your butternut squash halves on the baking sheet. The cut side should be down. Coat oil on the surface well.
- Roast for 40 minutes.
- Turn your squash with tongs on your baking sheet. Season with pepper and salt.
- Spoon the remaining oil from the pan over your squash.
- Let your squash cool. Scoop flesh into the bowl of your food processor. Now, add the broth. Puree to make it smooth.
- Transfer to your saucepan. Keep warm over low heat.
- Heat a tablespoon of butter in a saucepan with the remaining olive oil.
- Next, add the garlic. Cook for 1 more minute.
- Add the rice. Cook for a minute more, stirring constantly.
- Add the wine. Simmer over medium heat while stirring.
- Add a cup of the butternut-broth mix to your rice. Cook while stirring often. The broth should be absorbed almost completely.
- Keep adding the broth until you have ½ cup broth left for about 20 minutes. Stir often.
- In the meantime, melt the butter over medium heat in your skillet.
- Add the leeks. Cook for 10 minutes, stirring occasionally.
- Season with salt.

- Stir in the remaining ½ cup broth into the risotto.
- Stir in the parmesan and the remaining 4 tablespoons of butter into your risotto. Combine well.
- Spoon the risotto on plates.
- Garnish with the chopped hazelnuts and cranberries.

Nutrition Facts Per Serving
Calories 457, Carbohydrates 55g, Fat 23g, Protein 7g, Sugar 6g

52.   Coconut Curry

This could be your go-to veggie curry recipe. It has a lot of flavors and is also easy to prepare.

Prep Time: 15 minutes, **Cook Time**: 35 minutes, **Servings**: 4

Ingredients:

- 1 cup of red onion, chopped
- 1 tablespoon of coconut oil
- ½ teaspoon ginger, grated
- 2 cloves of garlic, minced
- ¼ teaspoon of coriander
- ½ teaspoon of cumin
- ¼ teaspoon of cardamom

- ¼ teaspoon of turmeric
- 2 cups of butternut squash, cubed
- 1 teaspoon of sea salt
- 2 cups of cauliflower florets
- 3 red Thai chilies or ½ jalapeno, sliced
- 1 can of coconut milk, full-fat
- 2 cups of sweet potato, cubed
- 2 tablespoons of lemon juice and also wedges for serving
- Black pepper, ground

Instructions:

- Heat oil over medium heat in your oven. Add the onion. Cook for 10 minutes. Bring down the heat to low halfway through.
- Mix together the ginger, garlic, coriander, cumin, cardamom, salt, and turmeric in a bowl. Set aside.
- Add the chilies, potatoes and butternut squash.
- Stir. Cook for 4 minutes.
- Stir the cauliflower in and then add your coconut milk and the spice mix. Simmer covered for 18 minutes. The veggies should be tender.
- Add the lemon juice. Stir. Adjust the seasoning.
- Serve your curry over rice with the lemon wedges and optionally sliced red onion and chili peppers.

Nutrition Facts Per Serving

Calories 161, Carbohydrates 23.9g, Cholesterol 4mg, Fat 6.7g, Protein 5g, Fiber 5.2g, Sugar 8.6g, Sodium 649mg, Potassium 698mg

53.   **Indian Shepherd's Pie**

A wonderful Shepherd's Pie with Indian spices. You will love this delicious dinner recipe surely.

Prep Time: 20 minutes, **Cook Time**: 45 minutes, **Servings**: 8

Ingredients:

- 4 tablespoons of vegan butter
- 32 oz. potatoes
- ½ cup of milk
- ½ cup of sour cream or plain yogurt
- 1 teaspoon of pepper
- 2 teaspoons of salt
- 1 teaspoon of yellow curry powder
- 4 tablespoons of olive oil

- 2-1/2 cups of lentils, cooked
- 4 garlic cloves, chopped
- 1 onion, diced
- 2 cups of celery, diced
- 2 cups carrot, diced
- 1 teaspoon of cumin
- 2 teaspoons of garam masala
- 1 teaspoon of coriander
- 2-1/4 cups of vegetable broth
- 2 teaspoons of fenugreek leaves, dried
- 1 cup of peas
- 1 teaspoon of cumin seeds
- 3 tablespoons of flour
- 1 teaspoon of fennel seeds

Instructions:

- Boil the potatoes in a pot. Lower the heat and simmer covered for 20 minutes.
- Keep the lentils in salted water for 25 minutes. Simmer to make them tender. They should not fall apart.
- In a large skillet, heat oil and sauté the onion for 3 minutes.
- Bring down the heat to medium. Add the garlic. Sauté for 2 minutes.
- Add the celery and carrots. Cook for 6 minutes.
- Add the cumin, salt, fenugreek leaves, garam masala, and coriander.
- Add the broth. Simmer covered on medium heat for 7 minutes. The carrots should be cooked through.
- Simmer the fennel and cumin seeds over medium heat in a pot.
- Add the flour. Whisk and stir for a minute.
- Whisk the veggie broth in gradually. Cook until it has thickened slightly. Now, add this gravy to your filling and also the drained lentils and peas. Combine well by mixing.
- Adjust the pepper and salt.
- Drain the potatoes. Save some hot potato water. Return to the pot.
- Mash with some oil and yogurt.

- Season with curry powder, pepper, and salt. Mash and whip to make it light, fluffy, and smooth.
- Place in your oven for 20 minutes.
- Garnish with cilantro, chives, and scallions.

Nutrition Facts Per Serving
Calories 383, Carbohydrates 49.6g, Cholesterol 41.3mg, Fat 15.9g, Protein 12.2g, Fiber 11.3g, Sugar 8.7g, Sodium 850mg, Potassium 24mg

<u>Seafood</u>

54.   **Low-Carb Fish Tacos**

Soft tortillas that are filled with taco sauce and fried fish.

Prep Time: 20 minutes, **Cook Time**: 40 minutes, **Servings**: 3

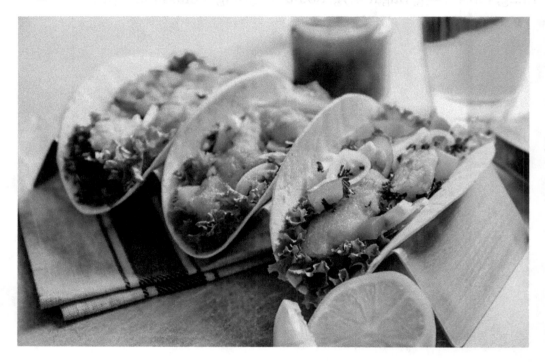

Ingredients:

- 1 tablespoon of lime juice
- 2-3 fillets of snapper, halibut, tilapia, mahi-mahi, or cod.
- ½ teaspoon of salt
- ¼ teaspoon of black pepper
- ½ teaspoon of cayenne pepper
- 2 eggs
- 3 tablespoons of flour

- Avocado oil or coconut oil for frying
- 1 teaspoon of paprika
- 1 avocado
- 1 tomato
- ¼ cup cilantro, chopped
- 1 red pepper, sliced
- 6 leaves of Batavia lettuce
- 2 tablespoons of mayonnaise
- 4 tablespoons of sour cream
- 1 tablespoon garlic, minced
- ¼ teaspoon of chili oil
- 3 tortillas

Instructions:

- Cut the fillets of fish into small pieces.
- Place them with spices and marinate in a bowl for 30 minutes.
- Chop, dice all the vegetables for the topping.
- Prepare your taco sauce by mixing all ingredients in a bowl. You can spread the sauce on your tortillas later or drizzle on the tacos from a bottle.
- Add the two eggs to a bowl. Mix well. Add the paprika over them
- Heat oil in a pot.
- Dip your fillets into the eggs. Coat well.
- Put the flour on another plate and dip the fillets into the flour.
- Add the fish to the oil once coated. Fry for a minute on each side. It is ready when you see the batter turn golden brown.
- Add the lettuce leaves to the tortilla.
- Drizzle the sauce over.
- Add the vegetables and fried fish and enjoy while still fresh.

Nutrition Facts Per Serving

Calories 613, Carbohydrates 27.6g, Cholesterol 178mg, Fat 39.7g, Protein 39.8g, Fiber 17.6g, Sugar 3.43g, Sodium 2656mg, Potassium 58.39mg

55.   Shrimp Scampi

This recipe is a favorite in many Italian restaurants. But you can now prepare it at home as well.

Prep Time: 20 minutes, **Cook Time**: 20 minutes, **Servings**: 4

Ingredients:

- 12 oz. plain or whole-wheat linguine
- 24 oz. shrimp in shells
- 3 garlic cloves, minced
- 1 tablespoon of olive oil
- 1 tablespoon of butter
- 2 tablespoons of chicken broth, low-sodium
- 1 tablespoon of parsley or chives, chopped
- 1/8 teaspoon of salt

Instructions:

- Thaw the shrimp. Peel and devein. Leave the tails intact.
- Rinse and pat dry using paper towels.
- Cook the linguine as per the pack instructions. Drain. Keep warm.
- Heat oil over medium heat in a skillet in the meantime.
- Add the garlic. Cook for 15 seconds while stirring.
- Add the shrimp. Cook for 3 minutes, stirring frequently.
- Transfer to your serving platter.
- Add salt and butter to your skillet. Cook while stirring over medium heat. Pour the butter mix over the shrimp.
- Sprinkle the chives. Serve over the linguine.

Nutrition Facts Per Serving
Calories 341, Carbohydrates 34g, Cholesterol 222mg, Fat 9g, Protein 29g, Fiber 1g, Sugar 2g, Sodium 1039mg, Potassium 274mg

56.　　**Rosemary Salmon**

Salmon will give you a lot of omega-3 fatty acids. Serve this simple recipe with asparagus, quinoa, or roasted potatoes.

Prep Time: 10 minutes, **Cook Time**: 15 minutes, **Servings**: 4

Ingredients:

- 2 garlic cloves, minced
- 2 red onions, sliced
- 2 garlic heads
- 1 lemon, sliced
- 2 teaspoons of Dijon mustard
- 1 teaspoon of lemon juice
- ¼ teaspoon of lemon zest
- ½ teaspoon of honey

- 2 teaspoon of rosemary, finely chopped
- ¼ teaspoon red pepper, crushed
- ½ teaspoon of kosher salt
- 16 oz. salmon fillets, skinless
- 16 oz. asparagus
- 2 tablespoons of extra-virgin olive oil
- Lemon wedges and rosemary sprigs for garnishing

Instructions:

- Preheat your oven to 425 F. Use parchment paper to line your baking sheet.
- Combine the minced garlic cloves, mustard, lemon juice and zest, honey, rosemary, red pepper, and salt in a bowl.
- Place the salmon on your baking sheet. Now, spread the mustard mix over your fish.
- Add the sliced onion, asparagus, sliced lemon and garlic heads (bottoms removed) around the salmon.
- Drizzle everything with the olive oil.
- Bake for 15 minutes. You should be able to flake the fish easily with a fork. The asparagus should be tender.
- Sprinkle with fresh rosemary sprigs. Serve with lemon wedges.

Nutrition Facts Per Serving

Calories 222, Carbohydrates 4g, Cholesterol 62mg, Fat 12g, Protein 24g, Fiber 1g, Sugar 1g, Sodium 256mg

57. Honey Garlic Shrimp

A healthy and easy dinner recipe for the entire family.

Prep Time: 15 minutes, **Cook Time**: 25 minutes, **Servings**: 4

Ingredients:

- 1 tablespoon and 2 teaspoons of olive oil
- 16 oz. florets of broccoli
- 1/8 teaspoon of pepper
- ¼ teaspoon of salt
- 1/3 cup of coconut aminos
- ¼ cup of honey
- 1 teaspoon ginger, peeled & grated, optional
- 4 garlic cloves, minced
- 16 oz. shrimp, peeled & deveined

- 2 teaspoons of lemon juice
- ½ teaspoon of corn starch or tapioca flour
- Lime wedges for garnishing

Instructions:

- Preheat your oven to 400 F. Use parchment paper to line your baking sheet. Spray oil and set aside.
- Whisk together the coconut aminos, honey, ginger, lemon juice, and garlic in a bowl. Keep half of this in a bowl for making the sauce.
- Add the shrimp to the remaining. Coat well by tossing.
- Refrigerate the shrimp to marinate.
- Cover and refrigerate the other marinade for later use.
- Roast the broccoli in the meantime. Add the broccoli to your baking pan. Drizzle olive oil. Sprinkle with pepper and salt.
- Bake for 10 minutes.
- Take out the pan from your oven. Push broccoli to a side.
- Add your marinated shrimp. Bake for 12 more minutes. The broccoli should be tender and the shrimp should become opaque.
- Prepare the sauce while it is baking. Place the reserved sauce in a pan. Whisk together a tablespoon of water and the tapioca flour.
- Add to your saucepan. Heat on medium while stirring. Set aside.
- Prepare white or brown rice while your broccoli and shrimp are baking.
- Serve with lime wedges, and the sauce.

Nutrition Facts Per Serving
Calories 1177, Carbohydrates 124.3g, Cholesterol 223mg, Fat 4.9g, Protein 24.6g, Fiber 0.3g, Sugar 17.5g, Sodium 4480mg, Potassium 33mg

58. Honey Glazed Salmon

Bake this salmon recipe in your oven for a wonderful meal.

Prep Time: 25 minutes, **Cook Time**: 25 minutes, **Servings**: 4

Ingredients:

- 1/8 teaspoon of black pepper
- ½ teaspoon of sea salt
- 4 salmon fillets of 6 oz. each, boneless & skin-on
- 16 oz. spinach
- 2 avocados, sliced
- 1 cup soy sauce
- 4 tablespoons of honey
- 3 garlic cloves, minced
- Juice from 1 lime

- 10 cups spinach
- Sesame seeds for garnishing

Instructions:

- Rest the salmon at room temperature for 20 minutes.
- Preheat your oven to 450 F in the meantime. Use parchment paper to line your baking pan. Set aside.
- Prepare the marinade. Whisk together the soy sauce, honey, lime juice, and garlic in a bowl. Set aside.
- Use a paper towel to pat dry the salmon.
- Keep on your baking pan. The skin side should be down.
- Season with pepper and salt.
- Coat each fillet with the prepared glaze. Leave out some that you will drizzle later.
- Bake for 16 minutes in your oven. Turn your oven to broil.
- Broil for 3 minutes. The top of the salmon should be crispy.
- Meanwhile heat oil in a skillet. Add the spinach and cook 3 minutes. Toss it continuously. Remove it from the heat.
- When the salmon is ready, take it out from your oven.
- Put the spinach on a plate. Add the salmon on top. Drizzle the sauce. Add the avocado slices near them. Sprinkle the sesame seeds.
- Serve with rice or other preferred veggies.

Nutrition Facts Per Serving

Calories 248, Carbohydrates 20.8g, Cholesterol 56mg, Fat 7.9g, Protein 25g, Sugar 17.4g, Sodium 70mg

59.   Blackened Salmon

A salmon recipe that tastes so yummy that everyone will think you ordered it from a restaurant.

Prep Time: 5 minutes, **Cook Time**: 10 minutes, **Servings**: 4

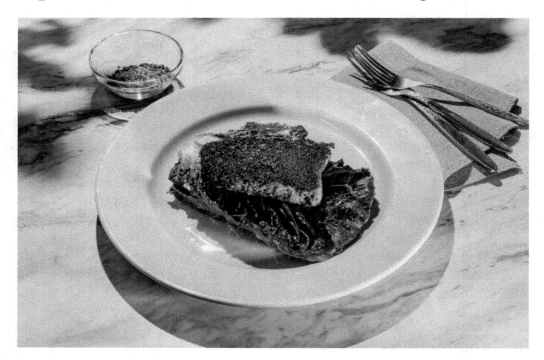

Ingredients:

- 2 teaspoons of cumin, ground
- 2 teaspoons of paprika, smoked
- 1 teaspoon of oregano, dried
- 2 teaspoons of garlic powder
- ½ teaspoon of black pepper
- 1 teaspoon of salt
- 1 teaspoon of onion powder
- 5 tablespoons of butter or olive oil

- ½ teaspoon of cayenne pepper
- 4 fillets of salmon, 6 oz. each
- 1 tablespoon of parsley, chopped
- Juice from half lemon

Instructions:

- Keep the cumin, smoked paprika, oregano, garlic powder, pepper, salt, and onion powder in a bowl.
- Use paper towels to pat dry the salmon. Spread the oil or butter on top.
- Now, dip each salmon piece into your seasoning. Push down. You should have an even, thick coat.
- Heat a skillet over high. Brush oil or butter lightly.
- Place the fillet when it is hot. The seasoning side should be down.
- Cook for 3 minutes on high heat.
- Mix the topping together in a dish.
- Flip your fillets once the salmon is crusty and blackened.
- Turn down the heat to medium.
- Brush the prepared mix on the top of each fillet.
- Cook for 7 minutes over medium.
- Take out from the heat. Serve immediately.

Nutrition Facts Per Serving
Calories 358, Carbohydrates 5.3g, Cholesterol 102.2mg, Fat 21.3g, Protein 38.9g, Sugar 1g, Fiber 1.1g, Sodium 720mg

60.   Mediterranean Cod with Roasted Tomatoes

A Mediterranean-inspired meal that will please you in every bite.

Prep Time: 5 minutes, **Cook Time**: 15 minutes, **Servings**: 4

Ingredients:

- 2 teaspoons of oregano
- 4 oz. cod fillets, skinless
- ½ teaspoon of salt
- 1 teaspoon thyme
- ¼ teaspoon of paprika
- ¼ teaspoon of garlic powder
- ¼ teaspoon of black pepper
- Non-stick cooking spray
- 2 garlic cloves, sliced

- 3 cups of cherry tomatoes
- 6 tablespoons butter, divided
- 2 limes, sliced
- 1 tablespoon of olive oil
- Parsley for garnish

Instructions:

- Preheat your oven to 450 F.
- Rinse the fish. Use paper towels to pat dry.
- Combine the thyme, oregano, garlic powder, salt, black pepper, and paprika in a bowl.
- Sprinkle half of your oregano mix on both sides of each fillet.
- Use aluminum foil to line a baking pan.
- Keep the fish on one side of the pan lined. Add the butter over it.
- Keep the garlic and tomatoes on the other side.
- Combine oil and the remaining oregano mix.
- Drizzle the oil mix over the tomatoes. Coat well by tossing.
- Bake for 10 minutes. You should be able to easily flake the fish using a fork.
- Stir the tomato mix once.
- Divide the roasted tomato mix and fish evenly among 4 serving plates.
- Add the lime slices and garnish with fresh parsley.

Nutrition Facts Per Serving

Calories 157, Carbohydrates 6.5g, Cholesterol 48.8mg, Fat 4.8g, Protein 21.6g, Sugar 3.6g, Fiber 1.8g, Sodium 429.2mg, Potassium 807mg

61. Fish Amandine

Use tilapia fillets to cook this quick dinner recipe.

Prep Time: 15 minutes, **Cook Time**: 15 minutes, **Servings**: 4

Ingredients:

- ¼ cup of buttermilk
- 4 tilapias, halibut, or trout fillets
- 2 tablespoons of parsley, chopped
- ½ cup of panko breadcrumbs
- ¼ teaspoon of salt
- ½ teaspoon of dry mustard
- 2 tablespoons of parmesan cheese, grated
- ¼ cup of almonds, sliced & finely chopped
- 1/8 teaspoon red pepper, crushed

- 1 tablespoon of melted butter

Instructions:

- Preheat your oven to 450 F. Grease your baking pan. Set aside.
- Rinse the fish and pat dry using paper towels.
- Pour buttermilk into a dish. Combine the parsley, breadcrumbs, salt, and dry mustard in another dish.
- First, dip your fish into the buttermilk and then into the crumb mix. Coat well. Place the fish into the baking pan.
- Sprinkle the parmesan cheese and almonds on the fish.
- Drizzle some of the melted butter.
- Bake 5 minutes for each half-inch thickness of the fish. It should easily flake with a fork.
- Serve with asparagus and lemon wedges.

Nutrition Facts Per Serving
Calories 209, Carbohydrates 6.7g, Cholesterol 66.9mg, Fat 8.7g, Protein 26.2g, Sugar 1g, Fiber 0.9g, Sodium 301.6mg, Potassium 413.8mg

62. **Shrimp Lettuce Wraps**

This is a fresh and healthy recipe packed with flavors. It can quickly become the favorite of your family.

Prep Time: 10 minutes, **Cook Time**: 10 minutes, **Servings**: 4

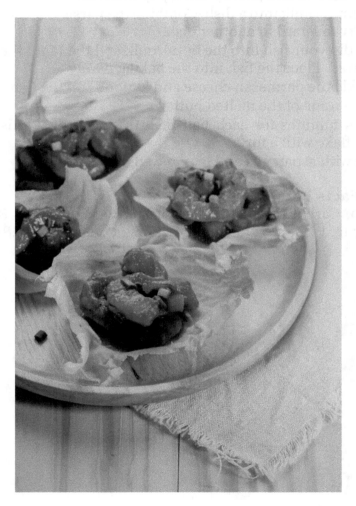

Ingredients:

- 2 cloves of garlic, minced

- ¼ tablespoons of butter
- 1 tablespoon of extra-virgin olive oil
- ¼ cup of hot sauce
- Kosher salt
- 16 oz. of shrimp, peeled & deveined, remove the tails
- 1 romaine head
- Black pepper, ground
- 1 can roasted tomatoes
- 1 red onion, chopped
- 1 jalapeno pepper
- 1 lime, juiced
- 1 small green chili, diced
- Chopped chives for garnish

Instructions:

- Prepare the sauce for the shrimps– melt the butter over medium heat.
- Add the garlic when it is completely melted. Cook for a minute.
- Add the hot sauce. Combine well by stirring.
- Turn the heat low.
- Prepare the shrimp. Season with pepper and salt.
- Add the shrimp to the sauce and cook it each side for 2 minutes. Coat well by tossing. Flip after a minute. It should be opaque and pink.
- Turn the heat off.
- Make the red salsa. Add the tomatoes, lime, onion, jalapeno paper and green chili to a blender and mix.
- Assemble the wraps. Add the salsa on top of the lettuce. Then place a scoop of your shrimp at the center of your romaine leaf.
- Add chopped chives for garnish.

Nutrition Facts Per Serving

Calories 265, Carbohydrates 9g, Cholesterol 253mg, Fat 11.5g, Protein 31.7g, Sugar 2.6g, Fiber 0.4g, Sodium 956mg, Potassium 684mg

63.　　Baked Salmon with Pesto

Serve this salmon recipe to your guests or have a hearty lunch. The pesto sauce, basil, and nutty flavor give it a unique taste.

Prep Time: 5 minutes, **Cook Time**: 30 minutes, **Servings**: 4

Ingredients:

- 8 tablespoons of green pesto
- 2 cups of Greek yogurt, full-fat
- 32 oz. salmon

Instructions:
- Put the salmon in your greased baking dish. The skin side should be down.
- Spread the pesto, pepper, and salt on top.
- Bake for 30 minutes at 400 degrees F.

- In the meantime, stir together the sauce ingredients (4 tbsp. green pesto, yogurt).
- Serve with salad and lemon slices.

Nutrition Facts Per Serving
Calories 1468, Carbohydrates 17.1g, Cholesterol 117mg, Fat 131.7g, Protein 57.1g, Sugar 4.8g, Sodium 526mg, Potassium 911mg

64.   Garlicky Shrimp & Spinach

Does it look better or taste better? Difficult choice!

Prep Time: 10 minutes, **Cook Time**: 15 minutes, **Servings**: 4

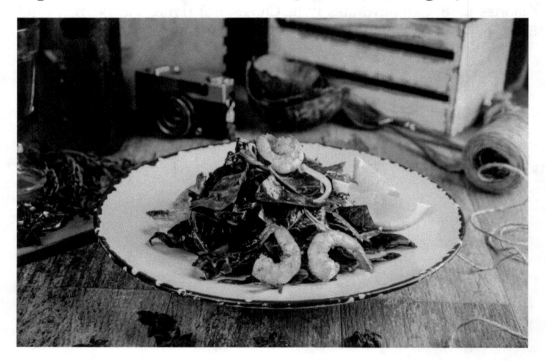

Ingredients:

- 6 garlic cloves, sliced
- 3 tablespoons of extra-virgin olive oil
- ½ teaspoon of salt
- 16 oz. of spinach
- 1 tablespoon of lemon juice
- 1-1/2 teaspoons of lemon zest
- ¼ teaspoon red pepper, crushed
- 16 oz. of shrimps, peeled & deveined
- 1 tablespoon of parsley, chopped

Instructions:

- Heat a tablespoon of oil over medium heat in your pot.
- Add half of the garlic. Cook for a minute.
- Add ¼ teaspoon of salt and spinach. Coat well by tossing.
- Cook for 4 minutes, stirring occasionally.
- Take out from the heat. Stir in the lemon juice.
- Transfer to your bowl. Keep warm.
- Increase the heat. Add the remaining oil to your pot.
- Add the remaining garlic. Cook for a couple of minutes.
- Next, add the red pepper, shrimp, and the remaining salt.
- Cook for 4 minutes while stirring.
- Serve shrimp over spinach. Sprinkle with parsley and lemon zest.

Nutrition Facts Per Serving

Calories 226, Carbohydrates 6.1g, Cholesterol 182.6mg, Fat 11.6g, Protein 26.4g, Fiber 2.7g, Sugar 0.7g, Sodium 444mg, Potassium 962.8mg

65.   Roasted Trout

Enjoy the delicate flavor of trout with herbs and citrus.

Prep Time: 10 minutes, **Cook Time**: 25 minutes, **Servings**: 2

Ingredients:

- 8 oz. trout, cleaned & butterflied
- 1 lemon
- Ground black pepper
- Kosher salt
- 1 tablespoon of extra-virgin olive oil
- 6 thyme sprigs
- 4 teaspoons of butter
- ½ shallot, sliced
- ¼ cup of walnuts

- Chopped parsley for garnishing

Instructions:

- Preheat your oven to 425 F. Use aluminum foil to line your baking sheet.
- Cut 1/3rd off the lemon and then into 4 slices. Reserve them all.
- Use a paper towel to pat both the inside and outside of your trout.
- Rub the fish entirely with olive oil. Season with pepper and salt.
- Keep on your baking sheet. The skin side should be down.
- Place three thyme sprigs. Layer the slices of lemon and the shallot over the thyme. Divide the shallots between your lemon slices.
- Add butter and more thyme sprigs on top.
- Fold the foil's top sheet to enclose your fish in a packet. Now, add the remaining pieces of lemon to the baking sheet. The cut side should be down.
- Bake for 14 minutes. The fish should be tender and flaky.
- Transfer fish to your cutting board with a spatula carefully.
- Reserve the cooking juices in the foil. Remove the lemons.
- Add walnuts to your baking sheet. Toast for 5 minutes.
- Transfer to a cutting board. Crush the walnuts into small pieces.
- Remove the filling from your trout. Reserve the shallots.
- Separate the trout fillets from the spine with a knife.
- Transfer the fillets to your serving plates. Scatter the shallots. Spoon cooking juices over.
- You can garnish with the crushed walnuts, fresh parsley and black pepper.
- Squeeze lemons over the fish. Add lemon slices when serving.

Nutrition Facts Per Serving
Calories 418, Carbohydrates 6.6g, Cholesterol 101mg, Fat 29.6g, Protein 34.2g, Fiber 3g, Sugar 1g, Sodium 175mg, Potassium 157mg

66.　　Grilled Halibut

Enjoy the mild halibut fish with this grilled recipe.

Prep Time: 5 minutes, **Cook Time**: 10 minutes, **Servings**: 4

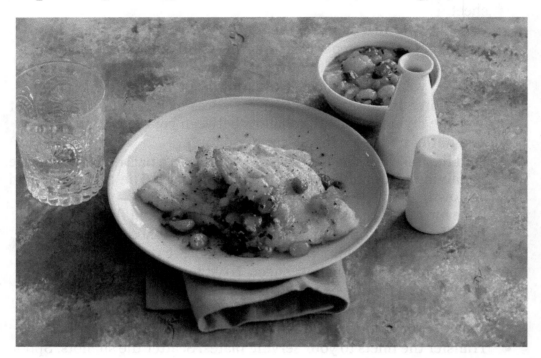

Ingredients:

- 2 tablespoons of extra-virgin olive oil
- 4 halibut steaks, 5 oz. each
- 1 red pepper, chopped
- 1 mango
- 1 minced jalapeno
- ½ red onion, diced
- 1 tablespoon of cilantro, chopped
- Juice from 1 lime

Instructions:

- Preheat your grill on medium heat. Brush oil on both sides of the halibut. Season with pepper and salt.
- Grill each side of the halibut for 5 minutes.
- Mix all the ingredients together for the salsa in your bowl.
- Season with pepper and salt. Serve the salsa over your fish.

Nutrition Facts Per Serving

Calories 892, Carbohydrates 18.1g, Cholesterol 220mg, Fat 23.4g, Protein 145.5g, Fiber 2.7g, Sugar 13.9g, Sodium 401mg, Potassium 245mg

67.   Creamy Oysters Rockefeller

Impress your guests without putting in a lot of effort. Prepare this recipe at home. Everyone will enjoy this fancy appetizer.

Prep Time: 10 minutes, **Cook Time**: 12 minutes, **Servings**: 24

Ingredients:

- 1 cup of spinach
- 2 garlic cloves
- ½ cup of parsley stems and leaves, chopped
- ½ cup of green onions, chopped
- ½ cup of softened butter
- 2 teaspoons of lemon juice
- ¾ cup of panko breadcrumbs

- 2 tablespoons of anise-flavored liqueur
- 1 tablespoon of extra-virgin olive oil
- ¼ cup of parmesan, grated
- 24 oysters, shucked & shells reserved
- 16 oz. coarse salt for baking
- Wedges of lemon for serving

Instructions:

- Keep a rack on the top third position of your oven. Preheat to 450 F.
- Add the spinach, garlic, parsley, green onions, butter, and lemon juice to your food processor. Pulse to chop finely.
- Combine the oil, parmesan, and panko in a bowl.
- Sprinkle the coarse salt on the baking sheet.
- Arrange the oysters in half shells in the salt.
- Next, divide the spinach mix among the oysters. Sprinkle the parmesan mix.
- Bake for 8 minutes. The spinach mix should be bubbling. The panko should be deep golden.
- Serve with lemon wedges.

Nutrition Facts Per Serving
Calories 160, Carbohydrates 6.8g, Cholesterol 125mg, Fat 8.2g, Protein 10.7g, Fiber 0.3g, Sugar 0.3g, Sodium 7807mg, Potassium 29mg

68.   Zingy Lemon Fish

The Gurnard fish is found throughout the Mediterranean Sea and the Atlantic Ocean. Prepare this wonderful seafood recipe with this fish. It is packed with rich flavors you will love.

Prep Time: 10 minutes, **Cook Time**: 16 minutes, **Servings**: 2

Ingredients:

- 3 tablespoons of butter

- 10 oz. of Gurnard fish fillets
- ¼ cup of almond flour
- 1 tablespoon of lemon juice
- 1 teaspoon of chives, dried
- 1 teaspoon of dill, dried
- ½ teaspoon of garlic powder
- 1 teaspoon of onion powder
- Pepper and salt to taste
- Dill sprigs and lemon slices to garnish

Instructions:

- Mix together the chives, dill, almond flour, garlic powder, onion powder, pepper, and salt on a plate. Spread evenly.
- Press one fish fillet at a time. Press into your flour mix.
- Turn and repeat. Keep on another plate once this is done.
- Heat half of the butter and half of the lemon juice in a pan over medium heat.
- Cook your fish for 3 minutes. It should soak up the lemony butter.
- Now, keep the remaining butter and lemon juice in a pan.
- Flip your fish in it for 3 minutes. Swirl the pan and your fish.
- Check whether the fish is ready with a fork.
- Remove from the pan.
- You can serve with steamed vegetables or just fresh dill, lettuce and lemon slices.

Nutrition Facts Per Serving

Calories 477, Carbohydrates 21.8g, Cholesterol 80mg, Fat 36.2g, Protein 18.2g, Fiber 2.3g, Sugar 0.8g, Sodium 659mg, Potassium 369mg

Poultry and Meat

69. Chicken Enchiladas

This could be your go-to dinner recipe. It is healthy and refreshing.

Prep Time: 15 minutes, **Cook Time**: 35 minutes, **Servings**: 6

Ingredients:

- 16 oz. chicken breasts, boneless & skinless
- 2 tablespoons of olive oil
- 1 teaspoon of garlic powder
- 1-1.2 teaspoons of cumin
- ½ teaspoon of black pepper
- 1 teaspoon of salt
- 3 garlic cloves, minced
- 1 diced yellow onion
- 1 can of black beans, drained & rinsed

- 1 can of corn, drained
- 1 can of red enchilada sauce
- 1 can of green chilies, diced
- 1 cup of shredded cheddar cheese
- 12 corn tortillas
- Cilantro, diced jalapenos, chopped chives for garnishing

Instructions:

- Preheat your oven to 350 F. Apply cooking spray on a casserole dish. Set aside.
- Heat olive oil over medium in a pan.
- Sprinkle garlic powder, cumin, pepper, and salt on the chicken breast. Keep in your pan with olive oil.
- Cook each side for 6 minutes over medium heat.
- Remove to your cutting board for cooling.
- Add the garlic and diced onion to your pan. Stir frequently. The garlic should be fragrant and onions translucent.
- Add the black beans, green chilies, and corn. Combine well.
- Bring down the heat to low. Cook while shredding your chicken.
- Shred the chicken breast with two forks.
- Keep in your pan with the corn mix and black beans. Combine well by stirring. Take out from the heat.
- Heat the tortillas for 30 seconds in your microwave.
- Next, dip each tortilla in a bowl with half a cup of enchilada sauce. Spoon ¼ cup chicken and the black bean mix into your tortilla.
- Fold the tortilla over the filling. Roll up.
- Place on the baking dish. The seam side should be down.
- Top enchiladas with the sauce and the shredded cheese.
- Bake for 15 minutes in your oven.
- Sprinkle with cilantro, chopped chives or diced jalapenos.

Nutrition Facts Per Serving
Calories 455, Carbohydrates 52.9g, Fat 13.9g, Protein 31.4g

70. Greek Chicken

Your entire family is going to love this Greek chicken. This recipe is easy to make as well so you can prepare it anytime you want.

Prep Time: 15 minutes, **Cook Time**: 35 minutes, **Servings**: 4

Ingredients:

- 24 oz. potatoes, cut into large pieces
- 16 oz. chicken breasts, boneless & skinless
- 1 red onion, chopped
- 3 tablespoons of red wine vinegar
- 1/3 cup of olive oil
- Juice from 1 lemon
- 3 cloves of garlic, minced
- ½ teaspoon of dried basil

- 1 teaspoon of dried oregano
- 1 tablespoon of honey
- ½ teaspoon of dried thyme
- ¼ teaspoon of pepper
- ½ teaspoon of salt
- Fresh oregano leaves and lemon wedges to top

Instructions:

- Preheat your oven to 400 F. Use foil to line your baking sheet. Set aside.
- Combine ingredients of the Greek marinade in a bowl. Whisk well.
- Add the potatoes and onion, and to another bowl.
- Pour half of the marinade over the vegetables. Mix well. Set the rest of the marinade aside.
- Now, pour the veggies with marinade on your baking sheet.
- Roast for 12 minutes in your oven.
- Prepare the chicken meanwhile. Trim the fat, cut the chicken in half along the length. Each breast should be half-inch thick.
- Add the chicken to the marinade you have stored. Coat well by tossing.
- Take out the veggies once the roasting is done. Stir well.
- Push the vegetables to one side of your baking sheet. They should not overlap.
- Place chicken on the other side. Bake for 16 minutes.
- Broil for 4 minutes. The potatoes should be slightly brown.
- Top with fresh oregano leaves and lemon wedges.

Nutrition Facts Per Serving
Calories 452, Carbohydrates 21.5g, Cholesterol 66mg, Fat 29.6g, Protein 27.8g, Fiber 3g, Sugar 9.6g, Sodium 51mg

71. Honey Mustard Chicken

A weeknight chicken dinner that is easy and healthy. It is tangy and sweet.

Prep Time: 10 minutes, **Cook Time**: 30 minutes, **Servings**: 4

Ingredients:

- 2 teaspoons of olive oil
- 24 oz. of chicken breasts, boneless & skinless
- ¼ cup of whole-grain mustard
- Pepper and salt to taste
- 5 tablespoons of honey
- 2 tablespoons of Dijon mustard
- 1 tablespoon of parsley, chopped
- 3 tablespoons of melted butter

Instructions:

- Preheat your oven to 375 F.
- Heat olive oil over medium heat in a pan.
- Season pepper and salt on your chicken breasts.
- Keep chicken in your pan. Sear both sides to make it golden brown.
- Whisk together the Dijon mustard, whole-grain mustard, butter, and honey in a bowl.
- Apply cooking spray on your baking dish.
- Spread half of your sauce on the dish.
- Keep the chicken breasts on the sauce. Drizzle the sauce over your chicken.
- Use a foil to cover. Bake for 18 minutes.
- Uncover. Bake for another 10 minutes.
- Sprinkle with parsley. Serve with rice and steamed broccoli.

Nutrition Facts Per Serving
Calories 349, Carbohydrates 22g, Cholesterol 113mg, Fat 15g, Protein 31g, Sugar 21g, Sodium 502mg, Potassium 569mg

72. Tuscan Chicken

Try making this Tuscan chicken at home. It's packed with flavors. It is also low-carb and healthy.

Prep Time: 10 minutes, **Cook Time**: 35 minutes, **Servings**: 4

Ingredients:

- 2 tablespoons of olive oil
- 4 to 5 chicken thighs, bone-in & skin-on
- 3 garlic cloves, minced
- 1 onion, diced
- ¼ teaspoon of pepper
- ½ teaspoon of sea salt
- ½ cup bone broth or chicken broth
- 2 teaspoons of tapioca

- 2/3 cup of coconut milk cream
- ½ cup of basil, chopped
- 10 oz. cherry tomatoes, drained & sliced

Instructions:

- Preheat your oven to 400 F. Heat a tablespoon of olive oil over high in your skillet.
- Season one side of your chicken. Keep in your pan. The seasoned side should be down.
- Sprinkle pepper and salt on the other side.
- Cook each side for 3 minutes.
- Take out the chicken. Keep on a cutting board.
- Reduce the heat to low. Add 1 more tablespoon of olive oil.
- Add the onions. Cook for a minute.
- Next, add the garlic. Cook again for 2 minutes.
- Add your chicken broth to the pan. Stir well.
- Return the chicken back to your skillet. Keep the skillet in your oven.
- Bake uncovered for 20 minutes.
- Chip the basil and tomatoes while it is baking.
- Mix your coconut cream with the tapioca starch in a bowl.
- Return skillet to a stovetop once the baking is done.
- Take out the chicken.
- Add coconut milk to your pan. Whisk well.
- Now, stir in the basil and cherry tomatoes. Simmer for a couple of minutes over medium heat.
- Return your chicken to the skillet. Cover with sauce.

Nutrition Facts Per Serving
Calories 402, Carbohydrates 13.8g, Cholesterol 128mg, Fat 18.7g, Protein 43g, Fiber 0.6g, Sugar 1.1g, Sodium 573mg, Potassium 476mg

73.   Thai Pork Salad with Dan Dan Noodles

Here's a delicious salad from Thailand with Asian flavors.

Prep Time: 10 minutes, **Cook Time**: 25 minutes, **Servings**: 2

Ingredients:

- 1 lb. Dan Dan noodles or ramen noodles

- ¼ red onion
- 2 garlic cloves
- 1 cup of cilantro leaves
- 1 teaspoon of sesame oil
- ¾ lb. pork, ground
- 1 tablespoon of fish sauce
- 1 tablespoon of coconut aminos
- ¼ teaspoon of chili oil
- 1 teaspoons of lemon juice
- ¼ teaspoon of black pepper
- ¼ teaspoon of Himalayan salt
- 2 teaspoons of dried chili pepper, sliced
- 1 cup toasted peanuts, chopped
- 2 spring onions, thinly sliced

Instructions:

- Mince the cilantro and garlic.
- Cut the noodles as they are very long.
- Boil a pot of water. Add the noodles.
- Boil the noodles according to the package instructions. Set aside the noodles.
- Heat the sesame oil in a pan. Add the pork and garlic.
- Cook the pork on medium heat until the meat is crispy and golden.
- Combine the meat and noodles in a bowl.
- Add the fish sauce, coconut aminos, chili oil, lemon juice, pepper, salt, and chili peppers.
- Mix so that the sauce covers the meat and noodles.
- Add the spring onions and peanuts on top. Toss well.
- You can serve with steamed greens.

Nutrition Facts Per Serving

Calories 332, Carbohydrates 10.34g, Cholesterol 72mg, Fat 24g, Protein 19g, Fiber 3.1g, Sugar 4.64g, Sodium 932mg

74.   Asparagus & Beef Stir-Fry

An easy-to-make stir-fry in Japanese style.

Prep Time: 15 minutes, **Cook Time**: 10 minutes, **Servings**: 2

Ingredients:

- 8 asparagus
- 10 oz. beef, sliced
- ¼ bulb of ginger
- 2 tablespoons of sesame oil
- 3 garlic cloves
- ¼ teaspoon of onion powder
- 2 tablespoons of coconut aminos
- ¼ teaspoon of Himalayan salt
- ¼ teaspoon of dashi powder

- 1/8 teaspoon of stevia powder
- ¼ teaspoon of black pepper
- ½ teaspoon of sliced red chilies, optional
- 1 tablespoon of sesame seeds, optional

Instructions:

- Combine the sauce ingredients in a bowl. Mix together.
- Peel your ginger bulk. Julienne. Mince the cloves of garlic.
- Cut off the asparagus stems. Cut into three.
- Heat sesame oil in a wok.
- Add the asparagus, garlic, and ginger. Fry for two minutes or until the asparagus is tender.
- Add the sauce and sliced beef to your pan. Mix everything and fry for 3 minutes. The beef should be cooked through.
- Optionally, sprinkle the sesame seeds and add sliced chilies.

Nutrition Facts Per Serving

Calories 536, Carbohydrates 17g, Cholesterol 96mg, Fat 37.5g, Protein 32.28g, Fiber 7g, Sugar 0.96g, Sodium 1075mg

75.Chicken and Feta Plate

This is an easy lunch idea that you can prepare very quickly. You will love this Mediterranean-style meal.

Prep Time: 5 minutes, **Cook Time**: 2 minutes, **Servings**: 2

Ingredients:

- 6 oz. of feta cheese, sliced
- 10 oz. of rotisserie chicken, cut into chunks
- 10 oz. of lettuce mix
- 2 avocadoes, cubed
- 4 tablespoons of olive oil
- Pepper and salt to taste
- Sesame seeds

Instructions:

- Arrange the feta cheese, rotisserie chicken, avocadoes, and lettuce mix on a plate.
- Season with pepper and salt.
- Drizzle olive oil and sesame seeds on top.

Nutrition Facts Per Serving

Calories 673, Carbohydrates 13.4g, Cholesterol 179mg, Fat 49.7g, Protein 47.9g, Fiber 2.4g, Sugar 7g, Sodium 1660mg, Potassium 386mg

76.   Chicken and Snap Pea Stir-Fry

This recipe is easy to make and tasty. It is healthier than those greasy restaurants or takeout meals.

Prep Time: 10 minutes, **Cook Time**: 10 minutes, **Servings**: 4

Ingredients:

- 1 bunch of scallions, sliced
- 2 tablespoons of vegetable oil
- 1 red bell pepper, sliced
- 2 cloves of garlic, minced
- 1-1/4 cups of chicken breast, boneless, skinless, and sliced
- 2-1/2 cups of snap peas
- ½ cup cashew
- 3 tablespoons of soy sauce

- Ground black pepper and salt
- 2 teaspoons of Sriracha, optional
- 2 tablespoons of rice vinegar
- 3 tablespoons of cilantro, chopped
- 2 tablespoons of sesame seeds, optional

Instructions:

- Heat oil in a pan over medium heat. Add the garlic and scallions. Sauté for a minute until fragrant.
- Now, add the snap peas and bell pepper. Sauté for 3 more minutes.
- Include the chicken. Cook for 5 minutes. The chicken should be fully cooked. The veggies should be tender.
- Add the rice vinegar, soy sauce, sesame seeds, and the Sriracha, optional. Combine well by tossing.
- Let it simmer for a minute.
- Stir the cilantro in. Garnish with cashew and optionally, sesame seeds.

Nutrition Facts Per Serving

Calories 200, Carbohydrates 16g, Cholesterol 16mg, Fat 10.1g, Protein 11.3g, Fiber 4.9g, Sugar 5.9g, Sodium 713mg, Potassium 393mg

77. Beef Ragu

Enjoy this authentic Italian dinner after a busy day at work.

Prep Time: 15 minutes, **Cook Time**: 2 hours, 30 mins., **Servings**: 10

Ingredients:

- ¼ cup of olive oil
- 64 oz. of chuck roast
- Ground black pepper and salt
- 4 garlic cloves, minced
- 1 sweet onion, chopped
- 2 stalks of celery, diced
- 2 carrots, diced
- 2 tablespoons of tomato paste
- 1 tablespoon of all-purpose flour

- 2 cups of red wine
- ¼ cup of balsamic vinegar
- 2 cups of beef stock
- 18 oz. of tomatoes, crushed
- 1 sage sprig
- 2 rosemary sprigs
- 16 oz. of tagliatelle pasta
- 5 thyme sprigs
- Finely grated parmesan cheese, to garnish

Instructions:

- Preheat your oven to 325 F.
- Season your beef with pepper and salt.
- Heat olive oil over medium heat in your Dutch oven.
- Brown all sides of the meat for 5 minutes in sizzling oil.
- Take out the beef. Reserve.
- Bring down the heat to medium. Add the garlic and onion.
- Sauté for 2 minutes. Add the celery and carrot. Cook for 5 minutes.
- Add the tomato paste and flour. Cook for 1 minute while stirring.
- Now, add the balsamic vinegar. Cook for 5 minutes.
- Pour the red wine. Simmer for 5 minutes. It should reduce by half.
- In the meantime, tie all your herbs with a kitchen string.
- Add the browned beef back when the wine is reduced.
- Also, add the beef stock and crushed tomatoes.
- Simmer the liquid over medium heat. Cover your Dutch oven. Transfer to your oven. Cook for 2 hours.
- Remove the bouquet garni.
- Now, shred your meat into very small pieces. Keep in the sauce.
- Adjust the seasoning.
- Cook pasta as per the pack instructions.
- Drain and reserve some pasta water.
- Spoon some tomato sauce over your pasta.
- Serve pasta with your ragu.
- Sprinkle some parmesan on top.

Nutrition Facts Per Serving
Calories 677, Carbohydrates 43.3g, Cholesterol 183mg, Fat 21.4g, Protein 67.6g, Fiber 4g, Sugar 5.8g, Sodium 302mg, Potassium 939mg

78.   Korean Beef Tacos

Korean beef tacos baked in an oven. Prepare your dinner quickly.

Prep Time: 10 minutes, **Cook Time**: 10 minutes, **Servings**: 8

Ingredients:

- 1 package of taco shells

- 2 packages of shredded beef
- 4 cups of Monterey Jack cheese
- ¼ cup of brown sugar
- ¾ cup of soy sauce
- 1 tablespoon of ginger
- ½ teaspoon of cayenne
- 1-1/2 tablespoons of sesame oil
- 1 red onion, sliced
- 2 scallion bunches, chopped
- 4 jalapeños, sliced
- 4 pickles, thinly sliced
- 4 radishes, sliced
- Cilantro leaves, optional.

Instructions:

- Preheat your oven to 400 F.
- Keep your shredded beef in a bowl.
- Now, mix the sauce ingredients. Pour over your beef. Combine well by tossing.
- Place the taco shells in a baking dish. They should be in two rows.
- Fill up 3/4th with the beef. Add cheese on top of each taco.
- Bake for 8 minutes. The cheese should be melted. The beef needs to be warmed through.
- Add onion, a couple of slices of jalapeno, and scallions on the top of each taco.
- Finish with sliced pickles and radishes and optionally, cilantro leaves.

Nutrition Facts Per Serving

Calories 329, Carbohydrates 11.3g, Cholesterol 69mg, Fat 21.7g, Protein 22.4g, Fiber 1.1g, Sugar 6.3g, Sodium 1678mg, Potassium 259mg

79.   Beef Burgundy Over Pasta

Serve this wonderful beef recipe. It has mushrooms, flavorful sauce, and tender beef. It will be delicious over pasta.

Prep Time: 10 minutes, **Cook Time**: 1 hour 10 minutes, **Servings**: 2

Ingredients:

- 8 oz. of beef sirloin steak, cut into 1/4-inch strips
- 2 teaspoons of butter
- 1-1/2 cups of mushrooms
- 2 carrots, sliced
- 2 tablespoons onion, diced
- ¼ cup + 2 tablespoons of water
- ¾ cup of Burgundy wine
- 1 bay leaf

- 3 tablespoons of parsley, minced
- 1/8 teaspoon of pepper
- ¼ teaspoon of salt
- 1 clove
- 1 tablespoon of all-purpose flour
- 1 pack of pasta of your choice, preferably tagliatelle
- ½ teaspoon of browning sauce, optional

Instructions:

- Heat butter in your non-stick skillet over medium heat.
- Sauté the onion and beef for a minute.
- Stir in the wine, mushrooms, carrots, 2 tablespoons of parsley, ¼ cup water, and the seasonings.
- Boil and then reduce the heat. Simmer covered for an hour. The beef should be tender.
- In the meantime, cook the pasta as per pack instructions. Drain.
- Mix flour with the remaining water in a bowl.
- Stir into your beef mixture.
- Cook for a couple of minutes. Keep stirring. It should be thickened.
- Discard the clove and bay leaf.
- You can stir in the browning sauce (if using).
- Serve the meat and sauce over your pasta.

Nutrition Facts Per Serving
Calories 571, Carbohydrates 49g, Cholesterol 158mg, Fat 14.6g, Protein 43.7g, Fiber 3.3g, Sugar 2.4g, Sodium 417mg, Potassium 783mg

80.　　California Avocado Chicken

You will love this grilled chicken. It is tender and yummy.

Prep Time: 10 minutes, **Cook Time**: 12 minutes, **Servings**: 4

Ingredients:

- ¼ cup of honey
- ¾ cup of balsamic vinegar
- 2 tablespoons of olive oil
- 3 garlic cloves, minced
- 2 teaspoons of Italian seasoning
- ¼ teaspoon of pepper
- ½ teaspoon of salt
- 2 diced avocados
- 2 red onions, sliced

- 4 chicken breasts, skinless
- ¼ cup of basil, chopped
- 10 cherry tomatoes, diced
- balsamic vinegar for drizzling, optional
- Spinach leaves, to serve

Instructions:

- Whisk together the honey, vinegar, olive oil, garlic, pepper, salt, and Italian seasoning in a bowl.
- Add your chicken breasts. Coat. Marinate for half an hour.
- Add the tomato, avocado, onion, pepper, salt, and basil to another bowl. Set aside.
- Heat your grill on medium. Grill each side of chicken for 6 minutes.
- Top with the avocado, and tomato basil mix.
- Drizzle with the balsamic vinegar.
- Serve with a spinach salad.

Nutrition Facts Per Serving

Calories 558, Carbohydrates 38g, Cholesterol 95mg, Fat 31g, Protein 33g, Fiber 8g, Sugar 27g, Sodium 621mg, Potassium 1123mg

81.Turkey Meatballs

This turkey recipe can quickly become your family favorite.

Prep Time: 10 minutes, **Cook Time**: 17 minutes, **Servings**: 15

Ingredients:

- 1 egg
- 16 oz. lean turkey, ground
- 1/3 cups of breadcrumbs
- 1/3 cup of parmesan cheese, grated
- 1 teaspoon of oregano, dried
- 1 teaspoon of basil, dried
- 2 cloves of garlic, minced
- ½ teaspoon of pepper
- ¼ teaspoon of red pepper

- ½ teaspoon of sea salt
- 15 mozzarella pieces, 1-inch each

Instructions:

- Preheat your oven to 375 F. Combine everything except the mozzarella in a bowl.
- Mix well. Roll into 2-inch bowls.
- Create a dent into each meatball to include the mozzarella piece.
- Keep 1-inch piece into the dent. Form your meatball around the cheese. Cover completely.
- Keep them on a baking sheet lined with parchment.
- Bake for 15 minutes. Set aside before serving.

Nutrition Facts Per Serving
Calories 128, Carbohydrates 2g, Cholesterol 40mg, Fat 8g, Protein 14g, Fiber 1g, Sugar 1g, Sodium 169mg, Potassium 101mg

82.   Quinoa Chicken Parmesan

It is packed with protein, crispy, and very healthy.

Prep Time: 10 minutes, **Cook Time**: 30 minutes, **Servings**: 4

Ingredients:

- 1 tablespoon of Italian seasoning
- 1 cup of quinoa
- ½ cup of all-purpose flour
- Black pepper and kosher salt, to taste
- 2 chicken breasts, boneless & skinless, cut in half
- ½ cup of mozzarella cheese, shredded
- 2 eggs, beaten
- ¼ cup of parmesan cheese, grated
- ¼ cup of thyme leaves

Instructions:

- Preheat your oven to 400 F. Apply non-stick spray on your baking sheet.
- Cook the quinoa in 1-1/2 cups of water in your saucepan as per the pack instructions. Stir in the Italian seasoning.
- Season your chicken with pepper and salt.
- Dredge the chicken in flour. Then dip into the eggs. Now, dredge into the quinoa mix. Coat well by pressing.
- Keep chicken on your baking sheet.
- Place in the oven. Bake for 25 minutes. It should be golden brown.
- Now, top with the cheese.
- Keep in the oven. Bake for 5 minutes more.
- Garnish with thyme and serve.

Nutrition Facts Per Serving
Calories 463, Carbohydrates 48.6g, Cholesterol 162mg, Fat 14.1g, Protein 33.7g, Fiber 5.1g, Sugar 6.1g, Sodium 393mg, Potassium 663mg

83.   Beef Stew

This is a classic beef stew from France. It can be very good comfort food for cold weather.

Prep Time: 15 minutes, **Cook Time**: 3 hours, 30 minutes, **Servings**: 6

Ingredients:

- 2 teaspoons of salt
- 1 teaspoon of black pepper, ground
- 48 oz. of beef chuck, boneless, cut into small pieces
- 3 tablespoons of olive oil
- 7 garlic cloves, peeled & smashed
- 2 yellow onions, cut into small chunks
- 1-1/2 tablespoons of tomato paste
- 2 tablespoons of balsamic vinegar

- 2 cups of dry red wine
- ¼ cup of all-purpose flour
- 2 cups of water
- 2 cups of beef broth
- ½ teaspoon of thyme, dried
- 1 bay leaf
- 4 carrots, peeled & cut diagonally
- 2 celery sticks, cut
- 1-1/2 teaspoons of sugar
- 16 oz. of potatoes, cut in half
- Rosemary leaves, for serving, optional

Instructions:

- Preheat your oven to 325 degrees. Set on the lower-middle rack.
- Pat dry your beef. Season with pepper and salt.
- Heat a tablespoon of olive oil in your Dutch oven over medium heat.
- Brown your meat in three batches, 5 minutes for each batch.
- Add a tablespoon of oil for each batch.
- Keep your meat on a plate. Set aside.
- Now, add the garlic, balsamic vinegar, and onions.
- Cook for 5 minutes while stirring.
- Add the tomato paste. Cook for another minute.
- Next, add the beef and juices back into the pan.
- Sprinkle some flour. Dissolve the flour well.
- Add the beef broth, wine, bay leaf, water, sugar, and thyme.
- Stir. Loosen the brown bits. Boil.
- Transfer to a preheated oven. Braise for a couple of hours.
- Take out from your oven.
- Add the potatoes, celery and carrots.
- Place back in your oven for an hour.
- Take out and discard the bay leaf. Adjust the seasoning.
- Serve your warm stew.
- You can garnish with rosemary.

Nutrition Facts Per Serving
Calories 539, Carbohydrates 32g, Cholesterol 143mg, Fat 18g, Protein 54g,
Fiber 4g, Sugar 8g, Sodium 1189mg, Potassium 1255mg

84.　　Chinese Beef & Broccoli Stir-Fry

This Chinese beef recipe is precisely what your family needs.

Prep Time: 45 minutes, **Cook Time**: 10 minutes, **Servings**: 4

Ingredients:

- 3 tablespoons and 2 teaspoons of soy sauce, low-sodium
- 2 teaspoons of cornstarch
- 4 teaspoons of sesame oil
- 2 teaspoons of rice wine
- ¼ teaspoon of kosher salt
- 16 oz. of sirloin steak, thinly sliced, without fat
- 1 red pepper
- 4 scallions, cut into small pieces
- 4 cups of broccoli florets

- ½ teaspoon of ginger, minced
- 1 tablespoon garlic, minced
- 1 tablespoon of soy sauce
- 2 tablespoons of brown sugar
- Sesame seeds

Instructions:

- Whisk together 2 teaspoons of soy sauce, cornstarch, 1 teaspoon of sesame oil, and the rice wine in a glass container.
- Sprinkle salt over your steak. Now, add the steak to your marinade. Coat well. Set aside for half an hour at room temperature.
- Boil water in a saucepan.
- Add the broccoli. Cook for a minute. Drain. Rinse in cold water.
- Heat your skillet over high.
- Add half of the steak and a teaspoon of sesame oil.
- Cook each side for a minute. Don't stir.
- Transfer to your plate. Repeat with another teaspoon of the oil and the remaining steak.
- Now, heat the remaining sesame oil. Add the scallions, red pepper, ginger, and garlic. Cook for five minutes.
- Add the brown sugar, broccoli, and the remaining soy sauce. Cook for one minute, while stirring.
- Add the beef. Cook for one minute.
- Take out from the heat.
- Sprinkle the sesame seeds on top.

Nutrition Facts Per Serving
Calories 266, Carbohydrates 16g, Cholesterol 69mg, Fat 10g, Protein 29g, Fiber 3g, Sugar 8g, Sodium 855mg, Potassium 735mg

85.   Turkey Loaf

Here's a kid-friendly meatloaf made with low-fat mozzarella, spinach, and turkey.

Prep Time: 10 minutes, **Cook Time**: 60 minutes, **Servings**: 6

Ingredients:

- 1 cup of Italian sauce
- 24 oz. of lean turkey, ground
- 1 onion, chopped
- ½ cup of breadcrumbs
- 2 tablespoons of parmesan cheese, grated
- 2 eggs, beaten
- ½ teaspoon of fennel seeds
- ¾ cup of mozzarella cheese, shredded, low-fat

Instructions:

- Heat your oven to 350 F. Apply vegetable cooking oil on your pan.
- Mix the turkey, breadcrumbs, ¼ cup of the sauce, eggs, onion, fennel seed, shredded mozzarella and parmesan in a bowl.
- Place the turkey mix in your pan.
- Bake for 40 minutes. Spoon the rest of the sauce over your meatloaf.
- Bake for another 15 minutes.
- Set aside for 10 minutes and then slice.

Nutrition Facts Per Serving
Calories 295, Carbohydrates 13.7g, Cholesterol 135mg, Fat 10.3g, Protein 36.8g, Fiber 3g, Sugar 4.9g, Sodium 520mg, Potassium 723mg

86.   Pork Chops with Tomato-Peach Salad

Serve these pork chops to your guests and expect to receive many compliments for your cooking skills.

Prep Time: 15 minutes, **Cook Time**: 20 minutes, **Servings**: 4

Ingredients:

- ¼ cup of Dijon mustard
- 4 pork chops, 8 oz. each, bone-in
- 2 tablespoons of honey
- 1 red onion, sliced
- ¼ cups and 2 tablespoons of red wine vinegar
- 2 tomatoes, cut into 1-inch chunks
- 8 tablespoons of extra-virgin olive oil
- ¼ cup of basil leaves, torn

- 3 peaches, sliced
- 1 cup of gorgonzola cheese, crumbled
- 2 tablespoons of pine nuts
- Ground black pepper and kosher salt

Instructions:

- Preheat your oven to 375 F. Keep the pork chops in a baking dish.
- Whisk together the red wine vinegar, mustard, 4 tablespoons of olive oil, and honey in a bowl.
- Pour the mix over your pork. Coat well. Set aside for 10 minutes.
- Place the peaches, tomatoes, and basil in a bowl.
- Whisk together the remaining 4 tablespoons of olive oil and the remaining 2 tablespoons of vinegar in another bowl.
- Drizzle the mix over your peach-tomato mixture. Toss.
- Season with pepper and salt.
- Heat a grill pan over medium heat.
- Grill the peaches 4 minutes on each side. Transfer them back to the bowl.
- Remove your pork chops from the marinade.
- Season with pepper and salt. Grill each side for 3 minutes.
- Transfer pan to the oven. Cook for 7 more minutes.
- Let it rest for 5 minutes.
- Roast the pine nuts in a skillet for 3 minutes.
- Serve the chops with peach-tomato salad. Garnish with basil. Add the pine nuts and gorgonzola cheese on top.

Nutrition Facts Per Serving

Calories 1148, Carbohydrates 23.3g, Cholesterol 202mg, Fat 93.2g, Protein 55.8g, Fiber 2.3g, Sugar 19.2g, Sodium 570mg, Potassium 1015mg

87.   Caprese Balsamic Chicken

You will get many delicious flavors in this wonderful chicken recipe.

Prep Time: 10 minutes, **Cook Time**: 15 minutes, **Servings**: 4

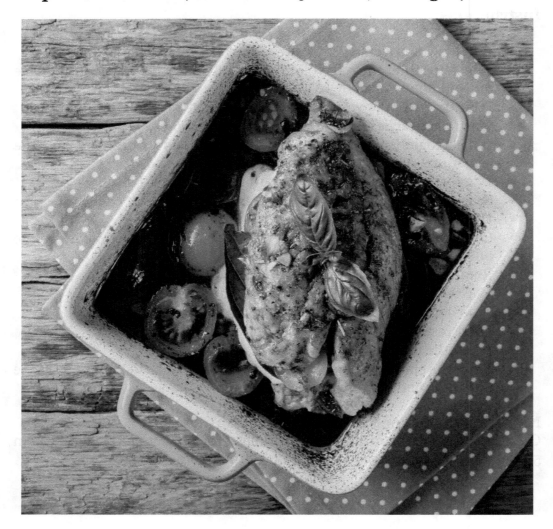

Ingredients:

- 3 tablespoons of balsamic vinegar

- ¼ cup and 2 tablespoons of Italian salad dressing
- 1/8 teaspoon of red pepper flakes, crushed
- 1-1/2 tablespoon of honey
- 2 tablespoons of olive oil
- 20 oz. of chicken breast tenderloins
- 4 mozzarella cheese slices
- Ground black pepper and salt
- 2 cups of cherry tomatoes, halved
- 1 cup of sun dried tomatoes, diced
- Basil leaves

Instructions:

- Preheat the oven to 350 F.
- Whisk together the balsamic vinegar, salad dressing, red pepper flakes, and honey in a bowl. Set aside.
- Cut a pocket into each chicken breast, without cutting all the way through.
- Season the chicken with pepper and salt. Drizzle it with oil.
- Fill each pocket with half of the fresh tomatoes, mozzarella cheese, sun dried tomatoes and basil leaves.
- Heat a skillet over medium heat. Cook the chicken 6 minutes. Add half of your dressing mix to the skillet. Coat your chicken well.
- Flip halfway through.
- Chop the tomatoes and asparagus in the meantime.
- Add half of your dressing mix to the skillet. Coat your chicken well.
- Transfer the pan to the oven and cook for 15 more minutes.
- Add the remaining dressing mix to the oven. Leave it for 3 more minutes.
- Serve the chicken on a plate with the remaining tomatoes, covered in hot sauce.

Nutrition Facts Per Serving

Calories 342, Carbohydrates 20g, Cholesterol 90mg, Fat 14g, Protein 33g, Fiber 4g, Sugar 15g, Sodium 351mg, Potassium 1021mg

88.   Sweet Potato-Topped Beef

You can cook and serve this recipe with pride. It is delicious, healthy, and easy to make at home.

Prep Time: 15 minutes, **Cook Time**: 1 hour, **Servings**: 8

Ingredients:

- 2/3 teaspoon of salt
- ½ teaspoon of pepper
- 32 oz. of lean beef, ground
- 1 onion, chopped
- 2 tablespoons of olive oil
- 8 oz. of mushrooms, sliced
- 4 carrots, sliced
- 2 tablespoons of all-purpose flour

- 4 cloves of garlic, minced
- 1-1/4 cups of dry red wine
- 2 teaspoons of herbes de Provence
- 4 sweet potatoes, cut into ¼-inch slices
- 1 can of beef broth, low-sodium
- 1/3 cup of parmesan cheese, shredded
- Minced parsley, optional

Instructions:

- Cook and crumble the beef for 7 minutes over medium heat. It should not be pink anymore.
- Stir in the pepper and salt. Remove from the pan.
- Heat oil in the same pan over medium.
- Sauté the carrots, onion, garlic, and mushrooms for 5 minutes.
- Stir in the herbs and flour. Cook for a minute.
- Now, stir the wine in and boil.
- Cook for a minute. Keep stirring for loosening the browned bits from your pan. Add the broth and beef. Boil.
- Reduce the heat. Simmer for 30 minutes covered. Stir occasionally.
- Remove from the heat.
- Meanwhile, keep potatoes in your saucepan. Add water. Boil.
- Reduce the heat and cook for 10 minutes. It should be uncovered.
- Drain. Set aside for cooling.
- Arrange potatoes over the stew. They must overlap slightly.
- Now, brush oil lightly and sprinkle with pepper and salt.
- Cook for 7 minutes. The potatoes should brown lightly.
- Set aside for 5 minutes. Sprinkle with parsley and serve.

Nutrition Facts Per Serving
Calories 313, Carbohydrates 18g, Cholesterol 74mg, Fat 14g, Protein 26g, Fiber 3g, Sugar 4g, Sodium 459mg

Snacks and Desserts

89. Almond Coconut Granola Bars

Delicious and healthy snacks you can have any time you want.

Prep Time: 10 minutes, **Cook Time**: 1 hour, **Servings**: 8

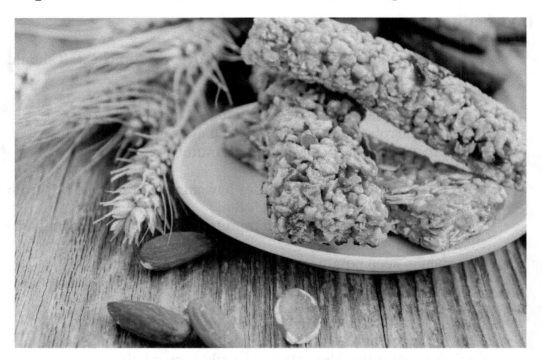

Ingredients:

- 1-3/4 cup of quick-cooking oats
- 1 cup of almonds, chopped
- ½ teaspoon of cinnamon, ground
- 1 cup coconut flakes, unsweetened
- 1 cup dried cranberries
- 1 cup of peanut butter or almond butter
- ½ teaspoon of salt

- 1-1/2 teaspoons of vanilla extract
- ½ cup of maple syrup or honey

Instructions:

- Line a square baker with parchment paper.
- Toast your almonds in a skillet for 5 minutes, stirring frequently.
- Transfer to a mixing bowl.
- Add the coconut flakes, oats, cranberries, salt, and cinnamon to the bowl. Stir to blend well.
- Measure a cup of almond butter. Add half a cup of honey to the top and then the vanilla extract. Blend well by whisking.
- Pour your liquid ingredients into the dry ones.
- Mix them together with a spoon. The wet and dry should be evenly combined. There shouldn't be any dry oats.
- Transfer this mix to your square baker. Arrange it evenly with a spoon. Pack the mixture down with the bottom of a round and flat surface. It should be firm.
- Refrigerate the baker covered for an hour at least.
- Lift out the bars from the baker.
- Slice the mix with a sharp knife into even layers or columns.

Nutrition Facts Per Serving
Calories 255, Carbohydrates 25.4g, Fat 15.4g, Protein 7.7g, Sugar 9.9g, Fiber 4.7g, Sodium 75.9mg

90.   Chia Seed Pudding

This can be the perfect healthy snack or breakfast. It is rich in protein, fiber, and is very satisfying. It is gluten-free too.

Prep Time: 5 minutes, **Cook Time**: 5 minutes, **Servings**: 1

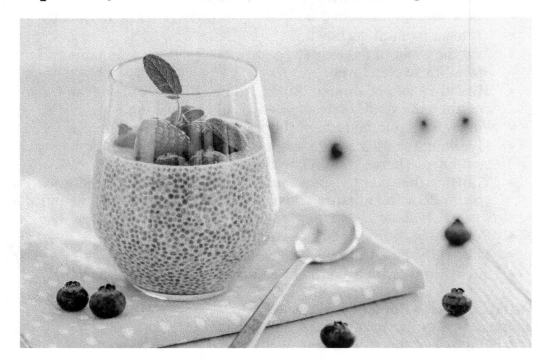

Ingredients:

- 1 cup of coconut or almond milk
- 3 tablespoons of chia seeds
- ¼ teaspoon of vanilla, optional
- ½ teaspoon of honey or maple syrup
- Fruits to serve

Instructions:

- Stir together the milk, chia seeds, vanilla, and maple syrup in a bowl.

- Let it set. Stir. This will break up any chia seed clumps.
- Cover. Refrigerate your mixture for a couple of hours.
- Serve with fruits on top.

Nutrition Facts Per Serving
Calories 271, Carbohydrates 26g, Fat 16g, Protein 10g, Sugar 6g, Fiber 16g, Sodium 248mg

91. Guacamole with Tortilla Chips

A Mexican delicacy! Prepare this guacamole recipe at home.

Prep Time: 10 minutes, **Cook Time**: 10 minutes, **Servings**: 1

Ingredients:

- 1/3 cup of lime juice
- 3 avocados
- ½ red onion, chopped
- 2 garlic cloves, chopped
- 1 tomato, seeded & chopped
- 1 red chili, chopped
- 1 bunch of coriander, chopped
- ½ teaspoon of cumin
- 1 pack of corn tortillas

- Ground black pepper and sea salt, to taste

Instructions:

- Halve the avocados lengthwise. Remove the seeds and scoop out the flesh into a bowl.
- Add the lime juice. Combine by mashing.
- Add the onion, garlic, tomato, chili, coriander, cumin, pepper, and salt. Mix well.
- Serve the guacamole with tortilla chips.

Nutrition Facts Per Serving
Calories 2368, Carbohydrates 160g, Fat 180.9g, Protein 36g, Sugar 10.7g, Fiber 31.2g, Sodium 1680mg, Potassium 171mg

92.   Pistachio Oat Squares

A yummy snack you can make with just 6 ingredients. It is gluten-free and vegan too.

Prep Time: 5 minutes, **Cook Time**: 12 minutes, **Servings**: 8

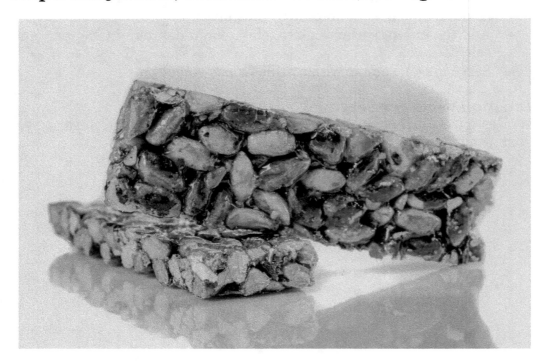

Ingredients:

- 1/2 cup of rolled oats
- 2 cups of pistachios
- ¼ cup of maple syrup
- ½ teaspoon of sea salt
- 2 tablespoons of olive oil

Instructions:

- Preheat your oven to 350 F. Use parchment paper to line your pan.

- Process the oats, and salt in your food processor for 30 seconds.
- Drizzle in the olive oil and maple syrup while the motor is running.
- Combine the dough with the pistachios into your pan evenly.
- Bake for 11 minutes. The dough should be cooked through.
- Don't overbake.
- Take out the cooled dough carefully from the pan.
- Cut into bars.
- Drizzle some maple syrup on the top.
- Let it cool and then serve.

Nutrition Facts Per Serving
Calories 131, Carbohydrates 12.5g, Fat 7.8g, Protein 3g, Sugar 4.6g, Fiber 1.9g, Sodium 84mg, Potassium 38mg

93.   Raw Carrot Balls

Carrot energy balls that taste just like your carrot cake. They are gluten-free, nut-free, and vegan.

Prep Time: 5 minutes, **Cook Time**: 10 minutes, **Servings**: 16

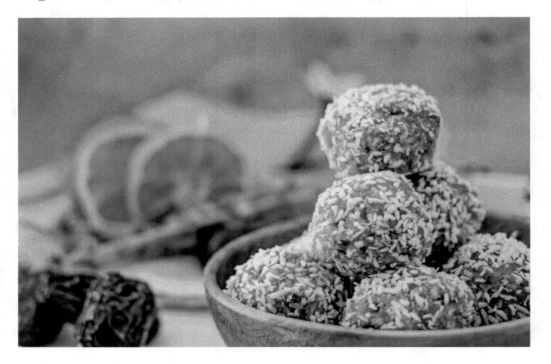

Ingredients:

- 1 cup of coconut, unsweetened, shredded
- 1 cup of sunflower seeds
- ½ teaspoon of sea salt
- ½ teaspoon of cinnamon
- 2/3 cup carrots, chopped
- 12 Medjool dates, pitted & soaked
- 2 teaspoons of maple syrup

Instructions:

- Bring together a cup of shredded coconut, sunflower seeds, salt, and cinnamon in your food processor. Pulse.
- Add the carrots and dates. Pulse again to make the mix combine well, until they stick.
- Add the maple syrup. Refrigerate for 20 minutes so it firms up.
- Scoop out the mixture with a tablespoon.
- Roll into 1-inch balls with your hands.
- Roll the remaining coconut for coating the outside if you want.

Nutrition Facts Per Serving

Calories 94, Carbohydrates 4.1g, Fat 7.8g, Protein 2.5g, Sugar 1.5g, Fiber 1.7g, Sodium 67mg, Potassium 17mg

94.   Crispy Roasted Chickpeas

This is a protein-packed snack. You will love its crispy texture.

Prep Time: 5 minutes, **Cook Time**: 30 minutes, **Servings**: 1-1/2 cups

Ingredients:

- 1-1/2 cups of chickpeas, cooked, drained & rinsed
- Olive oil, for drizzling
- Sea salt
- Curry powder, paprika

Instructions:

- Preheat your oven to 425 F. Use parchment paper to line your baking sheet.

- Spread chickpeas on your kitchen towel. Pat dry. Remove loose skins, if any.
- Mix the chickpeas with the curry powder, salt, paprika and oil. Mix them well.
- Transfer the chickpeas to your baking sheet.
- Roast your chickpeas for 25 minutes. They should be crisp and golden brown.
- Take out from the oven. Toss with additional spices of your choice (optional) while they are still warm.

Nutrition Facts Per Serving
Calories 609, Carbohydrates 91.6g, Fat 16.2g, Protein 29.1g, Sugar 16.2g, Fiber 26.5g, Sodium 270mg, Potassium 1337mg

95. Avocado Toast

This snack is very crispy and very satisfying.

Prep Time: 3 minutes, **Cook Time**: 2 minutes, **Servings**: 3

Ingredients:

- 2 avocados, ripe
- 3 bread slices
- 3 cherry tomatoes
- Red pepper flakes

Instructions:

- Toast the bread slices until it becomes firm and golden.
- Take out the pit from the avocados. Scoop out the flesh with a spoon.
- Place 1 avocado and a half in a bowl. Use a fork to mash it up. Make it smooth.
- Mix with 1/8 teaspoon of salt.
- Spread the avocado paste on your toast.
- Add the sliced tomatoes over 2 slices of bread.
- Add the remaining half of the second avocado, sliced, over the third slice of bread.
- Sprinkle everything with red pepper flakes.

Nutrition Facts Per Serving
Calories 237, Carbohydrates 21.4g, Fat 15.8g, Protein 6.1g, Sugar 2.1g, Fiber 8.6g, Sodium 413.3mg

96.   Baked Apples

Healthy and delicious apples for you.

Prep Time: 2 minutes, **Cook Time**: 60 minutes, **Servings**: 6

Ingredients:

- 6 apples, cored & sliced
- 2 cups of sugar-free orange carbonated beverage
- Cinnamon spice

Instructions:

- Preheat your oven to 350 degrees F.
- Place apples on a baking dish.
- Now pour your orange beverage over the apples.

- Bake for an hour. The apples should become tender.
- Sprinkle cinnamon on top before serving.

Nutrition Facts Per Serving
Calories 64, Carbohydrates 15g, Fat 0g, Fiber 2g, Protein 1g, Sugar 11g

97.   Popcorn Chicken

Kids, adults... everyone loves these popcorns!

Prep Time: 5 minutes, **Cook Time**: 10 minutes, **Servings**: 4

Ingredients:

- 4 oz. chicken breast halves, boneless and skinless
- ½ teaspoon paprika
- ¼ teaspoon mustard, ground
- ¼ teaspoon of garlic powder
- 3 tablespoons of arrowroot

Instructions:

- Cut the chicken into small pieces and keep in a bowl.

- Combine the paprika, garlic powder, mustard, salt, and pepper in another bowl.
- Reserve a teaspoon of your seasoning mixture. Sprinkle the other portion on the chicken. Coat evenly by tossing.
- Combine the reserved seasoning and arrowroot in a plastic bag.
- Combine well by shaking.
- Keep your chicken pieces in the bag. Seal it and shake for coating evenly.
- Now transfer the chicken to a mesh strainer. Shake the excess arrowroot.
- Keep aside for 5-10 minutes. The arrowroot should start to get absorbed into your chicken.
- Preheat your air fryer to 390 degrees F.
- Apply some oil on the air fryer basket.
- Keep the chicken pieces inside. They should not overlap.
- Apply cooking spray.
- Cook until the chicken isn't pink anymore.

Nutrition Facts Per Serving
Calories 156, Carbohydrates 6g, Cholesterol 65mg, Fat 4g, Protein 24g, Fiber 1g, Sodium 493mg

98.   Cranberry Tarts

Beautiful tarts packed with citrus and cranberry flavors.

Prep Time: 5 minutes, **Cook Time**: 25 minutes, **Servings**: 2

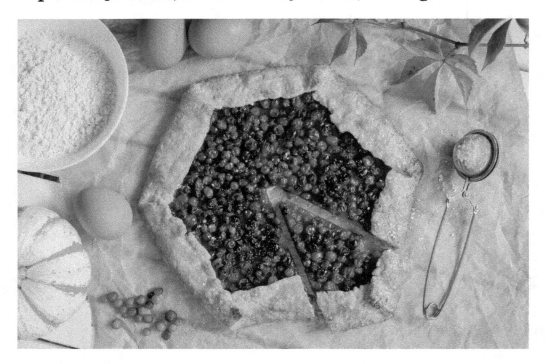

Ingredients:

- ¼ cup of all-purpose flour
- 1 cup of orange marmalade
- ¼ cup of sugar
- 4 cups of cranberries, thawed
- 1 egg white, beaten lightly
- 2 sheets of pie crust
- 1 tablespoon of coarse sugar

Instructions:

- Preheat your oven to 425 F. Mix the sugar, flour, and marmalade in a bowl. Stir in the cranberries.
- Unroll a pie crust on your baking dish lined with parchment paper.
- Spoon half of the mixture over the crust. It should be within 2 inches of the edge.
- Fold the edge over the filling. Leave a 5-inch opening at the center.
- Brush egg white in the folded crust.
- Sprinkle half of your coarse sugar.
- Bake for 20 minutes. The crust should be golden. The filling should be bubbly.
- Repeat with the remaining ingredients.
- Now, transfer the tarts to the wire racks for cooling.

Nutrition Facts Per Serving

Calories 2043, Carbohydrates 347g, Cholesterol 65mg, Fat 67.2g, Protein 16.4g, Fiber 14.1g, Sugar 233.3g, Sodium 1546mg, Potassium 687mg

99.   Biscochitos

Here are some traditional Mexican cookies you can enjoy all year round.

Prep Time: 15 minutes, **Cook Time**: 15 minutes, **Servings**: 11 dozen

Ingredients:

- 1 large egg

- 1 cup of sugar
- 1 cup of shortening
- ¼ teaspoon of anise extract
- ¼ cup of maraschino cherry juice
- 1-1/2 teaspoons of baking powder
- 3-3/4 cups of all-purpose flour
- ¼ teaspoon of salt
- Zest of one orange
- ¼ cup of confectioner' sugar

Instructions:

- Preheat your oven to 375 F. Cream the shortening and sugar in a bowl until it becomes fluffy and light.
- Beat the egg, anise extract, zest of the orange and cherry juice.
- Whisk the baking powder, salt, and flour in a second bowl.
- Beat into your creamed mix gradually.
- Divide the dough in half. Now, shape into a disk.
- Roll each portion of the dough on a floured surface into 1/4-inch thickness.
- Cut into a 2-inch star-shaped cookie.
- Keep on the baking sheet. They should be an inch apart.
- Bake for 8 minutes. The edges should start to brown.
- Take out from the oven. Dust with the confectioners' sugar immediately.
- Transfer from the pan to wire racks for cooling.

Nutrition Facts Per Serving
Calories 35, Carbohydrates 5g, Cholesterol 1mg, Fat 2g, Sugar 2g, Sodium 11mg

100.   Mexican Cinnamon Cookies

These are the traditional cookies from Mexico.

Prep Time: 10 minutes, **Cook Time**: 15 minutes, **Servings**: 12 dozen

Ingredients:

- 2 cups of lard
- 1 egg
- 3 teaspoons of baking powder
- 4 cups of all-purpose flour
- 1 cup oatmeal flakes
- 1 cup of sugar
- Dash of salt
- 1-1/2 teaspoons of cinnamon, ground
- Confectioners' sugar, optional
- 4 teaspoons of cinnamon, ground

Instructions:

- Keep the egg white in a bowl. Set aside for 30 minutes at room temperature.
- Preheat your oven to 375 F.
- Beat the lard in a bowl to make it creamy.
- Pulse the oatmeal flakes in a food processor, until they look like flour.
- Whisk the baking powder, flour, oatmeal flour, salt, and cinnamon in a second bowl. Beat into the lard gradually.
- Now, beat the egg white at high speed. Stiff peaks should form.
- Whisk in the egg yolk and sugar gently.
- Beat into the lard mix gradually.
- Turn on a floured surface. Knead 10 times gently.
- Scoop the dough and shape into small balls.
- Place them on an ungreased baking sheet. Flatten them on the backing sheet, 1-inch apart.
- Bake for 10 minutes. The edges should be light brown.
- Let it cool for a couple of minutes.
- Mix the cinnamon and sugar in a bowl.
- Roll your cookies in the cinnamon-sugar mix. Let them cool.

Nutrition Facts Per Serving
Calories 47, Carbohydrates 5g, Cholesterol 4mg, Fat 3g, Sugar 2g, Sodium 10mg

101. Tofu Nuggets

For those times when you don't want to have chicken.

Prep Time: 15 minutes, **Cook Time**: 25 minutes, **Servings**: 4

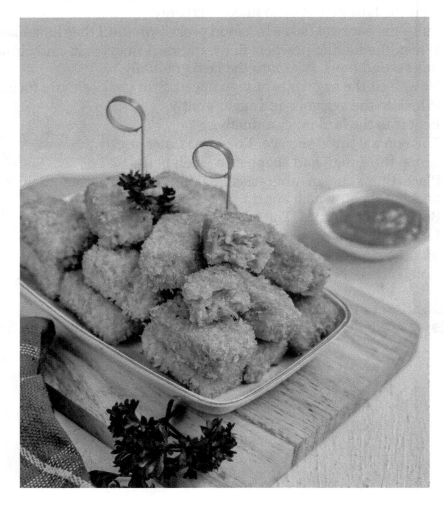

Ingredients:

- 1/3 cup of soy milk
- 1 block of tofu, firm, well pressed

- 2 carrots, shredded
- ¾ cup soy flour
- 1 tablespoon of nutritional yeast
- 2 tablespoons of mustard
- 1 teaspoon of garlic powder
- 1 teaspoon of onion powder
- ¼ teaspoon of black pepper
- ½ teaspoon of sea salt
- 1 teaspoon of dried parsley
- 3 tablespoons of coconut oil or vegetable oil
- ½ cup of panko breadcrumbs

Instructions:

- Pat your tofu block dry. Keep a cutting board on your tofu.
- Let it sit for half an hour.
- Chop the tofu and transfer it to a food processor.
- Combine the processed tofu with the shredded carrots in a bowl. Combine them with the soy flour, the mustard, soy milk, onion, garlic powder, nutritional yeast, pepper, salt.
- Keep your panko breadcrumbs in another bowl.
- Scoop mounds of the filling from the bowl.
- Next, dip into the breadcrumbs. Coat well.
- Place the nuggets on baking sheets. Transfer them to the freezer until they are firm.
- Take the nuggets out.
- Heat oil on medium in your frying pan.
- Place them in the pan.
- Fry your tofu pieces. Turn them over. All sides should be golden brown.
- Serve with ketchup or red salsa.

Nutrition Facts Per Serving
Calories 175, Carbohydrates 9g, Fat 10g, Protein 17g, Fiber 2g, Sodium 529mg

102.   Spicy Tuna Rolls

These beautiful tuna rolls can be the perfect snack you can have.

Prep Time: 10 minutes, **Cook Time**: 10 minutes, **Servings**: 8

Ingredients:

- 6-1/2 tablespoons of wild-caught tuna
- 1 cucumber
- 1/16 teaspoon cayenne, ground
- 2 slices of diced avocado
- 1/8 teaspoon pepper
- 1/8 teaspoon salt
- 1 teaspoon hot sauce
- 1 tablespoon mayo chili sauce
- toothpicks

Instructions:

- Slice the cucumber lengthwise. Make thin cuts.
- Flip the cucumber and slice the opposite side.
- Discard the outermost slices. There should be no seeds.
- Take a paper towel and pat dry. Set aside.
- Keep the tuna, cayenne, hot sauce, pepper, and salt in a mixing bowl.
- Combine well. Everything should mix well.
- Spoon out the tuna mix across the cucumber slices. Leave an inch on each side.
- Add the diced avocado on top of your tuna.
- Roll up the cucumber. Use toothpicks to secure the ends.
- Drizzle with mayo chili sauce before serving.

Nutrition Facts Per Serving
Calories 129, Carbohydrates 2g, Total Fat 9g, Protein 10g, Fiber 1g

103.   Lemony Quinoa

A healthy snack that will give you a nutty and lemony flavor.

Prep Time: 10 minutes, **Cook Time**: 10 minutes, **Servings**: 6

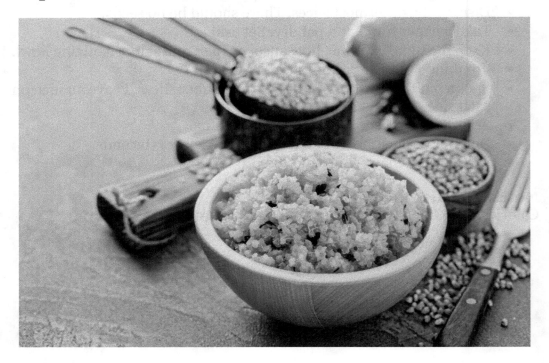

Ingredients:

- ¼ cups pine nuts
- 1 cup quinoa
- ¼ cup lemon juice
- Sea salt to taste
- 2 chopped celery stalks
- ¼ chopped red onion
- ¼ teaspoon cayenne pepper
- ½ teaspoon cumin, ground
- 1 parsley bunch, chopped

Instructions:

- Keep pine nuts in a skillet and toast over medium temperature.
- Stir. Keep aside for cooling.
- Combine water, salt, and quinoa in your saucepan.
- Boil. Bring down the heat.
- Cook till the quinoa has become tender. Water must be absorbed.
- Let it cool. Use a fork to fluff.
- Transfer to your serving bowl.
- Stir the lemon juice, pine nuts, onion, celery, parsley, cumin, and cayenne pepper in.
- Add some pepper and salt if required before serving.

Nutrition Facts Per Serving

Calories 117, Carbohydrates 21g, Fat 1g, Sugar 1g, Fiber 3g, Protein 6g

104.   Dairy-Free Brownies

Here's the recipe for the times when you want to have a brownie, but are wary of its sugar or dairy content. It is moist and yummy.

Prep Time: 5 minutes, **Cook Time**: 30 minutes, **Servings**: 8

Ingredients:

- ½ cup of cocoa
- 1 cup of white sugar
- ¼ teaspoon of salt
- ¼ cup of all-purpose flour
- ¼ cup of oil
- 2 eggs
- ½ tablespoon of vanilla
- 2 tablespoons of water

- ¼ cup of dairy-free dark chocolate chips, optional
- ½ cup of walnuts, chopped, optional

Instructions:

- Preheat your oven to 163 C or 325 F.
- Whisk together the cocoa, sugar, salt, and flour in a bowl.
- Add the oil, eggs, vanilla, and water. Mix to make it smooth. Your batter must look runny.
- Pour the batter with a baking spatula into your baking pan. Use parchment paper to line your pan.
- Bake for half an hour.
- Take it out. Cut after cooling.

Nutrition Facts Per Serving

Calories 259, Carbohydrates 31g, Cholesterol 42mg, Fat 14g, Protein 4g, Sugar 25g, Fiber 2g, Sodium 76mg

105.   Banana Cream Pie

A delicious banana cream pie that is gluten-free, vegan, fluffy, and crispy.

Prep Time: 7 hours 30 minutes, **Cook Time**: 30 minutes, **Servings**: 8

Ingredients:

- ¾ cup of raw almonds
- ¾ cup rolled oats, gluten-free
- 7 tablespoons of coconut sugar or cane sugar
- 1/3 teaspoon of sea salt, optional
- ¼ cup of coconut oil, melted
- 2 tablespoons of cornstarch
- 1-1/2 teaspoon vanilla extract
- 1-1/2 cups of plain almond milk, unsweetened
- 2 bananas, sliced

- 1 can of coconut cream
- 4 tablespoons of powdered sugar
- Coconut whipped cream

Instructions:

- Preheat your oven to 176 C or 350 F. Use parchment paper to line your baking dish. Set aside.
- Add almonds, oats, sugar, and sea salt (optional) to your blender.
- Pulse/mix on high.
- Remove the lid. Add ¼ of the melted coconut oil.
- Pulse on low to form a loose dough.
- Transfer the mix to your baking dish or pie pan. Spread evenly.
- Place parchment paper on top. Press down firmly with a drinking glass, spoon, or another flat-bottom object.
- Bake for 12 minutes. Increase the heat to 315 F. Bake for another 7 minutes. The edges should become golden brown.
- Take out from your oven. Set aside for cooling.
- Prepare the pudding in the meantime. Add the sugar, salt (optional), and cornstarch to a saucepan.
- Whisk in the almond milk.
- Keep over medium heat. Cook until you see it bubbling. Whisk frequently.
- Bring down the heat to low. Keep cooking for 5 more minutes. Scrape off the bottom and sides.
- Take out from the heat. Whisk in the vanilla. Set aside for 10 minutes for cooling.
- Transfer to your ceramic or glass bowl. Plastic wrap.
- Refrigerate for 2 hours.
- Meanwhile, keep a glass mixing bowl in your freezer for the coconut whipped cream.
- Take out the coconut cream from your fridge. Scoop out the top hardened portion and place it in your chilled bowl.
- Whip the cream for a minute with a handheld mixer.
- Add the vanilla extract and some powdered sugar.
- Beat for 2 minutes to make it airy and light.

- Refrigerate for chilling – 30 minutes' minimum.
- Add pudding to your coconut whipped cream once it is cooled.
- Stir lightly. Add the sliced banana to the bottom of your baked crust.
- Add the custard-coconut mix on top. Use a spoon to smooth the top.
- Refrigerate for 4 hours minimum.
- Top with sliced bananas to serve.

Nutrition Facts Per Serving
Calories 369, Carbohydrates 33.7g, Fat 25.9g, Protein 5g, Sugar 19.5g, Fiber 4.2g, Sodium 590mg

106.   Chocolate Zucchini Bread

A fudgy and moist chocolate zucchini bread recipe.

Prep Time: 15 minutes, **Cook Time**: 50 minutes, **Servings**: 16

Ingredients:

- 1-1/4 cup of all-purpose flour
- 1-1/4 cup of whole wheat pastry flour
- 1 tablespoon of baking powder
- 1/3 cup of cocoa powder
- 1 teaspoon of sea salt
- 1 teaspoon of baking soda
- ½ teaspoon of nutmeg
- 1 teaspoon of cinnamon
- 1-1/2 cups of almond milk

- 3 eggs
- 1 cup of maple syrup
- ¼ cup of coconut milk, melted
- 2 cups of zucchini, shredded & unpeeled
- 2 teaspoons of vanilla extract
- 1 cup of chocolate chips, semi-sweet

Instructions:

- Preheat your oven to 350 F. Apply non-stick spray on two loaf pans.
- Bring together the cocoa powder, flour, baking soda, baking powder, nutmeg, cinnamon, and salt in a bowl.
- Whisk together the almond milk, eggs, maple syrup, vanilla, and coconut oil in another bowl.
- Stir the zucchini in. Now, add your dry ingredient to the bowl.
- Stir to combine well. Do not overmix.
- Fold in your chocolate chips.
- Next, pour your batter into the pans.
- Sprinkle more chocolate chips. Bake for 50 minutes.
- Take out from the oven. Let it cool before serving.

Nutrition Facts Per Serving
Calories 498, Carbohydrates 56.1g, Cholesterol 31mg, Fat 28.8g, Protein 7.7g, Sugar 18.1g, Fiber 6g, Sodium 225mg, Potassium 456mg

Drinks

107.   Vanilla Milkshake

Prepare this low-carb milkshake with just 4 ingredients.

Prep Time: 2 minutes, **Cook Time**: 2 minutes, **Servings**: 4

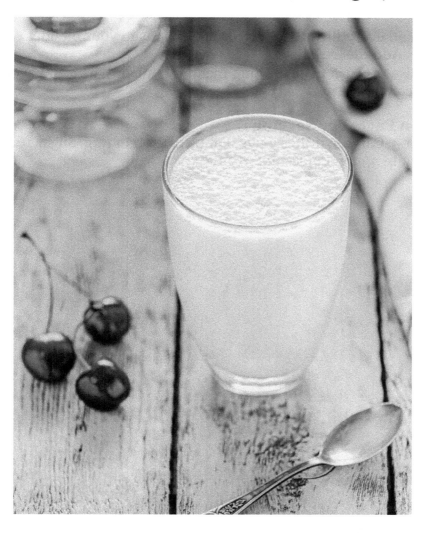

Ingredients:

- 2 teaspoons of vanilla extract
- 13 oz. of coconut milk
- ¼ cup of powdered fruit allulose blend
- 2 cups of ice cubes

Instructions:

- Blend everything together for 20 seconds in your blender except the ice. Add the ice cubes.
- Pulse to crush the ice. Don't blend too much. The ice may otherwise become watery.

Nutrition Facts Per Serving

Calories 105, Carbohydrates 24.7g, Fat 0.1g, Protein 1.4g, Sugar 19.8g, Fiber 0.6g, Sodium 43mg, Potassium 379mg

108.   Cucumber Strawberry Lemon Water

This could be the perfect drink for a hot day.

Prep Time: 5 minutes, **Cook Time**: 5 minutes, **Servings**: 6

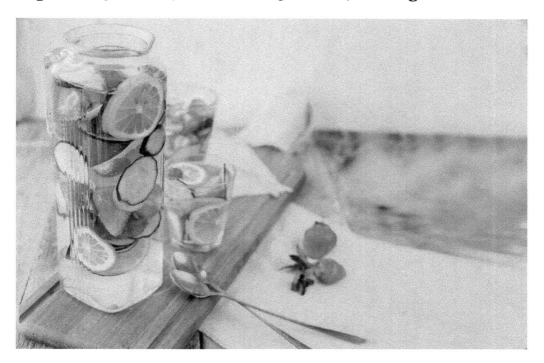

Ingredients:

- ½ cucumber, sliced
- 6 strawberries, sliced
- 6 cups of filtered water
- 1 sliced lemon

Instructions:

- Halve or slice your strawberries. Peel, slice your cucumber.
- Slice your lemon. Now, add everything to your pitcher or mason jar.

- Serve immediately or chill.

Nutrition Facts Per Serving
Calories 13, Carbohydrates 4g, Sugar 2g, Fiber 1g, Sodium 10mg

109.   Low-Carb Margarita

The recipe for preparing sugar-free, low-carb margaritas at home.

Prep Time: 5 minutes, **Cook Time**: 5 minutes, **Servings**: 2

Ingredients:

- 2 oz. of lime juice
- 3 oz. of tequila
- 1 tablespoons of sweetener, optional
- ½ teaspoon of orange extract
- Kosher salt for rimming, optional
- Crushed ice

Instructions:

- Combine the lime juice, tequila, sweetener, and orange extract in a measuring cup or cocktail shaker.
- Fill crushed ice into two margarita glasses.
- Divide the mixture between them evenly.
- Run a lime wedge and kosher salt around the outside of your glass.

Nutrition Facts Per Serving

Calories 57, Carbohydrates 8.3g, Fat 0.1g, Protein 0.3g, Sugar 0.6g, Fiber 0.6g, Sodium 25mg, Potassium 39mg

110.   Naturally Sweetened Lemonade

This drink is so soothing and refreshing.

Prep Time: 5 minutes, **Cook Time**: 5 minutes, **Servings**: 8

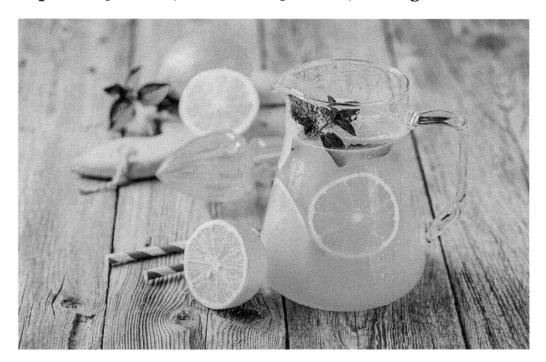

Ingredients:

- 1 lemon, sliced
- 6 lemons, juiced
- 2 quarts of water
- 1 teaspoon of liquid stevia
- 1 cup of ice cubes

Instructions:

- Slice the lemons. Squeeze out the juice and keep in a bowl. Remove the seeds.

- Add the juice to your pitcher. Add the water to your pitcher.
- Stir in a teaspoon of stevia.
- Slice a lemon. Add to your pitcher.
- Next, add the cubes of ice. Serve.

Nutrition Facts Per Serving
Calories 35, Carbohydrates 6.1g, Fat 1.7g, Protein 0.8g, Sugar 2.7g, Fiber 1.4g, Sodium 11mg, Potassium 72mg

111.　　**Honey Iced Tea**

This sweet and healthy tea is made with honey instead of sugar.

Prep Time: 5 minutes, **Cook Time**: 20 minutes, **Servings**: 8

Ingredients:

- 1/3 cup of honey

- 4 green or black tea bags
- 8 cups of water (4 cups cold, 4 cups boiling)
- 1/8 teaspoon of baking soda, optional

Instructions:

- Boil 4 cups of water.
- Add the baking soda (optional) and tea bags. Cover your pan.
- Take out from the heat. Allow it to steep for 12 minutes.
- Remove the tea bags. Pour into your pitcher.
- Add the honey. Stir. Pour the 4 cups of cold water. Refrigerate.

Nutrition Facts Per Serving
Calories 34, Carbohydrates 9g, Sugar 9g, Sodium 16mg, Potassium 5mg

112.   Pumpkin Spice Latte

Prepare a large batch of this latte for the entire week.

Prep Time: 2 minutes, **Cook Time**: 5 minutes, **Servings**: 2

Ingredients:

- ½ teaspoon of pumpkin spice mix
- 2 tablespoons of pumpkin puree
- 1 tablespoon of vanilla extract
- 1 tablespoon of sweetener, your choice
- 1 tablespoon of coconut milk, full-fat
- 240 ml of almond milk
- 2 shots of espresso
- Pumpkin spice mix and whipped cream for garnishing

Instructions:

- Heat your pumpkin puree with the pumpkin pie spice over medium heat in your saucepan. Keep stirring for 2-3 minutes.
- Stir in the sweetener. Mix to combine well. You can refrigerate the spice mix for 4 to 5 days.
- Pour in the milk. Summer until it is warm.
- Take out from the heat. Add the vanilla extract.
- Whisk for 30 seconds. It should be frothy and light.
- Pour espresso. Add your pumpkin spiced milk.
- Add some pumpkin pie spice and the whipped cream on top.

Nutrition Facts Per Serving
Calories 70, Carbohydrates 2g, Fat 1g, Sugar 1g, Sodium 163mg, Potassium 81mg

113.   French Coconut Lime Soda

Try this recipe and turn your Italian soda into French.

Prep Time: 2 minutes, **Cook Time**: 2 minutes, **Servings**: 1

Ingredients:

- 2 oz. of lime juice
- 2 oz. of coconut cream
- 8 oz. of carbonated water

Instructions:
- Mix everything together for an awesome drink.

Nutrition Facts Per Serving
Calories 145, Carbohydrates 7.9g, Fat 13.6g, Protein 1.5g, Sugar 2.8g, Fiber 1.5g, Sodium 12mg, Potassium 215mg

Sauces and Dressings

114.   Vegan Caesar Dressing

A hummus-based and creamy vegan Caesar dressing that you can prepare with a few simple ingredients.

Prep Time: 5 minutes, **Cook Time**: 5 minutes, **Servings**: 8

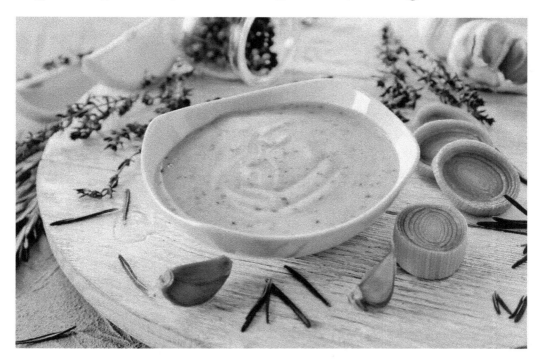

Ingredients:

- 1 teaspoon of spicy mustard
- ¼ cup of plain hummus
- 2 tablespoons of lemon juice
- ½ teaspoon of lemon zest
- 4 garlic cloves, minced
- 2 teaspoons of capers

- 1 pinch of pepper and sea salt
- 1 teaspoon of maple syrup, optional
- 1 tablespoon of olive oil, optional

Instructions:

- Place the spicy mustard, hummus, capers, lemon zest and juice, olive oil (optional), salt, pepper, and garlic in a bowl. Combine well by whisking.
- Add some hot water. Adjust the flavor if needed.
- Add the maple syrup. This will offset some saltiness.

Nutrition Facts Per Serving
Calories 19, Carbohydrates 2.8g, Fat 0.7g, Protein 0.8g, Sugar 0.4g, Fiber 0.54g, Sodium 69mg, Potassium 29mg

115.   Carrot Ginger Dressing

This salad dressing is creamy, light, and remarkable.

Prep Time: 5 minutes, **Cook Time**: 3 minutes, **Servings**: 8

Ingredients:

- 1/3 cup of rice vinegar
- 1/3 cup of extra-virgin olive oil
- 2 tablespoons ginger, peeled & chopped
- 2 carrots, peeled & chopped
- 1 tablespoon + 1 teaspoon of honey
- 2 tablespoons of lime juice
- ¼ teaspoon of salt
- 1-1/2 teaspoons of sesame oil, toasted

Instructions:

- Combine all of your salad dressing ingredients in a blender.
- Blend to make it smooth.
- Serve over greens or a healthy salad.

Nutrition Facts Per Serving

Calories 109, Carbohydrates 5.8g, Fat 9.3g, Protein 0.3g, Sugar 3.3g, Fiber 0.7g, Sodium 87mg, Potassium 90mg

116.   **Avocado Salad Dressing**

Prepare this healthy and delicious dressing in just 5 minutes.

Prep Time: 5 minutes, **Cook Time**: 5 minutes, **Servings**: 1 cup

Ingredients:

- 1 garlic clove, peeled
- 1 avocado
- 3 tablespoons of avocado oil or olive oil
- ½ teaspoon of lemon or lime juice
- ¼ teaspoon of ground black pepper and kosher salt each

Instructions:

- Add the avocado, garlic, lemon or lime juice, pepper, salt, and oil to your food processor.

- Process and make it smooth.
- Thin out your salad dressing by adding some water.

Nutrition Facts Per Serving
Calories 90, Carbohydrates 2g, Fat 9g, Fiber 1g, Sodium 68mg

117.   Green Tahini Sauce

One of the easiest sauces you can make all by yourself.

Prep Time: 5 minutes, **Cook Time**: 5 minutes, **Servings**: 2 cups

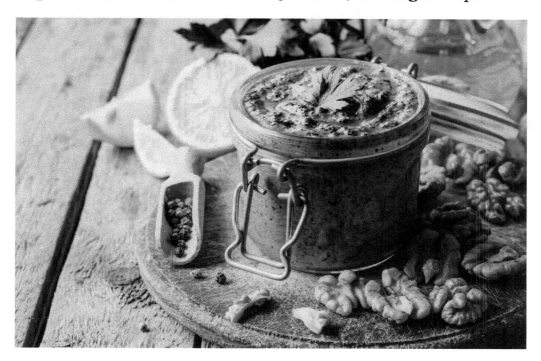

Ingredients:

- 2 serrano chilies
- 2 lemons
- 3 cups of parsley, chopped
- 2 cloves of garlic, crushed
- ½ cup of tahini
- ¼ cup of extra-virgin olive oil
- Kosher salt, to taste

Instructions:

- Grate the zest of a lemon and keep it in your blender.
- Cut both the lemons. Remove the seeds.
- Squeeze out the juice into your blender.
- Add the garlic, chilies, oil, parsley, and a half cup of cold water.
- Blend on high.
- Pour the mixture into a bowl.
- Add the tahini. Whisk well.
- Season the sauce with salt.

Nutrition Facts Per Serving

Calories 662, Carbohydrates 32g, Fat 58.8g, Protein 16g, Sugar 2.5g, Fiber 10.2g, Sodium 121mg, Potassium 839mg

118.   Curried Peanut Dip

You can pour this dip easily when it is warm. But it thickens when it is chilled.

Prep Time: 5 minutes, **Cook Time**: 5 minutes, **Servings**: 1 pint

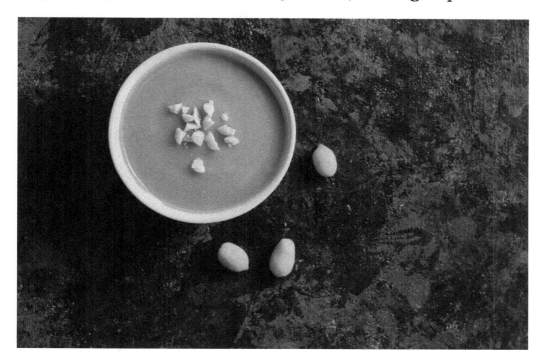

Ingredients:

- ¼ cup of red curry paste
- 1 tablespoon of vegetable oil
- ½ cup of peanut butter
- 1 can of coconut milk
- 1 tablespoon of fish sauce
- 3 tablespoons rice vinegar, unseasoned
- 1 tablespoon of honey
- Kosher salt

Instructions:

- Heat oil in your saucepan.
- Add the curry paste. Cook for 2 minutes, stirring frequently.
- Whisk in the coconut milk. Simmer for 3 minutes. The mixture should reduce slightly and turn darker in color.
- Remove saucepan from the heat.
- Whisk in the vinegar, peanut butter, honey, and fish sauce.
- Season to taste with salt.
- Cool at room temperature.

Nutrition Facts Per Serving
Calories 2164, Carbohydrates 78.1g, Fat 194.5g, Protein 42.6g, Sugar 43.7g, Fiber 16.7g, Sodium 5165mg, Potassium 1981mg

119.   Lemon Tahini Dressing

This could easily become your favorite salad dressing. It doesn't require any oil or dairy.

Prep Time: 5 minutes, **Cook Time:** 2 minutes, **Servings:** 10

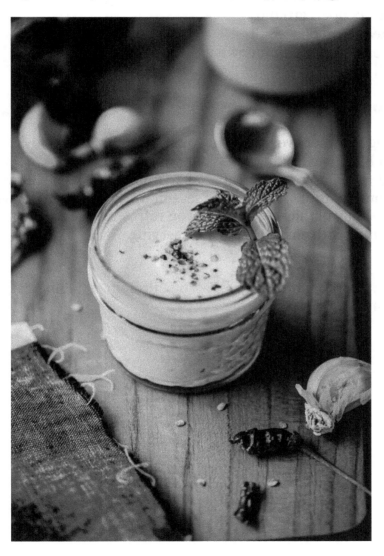

Ingredients:

- ¼ cup of water
- ½ cup of tahini
- 3 garlic cloves, minced
- 6 tablespoons of lemon juice
- Black pepper, ground
- ¾ teaspoon of sea salt
- ½ teaspoon of onion powder
- Chili flakes

Instructions:

- Bring together everything in your mason jar or bowl.
- Combine by whisking well.
- Add 1 tablespoon of water at a time until you see the dressing becoming thin. Adjust the seasoning if needed. Remember, the dressing will thicken up when you refrigerate.
- Sprinkle with chili flakes before serving.

Nutrition Facts Per Serving
Calories 73, Carbohydrates 3g, Fat 6g, Protein 2g, Fiber 1g, Sugar 1g, Sodium 179mg, Potassium 64mg

120. Cilantro Chutney

Have some extra cilantro at home? Prepare this chutney in 5 minutes.

Prep Time: 5 minutes, **Cook Time**: 2 minutes, **Servings**: ¾ cup

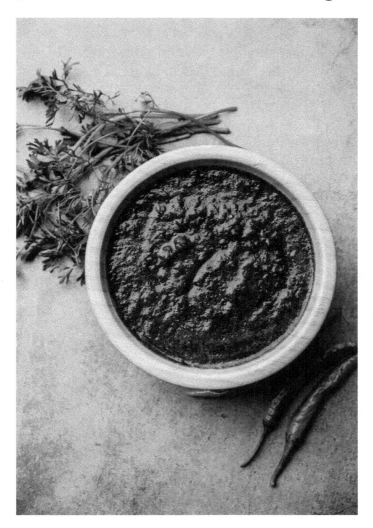

Ingredients:

- 1 green or serrano chili, chopped

- 1 bunch of cilantro, leaves & stems chopped
- ¼ teaspoon of sugar
- 2 tablespoons of lime juice
- Kosher salt

Instructions:

- Blend the chili, cilantro, sugar, and juice in your blender.
- Add some water if required. Make it smooth.
- Season with salt.

Nutrition Facts Per Serving

Calories 41, Carbohydrates 11.4g, Fat 0.1g, Protein 1.4g, Sugar 3.5g, Fiber 1.4g, Sodium 32mg, Potassium 362mg

Part 4: 2-Weeks Meal Plan

Here is a PCOS meal plan for 14 days to help you get started. It is an introduction to low carbohydrate cooking and a great way to control the symptoms. You may not see a huge change in just 2 weeks, but it's a good start. Keep eating healthy foods and you are sure to see positive changes.

The grocery lists below contain the ingredients that you would need for the number of servings from the menus. Please note that the recipes, as presented in Part 3, contain more servings than in the menus below. You can adapt the quantity of ingredients in the grocery lists as per your needs or servings you prefer.

Week 1 Menu:

	Breakfast	Lunch	Dinner	Nutritional Info
Day 1	Healthy Chicken Soup	Honey Garlic Shrimp	Stuffed Potatoes with Beans and Salsa	1923 calories, 41g fat, 192g carbs, 26g sugar, 71g protein
Day 2	Healthy Chicken Soup Leftover	Stuffed Potatoes with Beans Leftover	Mediterranean Cod with Roasted Tomatoes	903 calories, 41g fat, 74g carbs, 13g sugar, 68g protein
Day 3	Banana Oatmeal Pancakes	Mediterranean Cod Leftover	Chicken Tortilla Soup	1064 calories, 47g fat, 106g carbs, 25g sugar, 65g protein
Day 4	Low-Carb Biscuits with Jalapeno and Cheddar	Chicken Tortilla Soup Leftover	Chicken and Feta Plate	1696 calories, 109g fat, 98g carbs, 29g sugar, 97g protein
Day 5	Banana Oatmeal Pancakes Leftover	Quinoa Chicken Parmesan	Chicken and Feta Plate Leftover	1306 calories, 72g fat, 82g carbs, 13g sugar, 88g protein
Day 6	Low-Carb Biscuits with Jalapeno and Cheddar Leftover	California Avocado Chicken	Quinoa Chicken Parmesan Leftover	1307 calories, 71g fat, 92g carbs, 34g sugar, 77g protein
Day 7	Bacon Patty Cakes	California Avocado Chicken Leftover	Mexican Quinoa	1168 calories, 64g fat, 95g carbs, 31g sugar, 51g protein

Week 1 Grocery List:

Baking:

- 2-1/2 teaspoons of baking powder
- ¼ teaspoon of baking soda

Spices & Herbs:

- 1 teaspoon paprika powder
- 1/4 teaspoon cayenne powder
- ½ teaspoon of smoked paprika
- 1 teaspoon of onion powder
- ¼ teaspoon of garlic powder
- 1 tablespoon of chili powder
- 1 teaspoon of black pepper
- 2 tablespoons of black peppercorn
- 3 tablespoons of salt
- ½ cup of basil leaves
- 1 rosemary sprig
- 1 thyme sprig
- 1 teaspoon thyme
- 1 sage leaf
- 1 oregano sprig
- 1 bay leaf
- 2 teaspoons oregano
- 2 teaspoons of cumin

Condiments:

- 1 tablespoon of maple syrup or honey
- ¼ cup of honey
- 1 teaspoon of vanilla extract
- 1 teaspoon of apple cider vinegar
- 1 cup of balsamic vinegar

- 1/2 cup of salsa sauce
- 2 tablespoons of Italian seasoning
- ½ teaspoon cinnamon
- 1/3 cup of coconut aminos

Grain:

- 1-1/2 cups of oats
- 1 cups of almond flour
- ½ teaspoon of corn starch or tapioca flour
- 1 cup of all-purpose flour
- 1-1/2 cups of quinoa
- 4 corn tortillas

Meat:

- 26 oz. of rotisserie chicken
- 2-1/2 cups of chicken broth
- 1 cup of cooked chicken
- 3 chicken breasts
- 2 bacon slices

Vegetables:

- 1 carrots
- 4 garlic heads
- 2 medium potato
- 2 cups of mashed potatoes
- 2 sweet potatoes
- 1 yellow onion
- 2 cups of red onion
- 1/2 can of tomatoes with green chilies
- 2 cups of cherry tomatoes
- 1 can of tomato + juice
- 4 oz. florets of broccoli
- 4 jalapeno pepper

- 10 oz. of lettuce mix
- 1 cup of corn kernels
- 1 cup pf parsley leaves
- 2 cups of spinach leaves
- 1 teaspoon of ginger

Fruits:

- 2 bananas
- 3-1/2 avocados
- 3 limes
- 2 teaspoons of lemon juice
- 1 tablespoon of lime juice

Dairy:

- 4 eggs
- 1-1/2 cups of cheddar cheese
- 3 tablespoons of butter
- 3 tablespoons of dairy free butter
- 3 tablespoons of vegan sour cream
- 6 oz. of feta cheese
- ¼ cup of parmesan cheese
- ½ cup of mozzarella cheese

Fish & Seafood:

- 4 oz. shrimp
- 2 oz. cod fillets

Oil:

- 15 tablespoons of olive oil
- 1-2 teaspoons of coconut oil

Nut Products:

- 1/2 cup coconut milk
- 3 tablespoons almond milk
- ½ cup sesame seeds

Beans & Peas:

- 1 cans of black beans
- 1 can of pinto beans

Week 2 Menu:

	Breakfast	Lunch	Dinner	Nutritional Info
Day 8	Chicken Nuggets	Tofu Pad Thai	Fish Amandine	1323 calories, 68g fat, 94g carbs, 55g sugar, 81g protein
Day 9	Chicken Nuggets Leftover	Fish Amandine Leftover	Korean Beef Tacos	782 calories, 38g fat, 24g carbs, 9g sugar, 82g protein
Day 10	Taco Stuffed Sweet Potatoes	Chicken and Feta Plate	Korean Beef Tacos Leftover	1447 calories, 89g fat, 69g carbs, 14g sugar, 104g protein
Day 11	Vegetable Frittata	Chicken and Feta Plate Leftover	Buffalo Cauliflower Taco Salad	1169 calories, 86g fat, 47g carbs, 17g sugar, 65g protein
Day 12	Sweet Potato Hash	Buffalo Cauliflower Taco Salad Leftover	Stuffed Red Peppers	1086 calories, 44g fat, 143g carbs, 23g sugar, 40g protein
Day 13	Vegetable Frittata Leftover	Asparagus and Pancetta Penne	Stuffed Red Peppers Leftover	961 calories, 28g fat, 137g carbs, 19g sugar, 48g protein
Day 14	Sweet Potato Hash Leftover	Shrimp Scampi	Asparagus and Pancetta Penne Leftover	1066 calories, 35g fat, 124g carbs, 22g sugar, 67g protein

Week 2 Grocery List:

Spices & Herbs:

- 2-1/2 teaspoons of paprika
- 1-1/2 teaspoon of cayenne pepper
- 2-1/2 teaspoons of onion powder
- 4 teaspoons of garlic powder
- 2 tablespoons of chili powder
- 1-1/2 teaspoons of black pepper
- 1 teaspoon of sea salt
- 8 teaspoons of salt
- ½ teaspoon of coriander
- ½ teaspoon of dry mustard
- ½ tablespoons of cumin

Condiments:

- ½ cup of soy sauce
- ¼ teaspoon of agave nectar
- 1 teaspoon of tamarind paste
- ¼ cup of rice vinegar
- ¼ cup of granulated sugar
- ¼ cup of brown sugar
- ½ cup vinegar sauce
- ¼ cup of tomatillo salsa

Grain:

- 1 tablespoons of tapioca flour
- 4 tablespoons of gluten-free flour
- 1/3 pack rice noodles
- 4 taco shells
- 4 gluten-free taco-sized tortillas
- ½ cup of panko breadcrumbs

- 6 oz. whole-wheat penne
- 1 cup of bulgur
- 4 oz. plain or whole-wheat linguine

Meat:

- 8 oz. chicken
- 2 tablespoons of chicken broth
- 10 oz. of rotisserie chicken
- 1-3/4 oz. sausage
- 4 oz. turkey
- 1 packages of beef
- 2 oz. pancetta

Vegetables:

- 2 garlic cloves
- 1 baby Bok Choy
- 1 tablespoon of thyme
- ½ teaspoon of oregano
- 6 sweet potatoes
- 2 yellow onions
- 1 red onion
- 2 radishes
- 2 pickles
- 2 jalapenos
- 1 tomato
- 2 cups of cherry tomatoes
- 7 red bell peppers
- 2 zucchini
- 1/2 tablespoon of ginger
- 3 cups of spinach
- 14 oz cremini mushrooms
- 3 tablespoons of chives
- ¾ cup of cilantro leaves

- 3 tablespoons of parsley leaves
- 1 cup of basil leaves
- 1 tablespoon of dill
- 6 oz. asparagus
- 1 cauliflower head
- 1 cup of cauliflower florets
- 10 oz. of lettuce
- 6 cups of mixed salad leaves
- 4 scallion bunches

Fruits:

- 3 avocados
- 1 teaspoon of lemon rind
- 2 tablespoons of lemon juice

Dairy:

- 8 eggs
- ¼ cup of buttermilk
- 4 tablespoons of butter
- 4 tablespoons of vegan butter
- 1 cup + 1 tablespoon of milk
- 6 oz. of feta cheese
- 1 tablespoon of parmesan cheese
- 4 oz. tofu
- 2 cups of Monterey Jack cheese
- ½ cup of vegan yogurt

Fish & Seafood:

- 6 oz. shrimps
- 1 tilapias, halibut, or trout fillet

Oil:

- 12 tablespoons of olive oil
- 2 tablespoons of canola oil
- 1tablespoon of sesame oil

Nut Products:

- ½ cup coconut milk
- ¼ cup of almonds
- 1 cup of peanuts
- ¼ cup sesame seeds

Beans & Peas:

- 1 cup cannellini beans

Others:

- ¼ cup of white wine

Part 5: What's Next?

Changing your diet and eating the right foods is a great first step towards managing PCOS symptoms.

Next, change your lifestyle. Many studies have revealed that exercise and lifestyle changes can help immensely.

Women suffering from PCOS have a higher insulin resistance rate. Doctors believe, excess body weight and lack of physical activity can affect the body's ability of using blood sugar for energy. According to the National Institute of Diabetes and Digestive and Kidney Diseases, lack of physical activity and obesity are contributing factors for IR.

Of course, not all women who have PCOS are overweight. Physical activity will however reduce your risk and improve your ability to fight the symptoms. Besides, it will help you burn calories, build muscle mass, lower cholesterol levels, and reduce insulin resistance.

Cardiovascular workouts, interval training, and strength training will all help you. An analysis of 16 studies discovered that vigorous-intensity aerobic exercise can be the most effective (10) way of reducing BMI and insulin resistance in women who have PCOS. This study was published in the Frontiers in Physiology journal.

- Run, jog, bike, or walk for 30 minutes in a day.
- Take the stairs instead of the elevator.
- Park your car further away from work so you have to walk.
- Get off the bus one stop early.
- Swimming is a great exercise.
- Play a sport like tennis or squash.
- Play with your kids.
- Take a break from work. Go on a walk.
- Stop smoking and restrict alcohol consumption.

How to Up Your Game?

Stay focused and keep on the right track. Eat the right foods at the right time in the right proportions. Also, make sure to exercise regularly to stay healthy. You will be able to fight the symptoms of PCOS much better.

Also, remember to stay hydrated. Drink enough water and get adequate sleep. Good rest is very important for the human body. Wear comfortable clothing when you go to bed. Make sure that the room is clean.

Excessive stress is also a major problem. Stress can cause several health problems. So go on a holiday once in a while. Practice deep-breathing exercises. Do meditation and yoga. Or just dim the light, play some relaxing music to relax at home.

Prepare small milestones and reward yourself for achieving each one of them. For example, give yourself a prize if you can follow the PCOS diet for a month. It could be a material reward like buying something or an act of kindness like taking an afternoon off from work. Small rewards will keep you motivated to stay on the right track.

Conclusion

I have personally battled with PCOS and know how frustrating and agonizing it can be. But let me tell you this... like me, you too can beat PCOS and find relief from its symptoms.

All you have to do is learn about the condition, eat healthy foods, and lead a healthy lifestyle. It is not that difficult... really.

Do not take it lightly. Remember, PCOS is a serious condition that affects millions of women. Look out for its symptoms. Millions of women from around the world suffer from PCOS. It can cause many health issues. Yes, there is no cure yet, but lifestyle changes and food can go a long way in helping you manage the symptoms and prevent any complications.

I have shared many recipes in this book. You can easily prepare them at home, all by yourself. Eating homemade food is anyways always healthy than eating out. I have made every effort to keep the recipes simple by providing step-by-step guidance and a list of ingredients you will need. You will be able to find most of the ingredients in my recipes easily.

Thank you again for reading this book. I hope you have liked reading this book and found it useful.

Happy cooking! Lead a PCOS-free life. Thank you and good luck!

My kind request

Thank you for your purchase and I hope you enjoyed this book!

Reviews help me tremendously, so your feedback is greatly appreciated, as it lets me know how I am doing!

I can't wait to read your opinion!

References

Part 1: All About PCOS

1. Polycystic Ovary Syndrome By Fahimeh Ramezani Tehrani and Samira Behboudi-Gandevani
https://www.intechopen.com/books/contemporary-gynecologic-practice/polycystic-ovary-syndrome-

2. The prevalence of polycystic ovary syndrome in a community sample assessed under contrasting diagnostic criteria
https://www.ncbi.nlm.nih.gov/pubmed/19910321

3. Gestational Diabetes and Type 2 Diabetes in Reproductive-Aged Women With Polycystic Ovary Syndrome
A. E. Joham, S. Ranasinha, S. Zoungas, L. Moran, H. J. Teede
https://doi.org/10.1210/jc.2013-2007

4. Researchers reveal link between PCOS, type 2 diabetes
https://www.endocrine.org/news-and-advocacy/news-room/2017/researchers-reveal-link-between-pcos-type-2-diabetes

Part 2: Getting Started

5. An assessment of lifestyle modification versus medical treatment with clomiphene citrate, metformin, and clomiphene citrate–metformin in patients with polycystic ovary syndrome by Mohammad Ali Karimzadeh, Mojgan Javedani
https://www.sciencedirect.com/science/article/abs/pii/S0015028209005056

6. The role of insulin-like growth factor-1 (IGF-1) and IGF binding protein-1 (IGFBP-1) in the pathogenesis of polycystic ovary syndrome
R Homburg, C Pariente, B Lunenfeld, H S Jacobs
https://pubmed.ncbi.nlm.nih.gov/1283982/

7. Adult Ovarian Function Can Be Affected by High Levels of Soy
   Wendy N. Jefferson
   https://www.ncbi.nlm.nih.gov/pmc/articles/PMC3139237/

8. Effects of caloric intake timing on insulin resistance and hyperandrogenism in lean women with polycystic ovary syndrome
   Daniela Jakubowicz, Maayan Barnea, Julio Wainstein, Oren Froy
   https://pubmed.ncbi.nlm.nih.gov/23688334/

9. Dietary composition in the treatment of polycystic ovary syndrome: a systematic review to inform evidence-based guidelines
   https://academic.oup.com/humupd/article/19/5/432/611716

Part 5: What's Next?

10. Exercise Interventions in Polycystic Ovary Syndrome: A Systematic Review and Meta-Analysis
    https://www.frontiersin.org/articles/10.3389/fphys.2020.00606/full?report=reader

Index